The

Monstered

Self

The Monstered Self

Narratives of Death and Performance in Latin American Fiction

Eduardo González

Duke University Press   Durham & London

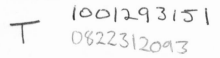

T 100129315\
0822312093

To Laura E. Scott

Contents

Acknowledgments

I owe much to Peter Batke, without whose magic the manuscript would have perished in dread of revision. John Irwin and Greg Lucente lent a hand that others could not take out of their pockets. Kyle McCarter received me with unbureaucratic patience to discuss Genesis and Exodus; Del Hillers, Jerry Cooper, Diskin Clay, and Lowell Edmunds tolerated my itinerant assault upon their crusty disciplines. Marta Paley Francescato offered me her copy of *Homeopatía*. I found support in many, including Peter Sacks, Pier Massimo Forni, John Russell-Wood, Mary Jane Hall, Ana María Snell, Meme Saccone, Jay Geller, Benigno, Karen and Elías Ramón Sánchez-Eppler, Steve Winfield, María Antonia Garcés, Nicolás Wey, Brian Doyle, Guillermo Carrascón, Daniela Capra, María del Rosario Ramos, Stephanie Sterner, Marc Spindlemann—and merciless Verónica. In an age of fake budgets and crumbling ideologies, Dick Macksey and Neil Hertz were hospitable signifiers. Ana María Codas and Juan Manuel Marcos provided assistance in approaching Roa Bastos and the living story of their Paraguay. Harry Sieber gave me neXT-J and some timely advice.

I am grateful to Daniel Balderston and Tom Campbell for their expert help and accuracy, and to Reynolds Smith and Gustavo Pérez Firmat for their faith in the project.

It is said that Jacques Lacan had a glimpse of the Unconscious while looking at Baltimore through a hotel window. On my part, I thought I saw it being thrown out at home plate in the crisp air of a late spring evening at Memorial Stadium: Richard Poirier chased from third base, Leslie Fiedler nailed the tag, Harold Bloom made the call—the appropriate one, I thought.

On behalf of the author, his family and pets, this book is dedicated to Laura E. Scott.

This book explores biographic matters of ethical interest in the fictional portrayal of individual fate. In each of the stories and novels discussed, grounds of reciprocity are established between death and transfiguration. Each of the stories in question regards what dies as interesting and what remains immutable as boring. In all of them, character implies a complex relationship between the settled and the mutable, between recognition and metamorphosis, and between life and death. Hence, the character of dying in character is the book's main theme, in which it is assumed that certain ethical constraints and notions of death may combine as responses to and representations of life-consuming change.

One may imagine change itself as a figure within which death lies disguised. Likewise, in the same figure, change might appear reflected as a death picture aping human character in the mirror of mutability. The fiction studied in this book confronts change as if it were death being caught in the act of imitating life. Dying and changing represent a minimal dancing and acting pair. They make up the dual character of performance in the plots studied. The performing and storytelling self (acting in death's borrowed weeds) constitutes character's main character in each interpretation attempted here. Metamorphosis or transfiguration envelops every significant attitude and practice considered in each story or plot.

An element of monstrosity inhabits the fiction chosen for analysis. For instance: a lonely bachelor, whose only apparent sin is smoking, becomes a rapist and suicidal murderer; some nameless individuals are possessed by a jargon of sickness and remedy that reduces them to the forlorn status of linguistic zombies; members of an isolated family are bound by the presence of an avenging predator in whom their own guilt and craving for self-punishment find expiation. Such uncanny and lethal experiences invade personal existence with unknown and sudden purpose. Metamorphosis resists ethical discourse: gesture and event insist on occurring out of the reach of moral or pragmatic conscience. Death remains unexplained: change protects it and gives it the character of fiction's herald and executor.

Besides such stories of merciless mutability, there are others in which individual transformation hinges on achieving a stylized and spectacular degree of self-consciousness, or in which monstrous change involves performance and eventually a sort of moral calculus stressing the active role of choice and reflection in human conduct. In this regard, the book explores two types of plots: one which strips a character of moral choice, and another which allows a character type to choose a life of its own, though one deprived of personal autonomy and held in ritual bondage to a group. In the second type, the agonistic (male) individual assumes a highly specialized role within a community held together by archaic notions of social solidarity; he engages in the selfish exploitation of the magician's prestige, or in the unselfish observance of ancestral beliefs. Individual (male) behavior reflects the interests of the group in two distinct yet related ways: it performs at the service of leadership and for the sake of sustaining group solidarity against alien encroachments upon its pristine identity. Acting on this basis, performative behavior may include heroic duty to the group, but the performer's heroic character may take on monstrous features as it finds a voice in self-deprecation and satire, or as it comes to rely on sacrificial self-ridicule and spectacular abjection. Such ritual heroism very often ends with a display of the character's agony as an act of self-destruction. Extremes of apocalyptic hope and nihilistic despair meet in shaping this performing self.

Outside of any strictly academic notion of performance, we wish to situate our illustrated sense of it in reference to the following characterization offered twenty years ago by Richard Poirier in *The Performing Self*:

> Performance may, in its self-assertiveness, be radical in impulse, but it is also conservative in its recognitions that the self is of necessity, if unwillingly, inclusive of all kinds of versions, absorbed from whatever source, of what that self might be. Performance in literature, life, or politics is allusive, and therefore historical. While I personally find the radical impulse more interesting than the conservative necessity—it is, I think, more revelatory of the boundaries of human possibility—performance, as I conceived of it, differs from what is called a happening by virtue of the fact that it is an action which must go through passages that both impede the action and give it form, much as a sculptor not only is impelled to shape his material but is in turn shaped by it, his impulse to mastery always

chastened, sometimes made tender and possibly witty by the re-calcitrance of what he is working on. Performance comes to fruition at precisely the point where the potentially destructive impulse to mastery brings forth from the material its most essential, irreducible, clarified, and therefore beautiful nature. (xiv)

Beneath the well-inscribed idioms of late-1960s politics and other cultural phenomena, one may detect in Poirier's characterization of the radical impulse a concern with boundaries similar to the anxiety that a responsible practice of intertextual criticism may feel toward the debilitating effect of too much allusiveness, of too extensive or involved a reflection on the inherent borrowedness of a writer's best work.

One may recall that intertextuality became fashionable as the fiction of Jorge Luis Borges gained currency. Poirier implies a negative awareness of intertextual fixation in saying that for him, "Borges is . . . too little concerned with the glory of the human presence within the wastes of time, with human agencies of invention, and he is too exclusively amused by the careers of competing systems, the failed potencies of techniques and structures" (44). In exploring some of the very features of impersonal pantextualism mentioned by Poirier, our goal has been to demonstrate the opposite: the stubbornly local and radically personal making of the human presence in Borges's essays, parables, and fictions.

At a distance of two decades, Poirier's counterpoint between "radical impulse" and "conservative necessity" seems to have collapsed into an amalgamation of person-bond tendencies within the radical impulse itself, on either the right or the left. Right or left, there now seems to exist a parallel radical investment in the force of character and personality. Beyond the overt issues of political correctness and its vicissitudes, a new radical impulse may come to reject most political agendas as inherently driven by leveling kinds of tokenism. Not too long ago, writing from the mounting shambles of the left, Richard Sennett warned against an inward turn toward authenticity and away from the preeminent needs of social intercourse and its reliance on alienated sincerity. "The Obsession with persons at the expense of more impersonal social relations [argued Sennett] is like a filter which discolors our rational understanding of society." Such an obsession, which in my view may include the spontaneous appropriation of art and fiction as if they were the same as routine existence, "obscures the continuing importance of class in advanced industrial society; it leads us to believe community is an act of mutual self-disclosure and to undervalue the community relations of strangers, particularly those which occur in cities" (*The Fall of the Public Man*, 4). Sennett's resistance to varieties of late-modern intersubjective utopias (or to a potlatch of commodified feelings passing as tokens of sincerity in the midst of public exchange) includes his liberal faith in urbane civility—and his own awareness of its decline. Such faith in civility is abandoned (or hyped into wild forms of self-advertisement within apparent self-effacement) in the sequence of plots discussed in the first part of this book, which runs from young Borges and late Walter Benjamin through early H. G. Wells, on to Borges's own pantheist image of Walt Whitman, and to Mario Vargas Llosa's invention of a nomadic and savage storyteller.

As the sequence unfolds, the city is either transformed into a labyrinth haunted by heroic and tribal ancestors or it is abandoned in search of some removed habitat in which such imagined ancestors may still be found alive and kicking. In either case, the character's quest moves him away from a democratic and class-mediated social order, an order in the best of cases ruled by compromise—but also by consensual, uncharismatic mediocrity. His flight takes him into a primitive and often criminal order based on genealogy, kinship, and various degrees of inherited and unquestioned solidarity with both ancestral peers and rivals, with kinfolk and enemies alike. The radical urge to engage in personal performance shifts from the protagonist's quasi-bohemian aesthetics of the tribal city to the cozy ethics of his assimilation into an actual tribe or gang. Such an assimilation is minimally but sufficiently kept from oblivion (of the sort that leaves no printed trace) by residuals of narrative irony, according to which personal transcendence lies in placing the performing self under observation by at least one of its previously established identities: the one committed to the elective pluralism of sharing stories with a universal audience through the mediations of writing.

The assimilation may seem elective because in the end it should embody the figure of a chosen self. And it may seem pluralist because it implies the existence of an unlimited audience of readers and listeners constrained by no prohibitions in their access to knowledge. As such, this could amount to a displaced liberal solution to radical urgings lying deep within layers of empowering egotism.

In establishing the radical impulse to perform and setting it against conservative necessity, Poirier neglects a rich tradition of eccentric egotism radically engaged in its own varieties of performance, such as when Harold Bloom defines his enabling sense of "brute contingency" by means of a verbal talisman that may at any moment explode in his own face: "*Facticity* would mean the state of being a fact, as an inescapable and unalterable fact. To be caught in facticity is to be caught in the inescapable and unalterable. The stances or positions of freedom are not available, and the text or event reads us more fully and vividly than we can hope to read it" ("The Sorrows of Facticity," 1). Whether negotiable or not, Bloom's inordinate facticity is both canon-bound and radically antinomian; it also strikes a radically undemocratic blow at canon pluralism. Bloom's creative self adopts an arrested stance in the face of predemocratic and genealogical compulsions, so awesome in nature that only their enforcement—at the head and tail of the canon's roll—can insure a worthy and memorable (self)punishment against the act of trying to break with them. Bloom's canon strife is tragic, prophetic, and satirical; its highest embodiment might lie in the Book of Ezekiel, or in some disguised Oedipal style of ethical suicide.

Facticity demands performance, just as it leaves almost no grounds for autonomous display and frivolous creation. Yet, if as Bloom so appealingly claims, *There is no method other than yourself,* the person who is pinned down and fixed by the weight of facticity should require charisma as well as the inborn yet epiphanic intrusion of the other, an intrusion different from the structured factualness of theories detested by Bloom on account of their meagerness of flesh and soul: "All those who seek for a method that is not themselves will find not a method, but someone else, whom they will ape and involuntarily mock. Poetry and fiction share with criticism the mystery that poststructuralist speculation seeks to deny: the spark we call personality or the idiosyncratic, which in metaphysics and theology once was called presence" (9). In the end, Bloom's ethical imperatives of risen personhood in the presence of religious legacies stand in radical kinship with Poirier's fragile aesthetics of performance in a postcountercultural context.

Rather than suggesting a synthesis between these positions, I will establish as this book's opening presence an irresistible maniac of facticity named Caius Martius Coriolanus. Indeed, my title alludes to a tremor in the quest for biographic autonomy. It comes from the following complaint:

> I had rather have one scratch my head i'th'sun
> When the alarum were struck, than idly sit
> To hear my nothings monster'd.
> (2.2.75–77)[1]

No other instance of *monstered* is known before this one. Shakespeare seems to have chosen *monster* (as in the action of being taken out of stubborn loneliness and displayed to a hungry mob) as he tried to render (in corrosive tenderness) the lethal consequences of being chosen by fame in a time of civic crisis. In any event, monstered Coriolanus echoes in the chambers of biographic memory mainly because of the *nothings* plucked from him and displayed by his crude solicitors: very rarely have self and pride been asserted with such seemingly nihilistic bluntness.

The central paradox explored in each of the following chapters grows out of a similar sense of individual uniqueness shaped in stories and novels in which personal identity is discernible only under the threat of individual obliteration. A sense of character persists even though the very notion of character proves virtually untenable; rather than being *shown*, as Coriolanus loathes to be, character is *nothing'd* by death or by intricate modes of passage into alien or bizarre forms of personal being.

In *The Lion and the Fox*, Wyndham Lewis accurately sees the quixotic character of this kind of furor in Shakespeare's view of heroic self-cruelty: "Timon, Coriolanus, Brutus, Hamlet, *are all Quixotes*. Only he sees them all, except perhaps Othello, more coldly than Cervantes saw his *hijo seco*, save when something like a sexual excitement seems to take possession of him, and he begins caressing and adoring his hero as though he were a woman—like another Antonio in front of a Sebastian, in *Twelfth Night*" (237). Caressing oneself in character, having one's head scratched, as if digging for a strange tenant within: for a mother, a feared lover, a wondrous host. With Gabriel García Márquez's great novel in mind, it could be said that one hundred ways of being lonely are the nothings monstered in the fictions analyzed in this book.

Some warning is required concerning the book's pace and organization. Each chapter represents an autonomous expository and narrative unit within a circular sequence. The first part introduces and develops themes that will recur in variation throughout the book. Starting with Benjamin and Borges, the figure of the storyteller is given composite shape as a privileged mediator between theories of narrative and the narrative of theory, or between essayistic allusiveness and the reflection of biographic desire in anecdote and story.

Taken together, Benjamin and Borges demonstrate a dialectical entrapment of stoic wisdom. Their protagonists are caught between, on the one hand, a struggle to secure individual ancestral honor and, on the other, instances of social conflict they perceive through an unyielding fascination with myth, ritual, and the power of the dead. The two aspirations are irreconcilable. The luster of genealogical ancestry and its shining names fades with each clustering of myth and its stereotypical redundancies of being and action. As a chosen mode of rendering knowledge individual and memorable, storytelling cannot unbind personal redemption from the catastrophes of solidarity nor individual memory from group mourning. In his attempts to cope with and to render vivid the authority of the dead, Borges creates an ironic celebration of pantheism in individuals like Juan Dahlmann and the *other* Walt Whitman. But his portrayal of the pantheist breaks down into a sublime and grotesque survey of narrative causality and of the trivial assumptions at the core of character as it is encircled by death. Borges's view of magic determinism at work in well-made plots will be tested against his own rendering of Wells's story of the Invisible Man. Wells's parable of threatened village life will then be found recast and expanded in Vargas Llosa's mythic biography of a full-fledged storyteller performing among savages.

The book's first rehearsal of intertextual progression (from an implied to an explicit *Life* of a master of stories) ends with *El hablador* (1987) and the parallel lives of Vargas Llosa's parrot storyteller and Aesop's cult as a sacred, dog-faced freak in the *Aesopica*. A monstered version of Aesop is thus found embedded in the myth of Gregor Samsa's awakening into the life of his living but deadened ancestors, as transposed from Franz Kafka's *The Metamorphosis* (*Die Verwandlung*, 1916) into the Machiguenga biography of a certain Saúl Zuratas. Hence, the first part moves from the fierce yearning to have oneself monstered to the militant acceptance of the monstered task of narrating as a personal offering to others.

The two chapters of the second part reinterpret two ongoing themes: the inherent perils of storytelling as personal (self)creation, and the ritual kinship between sacrifice and suicide in association with storytelling. In Vargas Llosa's *El hablador,* the first storyteller ever known in the mythic life of a community must be decapitated because each time he speaks in reference to someone, he transforms that person into an animal. The lethal remedy fails, and the severed head continues to *talk* people into becoming animals each time it utters their proper names. The talking head's rampant creationism—both poetic and sacred in kind—reemerges in Julio Cortázar's "Cefalea," examined here as a fable based on the peculiar shifts and reciprocities of pronoun identity. The identity of persons in pronoun form enters into conflict with feelings being expressed by human actors within the province of pain, where pronouns exist (and persist) in mourning of a lost companionship with actual persons, with beings situated outside the order of grammar. "Cefalea" represents a silent, black-and-white version of Cortázar's recurrent depictions of fantasy. This minimalist essay in formal and narrative autism resembles a manifesto on the melancholy basis of desire in Cortázar's fiction.

The second part ends with a comprehensive account of Cortázar's modes of fantasy, set within pastoral conventions evoked and ruined. Rising from the alienated idioms of "Cefalea," the elegiac growth of self-consciousness in pastoral settings reflects Cortázar's persistent nostalgia for the origins of art in the ancestral sacredness of childhood. Starting from a sacrificial sublime in close kinship with the allurement of female chastity ("Silvia," "Los venenos," and "Final del juego"), the pastoral progression moves to an incestuous attack against primal innocence ("Bestiario") and on to an unresolved obsession with fantasy that ends up entrapped in the dark aesthetics of suicide ("Las armas secretas").

As a translator of Poe, Cortázar experiences and re-creates his legacy as a struggle between unravished female candor and demonic male self-consciousness. A haunted virility encompasses both men and women: regardless of gender, no one can unite with only *one* side of sexual difference. At the heart of his best stories, Cortázar's representation of sexual union uncouples the specular duality of romantic solitude: erotic union exceeds the twin norms of dual sexual difference forever lodged in the parental couple. In marrying oneself in the telling of stories, one marries chimerically. The storyteller in Cortázar is a monstered bachelor; he is the son, the filial version of a brother-bridegroom who commits incest with his own sisterly, female demand for plural desire. In such terms, suicide represents the melancholy outcome of the character's struggles with both his narcissistic creation and his own femaleness.

The last part of the book offers a biographic reading of Augusto Roa Bastos's *Yo el Supremo* (1983). Beginning with Hamlet, the figure of the divided son is traced through various rituals of parthenogenesis, ranging from the idioms of alchemy to the voices of Paraguay's native myths and historical chronicles. To the extent that *Yo el Supremo* narrates the biography of an individual, it also recapitulates the life of a country, from birth to near destruction. Roa Bastos's novel may be seen as a secular instrument at the service of religious mourning: it serves a religion that blends Christian and Guaraní elements of natural piety, it is inspired by suffering, and it resists doctrinal closure through a combination of satire and prophecy. The blending of myth and history in Roa Bastos will be seen in contrast with James Joyce's monstering of ancestral voices in *Finnegans Wake* (1939).

The book's unfolding is then circular. *Yo el Supremo* expands into perilous complexity the notions of storytelling first seen in Benjamin, Borges, and Wells; it also gives farcical and encyclopedic shape to the encounter between myth and biography in *El hablador,* and it rethinks many of the affinities and aversions between tribal membership and national destiny debated in that novel. Among the several chimerical figures as tacit narrators of *Yo el Supremo,* our reading will enhance that of Chaucer's Pardoner and his exploitation of sermon rhetoric and myth. The storyteller becomes a wickedly brilliant, rat-tailed seller of pardons, who may also resemble a dwarfish, dog-faced wanderer who tells stories about talking animals, and also a birthmarked nomad who shares his face and voice with a parrot: the Pardoner becomes the *hablador* under Aesop's mask.

By virtue of its complexity and range, *Yo el Supremo* caps the sequence of interpretations developed in this book and sends the act of reading back to its beginning. In this regard, the reader should expect narrative rather than theory, and no argument that is not embedded in a given negotiation with specific stories. The book's argument lies in its sequential unfolding, in its growing through accretion, reiteration, and displacement. The argument is simply this: in narrative, the need for expressiveness goes hand-in-hand with (and may radically resist) the plain urge to communicate with others. Such is, nakedly, our monstered sense of ethical facticity and aesthetic performance.

Part

One

Myth

As

Mask

Counterfeit

Bewitchments:

The Storyteller

in Benjamin,

Borges, Wells, and

Vargas Llosa

*. . . I will counterfeit the bewitchment of some
popular man, and give it bountiful to the desirers.*
—*William Shakespeare,* Coriolanus *(2.3.100–102)*

Caius Martius of Corioles hates the mob and above all those who sway it
with fables and spells; but in Shakespeare's play he must live by the
word, and even his wounds become voices. Caius Martius is a warrior,
not a storyteller; he can have his "nothings monster'd" by the rumor of
fame that thrives among those who would have heroic deeds transformed into exhibitions and heroes themselves into things for tasting.
Stories swirl around Caius Martius as if he lived in the age of the media;
he is the only one among Shakespeare's tragic heroes to resemble a
commodity. His well-advertised likeness to a thing, a god, a dragon, or
just to nothing threatens to undo tragedy in him. George Bernard Shaw
thought that *Coriolanus* was Shakespeare's greatest comedy.

Roman citizens want to barter with the warrior's marked body as if it
were a fetish, a tool of oral greed. Thus the Third Citizen says of
Coriolanus:

> For if he show us his wounds and tell us his deeds,
> we are to put our tongues into those wounds and speak for them.
> (2.3.5–7)

and, he goes on:

> if he tell us his noble deeds, we must also tell him
> our noble acceptance of them
> (2.3.7–8)

The Third Citizen is an expert on monsters, crowds, and the melting
pot:

Ingratitude is monstrous,
and for the multitude to be ungrateful,
were to make a monster of the multitude;
of the which we being members,
should bring ourselves to be monstrous members.

(2.3.8–13)

By contrast with the would-be confidence man, monster Coriolanus
stands alone, and takes pride in being "author of himself"; his awful
virtues are parthenogenic, and his ranting phobia against all manner of
reference addressed to him would make Coriolanus a biologist of speech
in our present age. The "multiplying spawn" he sees around him act less
like people than like word-borne particles of tainted seed. Coriolanus
fears being brought from nothing to monster by the mob's gossip; he
hates to be born from words rather than from the sword's cruel path into
the aroused flesh of some worthy enemy.

This hasty résumé of an unnatural genius is meant to qualify Coriolanus as our counterfeit embodiment of the storyteller. I choose him as
my exemplary man due to his antithetical value as both an *adversary* of
stories and gossip and as a *generator* of them, in the shape of the myths
produced by his own charisma. As an engine of destruction, Coriolanus
inspires (as much as he would destroy them) those parasitic raids on
group dreams carried out by traditional storytellers and word enchant-
ers. He qualifies for the role of involuntary storyteller shown in a frightful and sacrificial shape. He is quite sensational, his fate is more performative than substantive, more memorable than tragic. Coriolanus is too
hot and proud to be a dictator and too real to be worshipped as a god.

Contrary to the impact caused by Coriolanus's deeds and words, most
stories cast a spell of their own, detached from the storyteller's person.
But the stories and plots examined here have been chosen in order to
uncover and examine the intrusion of a mouthpiece, a voice, a body, a
self performed and thus monstered. It will matter little if such an intrusion of the authors' surrogates in these plots is felt in written form or as
an effect of voice. In fact, the distinction between the oral and the
written will play only an accessorial role in the central issue of the
storyteller's involved presence in his material. At every significant twist
and turn in our study of a given tale, its teller will be implicated, his
handiwork transformed into a testimony of vulnerability and prowess,
of sacrificial vanity and elation.

Dissections of the Sacred

[T]he image of classlessness is put back into mythology instead of becoming truly transparent as a phantasmagoria of Hell. Therefore the category into which the archaic coalesces with the modern is far less a Golden Age than a catastrophe.—Theodor Adorno to Walter Benjamin, quoted in Richard Wolin, Walter Benjamin: The Aesthetics of Redemption

Adorno warned Benjamin in a letter against idealizing tribal solidarity. In his view, pristine societies found consensus in structures of domination mediated by a sense of material scarcity and the threat of external aggression. A dialectical view of archaic social bonding must reject the illusion of classlessness to which a nostalgic view of the primitive so often leads; a horizon of violence and internalized coercion encircles a modern political appropriation of myth. Adorno is responding to Benjamin's militant search for a collective subject in archaic society capable of offering a model of political action against fascist mobilization.[1] In "The Work of Art in the Age of Mechanical Reproduction" (1936), Benjamin reaches a bold synthesis of the views criticized by Adorno. The essay's main themes merge with the seemingly antithetical theses developed in "The Storyteller: Reflections on the Work of Nikolai Leskov" (1936). Taken together, both pieces of materialist analysis provide us with a counterpoint approach to the art of storytelling examined by Borges in two short essays that have come to share a common space in his poetics of fiction: "La postulación de la realidad" (1931) and "El arte narrativo y la magia" (1932).

A curious affinity between materialist and idealist views of aesthetic representation in Benjamin and Borges emerges if one examines not so much their explicit or implied doctrines as their respective fictional modes of rendering such doctrines vivid to themselves and their readers. In what follows, this fictional mode of illustrating argument will be explored in relation to the corporeal self's involvement in its own fictions (or the narrator's personal embodiment in the texture of either essay or story). The physical and the fictional will coexist at key moments in the acts of persuasion in which Benjamin and Borges involve the reader, of whom they represent the first recognized instance. The body in question will resemble a surface read, newly exposed, as when two pages from an old book are peeled apart to reveal faint traces of their print on each other.[2]

I will not be equating the act of reading with the activity of writing in a straightforward manner, nor with the notion of *écriture* in vogue at least since Roland Barthes's *Writing Degree Zero* (1953). In the specific case of Benjamin and Borges (leading up to Wells and Vargas Llosa), reading will be identified with a *mood*, with a mode of possession rather than with a professional activity. In fact, for the most part, reading of the sort imagined here should remain oblivious to writing of the *written* kind, although not to the wide phenomenon of *arche-writing*, insofar as what is written should not constitute a mere accessory to ideas or to the effect of their representation (see Derrida, *Of Grammatology* 51ff.). We are interested in naïve, possessed reading, in a mode of immersion not alien to trance and analogous to a sort of receptive alienation: self-absorption rather than professional zeal should define the essence of what we understand by reading. When, for instance, in the first preface to *Historia universal de la infamia* (1935), Borges speaks of his "re-readings" (*relecturas*) of Stevenson, Chesterton, "and also from Sternberg's early films," he makes it a point to identify his art with biography, and with the "sudden shifts [*solución*] of continuity, and the paring down [*reducción*] of a man's whole life to two or three scenes" (*Infamy*, 13). A mood of asceticism underlines his method of editing and *montage*, as if it were aimed at the surgical removal of superfluous and moody symptoms from the lives of his adopted characters. A "propósito visual," or visual aim, informs Borges's method: the stories "are not, they do not try to be, psychological" (*Infamy*, 13); and in this aim he coincides with Benjamin's assertion that "nothing . . . commends a story more effectively to memory than that chaste compactness which precludes psychological analysis" (*Discusión*, 91). As a result, Borges's implicit notion of reading may seem very much at odds with the one adopted here, for it seems to imply the opposite of absorption and randomness; even its profession of modesty suggests a discriminating sense of high alertness to the perils rather than the pleasures of passive assimilation. "Reading [insists young Borges] . . . is an activity which comes after that of writing; it is more modest, more unobtrusive, more intellectual" (*Infamy*, 13).

Fastidious or not, such a densely minimalist profession of reading aimed at nothing less than improving the already-written seems balanced by two strong disclosures about the fate of writing. In the preface to the 1954 edition of *Historia*, Borges defines baroque as "that style which deliberately exhausts (or tries to exhaust) all its possibilities and which borders on its own parody." He now sees *Historia* flaunting a style of late self-consciousness and parody through each of its pages; "to curb them," he adds, "would amount to destroying them" (11). Obviously, and regardless of other implications, by *baroque* Borges means a style of aristocratic defense at odds with candor and coolly in favor of authenticating what is written by alluding to motives so deep they escape the innermost reach of psychological understanding in an age where psychology may prove more egalitarian than democracy. Such an unpsychological notion of baroque will lend itself rather easily to its own redefinition in Borges's canon as the *classic* mode of storytelling in opposition to the *romantic* one, a crucial distinction that will be analyzed in depth soon.

Baroque's defenses lie in humor. Sometimes, as with Baltasar Gracián, humor appears unintended. However, with Donne, humor becomes "voluntario o consentido" (di Giovanni translates this as "deliberate, or self-conscious," but it may be rendered as "self-willed," "self-indulgent," or "spoiled"). But if it is true that baroque defends itself against passionate candor through near-suicidal humor, one may wonder if, albeit faintly, time has allowed humor—of the unwitting kind—to creep into the following declaration by Borges: "I inscribe this book [*Historia*] to S.D.; English, innumerable and an Angel. Also I offer her that kernel of myself that I have saved, somehow—the central heart that deals not in words, traffics not with dreams and is untouched by time, by joy, by adversities" (*Infamy*, 7).[3] More queer than baroque, Borges's English becomes self-conscious in spite of itself. It could be said that the adopted style of writing defends its writer· against the risks and flaws of voicing and gesturing, that as a form of hyper-writing baroque protects him against involuntary lapses between brain and mouth and a certain body impact. Such idioms of body voice and body gesture were inscribed as a passionate hoax on a platonized female, for it seems that baroque writing in young Borges (as revised by his older self) aims at several simultaneous women rather than at a single actress of the sublime. In terms of the present urge to regard reading as a diffuse state not disciplined by writing, the dedication to "S.D." can serve as evidence of how fragile the liberated conscience of the writer becomes when it journeys beyond feelings and desires which it then chooses to address indirectly, or in the medium of fictions actually written or read in preparation for their ultimate shaping into a story or essay.

With this keenly private and undisciplined view of reading in mind, I should argue that, in constructing a view of transcendent expressiveness in film and story, both Borges and Benjamin project their own peculiar feelings of surrogacy as fiction makers into the common space of storytelling. Each imaginary storyteller provides a space in which the author perceives a conflict between individual autonomy and the stereotypes of group solidarity found in magic and ritual. In so doing, the storytellers blur the conventional lines separating essay from story, and transform the relative autonomy of essayistic theory into the inherent captivity of the teller within his own fictions—whether in the form of essay or story. Such captivity—such a way of being caught as a character in one's own analytic fictions—suggests that the writer in Borges and Benjamin is perhaps mourning (through a parody of sacrificial elation or by seriously contemplating his own death-spectacle) the passing of an age in which he did not write, did not enjoy such a trained pleasure, an age when desire and pleasure appeared and disappeared and were thus absorbed and renewed only within the leisurely space of reading: a Golden Age.

If there is a certain hectic quality or a given rapport with violence in what the writer chooses to write while in such a state of elated mourning, his quickening of emotion could reflect an opposite posture, a bygone mood of leisure, a manner of vagrancy through which early readings escaped the work ethic, the potlatch, the orgy, and other forms in which culture already conspired to make one's actions either plainly or aberrantly useful and meaningful to others. Besides concerning itself with questions of individual autonomy and group solidarity, this notion of pristine reading in the style of a neophyte on spiritual holiday would seem to banish writing into the future, into an age of labor. Framed and ruled by an economy of usefulness, writing emerges in alienation of truly meditative experience and the exploitation of memory. As a matter of professional or cultivated loneliness, reading-as-writing may exist among the preconditions of modern pastoral and its aura of incestuous dwelling in the landscapes of remembrance.[4] The work of reading as a posture of false loneliness attempts to bypass the conditions of authority set in place by social contracts or by the regulations of business life. In a harmless sense, this kind of reading is indecent: it represents a cool and indefinite form of being horny, within oneself and yet in print.

In Benjamin's view, the age of mechanical reproduction—of which photography and film are the dominant media—brought about a devaluation of authenticity as a criterion by which one could measure the artwork's authority over its beholders. For him, the authentic in art "is the essence of all that is transmissible from its beginning, ranging from its substantive duration to its testimony to the history which it has experienced."[5] Although the thrust of his argument in the essay on mechanical reproduction differs from that in the essay on the storyteller, the notion of experiencing what has become transmissible on account of its authentic makeup and history leads to the notion of experience as the fundamental content and context of traditional storytelling. Just as the "aura" of authenticity vanishes in the age of mechanical reproduction, so does what Benjamin perceives as genuine experience, or the traditional stuff of which stories are made. For him, in the modern industrial world that centers on the First World War, the ability to exchange experiences has faded, human experience has "fallen in value," and newspapers convey information that in former times would have traveled from region to region by word of mouth in the form of stories laced with practical wisdom. Sheer information of the journalistic sort has replaced the type of person-to-person communication in which what was learned through direct experience was handed over to someone who then became the bearer of that experience in face-to-face encounters with different groups of listeners. Mechanical warfare during the Great War obliterated the old channels of personally traded information. Benjamin evokes a landscape of utter allegorical loneliness in the face of swift changes affecting the tenor of life after the war: "A generation that had gone to school on a horse-drawn streetcar now stood under the open sky in a countryside in which nothing remained unchanged but the clouds, and beneath these clouds, in a field of force of destructive torrents and explosions, was the tiny, fragile human body" (84). In a world shattered by the engines of mechanical reproduction and warfare, the storyteller of old (a man) comes into the essayist's mind like a figure of "full corporeality": man and tale form a single matter. Such weathered resilience contrasts with the way in which authentic experience has broken down, carrying with it all the bits of practical wisdom that it once conveyed to the listeners of tales.

Traditional tales used to reflect the values of "an artisan form of communication," performing such a duty in a manner now broken, as the tiny human presence is left facing an empty landscape from which all information value has been extracted. As conceived by Benjamin, in traditional times the artisan's image draws itself in tight rapport with its own means of production, its representation (or product) is reduced to a minimal art glued to the artisan's body. The artisanship of telling stories "does not aim to convey the pure essence of the thing, like information or a report"; its method of passing wisdom to the audience, says Benjamin, "sinks the thing into the life of the storyteller, in order to bring it out of him again. Thus traces of the storyteller cling to the story the way the handprints of the potter cling to the clay vessel" (92). This memorable nostalgic sentence expresses Benjamin's emphasis on use value and the way in which it may transform a sense of individual autonomy into one of communal adherence, or into signatures of material solidarity which yield a type of residual aura free from the inherent cult value that sustains the notion of aura when Benjamin illustrates its dissipation under mechanical reproduction.

The aura of authenticity in storytelling preserves both a sense of individual worth and of communal usefulness and solidarity with a group of virtual consumers. In moving from the very archaic setting of societies based on the authority of ritual and myth toward a socio-economic setting occupied by artisans, tillers of the soil, and itinerant merchants, Benjamin shifts his recovery of the past away from the conflict-ridden space in which solidarity, most likely of a tribal and religious sort, would have prevailed over wisdom and craft of a simple industrious nature. As a result of this shift of settings from the efferves-cence of tribal or homeric ways to the routines of medieval guild-labor, the traditional telling of stories as imagined by Benjamin never comes under the alienating effects of authority as defined by his own view of cultic awe, the death mask, and primitive soothsaying. The essay on the storyteller does not deal with such phenomena as archaic magic and the epic cult of the warrior, and instead offers a nostalgic picture of the anonymous habits of medieval artisanship. In counterpoint, the essay on mechanical reproduction claims that regressive links exist between the modern mechanical ensembles of persons and parts and the primitive arts of magic. The storyteller represents a plain artist, not a wizard, who shapes vessels and words for his own benefit and that of a small group of productive witnesses and consumers. In contrast, those figures whom Benjamin chooses either as victims or executors of mechanical reproduc-tion are seen caught in conflict with a host of unresolved dialectical forces, unresolved because their own force depends on never truly over-coming the struggle between autonomy and bondage that sets them in what amounts to perpetual motion. The enforcers and victims of me-chanical drive betray their kinship with a primitive and sacred creator of objects animated by an enchanting and frightful movement and whose aura was already a milder form of chaos, a tamed version of the awesome typhoon winds of cosmogonic times (of which the primitive swastika may have been a frequent emblem). Thus, when Benjamin's essays are read intertextually, a wizard (such as a demiurge, a counterfeit of primal violence in charge of storytelling and the stewardship of magic) stands as the prototype of mechanical illusionism and repetitive production. As we will see, something like film (or the filmic) seems to precede storytell-ing in Benjamin's imaginary realm of materialist evolution.

Along such lines, Benjamin's discussion of aura may be seen as an exorcism of charismatic fascism and its frenzied motions. He begins by identifying the phenomenon of aura in its presumed natural setting. In a restful summer afternoon, the eye wanders to the distant mountains, just as it may notice the shadow of an overhanging branch; distance and proximity create a haven for leisure, a place in which to enjoy reading and its random pauses. We are in a bower of solitude and ready to experience aura. Two factors in contemporary life will destroy such individual awareness, its passive reflection, and transcendent design. The masses want things brought closer to them, so they might overcome "the uniqueness of every reality by accepting its reproduction" (223). A collective fetishism devoted to equivalent qualities and exchange values sets in: "Every day the urge grows stronger to get hold of an object at very close range by way of its likeness," says Benjamin, in terms very similar to the ones that had been used by Sir James Frazer in defining the procedures of animistic magic in *The Golden Bough* (1890) discussed below. Soon, the approach through likeness becomes an assault aimed at the very core of what is desired: "To pry an object from its shell, to destroy its aura, is the mark of a perception whose 'sense of the universal equality of things' has increased to such a degree that it extracts it even from a unique object by means of reproduction" (223).

It should be noted that these preliminary assertions will lead to Benjamin's embrace of mechanical reproduction, particularly with respect to film, as a revolutionary means to shock the cult of commodity in bourgeois art and to bring down its illusions of subjective aesthetic autonomy. Film requires work in ensemble, it fragments its various components before final editing, it subjects narrative to the selective violence of *montage,* as it isolates and segments the actors from an audience of potential worshipers, at least at the moment of performance. Quite besides its incipient commodification in the cult of *stars,* film represents for Benjamin a weapon in the struggle to remove art from its service to ritual, magic, and religion: "For the first time in world history, mechanical reproduction emancipates the work of art from its parasitical dependence on ritual" (224). The urgency with which Benjamin brings his own political agenda into the breach opened between the artwork and its former cult value reflects his awareness of the renewal of precisely such ritual value under fascist ideology, with its program to introduce aesthetics into political life. However, Benjamin's dialectical thinking drives him beyond film's and the avant-garde's potential revolutionary use of the destruction of aura, as brought about by mechanical reproduction.

Thus, when he describes the *exhibition value* that replaces the old cult value in artworks divested of aura, Benjamin flirts with an enhancement of violence quite different from, but cognate with, the technological shocks to sensibility that he perceives in the filmic, as well as in other means of wrenching presence and authority generated by his own violence-specific, segmentary, and nonritual views on the mechanics of filmmaking.

Accordingly, Benjamin narrates a *petite histoire* of how photography drove the cult value of individual portraiture into one final effusion of aura emanating from the human countenance. Early on, photography replaced painting as the main token of ritual presence; the image of a face had a quality of timelessness akin to the one present in the death mask. But this "ultimate retrenchment" of personal aura disappeared from Atget's photographic work on deserted streets; exhibition value gained the upper hand in those views of Parisian locales empty of all human presence, like scenes registered in the wake of a crime. The "scene of a crime too is deserted; it is photographed for the purpose of establishing evidence"; with Atget, "photographs become standard evidence for historical occurrences, and acquire a hidden political significance" (226). With this hermeneutic anecdote, the invisible presence of violence begins to animate Benjamin's view of a certain transparency and weightlessness emerging at the point where the value of exhibition replaces that of cult, and whereupon the will to read meanings with piercing ingenuity would break loose from the ritual script of traditional authority and aura.

Events of crowded political significance should occupy the deserted crime and mystery places photographed by Atget. However, Benjamin's expectations of having history enter into the transparencies of forensic and detective space run into further illustrations of violence and displacement of a primitive prepolitical sort. Just as aura found final retrenchment in the photographic exposure of the human face, the process of filming obtains evidence of its own exhibition value by focusing on the human figure, but with different results since, rather than lending aura to the photographed countenance and its stoic charisma, film will cause the audience to identify with the camera itself—not with the filmed actor. This startling complicity turns the actor into a victim of mechanical isolation and deprives him of the public's immediate notice or pity. Relying on Luigi Pirandello's novel *Si Gira* (1915), Benjamin finds the film actor in exile, "not only from the stage but also from himself." With "a vague sense of discomfort," the actor "feels inexplicable emptiness: his body loses its corporeality, it evaporates, it is deprived of reality, life, voice, and the noises caused by his moving about, in order to be changed into a mute image, flickering an instant on the screen, then vanishing into silence." The actor migrates from the camera work to the projector, which "will play with his shadow before the public," as "he himself must be content to play before the camera" (229). Some sort of black magic or counterfeit metaphysics could obtain from such a view of metamorphosis in the silent cinema, but Benjamin is more interested in the dialectics between bondage to ritual (as in the theater) and the actor's new need (as in filmmaking) to rely on his own body while performing in a scene of freedom yet to be mastered. "For the first time, man has to operate with his whole living person, yet forgoing its aura. For aura is tied to presence; there can be no replica of it" (229). In contrast with dramatic tragedy, the film actor performs beyond the grasp of the audience but within that of the camera, but the camera registers no emanation. Filmic Macbeth amounts to a serial duplicate that is edited, extracted from a sequence of *takes,* and that appears uninhibited by any such gaps or elisions in its own making. The film actor represents a sheer product, a hidden contrivance of mechanical steps, and hence a crisis, a *shock* to the cult of presence.

It would seem that, with his narrativistic attention to factors of technique and production, Benjamin would place film closer to painting than to photography. After all, painters and filmmakers work at intervals and rely on repeated applications of technique and material; also, by Benjamin's time, painting had produced elaborate mediations of a technical and mechanical sort between the artist and the space of representation. It should be added that, as film increases its technical capabilities to simulate and enhance appearances, it becomes *painterly* to a degree of illusion and impact already achieved in Benjamin's lifetime by German expressionist cinema. However, it is precisely the narrativistic approach to what he sees happening to the human presence in the process of mechanical reproduction that causes Benjamin to leave painting outside any intriguing dialectical set of resemblances and proximate differences in connection with film. Benjamin's emphasis on the fragmenting procedures that film brings into play in order to reproduce human performance sidetracks his own dialectical recognition of the medium's access to the familiar and the uncanny. His highly defamiliarized version of film, with its elements of a monster story, takes Benjamin outside film events as such, or beyond the shape in which they might exist in any given movie either seen or imagined by him. Nonetheless, in the end, Benjamin's punctuation of theory with brief illustrations and analytic scenes works against the mechanical strangeness he tries to recognize in film whenever he contrasts it with the illusion of natural fluency already achieved in the traditional art forms of painting and the novel. For instance, it could be argued that, rather than destroying aura and ritual value as Benjamin claims, the film apparatus contributes to their emergence, as it gives a new appeal to the bodily motions of militant as well as hedonistic life. Aura itself might be a symptom of film culture rather than its notorious victim. A type of violent and charismatic performance (which one might attribute to the *filmic*) brings the machine into play outside film-space as such. In those images in which Benjamin's essay exploits a narrative repertoire of dualistic characterizations concerning specific types of mechanical and nonmechanical activity, a darker, phantasmagoric view of film culture and phenomena comes to the foreground and sets limits to his political optimism concerning the medium's potential value for revolutionary art. This is particularly true of his efforts to put the greatest distance between film and painting.

Since he begins by equating painting (as well as the novel) with the individualistic maintenance of ritual aura in bourgeois art, Benjamin goes on to enliven the gap between the techniques of the film cameraman and the brush painter with an example. He starts by seeing the masses attempting to "pry an object from its shell" in order to "destroy its aura"; then this image of violence (and violation) comes back as he compares the cameraman to a surgeon and the painter to a magician. In magic, the cure maintains "a natural distance" with the patient: the magician lays hands on the sick with all the power lent by authority. The surgeon's art "does exactly the reverse," for as distance ceases to mediate between cure and symptom, the surgeon penetrates into the patient's body, "his hands move among the organs." Hence, "in contrast to the magician—who is still hidden in the medical practitioner—the surgeon at the decisive moment abstains from facing the patient man to man; rather, it is through the operation that he penetrates into him." Thus "magician and surgeon compare to painter and cameraman," while the painter "maintains in his work a natural distance from reality, the cameraman penetrates deeply into its web" (233). The importance of bodily involvement in these contrasting practices receives further treatment in a footnote, where Benjamin describes the "boldness of the cameraman," as reflected in the "acrobatic tricks of larynx surgery" and in "the so-called endonasal perspective procedure" (248–49).

Any attentive reader of Benjamin would know that this is not an isolated instance of dramatic enhancement, that he uses narrative sketches whose imagistic effect defeats any synthetic approach to his theories. The sketch artist in Benjamin seems destined to outlast the theorist. Just as in the course of a life random memories of certain readings may embalm and bury their own writing, in Benjamin's essays the muse of memory interposes her body between two forms of regressive reading. Often one reenters his writings through a window that he once opened within his own reading of stories whose effect becomes the more striking when one has never read them. A collaboration between two types of readers ensues, one who remembers and one who surmises and invents. For instance, on the eve of his wedding, a miner dies at the bottom of a mine shaft; his bride mourns him for years until, one day, "a body is brought up from the abandoned tunnel which, saturated with iron vitriol, has escaped decay, and she recognizes her betrothed. After this reunion she too is called away by death" (94). Benjamin offers this picture (from Johann Peter Hebel) in order to illustrate how death supports all that the storyteller borrows from authority and then gives to the audience. Although the notion of aura is never mentioned in "The Storyteller," it is hard to imagine a better example of it. In fact, Benjamin demonstrates the transmissible form that stories take at the point of individual death by means of another illustration in which an audience raised on television and the movies would spontaneously recognize conventional elements of film narrative:

> Just as a sequence of images is set in motion inside a man as his life comes to an end—unfolding the views of himself under which he has encountered himself without being aware of it—suddenly in his expressions and looks the unforgettable emerges and imparts to everything that concerns him that authority which even the poorest wretch in dying possesses for the living around him. This authority is at the very source of the story. (94)

What nowadays might seem like a domestication of film differs radically from the violent means of mechanical reproduction that Benjamin isolates in filmic representation. What he sketches here with considerable novelistic sentiment evokes the environment of narrative painting and the engraved illustration of novels. If such viewing takes Benjamin away from film as the machine of the unfamiliar, it does so in a way that liberates the violent essence which he saw in the medium, in what we now might call the filmic.

The filmic may encompass the growth of film fantasies and events outside the screen; it alludes to a style of public and cultural experience closer to a sense of *screen* than to one of *space*. It could be argued that Benjamin upholds an explosively antispatial sense of film and of filmic environment:

> Our taverns and our metropolitan streets, our offices and furnished rooms, our railroad stations and our factories appeared to have us locked up hopelessly. Then came the film and burst this prison-world asunder by the dynamite of the tenth of a second, so that now, in the midst of the far-flung ruins and debris, we calmly and adventurously go traveling. (236)

Such would be the landscape of the filmic in its widest implications, one in which any individual may go reeling and screening through shifting surfaces, trying to match his or her horizontal motions with the vertical passage of frames that the screen renders invisible. The filmic escapes the sedentary condition of viewing, it involves the politics of flight. When Benjamin says that "all efforts to render politics aesthetic culminate in one thing: war," he mentions two violations of autonomy. In one, the masses are brought to their knees by fascism and the cult of the Leader; in the other, "an apparatus . . . is pressed into the production of ritual values" (241). If, as the rest of the essay implies, film embodies (and alienates) the apparatus of modern aesthetic violence, one can assume that such ritual values in themselves are, among other things, forms of film displaced, removed from any concrete mechanical means of production. Then it should not be surprising if F. T. Marinetti's embodiment of the aesthetics of war (as quoted by Benjamin from "Futurist Aesthetic of War" [1935]) looks like something torn out of a movie: "War is beautiful because it establishes man's dominion over the subjugated machinery by means of gas masks, terrifying megaphones, flame throwers, and small tanks. War is beautiful because it initiates the dreamt-of metalization of the human body" (241).

Marinetti's list of war objects and motions goes on, yet it remains focused on the point where it frames the metallic body of the warrior, as if his dynamic armature represented the parthenogenesis of the film apparatus resembling something like Coriolanus in war gear. There is no need to quote from Caius Martius's impressive catalogue of metallic hardness and fire tricks in order to claim that Benjamin's anatomy of filmic technical violence finds a dualistic mythic counterpart in his own quotation of Marinetti's manifesto on the mechanistic beauty of war. What matters is not placing Benjamin's views within the war aura that emanates from an entire era of filmmaking subsequent to his death, or seeing in his views the unintended forecast of how much of film's thematic and technical violence has promoted the medium's overwhelming popularity. What matters is the recognition that Benjamin's film apparatus shocks because it is closer to a mythic beast and a war hero than to an inorganic machine. His implicit narrativistic film demonstrates the symbolic, magical, and exhibitionist equivalences that may exist among such entities of besieged solidarity as the ones found in moviehouse and public square. His film is tribal; it hums and flickers with sacredness. Unlike the storyteller, film wizardry has little to do with dying or even with death. Film *narratronics* makes ritual and magic war on the senses: it pierces, but in a strange way it never kills, simply unsettling old forms, creating new ones, and then coiling back upon itself like a toy dragon consuming reenchanted versions of the primitive.

In the end, if film comes to share with magic the phenomenon of aura under new conditions of technical alienation, Benjamin may demand that the mechanical metamorphoses of the filmic should exhibit themselves bluntly, as if they were incisions and not sacred wounds manifested in the charismatic body of society. Benjamin's aesthetics of estrangement would transform magic display into the forensic art of exposing inferences of latent general consent in the connecting tissue of group solidarity. If, like Don Quixote, the storyteller should die at home surrounded by neighbors, film may not. Film may never die; it should (like myth) recompose itself endlessly through a shameless rearrangement of its parts.

Inferences and Wounds

La poesía está en el comercio del poema con el lector, no en la serie de símbolos que registran las páginas de un libro. Lo esencial es el hecho estético, el thrill, *la modificación física que suscita cada lectura.*
[Poetry lies in the poem's commerce with the reader, not in the series of symbols registered by the pages of a book. The essential lies in the aesthetic event, the thrill, the physical modification that each reading arouses].—Jorge Luis Borges, Obra poética

During the same years (1936–39) in which Benjamin walked the line between film and magic and offered a memorial to the art of storytelling, Borges persisted in the apprenticeship of prose fiction under a syllabus of his own making. Emerging from his poetry of the previous decade, he published essays and a biography of a man and his neighborhood (*Evar-*

isto Carriego, 1930), a celebration of criminal heresies (*Historia universal de la infamia*, 1935), and a wicked recognition of Plato and various other antidotes to mutability (*Historia de la eternidad*, 1936). After almost a decade in Europe around the time of the Great War, Borges returned to Argentina and rediscovered Buenos Aires and its suburbs. The period up to the writing of "Pierre Menard, autor del Quijote" (1939) represents the ethnographic present in Borges's biography, a time of mythic signifi-cance in which a man's life and his work become reciprocal as they achieve the status of fiction, or *mytho-history*, as Edmund Leach prefers to call this peculiar thickening of evidence concerning the cultural biogra-phy of an individual or a cult (see Leach and Aycock, *Biblical Myth*, 35). One is reminded of the months that Thomas De Quincey spent in London as a truant and homeless teenager in 1802, which he would recollect in *Confessions of an English Opium-Eater* (1821).

In a brilliant piece of hagiography, Emir Rodríguez Monegal (*Borges*, 130–43) associates the death of Borges's father in early 1938 with the son's creative mourning and the iridescence of artistic guilt. Jorge Luis sets out to redeem the unfulfilled career of a paternal and homely writer whose work had been defeated by blindness. Moreover, at the moment when mourning for the father still must have been at the critical point of lacking a genuine creative outlet, on Christmas Eve, 1938, Borges suf-fered a head wound and almost died of septicemia. Much later, the ordeal would find fictional resolution in the story "El Sur" (1953), but in his "Autobiographical Essay" (*The Aleph*, 242–43), Borges mentions his portrait of Pierre Menard as the direct response to the hallucinations and horror produced by the fever that almost killed him. Rodríguez Mone-gal interprets what amounts to a rite of passage (or an episode of conversion) in terms of Borges's "aesthetics of reading." In the figure of Pierre Menard, he argues, the emerging writer of the combined and recycled fictions of others finds a character that allows him to conceal "the shunning of paternity," and that gives him the chance to engender himself within the father's symbolic realm, to acquire a new life in-formed by the knowledge of death.

It may be argued that the large role played by the notion of inference in Borges's poetics of fiction develops from the common association between the ghost of paternity and the combined acts of paternal as-sumption and filial confidence, as when he writes: "Reality as pro-pounded by classical writers, like fatherhood to a certain character in Goethe's *Wilhelm Meister*, is largely an act of faith" [La realidad que los escritores clásicos proponen es cuestión de confianza, como la paternidad para cierto personaje de los *Lehrjahre*] (*Prose for Borges*, 197). The two faces of inference (the naïve and the cunning) blend together in the tokens exchanged between filial confidence and paternal recognition, or in the assumption of negotiated love through the inherent fictionality of fatherhood. The all-too-familiar oedipal business may lead to the endless fluctuations of hope and despair experienced by a son trying to outlive his father's spiritual injuries in the heroic actuality of a physical wound. As will be examined shortly, inference, assumption, and injury—both physical and spiritual—are closely linked in Borges's representation of reality and in his own analytical understanding of fiction and mimesis. Inference extends its implications until it becomes the linchpin holding together the naked candor of the writer and the masked skepticism of the reader. A good deal of Borges's tragic and comic sense of character, author, and plot issues from his conception of these two binding and bonded individuals: the one reading and the one who holds what is being read to the mirror of his own writing.

A tension develops between, on the one hand, the simultaneous and specular view of reader and writer as a single but split being and, on the other, their relationship as two individuals who remain spaced-out, marked by difference, and kept apart by deferral. In this case, the reader reviews, emends, and takes delight in displacing the actions of the writer. Also, their split condition with respect to a single subject widens. Thus, instead of the specular bonding that reflects their essential identity, a chasm opens between them. As suggested by Rodríguez Monegal, such a widening gap includes elements of mourning and reparation, but in a way that is both covert and blatant. Irony of the most cunning sort mediates between both postures, since Menard (the author) is also a counterfeit on display, whose writing of *Don Quixote* appears different from the act of reading Cervantes by just a minimum degree of exertion. If the act of replacing the recognized father of a text represents an ironic transumption of mourning into joy, it also implies a passage from envy toward narcissism. Rather than internalizing the enduring prestige of a book through repeated readings, Menard displays the book and, unlike its original author, *wears* it. In a footnote to Thomas Carlyle, Menard disavows any residual form of modern(ist) melancholia through an act of sartorial cynicism.

Further parallels exist between psychoanalytic themes and the situation of the split storyteller in Borges. Inference (under the specific heading of *assumption* [*postulación*]) implies two distinct areas of psychoanalytic speculation concerning the male subject. It may open the question of fetishism, if either fear of castration or resistance against the mother's lack of a penis seem relevant in defining instances of trauma or specific cases of defense against loss. Inference may also open the question of mourning and melancholia if the same signs of trauma and countervailing defenses demand a kind of relevance differently attached to the question of love loss. If the matter of fetishism comes to the foreground, the specific imaginary contents involving sex, desire, and erotic thrills could underscore the presence of masochism and its contractual solution to feelings of fear and impotence. The son seeks refuge within a performance or ritual in which the intrusion of chance is not desired, and in which the mother should play a disguised role in the company of some phallic paraphernalia. At least in a vulgar sense, masochism of this sort reveals the animating presence of sexual anguish and perversity in rather obvious ways; it also corresponds to the imaginary specular identity already noted between reader and writer, because it hinges on a latent structure of simultaneous and contradictory beliefs. Namely, the fetishist consents to the mother's phallic nature at the same time that he counterfeits her lack of a penis by adopting some substitute object on behalf of the phallus. According to Freud, upon the adoption of a certain substitute object as a fetish, in the subject's mind "the woman *has* got a penis, in spite of everything; but this penis is no longer the same as it was before. . . . The horror of castration has set up a memorial to itself in the creation of this substitute" (*Works*, 9:154). If the matter of mourning displaces that of masochism, however, the role and character of the fetish could shift away from the scene of perversity and contractual ritual in which a mother figure and her son enact a liturgy of endurable punishment on behalf of the absent (paternal) phallus. Away from such a scene, the object could find a dwelling area inside the mourner and thus become lodged, lost, introjected in it. From being a rather plain thing, the fetish would become an inward object and, at various moments, it would be cast out, jettisoned into the mourner's surrounding reality, in which it could regain a sudden fetishistic allure. In a sense, the object of mourning never had the chance to become a fetish, or to be a token made for worship; but the object may later on withdraw from the mourner and be projected into his surrounding habitat, thus becoming an invested thing akin to a fetish.

Assuming that both masochism and mourning engage in a certain construction of sacredness, their respective procedures might involve a different rapport with death and also with aggression. In masochism, death remains imaginary or choreographic. Even if such a perverse mode of animating things seems to grant them the ability to die, what may actually happen is that, for the masochist, all manner of absence, including the one resulting from death, comes to signify at least three things: (1) loss, (2) the peculiar place of residence (the uncanniness) of what is lost, and (3) the necessary points of bodily attachment to which the object of loss belongs. In masochistic passivity, the individual finds rest under a contract to celebrate, to deck himself with, and to cover up such places and points of suture with the help of his consenting mistress or master. But in mourning activity, the status of being passive answers to a condition of harbored permanence, of prolonged rumination; it matters that mourning should persist, and that it should prove so refractory to any ritual articulation in erotic gear. It matters even more that mourning should in some cases punctuate its enduring vigil and its tendency to avoid untheatrical orgasm with bouts of sadistic frenzy. Insofar as any of these psychoanalytic speculations may inform the understanding of Borges's views on fiction in more than a casual way, one should explore two forms of displacement: displacement from a masochistic scenario (and the role of fetishism within it) to the space of mourning, and displacement from a ritual compromise with passivity to a hazardous coexistence with sadism and violence.

Although properly translated as "The Assumption of Reality," the title and arguments of "La postulación de la realidad" should promote inferences concerning *asking, soliciting,* and *pretending* present in the Latin verb *postulare* (Corominas, *Breve diccionario,* 471). Rather than being a simple question of etymology, the innocent and conniving actions implicit in *postulación* are found at the heart of Borges's arguments and of his view of the central role played by the spontaneous phenomenon of inference in narrative understanding. Upon reading the essay, the title could be awkwardly paraphrased as "On Inference, or, Begging Reality." Whether in the act of writing or reading a story, a given sense of reality takes shape; it typically involves a wealth of assumptions and inferences upon which both writer and reader depend, as well as a tacit consensus regarding the shared nature of what might be taken for granted as constituting the real. In his short meditations on fiction and the behavior of reading, Borges is far from demanding deep involvement with any theoretical issues in what is nowadays conceived as narratology, but the issues he raises correspond to recent topics in the study of narrative and its reception. For instance, when he contrasts the *classic* and *romantic* modes of expressing reality in writing, he sees each type of writer addressing a world that should be familiar to a perennial audience, to a group that speaks and understands a common language. What is different according to the essay is not the real as such, but the contrasting ways in which so-called classics and romantics articulate and express universal expectations concerning the nature of social reality. Implicit in this view is the notion that writers alter narrative textures against a background of routine expectations and the inclination to agree with what everyone else already believes. Before examining the contrast between the classic and the romantic modes, it seems appropriate to offer a brief preview of the interpretation that will be followed here.

I shall argue that the essence of what Borges means and implies by *postulación* corresponds to Benjamin's problematics of *aura*, that, in the context developed by Borges, assumption and inference involve an encounter with the related orders of ritual, magic, and communal solidarity as imagined by Benjamin. I shall further attempt to show how a particular notion of inference (as found within the general one of assumption) comes to rest upon the dominant figure of a man whose thematic prominence as a single individual makes him a lightning rod struck by irrational forces latent in communal solidarity. This figure may eventually transform the realm of inference into a person-specific affair in which the thematic substance of his character breaks down into dualistic particles gathered by lethal aggression. Just as in Benjamin the notions of aura and magic are said to suffer a violent breakup when exposed to film's mechanical reproduction, in Borges the rapport between magic and inference finds ground in violence and performance. Because both aura and inference manifest the ritualized existence of communal beliefs, they represent the threshold, the unveiling of social consensus spectacularly celebrated and advertised in sublime or prestigious modes of activity and production. Being trivial but also sacred, these instances of aura and inferential power may reward those individuals ready to experience their own sense of being elect and unique. At the same time, behind such a gift of mediated charisma, the parallel acts of hosting aura and engaging in assumption translate themselves into kindred forms of surrender. The individual loses autonomy and participates in group solidarity, actually or vicariously joins a tribe, a clan, or a mob, and may at times become a sacrificial victim in the affair. The discovery of violence in human shape—beneath both aura and inference—could represent a reaction, a defense staged by the individual who uncovers (in himself and in a specular adversary) the stripped-down or naked figure of someone who embodies the aggressive basis of ritual solidarity and bondage to magical practices. In Benjamin, the film apparatus transforms primitive aggression by means of its own technical violence, but it releases in the filmic a picture of magic and ritual that it both disenchants and rechannels, subverts and enhances. In Borges, the reading of stories is never far from a given sense of film. This feeling for film finds a mirror in the narrativistic violence that his stories so often depict, the same violence that his views on fiction uncover while disclosing the inner workings of narrative assumption and inference. In this context, whatever separates the two authors begins with Benjamin's attempt to transcend the primitive aggression inherent in social solidarity by means of a dialectical assumption (for revolutionary purposes) of the technical violence and visionary estrangement that he identifies with the film apparatus. Then, their separation culminates when Borges shows no such political agenda. On the contrary, Borges's view of gaucho violence, of *compadrito* dueling, and of other effusions of mythic or folkloric virility celebrates a heroic and tribal past whose obsolescence the storyteller mourns with dry but fervent tears distilled with irony.

Turning now to "La postulación de la realidad," the gist of the contrast it offers between classic and romantic writers consists in arguing that the former *trust* the expressive power of language, while the latter *thrust* themselves upon it. Classics rely on the "sufficient value" of each symbol, while romantics enlist language in an incessant striving for expression. Borges intends no historical connotation; hence, the term *classical* will be avoided here in order to prevent an unmediated identification with writers from antiquity. Borges uses each label to signify two "arquetipos de escritor," two paths ("procederes") followed by the art of writing (*Discusión*, 67). In fact, he gives no examples of the romantic proclivity toward expressiveness. The whole essay is devoted to demonstrating Benedetto Croce's mistaken identification of aesthetics with expression ("la identidad de lo estético y de lo expresivo"). Moreover, in showing how "writers of a classical [sic] turn of mind tend to eschew expression or . . . take it for granted" (*Prose for Borges*, 194), Borges implies that *clásicos* reject the impulse to express their own selves at every imaginable moment of rhetorical choice. It is as if the romantic instinct to express individual uniqueness—rather than just allowing language to express itself—constituted a spontaneous personal choice against which a certain adherence to the anonymous wisdom of rhetoric takes effect every time a classic writer writes. Abstinence from expression, however, does not represent a refusal to dwell in the thickness of rhetoric. In being a classic, one abstains from oneself rather than from the pleasures of linguistic expression. By implication, romantic expressive hedonism anx-iously abandons itself to hollow pleasures. Romantics confuse the real with themselves and fail to fully recognize their own representative or allegorical character in language. In not being content with *recording* reality and in trying instead to *represent* it, romantics seek "los primeros contactos de la realidad," rather than awaiting "su elaboración final en conceptos" (*Discusión*, 68). At the core of being romantic, one refuses the elaborate company of rhetoric's conceptual negotiations with the real. Rhetorical negotiation and desire resist intellectual abstraction and seek instead the flesh offered by a sort of inference supported by the testi-mony of other minds and by the impact upon the individual of bodies other than his own (the implicit writer here is gendered male). The assumptions in which classic writing dwells draw their heat from the ancestral routines of keeping pace with other minds and bodies engaged in countless activities, including battles, feasts, and the pleasures and perils found in bed. Although he does not use the word, it is rhetoric and not only style that Borges addresses; but rhetoric, of the classic sort, is not meant to exceed the inherited practical wisdom registered in the means it employs in order to offer a *record* of reality. The language of classic representation works with someone else's tools, fights with some-one else's weapons, and lies in someone else's bed (with a lover who bears someone else's love). The original genius of the classic writer is married to custom. If chaste rhetoric represents the classic's bride, myth has brought her to the altar.

Next to various sorts of war, one may find marriage, sacrifice, and burial as the three significant, interlinked rituals that inform Borges's mythic sense of classic rhetoric. His first example comes from Edward Gibbon's *The History of the Decline and Fall of the Roman Empire* (1776–88). It begins by depicting the aftermath of a battle between Roman forces and Attila's Huns, and ends with a quick picture of the subsequent plunder and rape carried out by the Thuringians:

> They massacred their hostages, as well as their captives: two hun-dred young maidens were tortured with exquisite and unrelenting rage; their bodies were torn asunder by wild horses, or their bones were crushed under the weight of rolling wagons; and their un-buried limbs were abandoned on the public roads as a prey to dogs and vultures. (quoted in *Prose for Borges*, 194)

Borges chooses a sober account of mayhem in order to illustrate how the classic writer exercises the craft of recording a series of events and actions.

He does not mention Gibbon's reliance on sources, or the likelihood that such sources might never have actually witnessed the events in question; his assumption regards such mediations as inherent in classic discourse. If, as Borges argues, such discourse translates raw experiences into concepts and symbols, it may matter most that the way in which he first put this in writing suffered changes in English translation, presumably with his consent. In quibbling with di Giovanni's rendition and in supplying brackets to what he has altered and even omitted, one plays the role of the same kind of audience on which, according to Borges, the classic writer relies (omissions are placed in double brackets):

> The bare statement "after the departure of the Goths" is enough to make us aware of the intellectual nature [carácter mediato] of this writing [de esta escritura, [generalizadora y abstracta hasta lo invisible]]; the complicated facts of what actually happened have been made into ideas. The writer has given us [nos propone] a set of symbols, which, though skillfully organized, do not convey the immediacy of reality [[cuya animación eventual queda a cargo nuestro]]. Gibbon is essentially expressionless; his aim is to record [registrar] reality, not to represent it. The many events to which he alludes [los ricos hechos a cuya [póstuma alusión nos convida]] were compounded of highly charged individual experiences, perceptions, and reactions. These may be inferred from the narrative but are not in it. In other words, Gibbon sets down not the first raw feelings of reality but their final elaboration into ideas [conceptos]. This is the classical method, the one followed by Voltaire, Swift, Cervantes. (*Prose for Borges,* 195)

The translation is less faulty than chaste. Three missing words need mention: *invisible, animación, póstuma.* Taken together, these *voces* represent the marrow of idiomatic Borges, they are the *narrative* kernels of the entire argument. To remove them betrays the working of certain assumptions very much at odds with the material sources from which, according to Borges, concepts usually spring, and from where they begin to act, to impinge on other minds and sensibilities. If words like these are expunged or replaced with others, their sublimation into concepts not only loses its sources in actual material life, it also breaks loose from the path it might have followed in coming *from* other minds and bodies into the work of any actual writer of the classic sort. Words like *invisible, animation,* and *posthumous* allow for dual embodiment, mediated by the passage of generations.

In Borges's classic genealogy, there is a distant source that already embodied such words, as well as another, currently available as a source akin to the older one in the way it (still) phrases these (same) words. In Borges's sense of classic rhetoric, characters fall within a lineage of parent sources which break up into elements of myth and allegory.

It might be said that Borges's imagined reader of classic sources *animates a posthumous allusion to the invisible*. A more complex formula might propose that in classic discourse *the invisible represents the real in posthumous allusion to itself*, insofar as the *real* springs from what other minds have already recorded and other bodies suffered or enjoyed in providing actual or imaginary substance to such recording. It all boils down to a matter of record: more than merely having been felt, said, or done, everything in classic sources has already been recorded. Animation occurs in reading, not in writing. At any given moment, when one is about to resume reading, recorded things stand at the point of requiring animation. Thus the real lies in present suspension and the past seems dead but about to be animated by a citation effectively veiled as an original phrasing. Like Hermione's statue, the real always returns as if from among the dead in order to replace, through animation, the otherwise disembodied presence of death among those still living.

In the second example given, Borges quotes Cervantes's exemplary novel, *El curioso impertinente,* as an "almost abusive" instance of classic reliance on the reader's supplying of missing points of reference. Lotario has been charged with the task of tempting rather than seducing Camila. Already madly in love with her and yet still outwardly faithful to the instructions of his best friend, Lotario mounts a verbal assault upon Anselmo's chaste wife, now transformed by the magic of words into a *fortress* and, like many other beauties, made more vulnerable by the very language that compares her to a bastion. Cervantes's past tense has it that the lover *cried, begged, offered, flattered, argued,* and *feigned,* until Camila joined him in passion. The hint that Camila's vanity is pierced by such an assault implies that, at least in her case, the lovers' mutual appetite has a supplementary source in self-passion. Borges is not interested, however, in such moral or psychological assumptions; he seems more concerned with the license to take things for granted, and he marvels at the implied quantity of such things, even in a passage as brief as the one found in Cervantes. Borges delights in the instant "simplificación conceptual de estados complejos" (*Discusión,* 68) at work in this, as well as in most other instances of high and low literature. (In implying that such simplification is almost universally common, his view of classic writing threatens to become an account of myth's instant access to consciousness by way of stereotypes.) Since, if not betrayed in translation, he might have agreed to have his words rendered as "The translation of sensory perception into concepts is instantaneous" (*Prose for Borges*, 196), the seemingly slight change (*translation* for *simplificación*) and the addition of *sensory* and *perception*) create notions of experimental psychology that might puzzle the best practitioners of that science. The passage from Cervantes, however, belongs to a different context, one about to emerge in the essay. It involves the replacement of psychology with allegory, and a further step toward a tacit recognition of the perennial influence of myth in narrative.

Passages like the one from Cervantes seem ineffective only when one expects them *not* to simplify complex behavior and specific conditions of awareness. In so doing, one expects from them—and from narrative in general—more accuracy and detail than what obtains in one's own awareness of spatial and corporeal actuality. It being the case that in actual experience a "deliberate omission of what is uninteresting" may eliminate random impressions, it could be that, if not actually "posthumous," the degree of attention involved in one's own corporeal motions may be controlled by a given set of stereotypic memories and expectations shared by many other human beings. It seems fancifully accurate to say that such typical human beings belong among the dead (past and future) and that they far outnumber human beings alive at any given moment. The fact that one sees and hears through the medium provided by memories, fears, and anticipations implies that when it comes to matters of the body ("lo corporal"), unconsciousness is a necessity embedded in physical acts: "La inconsciencia es una necesidad de los actos físicos" (*Discusión*, 69). The argument cuts deeper than what the polite translation of *inconsciencia* as "inattentiveness" seems ready to tolerate (*Prose for Borges*, 196). It does not imply the rather tedious notion that one *reads* reality, but that one actually may *live* and *die* through reading. The "body knows," says Borges, "how to articulate this difficult paragraph; it knows how to deal with staircases, with knots, overpasses, cities, rivers in torrent, dogs"; it knows, he adds, "how to cross a street without being destroyed by traffic; it knows how to engender, breathe, sleep; it perhaps knows how to kill"; but it is "our body, not our intelligence," that learns to cope with these obstacles and incitements. The condition of living represents "a series of adaptations," an "education in forgetfulness" (*Discusión*, 69–70).

Borges's narrativistic unconsciousness feeds (and is fed) in the midst of such motions and hazards. *Inconsciencia* gains ground the more one accelerates through references, inferences, and the unfolding (and reeling) of cities. Obstacles thrust themselves upon the rushing self of a person who forgets that it is running through accidents, until one such person becomes *an* accident, at which point the person would have collided with (a) memory, or with something it has learned to forget. It would be as if an indefinite condition of running through invisible gates or thresholds were to find such passages closed and demanding a toll, a sudden recognition of their presence. At such a moment, the self is brought to a halt, it is placed beside itself, or forced to share its material existence with things or with the general order of things lying outside the individual.

Somewhat like Benjamin (see Menninghaus, "Benjamin's Theory of Myth," 305), Borges ascribed to mythic forces in modern life an urban topography segmented by thresholds and boundaries, as if such stations were the only things left standing after the collapse of ancient ritual labyrinths:

> The city, at seven in the morning, had not lost that air of an old house lent it by the night; the streets seemed like long vestibules, the plazas were like patios. Dahlmann recognized the city with joy on edge of vertigo: a second before his eyes registered the phenomena themselves, he recalled the corners, the billboards, the modest variety of Buenos Aires. In the yellow light of the new day, all things returned to him. (*Anthology*, 18)

Throughout the small plot of "El Sur," Juan Dahlmann encounters an ordeal in animation; he experiences a posthumous reawakening of memories as he moves from Buenos Aires into the pampas following a course parallel to the one chaotically indexed by Borges in his account of the body's unheroic education in forgetfulness. Dahlmann is wounded in the forehead while hurrying upstairs in darkness and with his mind elsewhere, perhaps dwelling on books. His accident compares with the one suffered by Borges when he too strayed from the smooth path of well-educated forgetfulness and ran up a stairway to meet a young woman (believed to have been María Luisa Bombal) at his mother's kind behest (Rodríguez Monegal, 131–32). In terms of Benjamin's mythography of modern urban types, Dahlmann is anything but a *flâneur*, and yet his two possible ways of dying (of infectious fever *and* in a knife duel with a *compadrito*) have the aura of being fitting acts of retribution, in which emblematic figures of the genius of place (either in sinister or hieratic shape) strike down the sauntering virtuosity of the *flâneur*, with his exquisite taste for untraveled places and neglected thresholds:

> The grand reminiscences, the historical shudder, are even rubbish to the *flâneur*, who gladly relinquishes them to the traveler. And he gives away all of his knowledge about artist's lodgings, birthplaces, or royal domiciles, for the scent of a single threshold or for the tactile sensation of a single tile, as any house dog carries it away. (quoted in Menninghaus, 306)

The antithetical rapport between the epiphanic aestheticism attributed by Benjamin to *flânerie* and the stoic inattentiveness of Juan Dahlmann's *argentinismo* requires close scrutiny in order to articulate the full implications of Borges's apology for classic representation.

The *flâneur* should be at home in Rome, and yet it is in Paris that Rome haunts him, or where he, unknowingly, finds her likeness. Paris invented the *flâneur*, but he belongs to ancient Rome as grasped in certain corners and spots of the modern city (see Menninghaus, 306). Dahlmann's seemingly unaesthetic familiarity with Buenos Aires offers the best clue to the antithetical nexus between him and Benjamin's anonymous *flâneur*. Dahlmann is at home in the same city where Borges, years after writing the story, learned to walk in almost complete blindness, as if he were touching the walls of his own house. A vertical line divides Dahlmann into genealogical halves, it divides his ancestry according to a "discordia" between two lineages so ancestral that his parents seem to count less than his grandparents and their parents. Leaping over father and mother, Dahlmann harks back to an atavistic pair: a paternal German grandfather and a maternal trueblood *abuelo criollo* named Francisco Flores. These two vanished fathers define Dahlmann's brand of nostalgia. Juan has chosen the *romantic* ancestor, the soldier who died fighting Catriel Indians in the frontier, but the choice issues, perhaps, from his striving Germanic blood.

Presumably, the "classic" austerity of Johannes (the maternal [grand]-father who was a church minister) contained elements of German romanticism in check. Fathers (rather than grandfathers) may be designated as *maternal* even within patriarchal descent rules in a sense having little to do with the *motherly* manner of their being fathers. Since neither fathers nor mothers are directly mentioned in "El Sur," their narrative absence represents an instance of classic assumption (a typical "postulación de la realidad"). If classicism, as argued by Borges, concerns the mastery of the typical over the personal, of the universal over the particular, and of traditional consensus over present individual oddities, one may assume that classic parents are like grandparents, that their lineage-based status is stronger than the tenor of their marriage-based role as mere fathers and mothers. The classic assumption of reality, be it German or Argentine, begins at the atavistic point marked by two grand-sires. This may imply that a certain degree of romantic or personal expressiveness binds together children and parents, just as an equal degree of classic racial or cultural typicalness defines those links that bind the same children to their parents' parents. Therefore, no matter how romantic they might actually seem, grandfathers are classic; they represent more than mere individuals, they embody figures of *race* rather than just tokens of exogamous kinship.

If this seems too abstract or speculative, one can always turn to Borges for help. In a footnote to *Evaristo Carriego* (1955), he affirms that "only countries that are new have a past," that only in them one finds an "autobiographic memory" of the past, and that such countries possess "historia viva" (21). As proof, he mentions how one of his grandfathers "was able" to lead the "last battle of importance against the Indians" in 1872. Then, he adds something memorable—and truly romantic:

> Time—a European emotion true of men teeming with days, and acting as their vindication and crown—enjoys a more *shameless* circulation in these republics. The young, to their regret, feel it. *Here, we belong to time's same time, we are his brothers.*
>
> [El tiempo—emoción europea de hombres numerosos de días, y como su vindicación y corona—es de más *impudente* circulación en estas repúblicas. Los jóvenes, a su pesar lo sienten. *Aquí somos del mismo tiempo que el tiempo, somos hermanos de él* (*Evaristo Carriego*, 21; italics mine).]⁶

Colonial affairs linger; their persistence in Argentina includes the struggles of many civil wars in the wake of independence, of battles between armies and tribes in which soldiers and gauchos are made brothers by their swift fury, and in which savages and *criollos* share their spilled blood within a single barbarous *gens*.

Borges's footnote reveals other assumptions. In the realm of classic inference, the young might feel like brothers to their own grandfathers, for fraternal laws are atavistic. It may be recalled that in *Totem and Taboo* Freud allows rejected sons to become brothers to each other upon killing their father, a creature so indiscriminately incestuous as to stand guilty of also being his own sons' grandfather. Although father-daughter incest offers the clearest possibility of an aberrant *maternal* father (*my mother's father is my own father*), the truly rare mother-son incest may seem equally mother-specific. As long as the womb represents what is violated in such acts, incestuous fathers remain implicated in something awfully maternal. These collapsing issues within the realm of classic ancestral neighborliness are shunned (but also inferred) in Borges's biographic (Argentinean) spirit of partaking time with Time. Also, Juan Dahlmann's need to embrace one distinct lineage—while being inspired in his choice by the blood of the one lineage he rejects—provides another classic assumption. Juan, an eternal bachelor, seems involved in the discriminating actions typical of a man who is about to choose a wife with holy scruples, as if in fear of possible incest.

Before assessing Juan Dahlmann's itinerary and his choice of death over perpetual celibacy, attention must be paid to the manner in which Benjamin's *flâneur* combines his marriage to the solitude of thresholds with a heightened sense of what such places disclose concerning the sacred ancestry of social space. Like Dahlmann, the *flâneur* experiences moments of epiphany in the bridal company of loneliness, but unlike Juan, Benjamin's pilgrim does not have to face what turns out to be a lethal choice of bloodlines between grandsires. The *flâneur* does have to undergo a transformation of genealogy and habitat from romantic desire into the celibate fear that places can kill, that they can bring retribution particularly upon those sensualists of *gestalt* so capable of feeling eternally at home in the midst of transience. In other words, Dahlmann's attachment to a place of fixation *and* mutability appears blood-mediated, while the *flâneur*'s fondness for out-of-the-way privacies seems free of blood connections. Unlike Juan, the *flâneur*'s epiphanies seem unsullied by any direct link with the complex genealogies of deities and ghosts, creatures ancient enough to have already settled their ancestral scores with the localities which they own and protect. The *flâneur*'s aesthetic intercourse with the ancient and the sacred seems the opposite of incest when compared with Dahlmann's ethical choice of bloodlines and his spiritual, ascetic marriage to remembrance.

In the *flâneur*'s enjoyment of myth's urban persistence, the thrills of religious awareness have become detached from their place in domestic rationality. The *flâneur*'s deities are public, no matter how privately he might enjoy the lingering effect of their presence under the uncanopied cityscape. But in Dahlmann's case the lonely aesthete cannot yet separate public from private sacredness. Dahlmann belongs to the *uncanny,* that zone of experience in which, according to Freud, the homely and the unhomely remain primitively joined in conspiracy against mature adulthood. The uncanny marks a regressive accident; it signals the return of the intimate rapport between child and place. In their suddenness, uncanny experiences evoke epiphanies, but their arresting quality comes from beneath the sublime. Uncanny trials usually end up on the down side of omnipotence. The uncanny is a way of coping with loss in the adult possession of space. That which suffers loss in adult spatialness includes an extended notion of family law. Juan Dahlmann encounters the uncanny, in part, because he cannot break with a family-oriented habit of negotiation with public spaces. At the heart of his asceticism and indifference toward wealth and possessions, there is the assumption that all public property may in fact be private and, further, that such privacy offers safe passage only to the elect few who know how to enjoy the mysteries of civic property.

Instead of recognizing the laws of the city as universal expressions of commonwealth and state rule, Dahlmann practices a naïve and saintly socialism of inner experience. He believes in the possibility of recovering feelings of community from within his own memories, but his wisdom lies in recognizing that such memories were the prior possession of others from whom he may inherit them. Dahlmann's affirmation of nobility and lineage contains a core wish to affirm his own brotherhood with all Argentineans of heroic breed, including gauchos.

In contrast, and whether in Paris or Berlin, Benjamin's anonymous *flâneur* enjoys what the transition from Rome's domestic to civil religion has bequeathed to his cult of places. For him, architectural remnants of religion still emanate feelings of ancestral family bonds. He seems content with letting such remnants possess and thus represent all that may belong to family kinship and to a host of primal entanglements of bloodlines and disputed places:

> Beneath the *plebs deorum* of the caryatids and atlantes, the Pomonas and putti . . . are his favorite figures, those at one time ruling, now having become penates, unseeing Gods of private thresholds, who are the guardians of the *rites de passage,* dusty on stairway landings, namelessly quartered in corridors; who once accompanied every step across a wooden or metaphorical threshold. He cannot break free from them and he still feels the breath of their presence, where their likeness have long since disappeared or become unrecognizable. (quoted in Menninghaus, 307)

The *flâneur* enjoys all by himself what others as a group should but fail to see. He is in possession of a common inheritance from another age too far removed to be his sister, an age now seen in unmournful memorials celebrated by one individual *flâneur* at a time. Paradoxically, such inability to "break free" from the old guardians of place implies the opposite of sacred misprision. In a classic sense, a religion of one constitutes an aberration. So it is Dahlmann, with his blending of kinship mourning and patriotic nostalgia, and not the *flâneur* who can experience the binding force of sacredness present in those moments of elation that both he and the *flâneur* are capable of tasting. From Borges's vantage point, the single *flâneur* is a romantic turned modern, a redundancy that may imply that he is dangerously close to being a professional unless he turns into a recessive modernist like the hermeneutic sleuth and quintessential amateur Erik Lönnrot, a man with a fatally transposed character who carries a cluttered romantic head atop a classic structural heart.

In order to distinguish Dahlmann's rear-guard modernity from the precocious avant-garde spirit of *flânerie,* we must review his transit from city to countryside, or his crossing of the borderline where the mythic South begins. At this point, the issue of professional method versus improvisational intuition comes to the foreground as one approaches the farthest shores of classic assumption. The contrast involves certain parallels between Dahlmann's redemptive journey into the pampas and Erik Lönnrot's detective exodus to the villa of Triste-le-Roy in "La muerte y la brújula." The strong antithesis between Lönnrot's husbandry of superstitious details and Treviranus's divorce from the cult of higher trivia compares with what has been described as Dahlmann's devotion to family memories and the *flâneur*'s unencumbered dwelling amid religious landmarks. It is assumed that both Lönnrot and the *flâneur* engage in their own education in forgetfulness, and that this education includes their coming face-to-face with tokens or remnants of sacred authority, whose riddles they approach with different but related aims and results.

In facing a combination of sacred and demonic sublimity, the detective and the *flâneur* might be said to exchange dress as they straddle the wavering line that separates the exercise of classic assumption and rhetoric from a jumbled notion of myth. When Borges *rereads* ("releo para mejor investigación de lo clásico") the passage from Gibbon already quoted and discussed, he notices the "inocua metáfora" that alludes to "el reinado del silencio" [*the vast silence that reigned over the plains*] (*Discusión*, 70). He comments on the *invisibility* of the metaphor, and on how classic assumption takes for granted that once an image is forged ("fraguada"), it becomes a "bien público," or a part of the public patrimony (*Discusión*, 70). Such is the fate enjoyed by images like the ones found in the passage from Cervantes (which Borges views as anything but unique). Such images are typical of "the great majority of universal literature" (*Discusión*, 69). Borges argues that coined metaphors become invisible parts of the public domain, and that they support the confidence proposed by classic writers, whose dominant model is the mutual recognition of paternity between writers from different epochs. This general consensus is broken by romantic writers with their "carácter impositivo" and their fondness for excessive emphasis on expressing themselves rather than literature, which remains always a single one: "la pluralidad de los tiempos y de los hombres es accesoria, la literatura es siempre una sola" (*Discusión*, 70). If literature is always one and the same, it may share with myth a dominant attribute that postromantic thought confers upon mythology, its being a universal and ageless mode of expressing a romantic invention called consciousness, with its deep-seated realities (see Detienne, *The Creation of Mythology*, 1–22).

Erik Lönnrot is possessed by the murderous antithesis of two modes of consciousness and contrasting rationalities. He is a cool structuralist reader and intertextualist and a would-be charismatic writer and cryptic criminal. His fractured sentimental education deals with space, with points of passage and arrest, and with boundaries discovered and transgressed. His passage through a composite city evokes Benjamin's review of Franz Hessel's *Spazieren in Berlin,* as he speaks of the city having "few gateways," and of the *flâneur* as "the great threshold connoisseur" with his knowledge of "the minor crossings which contrast city against lowland, and one quarter of the city against the other: constructions sites bridges, city railroads loops, and city squares" (quoted in Menninghaus, 307). But the affinities between Lönnrot and the *flâneur* involve a further affinity with Dahlmann, for whom "the South begins at the other side of Rivadavia . . . whoever crosses this street enters a more ancient and sterner world." As Dahlmann travels inside a carriage to a railroad station he sees, "among the new buildings, the iron grille window, the brass knocker, the arched door, the entranceway, the intimate patio" (*Anthology,* 18). The sequence of things sighted and recalled by Dahlmann and elsewhere by Lönnrot (as they moved toward the site of their violent deaths) runs on the near side of the random and increasingly chaotic list from "La postulación de la realidad," which illustrates how the body learns to "deal with" spatial accidents:

> En lo corporal, la inconsciencia es una necesidad de los actos físicos. Nuestro cuerpo sabe articular este difícil párrafo, sabe tratar con escaleras, con nudos, con pasos a nivel, con ciudades, con ríos correntosos, con perros, sabe atravesar una calle sin que nos aniquile el tránsito, sabe engendrar, sabe respirar, sabe dormir, sabe tal vez matar.

> [In the corporeal, unconsciousness is a necessity of the physical acts. Our body knows how to articulate this difficult paragraph, it knows how to deal with stairways, with knots, with overpasses, with cities, with streaming rivers, with dogs, it knows how to cross a street without us being annihilated by the traffic, it knows how to breathe, it knows how to sleep, it knows perhaps how to kill. (*Discusión*, 69–70)]

It should be noted that "*tratar con*" (*to deal with*), as used by Borges, is oddly pathetic in reference to dealing with things, for it commonly applies to social intercourse with persons. Thus unconsciousness (rather than consciousness) implies (and negotiates with) an environment made up of animistic obstacles which have been deadened (and civilized) by habit into automatism.

Noting also that the last item on the list is the verb *to kill* ("*tal vez matar*"), Lönnrot's traveling through his own peculiar *Listenwissenschaft* of spatial clues may suggest that he is moving through the unchanging limbo reserved for those whom irony kills short of heroic reward. He too travels on a train "South of the city" and crosses "a blind little river filled with muddy water" (*Anthology*, 8). Dahlmann once "saw unplastered brick houses, long and angled, timelessly watching the trains go by; he saw horsemen along the dirt roads; he saw gullies and lagoons and ranches; he saw great luminous clouds that resembled marble" (*Anthology*, 19); Lönnrot, too, "saw dogs, he saw a wagon on a dead road, he saw the horizon, he saw a silvery horse drinking the crapulous water of a puddle" (*Anthology*, 9). The past tense that tells what Lönnrot and Dahlmann *see* translates a vanished *presentness*. But the past may also signify that even at the ever-present but instantly distant moment when experience held sway, things happened as if posthumously recorded. Such a memory-ridden way of traveling through the canon of forgetfulness represents a phenomenology of involuntary mourning in the realm of classic assumption. In perceiving reality, one alludes to it through a temporal deixis, a pointing at memories of things past. In the classic mode, one mourns what never dies, one lives in the past in which the present expires each time language alludes to actuality, as if unknowingly recording the sight of a vanished event.

Such a revolving spectrum of classic sight and site may resemble the way in which certain stories and myths recycle past experience, particularly in reference to the dead and their surviving legacy. Before returning to Dahlmann's and Lönnrot's parallel experiences, I should like to establish a context for the religious substratum of the *flâneur*'s city, in which I see a rich paradigm of ancestor worship and the cult of the dead most relevant to Borges. I have already suggested that Dahlmann's rapport with public spaces endowed with potential religious significance differs from the *flâneur*'s joyful experience of similar spots in terms of each man's style of expressing mourning. I have also argued that Dahlmann's bifocal family history is inextricably involved with his posthumous re-ception of spatial clues, and that his experience of public passages evokes Freud's notion of the uncanny. I also contrasted Dahlmann's family-grounded perceptions with the *flâneur*'s awareness of religious decor and with his receptiveness to epiphanic thresholds, in which he allows any sense of private genealogy to be divested into the hands of the deities of place or to locate itself in statuary and in corners of the city.

I shall now propose that Benjamin's *flâneur* enjoys unmediated (if imaginary) access to remnants of ancestor worship, and that this liber-ates him from the clutches of Freud's uncanny, in whose direction he glances with aesthetic irony. In contrast, Dahlmann's terse melancholia could reflect his migrant alienation from the external, European histor-ical objects of ancient ancestor worship, which he has introjected in a land where ancestors are still familiar in spite of the monuments that already proclaim their civil worship. In both cases, mourning involves the thrills of individual elation in rapport with the awakened past. In Dahlmann's case, however, such elation serves as a prelude to his death by duel with a figure sprung from a forgotten or illegitimate corner of the space of mourning. It would seem as if Benjamin's *flâneur* could be a Dahlmann-in-waiting, a modern man awaiting passage to a remote land in which classic assumptions hinge on the need to defend virile honor, mainly against a bastard progeny, like that of a drunken macho, a minor piece represented by a barbarian *mestizo* field hand, a *pawn* or *peón:*

The tough with the Chinese look [*cara achinada*] staggered heavily to his feet. Almost in Juan Dahlmann's face he shouted insults, as if he had been a long way off. His game was to exaggerate his drunkenness, and his extravagance constituted a ferocious mockery. Between curses and obscenities, he threw a long knife into the air, followed it with his eyes, caught and juggled it, and challenged Dahlmann to a knife fight. (*Anthology*, 22)

Besides being a "cuestión de confianza, como la paternidad," the reality proposed by classic writers rests on "the long working out of brief, laconic facts that cast a long shadow" [*el desenvolvimiento o la serie de esos pormenores lacónicos de larga proyección*] (*Prose for Borges*, 199). The phrase could serve as a cryptic definition of a chess move. Indeed, in the present context, chess extends things to the farthest reaches of calculated assumption (in Borges's poem on Adrogué, the model for Triste-le-Roy's courtyard is seen as "patio ajedrezado"). Hence, those whom the game mistreats as orphans of its causal (that is, paternal) laws may not be blamed if they end up confusing the game with "el asiático desorden del mundo," to which Borges refers elsewhere (cf. *Prose for Borges*, 214: "The overwhelming [sic, *asiático*] disorder of the real world"). In "El arte narrativo y la magia," which is virtually a pendant to "La postulación de la realidad," *causality* is identified as the central problem in novelistic narration: "el problema central de la novelística es la causalidad" (*Discusión*, 88). This formula follows a quotation from Poe in which a knife left no traces of its passage "athwart the veins" of water, unless the blade "was passed down accurately between the two veins," in which case "a perfect separation was effected, which the power of cohesion did not immediately rectify" (*Prose for Borges*, 213). Precise tribal wounds in Antarctic waters seem remote from Asian turmoil. However, one should not downplay the reach of classic inference across a vast paternal domain punctuated by chaos.

In fact, by the time Borges comments on Poe's passage on tribal surgery, the overt theme of classic assumption has gone underground to be replaced by the procedures of magic, but without driving away the issue of causality. Thus the "morosa novela" based on character development grinds out causal, trivial motives of the sort one may find in real life. It is as such that the strictly fictional and mythic counterpart of romantic expressiveness is found. Psychological realism inherits and codifies the romantic scrutiny of sentiment as it establishes a mimetic compact with common life. It is in the novel of adventures, in the short story, and in "the infinite spectacular novel contrived by Hollywood— with Joan Crawford's silvery idols [plateados *idola*]" that a genre akin to

classic assumption is found. A "very diverse order" rules over these pro-
ductions: "a lucid and atavistic order [lúcido y átavico]" in which lies
the "primitiva claridad de la magia" (*Discusión*, 88). The atavistic and
the mythic in Stevenson, Kipling, and primitive Hollywood heal the
wounds opened by classic inference's strict tracing of the paternal lineage. But there are other wounds yet to be considered.

The *pawn*—the footman or *peón* who staggers into Dahlmann's
path—comes at the end of a series of allusions to effigies or *idola*
standing guard in between the native land and the realm of myth. First
comes "an enormous cat which allowed itself to be caressed as if it were a
disdainful divinity," and which prompts Dahlmann into thinking that
"man lives in time, in succession, while the magical animal lives in the
present, in the eternity of the instant" (*Anthology*, 18–19). Then, already
inside the general store, Dahlmann beholds "an old man, immobile as an
object," whose "years had reduced and polished him as water does a
stone or the generations of men do a sentence," and who "was dark,
dried up, diminutive, and seemed outside time, situated in eternity" (21).
Like the Penates and idols of old Rome, the "old ecstatic gaucho"
belongs to "a corner of the room"; it is from such liminal and forgotten
spatial readiness that he hurls at Dahlmann the naked dagger to fight the
peón. Beneath Roman figures and statuary (whose presence Benjamin
infers from the *flâneur*'s cult of thresholds) lie the presence of such idols
in the family's ancestor worship.

It is hard to imagine that Benjamin might not have read Numa-Denis
Fustel de Coulanges's classic, *La Cité antique* (1864) [1960]). In any
event, around the Roman hearth gathered a host of demons, Lares,
Penates, and *larvae* (as malignant Manes were called), who in Fustel de
Coulanges's account give evidence of how the cult of the dead and the
worship of fire merged in one complex "ancient religion that did not find
its gods in physical nature, but in man himself, and that has for its object
the adoration of the invisible being which is in us, the moral and
thinking power which animates and governs our bodies" (33). Besides
the purity of the Vestal fire (given female form on account of the altar's
feminine gender), "each family made gods for itself, and each kept them
for itself, as protectors, whose good offices it did not wish to share with
strangers. . . . [A]s soon as a family, by personifying a physical agent, had
created a god, it associated him with its sacred fire, counted him among
its Penates, and added a few words for him in its formula of prayer"
(124). In Fustel de Coulanges's view, the Roman family absorbs within
its sacred domestic nomenclature deities who otherwise stand in the

civic domain under public and "higher" names. A similar dialectic between domestic and public precincts comes into play in Benjamin's depiction of the *flâneur*'s disregarding the *plebs deorum* and seeking the company of threshold idols, as if intruding into someone else's house.

Nevertheless, going into a plebeian's shelter, the *flâneur* should find little to be thrilled with, for these creatures so despised by Caius Martius of Corioles must have done most of their praying outdoors. Fustel de Coulanges has them "without a hearth" and, by his account, plebeians "did not possess . . . any domestic altars." Enemies "were always reproaching them [the plebeians] with having no ancestors"; this meant that "they had not the worship of ancestors, and had no family tomb where they could carry their funeral repast." In short, plebeians had no father: "They ascended the series of their ascendants in vain; they never arrived at a religious family chief"—*gentem non habent,* plebeians had no people of the recorded sort behind them, they had no past: "Sacred marriage did not exist for them" [232]). In the eyes of patricians (and even more so in those of Coriolanus), plebeians were no better than animals: *Connubia promiscua habent more ferarum* was said of them. It seems that plebeians would have a hard time carrying on with allusions (or assumptions) in the classic style, but this does not make them romantic. At best, their bastardness puts plebeians at the folkloric pedestal of political hero worship.

Rather than just saying that the *peón* who kills Juan Dahlmann is a fatherless crypto-fascist plebeian, I should turn to another realm of Roman inferences, most relevant to the suicidal death of bachelors of the classic sort in Borges's fiction. As Erik Lönnrot crosses the threshold into the villa of Triste-le-Roy, the decor around him becomes uncannily Roman: "a glacial Diana in one lugubrious niche was complemented by another Diana in another niche"; even the "two-faced Hermes" who casts a "monstrous shadow" upon the scene reemerges (inside Scharlach's account of his season in hell) transformed into Janus:

> Nine days and nine nights I lay dying in this desolate, symmetrical villa; I was racked with fever, and the odious double-faced Janus [*Jano bifronte*] who gazes toward the twilights of dusk and dawn terrorized my dreams and my walking. I learned to abominate my body. I came to feel that two eyes, two hands, two lungs are as monstrous as two faces. (*Anthology,* 11)

Turning to Frazer's commentary on Ovid's *Fasti* (1:89), one finds evidence affirming Janus as a divine embodiment of thresholds. Frazer leans in favor of Forculus being the older guardian of doors among Romans (in association with the common name *foris*), while he sees Janus as a divine doorkeeper who in more ancient days was nothing less than a "God of gods," the first deity to receive sacrificial offerings, being regarded "as the god of beginnings," who "in the character of an usher or beadle" headed divine processions (1:91–92). In the less common word for door (*ianua*), Frazer finds an adjectival trace derived from Janus. But more intriguing—in reference to the mythic decor at Triste-le-Roy—is *Dianus*, Janus's older name as the male counterpart of Diana, the moon goddess. In both cases, the original *Di* (the Indo-European root for *bright*) would have changed into *Ja*, for which Frazer cites Varro's reference to country people speaking about "the waxing and waning of Jana, where educated folk would have seemingly have said Diana, meaning the moon" (1:93). Finally, the figure of Janus is made to reveal associations with other beings from primitive religions. Frazer mentions "the double-headed fetish at the gateway of Negro villages in Surinam," standing guard like "the double-headed images of Janus, which, grasping a staff in his right hand and a key in his left, stood sentinel at Roman archways (*iani*)" (1:96).

Frazer's commentary is enough to support Janus as the ancient divine ruler behind Benjamin's modern mythography of threshold passages. Moreover, the commentary provides a clue to how Dahlmann's negotiations with the spatial idioms of myth (while on his way to one final door) combine with the nightmare of religious decor that surrounds him in Triste-le-Roy. If the divine cat and the ecstatic gaucho herald Dahlmann's entrance into the realm of myth, they do so while allowing for the individual's assumption of atavistic identity within the framework of a *rite de passage*. Even if the *peón* is not seen as a sacred avenger rising from the woodwork of plebeian illegitimacy to destroy Dahlmann's personal myths of descent, his own miserable demeanor would seem to lend him, as a pawn of fate, the stereotypic human stamp needed by Dahlmann to recognize that he is being killed at home. In other words, either as a pawn in the allegory of a fatherless son who kills the atavistic issue of a heroic grandfather, or as a plain "cur" (as Coriolanus would have called him), the nameless *peón* lends paternal coherence and a sort of prepolitical intimacy to Dahlmann's dying of familiar wounds.

Lönnrot's death by the gun of another plebeian turned mobster destroys such intimacy, as it reveals a different one. Although unrelated by blood, the evenness and clasping reciprocity binding Lönnrot's and Scharlach's calculations would seem to suggest that they are members of two feuding families, which in the end (as their names suggest) would emerge as transposed elements of a single clan. Glacial Diana and bifrontal Janus make up the mythic and sculptural enigma that the rationality of exogamous exchange would have to unravel, as it comes face-to-face with a pair of divine siblings in potential primal incest. Janus's cardinal duplicity, and his manner of being symbolically layered as both an open door and heaven's vault, should warn any of his putative sons against the perils of divine individuation and the ageless fixtures attached to sacred guardianship. In more ways than one, Janus is a place, a *locus primitivus,* a perennial allusion to the most archaic. If instead of meeting death in the face of a drunken cowhand Dahlmann had encountered Janus's facial double-door, he might not have died in the open (yet homely) pampas. Meeting Janus, Dahlmann would have been framed at the threshold that eternally leads outside but never reaches it, for the last door faces an empty sky.

On Diana's part, the perennial son/orphan couplet faces another riddle. "El Sur" presents a basic structural parallel with Freud's account of the threshold birth of fetishism. Just as the fetishist holds on to the simultaneous and contradictory beliefs that the mother possesses and lacks a penis, Dahlmann must appear as one undergoing death from infectious fever in a hospital, while also dying in a knife fight in the South. Freud refers to the traumatic sighting of the mother's *castrated* genitals and to the son's instant phallic reparation as he displaces the missing part and fixes it on a piece of apparel, typically situated on the lower limbs of the body. Early on, Dahlmann discovers his wounded condition upon coming face-to-face with a female: "On the face of the woman who opened the door to him he saw horror engraved, and the hand he wiped across his face came away red with blood" (*Anthology,* 17). Borges's account of his own accident (and his mother's version of it) make it clear that the woman in question could not be señora Borges (Dahlmann's story gives no signs as to the woman's features or identity). Only through a classic psychoanalytic narrative based on timely inferences could this face be associated with the missing mother endowed with a missing part. In the midst of the fever that almost kills him, however, Scharlach sees glacial Diana, the prototype of the cold mistress with whom the masochist reaches a contract based on her supplying him with endurable punishment. Besides, as Frazer's commentary would have it, the association of Diana-[*ianua-Dianus*]-Janus includes that of a female-moon–open-door–male-god-of-lintels entity, of which the psychoanalytic inference might suggest that in Janus's double *rostrum* and in his open gates the cyclic moon goddess finds and enjoys more than just a sibling consort. The Moon enjoys, all at once, her phallic framing and the legged openness that gives (but also may bar) access to her dual mysteries and baneful powers over some of her sons. Thus Frazer's suggestion of an African Janus cognate in the form of a double-faced fetish ties in with Triste-le-Roy's sacred fetishistic decor. Frazer's Janus/Diana primal pair also supports the structural analogy between Borges's story about Dahlmann's contradictory and simultaneous deaths and Freud's narrative of the fetishist's simultaneous view of the mother's primitive and dual sexual character.

In one of the most novelistic chapters of his biography, Rodríguez Monegal includes Borges's acknowledgment that

> Triste-le-Roy, a beautiful name invented by Amanda Molina Vedia, stands for the now demolished Hotel de las Delicias in Adrogué. (Amanda had painted a map of an imaginary island on the wall of her bedroom; on her map I discovered the name Triste-le-Roy.) (*Borges*, 64)

This remembrance may give us the opportunity to close the endless spawning of classic allusions.

Adrogué lies in the southern outskirts of Buenos Aires, near places over which (as Borges writes in the poem "Sur") "las puestas de sol *criminan* de sangre" [sunsets *criminate* with blood] (*Otras inquisiciones*, 48; emphasis added). The rare and virtually obsolete use of the verbal phrase *criminar de* echoes Latin (and perhaps English), and represents a resonant *cultismo* with some semantic consequences.[7] A flaw and a crime usually *incriminate*, but in Borges the tenor of allusiveness (inherent in the prefix *in-*) is modified: as if one could *criminate* in the same sense in which one could *reek of* or *bleed from*, or as if allusion itself were an *exuding*, an *emanative* or *effluvious* phenomenon, resistant to any manner of detachment from the body in which it originates. It is doubtful that the expression of cosmic mourning desired in the poem actually finds any particular *crime* in the sun's *criminating*. The poet conveys the vast assumption that what he sees in the sunset is the *alluding* drama that replaces the common pathetic illusion of human guilt being implicated in particular crimes, as portrayed in landscapes or any given locale. For instance, if one looks at the poem as an expression of *allusive* pictorialism, it becomes an extended pathetic fallacy: fields are *servile*, puddles are *abandoned*, barriers are *doleful* and *exalted*, houses *tedious*, and trains *discurren* (implying both their *passage* and *discourse*). The same landscape through which Dahlmann and Lönnrot travel to their respective deaths is all at once seen and remembered as a series of battlefields held under the law of antithesis: "a military precision of time and signals" and "a military disorder of fighting alternatives." Nonetheless, the poetic vision expressed here suggests the desire to reverse illusion, to have things themselves point at (or allude to) an author who, in expressing himself through them, should be *quoting* them, as if they stood before his glance already quoted by someone else. If the poem is held under the light of a classic covenant with prior (paternal) authority, it ought to suggest that a classic work should have no (single) author. However, this should imply the opposite of *the death of the author,* as recently conceived, for what survives is *the* author, the perennial *auctor* assumed by the inexpressive quality of reading that Borges wants to reproduce in writing. On the side of writing, classic assumption concerns the *auctor,* while on the side of reading it involves an *ad hominem* operation in which the *actor* emerges in performance (at times deeply embedded in a relationship with femaleness).

Once situated in the poem on Adrogué, it becomes evident that the elision of authorship to which Borges aspires can be found most directly in the mournful attribution of present meaning to the dead: "My step looks for and finds the awaited threshold" (*Otras inquisiciones,* 219). Time in Adrogué is *named* by the "ancient smell" of the eucalyptus trees and by each detail mentioned. Those who sleep beyond each door are "visionary owners" of whatever communicates vastness in belonging to yesterday and representing dead things. It is easier to identify the explicit unrealness of things past than to grasp the covert reality with which they burden and possess the present. In his mourning the actuality of the dead, the poet begs ghosts to concede to him that they are not the best mourners, and to confirm to him that he is not yet a ghost in becoming author of the oldest among the many forms of allusion, the one that sings of grief, the one that points at the pointedness of familiar death, or that mourns as well for the awesome fact that most deaths are *not* familiar. If at the heart of classic allusiveness there is mourning, then the maintenance of the familiar in relation to the dead may represent a yearning for the mother, for the earliest relation and point of pain and joy.

Under the sign of the mother, mourning and moon come face-to-face. Perhaps the moon transcends all other objects of mournful desire in Borges. It is she who allows meditative bliss to join formal melancholia as the poet addresses her. Borges's rapport with the moon ("mi largo comercio con la luna") is not erotic, and yet it approaches absolute intimacy, as when it combines the rhyming femaleness of *luna* with *una*, and with the complex writing ("compleja escritura") of that "rare Thing we are, numerous and one" ("esa rara / Cosa que somos, numerosa y una"; cf. Edwin Honig's rendering: "the rare / thing we all are, multiple and unique" [*Anthology*, 198]). In "La luna," the poet begins with the story of a man who undertook the project of trying to put the universe in a single book ("cifrar el universo / en un libro"), and hence built something like a tower of Babel: "built [*erigió*] his high and mighty manuscript." Upon lifting his eyes after *filing* (*limar: polish, file*) and declaiming the final line, he "saw / a burnished disk upon the air" (*Anthology*, 196), and thus realized that he had forgotten the moon. The poet goes on to review instances of the moon in his readings and in his own attempts to define her in his poetry. Between *una* and *luna* lies a secret: the word alluding to moon must be humbly employed. That it should be *one* word and yet also *una* means that in *luna*'s inherent rhyme with itself, there lies a plural *oneness*, a (one/*una*) thing that means *many* and means *female-one-ness*. While being in a sense like literature, this one word lies beyond the poet's literature: "más allá de mi literatura." Writing "Luna," the poet declares a resembling yet inverse relationship with melancholy gloom:

> Ya no me atrevo a macular su pura
> Aparición con una imagen vana;
> La veo indescifrable y cotidiana
> y más allá de mi literatura.

Though less odd than *criminar*, "macular" is nevertheless a *cultismo*. The verb manages to *quote* what *manchar* (or other vernacular equivalents of staining or defiling) could not: the *immaculate* (as in Honig's substitution and displacement of "macular" in "I do not dare stain its immaculate / appearance" [*Anthology*, 190]). Also, the one (pure) rhyme of *una/luna* is mirrored in that of *pura/literatura*.

Besides framing a reflection, the mythopoetic mirror might be said to quote or represent an alluding *thou*, a speckled (pure/impure) pointing, a posthumous allusion to oneself and *una*, framed in the *luna del espejo*. If mirror and speculation together suggest a verb in *moon*, they may also suggest the fear and peril in *maculate*, in the act of (self)interpretation in which the poet would face himself/herself in the moon-mirror. The classic assumption of reality bears a signature of imagistic *facialness,* on behalf of which I shall propose that, in alluding, assuming, and inter-preting, the romantic seems *specular* as the classic seems *speckled,* a differ-ence in modes of self-recognition that plays a crucial role in Borges's personal poetics and mythology of composition.

As already seen, the last item in the seemingly random list of con-tingencies negotiated by the "education in forgetfulness" is "perhaps to kill." The Spanish word for a *moral stain* is *mancilla,* a diminutive of the Latin *macula,* which proceeds in part from *macellare:* to *kill* or *sacrifice* (Corominas, *Breve diccionario,* 377). In defining one of the forms taken by the classic assumption of reality, Borges quotes a heroic fragment from Tennyson's "Morte d'Arthur" as an example of "imagining a reality more complex than the one given to the reader and then revealing, in an offhand way, details and facts not directly stated":

> [*So*] all day long the noise of battle roll'd
> Among the mountains by the winter sea;
> Until King Arthur's table, man by man,
> Had fallen in Lyonnesse about their Lord,
> King Arthur: then, [*because his wound was deep*],
> The bold Sir Bedivere uplifted him,
> Sir Bedivere, the last of all his knights,
> And bore him to a chapel nigh the field,
> A broken chancel with a broken cross,
> That stood on a dark strait of barren land.
> On one side lay the Ocean, and on one
> Lay a great water, [*and the moon was full*].[8]
> (quoted in *Prose for Borges,* 197, emphasis and brackets added)

According to Borges, three items in Tennyson "assume a more complex reality" than the one actually given to the reader:

(1) "So" (a mere verbal trick);
(2) "because his wound was deep" (indirectly supplying a fact); and
(3) "and the moon was full" (an unexpected addition).

Borges does not explain what such "inesperada adición" might bring in its wake. Therefore, in adherence to his own method, I shall quote Tennyson following the presumed path of Borges's suspended allusion to the rest of "Morte d'Arthur."

It should be kept in mind that, in adding materials to *Idylls of the King* between 1835 and 1874, Tennyson framed "Morte d'Arthur" by means of "The Epic," which provided the setting in which the poem was first performed: on Christmas eve, a group of friends are gathered round the fire and end up "harping . . . / Upon the general decay of faith" (15, 18). One friend has rescued from the hearth the "eleventh" among twelve books of "faint Homeric echoes," which a poet has already found useless:

> "Why take the style of those heroic times?
> For nature brings not back the mastodon,
> Nor we those times, and why should any man
> Remodel models?"
> (35–38)

Before the poet-narrator wakes up from what turns out to be a dream, as "The clear church-bells ring of Christmas morn" (303), the "Morte d'Arthur" has been read by a friend:

> "Read, mouthing out his hollow oes and aes,
> Deep-chested music."
> (50–51)

Read just as Tennyson is known to have read the poem for the first time to a group of friends in 1835. The *mouthing* of heroic lines expresses the performing essence of the oral/aural forging of memory.

It is in such a tonal spirit (and heroic tenor) that the highest instances of classic assumption in Borges should be addressed. Beyond (and within) the additional allusion to the full moon noted by him (in what he regards as the opening stanza of "Morte d'Arthur"), the one word (*moon*) should resonate (and thereby be quoted and assumed) by other words themselves, performing as *mouthings*. Thus the *wound* that was so deep may in fact quote (besides being its proleptic echo) the *moon* that was full; just as the "moon athwart the place of tombs" (46) *mouths* itself and is in turn *mouthed* in what may come at the end of a sort of unique assumption, of a single (*una*) line actually inscribed in lines ending in *wound, moon,* and eventually *tombs*. Image and phrased voices work within a complex reality *begged* (assumed) in classic incantation. Thus mouthed, sound constitutes a minor and sufficient epoch. Heroic recital moves on through fragments of arrested resonance, whose echo testifies to a grand illocutionary vibration punctuating heroic reference. When "Bedivere" at last hurls "Excalibur" to the waters, the moon-sound strikes the air:

> The great brand
> Made lightnings in the splendor of the moon,
> And flashing round and round, and whirled in the arch,
> Shot like a streamer. . . .
> (136–38)

The sound also alights itself upon the face of the sad King:

> for all his face was white
> And colourless, and like the withered moon
> Smote by the fresh beam of the springing east. . . .
> (212–14)

A face turns cosmic:

> And the light and lustrous curls—
> That made his forehead like a rising sun
> High from the dias-throne—were parched with dust."
> (216–18)

The central motif of "Morte" refers to how " 'The old order changeth, yielding place to new' " (240). A moon that once was full may become a "withered moon" upon a "grievous wound" (213/264). Before it breaks down into structural themes and citations, heroic myth educates memory through insistent mouthings.

In the prologue to his *Antología personal* (1961), Borges comes back to the essential argument he made in "La postulación de la realidad." Once again, he mentions Croce's notion that "art is expression," and blames "a deformation of this exigency" for "the worst literature of our time" (*Anthology,* ix). He returns to Tennyson and quotes the last lines of "Morte d'Arthur," where Bedivere sees the King vanish toward Avalon:

> . . . saw,
> Straining his eyes beneath an arch of hand,
> Or thought he saw, the speck that bore the King,
> Down that long water opening on the deep
> Somewhere far off, pass on and on, and go
> From less to less and vanish into light.

For the aging Borges, these are "verses which reproduce a mental process with precision" (*Anthology,* ix). The paradoxes generated by his examples of inexpressive eloquence suggest that for Borges the classic temper always stood for experience gathered from a past age made ancient by heroism and as such renewable at least in verse. His return to Tennyson and to Arthur implies more than a technical or cognitive interest in heroic vision or the veils of allusion. Whether or not he knew of Tennyson's manner of "mouthing" myth, one can imagine Borges singing the same lines in which he wryly isolates values proper to the sovereignty of sight. Traces of romanticism adhere to his quotations, traces that become classic the moment one remembers how his most memorable instance of visionary stillness, in "Nueva refutación del tiempo," silently quotes the singing of Keats's nightingale.

Dr. Jekyll's Hide

I am that which unloves and loves; I am stricken, and I am the blow.—Algernon Swinburne, "Hertha"

I announce adhesiveness, I say it shall be limitless, unloosen'd, I say you shall yet find the friend you were looking for.—Walt Whitman, "So Long!"

As an incidental biographer of the poet's lives, Borges refers to a few essences of character and leaves a lot for the reader and listener to gather in his wake. His "Note on Walt Whitman" in *Otras inquisiciones* (97–104) is a panegyric on immense emotions, rather than merely on the man who sang them. Borges is very much a witness to that man and to himself; his admiration for Whitman tests the limits of what he regarded as a life unbound and yet controlled by form. If by the time he cast a second glance on Whitman (1947), he still believed in laconic expressiveness, as he must have, then what he says about "an almost incoherent but titanic vocation to happiness" in the poet should disclose to what extent Borges felt moved by elements of effusion to which he seemed otherwise opposed. As Coriolanus does in the earlier sections of this essay, Whitman comes now into the picture as a point of reference, a model, of the storyteller in performance. Obviously, neither man directly represents storytelling in action, nor does either resemble any ancestral shape actually engaged in telling stories. The link between them works otherwise: it functions as gusty elements of transience do in the turbulent effect that Coriolanus and Whitman bring upon their respective realities, for in elements of such force Borges perceives the continuing life of stories. In a nutshell, both the warrior and the poet command a space of performance, and both, no matter how differently, collide and collude

with other bodies. Their exemplary value begins with the blunt requirements that their pride imposes on those around them, and it ends with
the transformation of their self-love into two contrasting modes of
persuasion: the warrior lending nobility to his hatreds and the poet
bestowing fury upon his loves.

Borges selects two opinions on Whitman he wishes to combine with
his own. In one (Lascelles Abercrombie's), the poet is said to rank
among the few great things in modern literature because he extracts
from life his own figure ("la figura de él mismo"); in the other (Edmund
Gosse's), there is no true Whitman because he represents literature as
protoplasm, being an intellectual organism so simple that it merely
reflects those who come near it. Most views on Whitman run into two
errors: identifying the man of letters with the demiurge, and adopting
the style and vocabulary of his poems. (Borges first read Whitman in
German in 1917, while in Geneva; he held the lifelong ambition of
translating *Leaves of Grass* [Rodríguez Monegal, *Borges,* 457].) As a rule,
biographers try to obscure the fact that there are two Whitmans, hence
Borges delights in uncovering clues of their presence and passage: there
is *éste* (the poor writer), and there is *aquél* (the "friendly and eloquent
savage" of the poems). *Éste* was "chaste, reserved, and rather taciturn,"
while *aquél* was "effusive and orgiastic" (99). As a nomadic hero of
happiness, Whitman finds a precursor in Nietzsche's Zarathustra, a
"happy pedagogue" whose only defect was never to have existed. There
are other romantic heroes (besides Vathek, "the first in the series") who
impose their uniqueness on the world. Whitman comes close to them,
but mainly through his democratic pantheism: he wants to resemble
everyone, to be a great collective individual.

Such a wild and noble view of pantheism in Borges implies, above all,
miscellaneous manifestations of godliness and also of individual sympathy
toward random instances of the beautiful; pantheism represents plato-
nism gone rampant. He quotes Emerson's "When me they fly, I am the
wings" (from "Brahma"), as he might Swinburne's "The deed and the
doer, the seed and the sower, the dust which is God" (from "Hertha,"
inspired by Emerson's poem). Whitman takes these cosmic declarations
into the streets and, "with ferocious tenderness," seeks to merge with
every passerby—but not "in mere history" ("la mera historia"), but "in
myth" (102). In the company of this Whitman, the cosmos saunters:

Walt Whitman, an American, one of the roughs, a kosmos,
Disorderly, fleshy and sensual . . . eating, drinking, and breeding.

Borges leaps from this quotation into prophecies of his own nostalgia, which he believes to be shared by others ("En nuestra verdadera nostalgia, creada por estas profecías que la anunciaron"):

Full of life now, compact, visible,
I, forty years old the eighty-third year of the States,
To one a century hence or any number of centuries hence,
To you yet unborn these, seeking you.

Borges starts with two Whitmans who then merge into a third one ("When you read these I that was visible am become invisible"). The third figure is in fact a third *you*, since every *I* becomes invisible by merging with *thou*, who is the *I* who listens, who is a *thou* possessed, *moved* by *I*. The link between sentiment and motion is central to prophetic intimacy. Borges says: "We are moved by the poet's being moved in foreseeing our emotion" ["Nos emociona que al poeta le emocionara nuestra emoción," 102]. A quotation from "So Long!" follows, a poem in which Whitman uses a novel phrase for farewell, defined by him as "a salutation of departure, greatly used among sailors, sports, and prostitutes. The sense of it 'Till we meet again,'—conveying an inference that somehow they will doubtless so meet, sooner or later" (Whitman, *Leaves of Grass*, 502n). Whether or not Borges was aware of these remarks, he quotes the poetry as if making a *motion* out of his own congeniality with Whitman's poetic character; he makes a motion on behalf of being a part of the poem's poet. One wonders, however, whether Borges, as a third entity in the affair, either recognizes or cares for *one* of the loves felt by *both* Whitmans (italics in brackets mark what his quotation leaps over):

Camerado, this is no book,
Who touches this touches a man,
(It is night? are we here together alone?)
[*It is I you hold and who holds you,*
I spring from the pages into your arms—decease calls
                                        me forth.
O how your fingers drowse me,
Your breath falls around me like dew, your pulse lulls
                                        the tympans
        of my ears,
I feel immerged from head to foot,
Delicious, enough.
Enough O deed impromptu and secret,

> *Enough O gliding present-enough O summ'd-up past . . .*
> *I receive now again of my many translations, from my avataras*
>   *ascending, while others doubtless await me . . .*
> *Remember my words, I may again return,]*
> I love you, I depart from materials, [me despojo de esta
> envoltura]
> I am as one disembodied, triumphant, dead.
> (*Leaves of Grass*, 505–6; bracketed italics indicate Borges's omission)

Most of what is left out by Borges may persuade some readers about the homoerotic tenor of Whitman's real and recorded loves. In this regard, the closest male companion whom Borges assigns to the poet is the *other* Whitman, the one who could not have written such great poetry, being just a happy drifter. For it must be understood "that the mere happy vagabond proposed by the lines of *Leaves of Grass* would have been incapable of writing them" (99). Yet, being a great poet must be about the only thing of which the other Whitman remains incapable—and I use the term *remains* because poetic immortality is certainly one thing of which this same other Whitman is quite capable. There are two persons: one, a great poet, who was "casto, reservado y más bien taciturno," who was "Walt Whitman, hombre," who was "director del *Brooklyn Eagle*," who read "sus ideas fundamentales en las páginas de Emerson, de Hegel y de Volney"; and then there is another, who could not have been such a great poet, who instead was a "personaje poético," who educed [*edujo*] those same ideas "del contacto de América," a contact he illustrated "with imaginary experiences in New Orleans bedrooms and on the battlefields of Georgia" (99, 103). Since false facts can be essentially true ("Un hecho falso puede ser esencialmente cierto"), Borges gives other examples of mythic contacts with America, but never mentions that from those imaginary experiences in New Orleans, seven brown Whitman children might have come into the world.

The other Whitman is no mere double; he emerges from the *avataras,* from the eternal return. Borges recalls how Nietzsche made fun of Pythagoras's notion of history repeating itself, only to hit upon the same idea while walking in a forest a few years later. It would be vulgar to speak of Nietzsche's plagiarism, says Borges, thus setting the stage for the poet's version of eternal return. In Whitman's case, the poet's immortality comes from a "personal relationship with each future reader; he confuses himself [*se confunde,* which means to *merge*] with the reader, and "dialoga con el otro, con Whitman" (104). Legend returns to legend, carrying with it a plural body that includes among its pantheistic alloys immortal Borges confused with eternal Whitman. Before ending with One-of-the-numberless-many, this kind of effusive pantheism reveals three figures: the poet, the poet's character in his poems, and the reader—who in fact looks at the *auctor* (or *poet*) only through a prior immergence in the *actor* (the *poetic character* confused with the *reader*). In essence, the best promise of memorable otherness is achieved through acting as distinct from writing poems.

Darker forms of redemptive pantheism exist in Borges's repertoire. In reviewing the 1941 version of *Dr. Jekyll and Mr. Hyde,* he rejects the film as Hollywood's latest defamation of Stevenson's name. The book makes it clear that Jekyll's moral duality resides in everyone, except in the "unalloyed" evilness of his "hypostasis"—Edward Hyde (*Ficcionario,* 181–82). The film disjoints Stevenson's moral theology into scenes from a sexual masquerade: a young pathologist "exercises chastity" while his drugged surrogate preys on women like a "sadist and acrobat." The "Good" in Hollywood consists in holding hands with Lana Turner, the "Evil" in having clandestine affairs with Ingrid Bergman and Miriam Hopkins. Stevenson's Jekyll is a sensualist hypocrite, whom the film reduces to a beastly suggestion of sexual mania. Borges declares that "ethics does not encompass sexual matters, unless betrayal, greed, or vanity contaminate them" (*Ficcionario,* 182). His own *Jekyll and Hyde* (under a dissembling title) would have two well-known actors facing some police problem. George Raft and Spencer Tracy would use analogous words and suggest through some timely references that they share a common past. When the problem becomes intractable, "one of them takes the magic drug and turns into the other." Instead, Borges is reviewing a movie in which, upon drinking the fickle beverage, Spencer Tracy becomes Spencer Tracy under a different wig and featuring "negroid" traits. The review ends by suggesting yet a third film: beyond Stevenson's "dualistic parable," one may imagine a "film panteísta," in which many characters evolve into a single enduring one, like the birds in 'Aṭṭār's *Manṭeq oṭ-ṭeyr* (*Conference of the Birds*), who migrate in search of their king Simurg and, after dying in droves, discover that they themselves are Simurg—and he is each and all of them at once. However, this full reference to what happens in 'Aṭṭār's poem belongs to the essay on Whitman, as does a broader sense of pantheistic survival than the one summarily requested in the closing of the film review.

Pantheism is quite visible throughout Borges, yet some disguised instances of it require discussion. In the preceding analysis of inference in "La postulación de la realidad," one last mode of classic allusion was not considered, since its full explanation depends on the notion of magic explained in "El arte narrativo y la magia." In fact, the two essays link by way of a curious account of latent pantheism. Borges points out that "the hardest to achieve and most efficient" scheme in classic narration involves *circumstantial invention*—possibly leading to a *"fantasmagoria circunstancial"* (*Discusión*, 72). For instance, in a certain novel, soup arrives at the dining table in a "padlocked tureen," a detail from which a broad scenario of domestic frugality, hungry servants, and winding corridors may be drawn. Borges adds a footnote on a better example of the method, found in H. G. Wells's *The Invisible Man* (1897). As it happens, an unfortunate man becomes invisible and then dies overwhelmed by the task of keeping others from *seeing* that he is invisible, or rather from seeing exactly *how* the invisible itself works on one of its human surrogates. Then, from such a grand opening assumption concerning invisibility some troubling particulars soon subtract themselves. What Borges means by *circunstancial* has a lot to do with how a diffuse order of phenomena (such as invisibility) makes sense only as it may be invented by a specific set of circumstances and constraints. In other words, the invisible may exist but it must be narrated, narrated to the point in which it becomes a counterpart of narration itself.

Perhaps in their manner of being awesomely local, some particular things begin to appear universal. Such is the case with the Aleph, which is both a pantheistic exhibit and a great instance of circumstantial invention. Upon remarking that, "what eternity is to time, the Aleph is to space," Borges mentions Wells's use of invisibility as that *one* fantastic element in itself sufficient to generate an entire narrative. Then he adds:

> My chief problem in writing the story lay in what Walt Whitman had very successfully achieved—the setting down of a limited catalog of endless things. The task . . . is impossible, for such chaotic enumeration can only be simulated, and every apparently haphazard element has to be linked to its neighbor either by secret association or by contrast. (*Ficciones*, 190)

The last requirements needed to camouflage chance by means of a visible yet secret appeal to either sympathy or aversion may be found in magic, as conceived by Borges under Frazer's influence. In magic (chance being ruled out) causality becomes binding, either through likeness or difference. In either case—whether as the lure of the same or the spell of the alien—procedures of magic exploit causality as a question of resemblance, no matter how farfetched or disguised. In what Frazer dubs homeopathic and contagious kinds of magic, differences disclose resemblances and nothing is ever random or ultimately strange. Crassly metaphoric, Frazer's magic creates differences only as it *unlikens* likeness from itself. As a result, resemblance and contiguousness traverse the spectrum of any imaginable differences.

Before reviewing another key element in Frazer's account of magic, some features of *The Invisible Man* need to be explored by situating them next to Borges's fascination with a paradox inherent in pantheism. As it is felt in Whitman's poetry, pantheism gathers together beautiful and sublime elements given convincing and charismatic appeal by a central poetic character. But, as is proven in the case of the man turned invisible, a potential source of sublime elation and unpredictable power unravels such elements of beauty, of *adhesiveness,* as Whitman would say, and transforms them into grotesque compounds, into chaotic animation, uncontrolled causality, and a stubborn regression to primitive dualities. The paradox of beauty degenerating into spectacular motions of cruelty represents a case of pantheistic yearnings ruined, of which *The Invisible Man* is a prime example.

The young chemist named Griffin wearing the dress of invisibility is the embryonic model of the transcendental victim in Borges's fiction. His plight has been keenly observed by Bernard Bergonzi:

> Conceived in strictly mythical terms, Griffin, at the point of his death, has become a scapegoat figure hunted out of society: it is perhaps not altogether fanciful to suppose that what is being "cast out" is not merely the dangerous pretensions of contemporary science, but also the young Wells's own identification with a highly romanticized kind of scientist-magician. . . . The point is underlined by the introduction into the story of the calm and pragmatic figure of the "orthodox" scientist, Dr. Kemp. (Early Wells, 120)

In archaic fashion, scapegoat victim and magician conspire to undo progress in a scientific spirit (a soul) which is banished from Griffin's body and comes into dull possession of Dr. Kemp's mind. Griffin's will is at odds with the ancient notion of the soul, which he has dismally managed to bring out before the eyes of society, where it is transformed into a terrible show of retribution upon his corporeal transparency. The soul's bewitchment happens as if the psyche had surfaced at the skin and played counterfeit with her routine invisibility, which is brought blow by blow back to light and into a life capable of eroticism, at which point the marvelous yet monstered thing is lawfully murdered. Griffin's broken body resurrects just as much as it becomes, in being at last pitifully visible, an awful yet proper corpse ready for burial:

> And, so, slowly, beginning at his hands and feet and creeping along his limbs to the vital centres of his body, that strange change continued. It was like the slow spreading of a poison. First came the little white nerves, a hazy grey sketch of a limb, then the glassy bones and intricate arteries, then the flesh and skin, first a faint fogginess, and then growing rapidly dense and opaque . . . there lay, naked and pitiful on the ground, the bruised and broken body of a young man about thirty. His hair and beard were white,—not grey with age, but white with the whiteness of albinism, and his eyes were like garnets. His hands were clenched, his eyes wide open, and his expression was one of anger and dismay.[9]

An abject marvel, Griffin is the residual object left over by a ritual farce. Restored to sight, the albino student becomes the freakish equivalent of vomited matter, something that could not be assimilated by the group, just as his own ingested food could not become invisible excrement fast enough to escape grotesque detection. When Mr. Marvel (named *Thomas* like the apostle) feels Griffin's body with his fingers, he can see a rabbit clean through him "arf a mile away," and, much closer, some bread and cheese in midair, "not quite assimilated into the system" (33).

Borges takes compositional delight in brilliantly sketching the hazards encountered by Griffin's unraveling mimicry. He mentions "a hasty overcoat and autonomous boots," a shady target "preferred" by traffic accidents, and so on. At times, Wells writes of Griffin as if quoting Borges: "a sporadically rosy face beneath a furry silk hat" (37). However, the face in question (which for an instant may seem like Griffin's) belongs here and elsewhere to Mr. Marvel, or to "a short and corpulent little man with a nose of cylindrical protrusion, wiry hair, and a sporadic rosiness of visage" (109) who acts as Griffin's involuntary helper. Nevertheless, Marvel's accessorial role under Griffin's tyranny transcends such touches of caricature. Indeed, his semblance could be that of the Invisible Man himself, moving inside a hastily borrowed outfit. Reading the story, one observes how garments may come to agree or blend with the somatic character, with the flesh of those who wear them. Clothes quote the visible individual, as they misquote the invisible one, as he is prone to arouse fear all around his structural nakedness. Just as Griffin's is a case of animated attire in amalgamated flight, those persons in closest contact with him may enact a sort of mimicry: they cannot but dress up his present nakedness by proxy, as he must eventually seek a dress all by himself.

Griffin's nakedness is the reverse image of prelapsarian unblemishness. The one person who should not have to be ashamed of being naked turns out needing clothes, getting notoriously dressed, and thus becoming a target of corrective aggression. What marvels Borges about the "circumstantial" behavior in Wells's parable includes this spontaneous affair of bodies not so much relating to each other as relentlessly quoting their own disguises through a sort of sartorial broken syntax.

As in the case of Dr. Jekyll with Edward Hyde, Mr. Marvel is driven by the Invisible Man, he is jerked around in broad daylight, "moved with a sort of reluctant alacrity" that answers to a naked, unseen force bound to a voice. This "Voice" belonging to Griffin naked and empty of all food strikes a note of sudden specular agreement between two of the villagers: "He looked into the face of Cuss, close to his own, and each saw a horrible reflection of his own sickly astonishment" (38). The men have felt the grip of fingers besides the Voice, but they are being watched also from a point of view that may be part of what Borges means by circumstantial invention. There is here a pure effect of *being seen* in which Lacan once located the now quite familiar (and abused) notion of the gaze. What besieges these men includes commanding sound, as in: " 'Since when did you learn to pry into an investigator's private memoranda,' said the Voice; and two chins struck the table simultaneously, and two sets of teeth rattled" (38). Voice also involves the multiple circumstantial effects of sight. The two comic victims are seen by each other, by the Voice, by the reader who hears and watches them, and by the phenomenal or structural effect of being thus witnessed from a point of view that relates to all the others and yet is detached from them, a point of view that may quite well emerge as a perspective of pure filmic enjoyment.

Mr. Marvel inherits the books, memoranda, and money left behind by Griffin's death. He becomes a landlord and remains a "bachelor man," for "his tastes were ever bachelor, and there are no women folk in the house" (109). From the wasted depths of Wells's parable rises the notion that Griffin faces some older men as would a guilty and criminal son, but that he couples with Mr. Marvel embodying some alienated and weirdly enacted female role. Certainly not the role of *a* woman, and not even that of a transvestite, but of some excessive being dragging *woman* into exposure and self-mimicry. In confessing to Dr. Kemp, Griffin discloses the absurdity of being helpless and yet capable of obtaining "things a man reckons desirable"; no doubt, he says, "invisibility made it possible to get them, but it made it impossible to enjoy them when they were got." Concerning raw ambition he asks: "What is the good of pride of place when you cannot appear there? What is the good of the love of woman when her name must needs be Delilah?" (88). His question requires some thought. The woman thus obtained takes one's power away, but by dint of cutting one's hair, which is the same added gear worn by invisible Griffin as a necessary wig. On one hand, Delilah stands for the lethal gifts obtained through being invisible, while on the other she is a token of the headgear that the invisible man must put on in order to assume his own wondrous vulnerability. He has no choice but to dress and wig himself with what Delilah wants, instead of chasing after her madly and invisibly naked. One may ask: Is Delilah, then, an external enemy of the one who is invisible, or is she what the invisible one already wears? Is she what comes to wear down the man and undress his head, or is she the wear-on piece that wears down its wearer? Would Griffin be better off being Delilah—in drag?

The theatrical Griffin or would-be transvestite plays an occluded role in his confession to Dr. Kemp. In traditional Freudian terms, the doctor stands for the superego; he represents the authority figure before whom the guilty son appears after committing a crime and upon encountering two figures of primitive paternal tyranny. Griffin stole money from his real father, who killed himself out of shame. The father's burial affords a sinister preview of the Invisible Man's ambulatory fate:

> I remember walking back to the empty home, through the place that had once been a village and was now patched and tinkered by the jerry builders into the ugly likeness of a town. Every way the roads ran out at last into the desecrated fields and ended in rubble heaps and rank wet weeds. I remember myself as a gaunt black figure, going along the slippery, shiny pavement, and the strange sense of detachment I felt from the squalid respectability, the sordid commercialism of the place. (67)

Back in London, the guilty son's landlord is "an old Polish Jew," who with his "old hag of a woman" and his two stepsons keeps a suspicious eye on his tenant's doings. Such a setting puts Griffin in the role of an estranged and superior being surrounded by "Yiddish and Cockney English" and a grotesque cast of domestic spies (70–73). Griffin's second crime (after causing his father's ruin and shame) is to set the landlord's house on fire before fleeing, invisible and naked, into crowded Oxford Street. The third crime against an increasingly brutish figure of parental authority comes when Griffin seeks refuge in "a dirty, fly-blown little shop in a byway near Drury Lane, with a window full of tinsel robes, sham jewels, wigs, slippers, dominoes and theatrical photographs" (83). Here Griffin haunts a simian presence, "a short, slight, hunched, beetle-browed man, with long arms and very short bandy legs," whom he regards as an "infernal little brute" (83, 85). Griffin knows that the "hunchback had been alone in the house for some time," a condition that increases the stark, one-on-one territorial battle between the unseen guest and his unwilling host. The movements of the ghostly intruder add a third presence to the encounter, however, for when the old man hears noises he says: " 'It must have been her. . . . Damn her' " (85). After being locked for a while in a room by the man, Griffin manages to beat him into unconsciousness and then, before fleeing, he gets down to business:

> I had thought of painting and powdering my face and all that there was to show of me, in order to render myself visible, but the disadvantage of this lay in the fact that I should require turpentine and other appliances and a considerable amount of time before I could vanish again. Finally I chose a mask of the better type, slightly grotesque but no more so than many human beings, dark glasses, grayish whiskers, and a wig. I could find no underclothing, but that I could buy subsequently, and for a time I swathed myself in calico dominoes and some white cashmere scarfs. I could find no socks, but the hunchback's boots [Borges's *botas autónomas*] were rather a loose fit and sufficed. (86–87)

It might be recalled that for Borges a dead metaphor ("inocua metá-fora") belongs to the public domain ("bien público"), that metaphors are justified in classic writing by their "invisibilidad" or conventional character (*Discusión*, 70). Hence, expressions like "fly-blown" may have become rather invisible upon losing their specific early meaning of *to corrupt* or *taint* by means of dropping eggs, as flies may do on meat. Nonetheless, places like the "fly-blown little shop" where Griffin becomes "grotesque to a theatrical pitch" (and where his noises are attributed to "her" by a brutish, lonely man) may restore life to dead meanings and lend to invisible metaphors (in this instance of clandestine and tainted parenting) a definite allegorical hue.

As with Henry Jekyll's "Full Statement of the Case," Griffin's confession to Dr. Kemp opens the heart of the story. It begins with this I.D. picture: "'Griffin,' answered the voice—'a younger student, almost an albino, six feet high, and broad, with a pink and white face and red eyes,—who won the medal for chemistry.'" (56). The albino's fascination with light—"*Light* fascinated me" (63)—drives him to experiment with photogenic effects until he finds "a general principle of pigments and refraction," and discovers that either "a body absorbs light, or it reflects or refracts it, or it does all these things," and that "the whole fabric of man except the red of his blood and the black pigment of hair, are all made up of transparent colourless tissue," so that "for the most part the fibres of a living creature are no more opaque than water" (63–65 passim). He decides then "to transcend magic" by creating "an animal— a tissue—transparent . . . invisible . . . all except the pigments" (66). Griffin's inaugural obsessions must be linked with the nature of beauty and pain, as expressed in Wells's early fiction and essays. At the same time, these themes should be compared with the "victoria total de ese panteísmo idealista" examined in "Tlön, Uqbar, Orbis Tertius" (*Ficciones*, 26).

Pain and Griffin are inseparable. While he secretly tries to make a white cat invisible, his landlord suspects him of being a vivisectionist. Griffin is accused of the same activity that Dr. Moreau takes to a remote island, but the association runs deeper: what Griffin is to light, Moreau is to pain; and pain is to light what the grotesque is to the sublime, its lower form. Doctor Moreau has a theory:

> Pain is simply our intrinsic medical adviser to warn us and stimulate us. Not all living flesh is painful; nor is all nerve. There is no tint of pain, real pain in the sensations of the optic nerve, you merely see flashes of light. (*The Island of Dr. Moreau*, 135)

In 1894, Wells published "The Province of Pain," an essay in which he tried to show that pain is "a phase through which life must pass on its evolution from the automatic to the spiritual" (*Early Writings*, 109). The phrase offers an epitaph to Griffin's failure in not being able to transcend the mechanical infliction of pain, of which he is both master and victim. But his is a failure in which sublime expressions of unbound invisibility come into imaginary view. Moreover, in Wells's imagination pain coincides with notions of tincture, it lends pigment and color to the somatic register of sensations, constituting a primitive evidence of the *seen felt* and of the *unfeeling seen*. Pain paints, it colors and hues the skin, it implants its message on the mind, which otherwise should be like a pure tissue. Wells believed that only the stuff of nerves, particularly the optic one, are *untainted* by pain. By the same token, when it affects surfaces, pain may seem like a *taint*. Therefore, being an albino is like having a skin that ought to be free of pain, as blood perhaps would be if it could be decolored white. As Griffin puts it: " 'You know the red colouring matter of blood; it can be made white—colourless—and remain with all the functions it has now!' " (66). In wanting to turn blood white and colorless, like himself, Griffin implies the higher wish of finding in invisibility a final release from pain, perhaps from the pain itself of being colorless. The contradiction is dialectical and cruel: white blood and skin should represent the absence of pain, but the wish to transgress from such lack into the invisible (with its promise of power) comes from experiencing albinism as shame, or as the spiritual cognate of somatic pain.

Anticipating Moreau, Wells writes: "The probabilities are that neither is life nor nervous structure inseparably tinted by the possibility of pain. . . . Most of the impressions of sight are devoid of any decided flavour of the kind, and most sounds, and all those many nervous impressions that never awaken consciousness; those that maintain the tonic contraction of arteries . . . are painless" (*Early Writings*, 194). In his experiments Griffin obtains a transparency of consciousness reduced to its chemical networks and pathways. In-between being commonly visible and totally transparent, his body passes through a state of arboreal crystallization in which he looks like an anatomical illustration of light layered and refracted beneath the outward membrane of the skin. Griffin's alertness to other bodies is also an alertness to pain, as if he were the mind exposed or dislocated to the skin. In man, writes Wells, the province of pain "is merely the surface of his body, with 'spheres of influence,' rather than proper possessions in the interior, and the centre seat of pain is in the mind" (*Early Writings*, 196). Wells associates physical pain with the "painful possibilities" and the "watch against injury" located on the surface of the body. Hence, "savages" are *painful*, they remain always on skin-guard, and thus primitively attuned to a threatening reality of mindless urgency. Wells attributes what might be called *suffering* (as distinct from pain) to civilized humans. It could be that, in partaking of both pain and suffering, Griffin reveals his kinship with angels and women.

In a curious aside, Wells comments on Cesare Lombroso's *La donna delinquente* (1893) and its thesis that women feel physical pain less acutely than men. Wells observes (against "all the militant feminine") that "there being a direct relation between emotional and physical sensibility," women's greater endurance of pain should be a sign of mental depth: "Their pains are more intense mentally, but less so physically" (*Early Writings*, 196). Griffin might be said to enjoy this mark of in-depth and mindful pain driven into ruinous details of masochistic grandeur. It is in this regard that his angeleology deserves notice.

As Bernard Bergonzi has shown (90–92, 115), the Angel in *The Wonderful Visit* (1895) gives Wells the satirist a chance to gently mock life in a small village situated in the same part of Sussex as the one in *The Invisible Man*. Wells wrote that with the story of the visiting Angel he "tried to suggest to people the littleness, the narrow horizon, of their ordinary lives by bringing into sharp contrast with physical characters a being who is free from the ordinary human limitations" (quoted in Bergonzi, 91). Ruskin once remarked that men would shoot an angel if it ever arrived on earth; a worse fate than this is encountered by Griffin in his own mangled epiphany. Wells contrasted his "Angel of Art" with angels in religious and popular beliefs; his is not the biblical angel of Milton, "a vast winged strength, sombre and virile," but more like "the Angel of Italian art, "polychromatic and gay" (*Early Writings*, 231). Griffin might have achieved a similar radiance, but his is the uncanny catastrophe of a would-be angel. And yet, in being antithetical to angelic beauty, he reflects it. He might not be an angel "plain and coloured," but, in a pathetic way, he aborts the angelic in himself. Eventually, the Angel in *A Wonderful Visit* comes close to Griffin's own predicament of dress, when he is brought into the Vicar's house wearing a colored garment that allows his bare legs to show, and provokes the females in the house into thinking that the Curate has brought home a young woman in short skirts. In the end, as Bergonzi points out, the beautiful Angel "himself is made a grotesque figure by having to be dressed, for reasons of propriety, in clothes belonging to the Vicar" (92).

More than a born-again man, Griffin represents a living essay on the perils of rehearsing one's own biological and representational conception and uniqueness of being. Wells approached biology in a philosophical and broadly inquiring spirit, much like Borges did in dealing with the theory and philology of fiction. Looking into the biology behind *The Invisible Man,* one soon discovers deep correspondences between the science of life and the life of words, and between the "sujeto indivisible" (as conceived in Borges's Tlön) and Wells's notion of "The Rediscovery of the Unique" (1891), proposed in an essay originally entitled "The Fallacy of the Common Noun" (*Early Writings,* 22–34). Like Borges,

Wells operates at his witty best when he breaks down and exposes some of the unsettling consequences of organized belief, of systems of thought which he finds persuasive but in some hidden fashion ruinous, as Borges does in "Tlön, Uqbar, Orbis Tertius" with the main tenets of George Berkeley's idealism.[10]

Common nouns have no purchase in Tlön's orthodox *Ursprache,* verb compounds and adjectival word strings have replaced them. Therefore, instead of saying or (if possible) writing *luna,* one refers instead to a given aspect of represented motion and enunciates something like "*Upward, behind the onstreaming it mooned,*" or maybe like "*aéreo-claro sobre oscuro-redondo,*" and so on. In certain regions of Tlön, things may not be *found* or *lost,* since this presupposes that objects survive their enunciatory existence unchanged (the stuff of such enunciations being the only matter that matters in Tlön). A pantheism absorbed in sensations replaces the problem of *having* coins which may not be either lost or found. Materialist heretics have tried in vain to persuade orthodox Tlönians that in gathering rust coins gain physical independence from the epistemic constraint that locates *coins* in the unchanging realm in which imprints on the mind are bound to their enunciation as words. The same is true of feelings and sensations. Pain afflicts nine men in nine successive nights, but the pain cannot be the same. But, again, pain may be all that matters in the end, as when all men engaging in intercourse are the same man, or those quoting a line from Shakespeare are Shakespeare (*Ficciones,* 24–25). As John Sturrock points out (*Paper Tigers,* 121), the whole line of demonstrations about Tlön begins when someone (perhaps Bioy Casares) misquotes *copulation,* putting it in place of *fatherhood,* which would be like opting for *intercourse* instead of *man,* or *line* (or *poetry*) instead of *Shakespeare.* Particularly in the latter case, one is back at the point where confidence in paternity sustains the assumption of authority in classic writing: quoting something, one quotes the author by becoming him—*besides him.* One wonders also about instances in which, rather than just being felt or suffered ("padecen un vivo dolor"), pain might be experienced upon actually being inflicted by someone— even by the same person who feels it. Can a country in which things cannot be lost or found tolerate a causal link between pain felt and pain given?

Wells's ironic approach to *the unique* parallels Borges's various narrative rehearsals of idealism. Idealism turns its own unrecognized backside on the trivial and unique, on pain and the all-too-solid noises of moaning. In such terms, the unique implies that where there is pain felt, there is pain given. Ironically, all that is unique predicates a singularity that transcends any instance of uniqueness: there are pains *here,* because there is pain *anywhere. All being is unique,* affirms Wells, "nothing is strictly like anything else." This implies that "we only arrive at the idea of similar beings by an unconscious or deliberate disregard of an infinity of small differences," a proposition not unlike the one made by Borges regarding the education in forgetfulness in which a person negotiates a path through space unhalted by any notice of the unique, moving along or gliding through things with the aid of memory in a manner corresponding to what Wells calls "to slur over uniqueness" (*Early Writings,* 26). The doctrinaires of Tlön do not "slur" over the unique; instead, they are its sentinels. It is even doubtful whether their language would recognize as one and the same individual the man who arrives back from a walk and the one who a half hour earlier left for it. In relation to a similar doubt, Wells offers his own theory of language, the gist of which concerns the *common noun,* or how the noun is "really the verbal link of a more or less arbitrarily determined group of uniques," so that when one takes "the term [the noun] distributively the boundaries grow suddenly vague"— hence the slurring (24). Wells's essay contains its own *Ursprache:* "The first substantives of primitive man were almost certainly not ordinary common nouns. They were single terms expressive of certain special relationships between him as the centre of the universe and that universe" (26). What is meant is that all nouns were at the start all at once both proper and common, but only in the sense that they stood for functions rather than persons who could be detached from them: *father* was *the-one-who-feeds; man, the one who might come to kill me,* and so forth. Such particularism eventually breaks down and the collapse of the unique is nowhere in worse evidence than with numbers. Wells had in mind a situation not unlike that of Funes the memorious (without his talent of total recall), in which "out of a jumble of broken-down substantives and demonstratives grew up the numbers—grew and blossomed like a grove of mental upas trees. . . . When we teach a child to count, we poison its mind almost irrevocably" (26). Funes goes against the grain of such teaching: he has a proper name for each number and he remembers them all. In Funes's case, however, names could not behave as they do with persons limited by a memory of the common sort. Funes's array of proper names must lead to a degree of connectedness falsely obscured by the fact that his memory seems to be atomistic, when in reality it must be endlessly gathering individual references into DNA-like spirals of timeless associations. Funes's sense of the familiar is interminable, his predicament is a philological version of Griffin's biological search for the unique.

In testing the ability to turn bodies invisible, Griffin began by giving the drug to a white female cat. What happened to the poor creature, as told to the horrified Dr. Kemp, leads straight to the biological matrix of the *unique*. Four hours into the experiment, the cat was almost gone from sight, "the bones and sinews and the fat were the last to go, and the tips of the coloured hairs" (69). However, something uniquely stubborn remains: "[T]he back part of the eye, tough iridescent stuff it is, wouldn't go at all. . . . I remembered the shock I had when striking a light—there were just the round eyes shining green—and nothing round them" (69). The tissue that resists being deprived of reflecting light is "the pigment stuff . . . at the back of the eye in a cat," the so-called *tapetum*. This membrane prevents the cat from being wholly invisible, but it should be noted that it shines because it lacks black pigment. The tapetum makes an irregular (colorless) sector in the choroid membrane lining the eyeball, which is related to the *chorion* or outermost membrane. As with the fetus, the chorion is the *shell* that is present, for instance, in names like *Coriolanus*. The word is not mentioned in Griffin's account of the tapetum, but the notion of uncovering the *unique* is warranted (uncovering it as the skin that reidentifies Griffin's albinism by relocating it inside the eye). A microcosmic picture of reflected uniqueness emerges in which the albino man who lacks the tapetum's unique colorlessness can become invisible (and humanly unique) while contemplating a mirror of albinism deep inside the cat's eye.

In "The Rediscovery of the Unique," Wells considers "the most indisputable corollary," namely, "the destruction of the atomic theory," for there is "absolutely no ground in human experience for the presumption of similar atoms, the mental entanglement that created one being now unravelled, and similarly the certainty of all so-called laws of physics and chemistry" (*Early Writings*, 27). Atoms are rediscovered as "unique things each with its idiosyncrasies," and then, if "the mad atom comes along, the believer in the unique remains tranquil, while the ears of the chemist get hot, his manner becomes nervous and touchy, and he mumbles certain unreasonable things about 'experimental error'" (28). Griffin is no ordinary chemist, he craves after the unique and is ready to make use of himself as its pawn. He is somewhat like Funes, who found in his ability to recall everything a unique mode of being arrested by the uniqueness of every detail he experienced. Ireneo Funes's confession to the narrator of Borges's story reflects a condition of linguistic obliviousness to generality. For him, each word or number represents an atom of disabling singularity. In the case of Griffin's confession to Kemp, one discovers biological evidence of yet another consequence of having found the unique: flight, pursuit, and the genetic equivalent of Funes's amazing dictionary of memory-terms. Either in biological or philological terms, the sense of the unique in Borges and Wells is at odds with the notion of a particular language whose uniqueness would not represent the virtual exclusion of any other competing language. Each memory trace registered in Funes's mind is unique and even denies the possibility of sequential or systematic memorization. What Griffin discovers in the female cat's eye is similarly shrouded in infinite self-reference.

In "The Biological Problem of To-Day" (1894), Wells grappled with the mysteries of redundant biological uniqueness while dealing with August Weismann's theory of "germ-plasm." In such a genetic context, the tapetum would offer evidence of ancestral stubbornness in the renewed life of certain cells. In other words, more than being Griffin's sacrificial double, the white (tapetum-specific) female cat could be the embodiment of the albino's own staggered genetic ancestry. As Wells explains it, Weismann's theory advanced "the idea that seeds or eggs contained a peculiar substance, different in kind from the prevailing living protoplasm of plants and animals, and that they could arise only from those parts of the body in which resided a stock of the peculiar material originally derived from the parent" (*Early Writings*, 125). Already, a resemblance appears between the exceptional status of what Weismann called germ-plasm and the tapetum's unique standing within its surrounding tissue. Wells adds that as the idea grew in "Weismann's fertile imagination," the germ-plasm "bore exotic fruits." Weismann insisted

> on the complete separation between the hereditary material and the material of the tissues of the body. A portion was used in the formation of the new organism; the remainder was secluded in the tissues of the organism undisturbed and uninfluenced by all the shaping and molding influences that affected the organism during life, and was handed on unaltered to the next generation. (125)

Wells's distaste for the notion that acquired traits should not pass from parents to children is of little interest here. What matters is the composition and place of residence of what is always preserved and passed on to each generation. Besides being located in the cell's nucleus, "the germ-plasm is composed of a number of separate pieces, each piece being a veritable microcosm corresponding to some separate ancestor, and each being composed of innumerable particles" (125). This could serve as a description of Funes's memory, broken down into philological particles, each bearing microcosmic and self-sufficient information about its ancestral impact upon Funes's consciousness, each a module of ancestor worship. As quoted by Wells, the germ-plasm endures in the "'architecture'" inside each cell, until, at each cell division, it "'partially disintegrates, and to the cells resulting from the division there are handed on different and appropriate groups of particles corresponding to different qualities'" (126). Being made of fractions of themselves, such cells can only give rise to cells of their own kind, thus new organisms "can arise only because a number of the complete ancestral pieces of the germ-plasm were preserved with their architecture untouched" (126). It could be that if the tapetum contains a cellular architecture that uniquely resists invisibility and does so in microcosmic resemblance with Griffin's color-less skin, and if both Griffin and the cat are white, then a unique (and shameful) white skin (Griffin's) is pursuing its own invisibility by confronting a colorless membrane in the cat's eye that performs the opposite—that is, it remains hostage to visibility, but only insofar as it stays out of sight as the inner lining of the womb, or as a womblike retinal habitat. In rejecting the invisible, the eye's membrane rejects Griffin, but it rejects him as a womb-unique token of Griffin's own similarity to his ancestors.

The unique tapetum is a specular and biogenic quotation of Griffin's present condition composed of ancestral singularities. The counterpart of attaining pure invisibility or pure colorlessness is for the individual to split into ancestral atoms, which is perhaps what the teeming streets of London fantastically evoke in Griffin's paranoid consciousness as he runs naked and unseen over his own muddy and excremental footprints. In contrast, instead of flight, Funes knows only lethargic rest, living imprisoned in the involuntary mourning of ancestral experiences kept alive in his definitive memory. Both men die as if stricken by a biological/philological hybrid disease known as ancestry. Their respective confessions and deaths replace erotic experience (of whichever sort) with a parody of orgiastic intercourse. A singularly dense amount of experience goes from one man to the other as if to obscure the fact that they are two very lonely beings. In terms of their narrative defenses, sporadic Mr.

Marvel, tight-assed Dr. Kemp, wild boy Griffin, aboriginally hybrid Funes, and his civilized interviewer are all immuno-plethoric instead of deficient organisms. These men make up a row of bachelors in whom the blessings and curses of storytelling and mythmaking confess their uniqueness, part of which consists in a certain paranormal pride against the sociobiological advantages of domesticity and breeding. Their maleness is monstered by a pride as old and pristine as the glaring envy and blasted beauty of Milton's Satan.

Anthony West has written something about *The Invisible Man* that Borges might have found challenging:

> The title proves to be misleading: the story does not deal with an invisible man's interaction with the world we know, but with what befalls an invisible madman, a person impenetrably concealed within his own special frame of private references, resentments, obsessions, and compulsions, and altogether set apart from the generality of mankind. When my father had done with the story he was aware that he had come very close to a complete success in the realm of the *tour de force,* but he had not convinced himself, and he was well aware of the extent to which the shadow of the arbitrary lay across his fiction. (*Aspects of a Life,* 234)

Borges's respect for "el primer Wells" rests on slightly different assumptions, he sees the shadow of the arbitrary summoned and then being thoroughly defeated by the storytelling powers of a writer who inherited the concisions ("las brevedades") of Swift and Poe, and who, "like Quevedo, like Voltaire, like Goethe . . . is less a man of letters than a literature" (*Otras inquisiciones,* 125, 128). In calling early Wells a classic, Borges would not hesitate in reinforcing that notion with a proper view of the author's derivative genius. What Anthony West calls the tour de force in his father's romance implies that a certain preestablished model has been taken to new lengths and altered without breaking it. His description of Griffin's turbulent depth leans perhaps too heavily on the dark self inside the man, and not at all on those redemptive possibilities that Griffin's mad project could not but adumbrate. West seems to be describing the same one-sided evil character that Borges deplores in his review of *Dr. Jekyll and Mr. Hyde.* But there is a way in which invisible Griffin becomes not so much Jekyll-in-Hyde as his magic mantle.[11] Under this mantle quickly hardened by the involuntary envy of vulgar minds, fears, and expectations, the monstered self hides in order to commit suicide through exposure, or for the sake of having his *I*—not his *Je* but his *moi*, as if from elsewhere—killed. Killed not by the *eye* that kills, but by the eyes of all his ever-present ancestors. Performing a tragic farce upon Freud's *Totem and Taboo*, Griffin runs and bumps his way toward an invisible elsewhere, where he hopes to die (of himself) while being purged of all ancestry. Accumulated ancestry kills in him the sublime possibilities of pantheistic experience.

The narrative elements and situations chosen by Wells are so purely eventful (and as such mythic) that they exempt Griffin from rhetorical gravity, from all those heavy theological formulas that Stevenson puts in Jekyll's priestly confession. The Invisible Man confesses to Dr. Kemp, a modern, unimpressive man. All the primitive and archaic persons Griffin ever knew (including himself) are thus sealed in his words. In parallel contrast, Henry Jekyll confesses to himself—and only in such fashion to God. Henry's disclosures multiply and enhance him, even if posthumously: "I concealed my pleasures; and then when I reached years of reflection, and began to look round me and take stock of my progress and position in the world, I stood already committed to a profound duplicity of life. . . . My scientific studies, which led wholly toward the mystic and the transcendental, reacted and shed a strong light on this consciousness of the perennial war among my members" (81–82).[12] As his reflections deepen, Jekyll would seem to be alluding to his own view of a body about to transcend itself into the invisible, or into a similarly etherealized condition: "I began to perceive more deeply than it has ever yet been stated, the trembling immateriality, the mist-like transience, of this seemingly so solid body in which we walk attired. Certain agents I found to have the power to shake and to pluck that fleshly vestment, even as a wind might toss the curtains of a pavilion" (82). Jekyll's descriptions lend value on his own self as they account for those virtues and defects from which Henry is now released, but which still hang on him as they would on a ritual offering: "I . . . recognized my natural body for the mere aura and effulgence of certain of the powers that made up my spirits," or "I knew well that I risked death; for any drug that so potently controlled and shook the very fortress of identity, might by the least scruple of an overdose or at the least inopportunity in the moment of exhibition, utterly blot out that immaterial tabernacle which I looked to it to change" (83). In confessing with such an effusion of ritual self-designation, Jekyll seems to be dressing himself with formulas as a victim of sacrifice. Already in defeat, he does not let go of words, as if they were still magic weapons. As opulently written as they seem, his sentences could be rendered oral just by shifting them to the present tense. As a speech act in present illocutionary shape, Jekyll's words would become a performative utterance signifying the victim's confessional self-enhancement at the moment just before immolation. This voice, speaking at the (self-pointing) occasion of sacrificial readiness, may also reveal how much the words and verbal tense of what has actually been written stand gravely in place of a story, a *mythos* of personal calamity that a given storyteller might impersonate. As will be explored further in reference to Vargas Llosa's *El hablador,* the performing storyteller may always be referring to himself, or may be drawing mainly from his own personal repertoire in telling any given story. These self-references, however, may not concern an individual unless they come mediated by voices regarded as inherently ancestral. A broad area of mediation between one individual and another (or between an individual and his/her group ancestry) lies across such sacrificial fault.

As already suggested, Borges's notion of atavistic order in narrative discourse borrows from Frazer's *Golden Bough* the distinction between homeopathic and contagious magic. Frazer's two modes of influencing reality and Borges's own "magic" ways of assuming it rest on a prior duality between two men, closely and at times indistinctly combined, both of whom function within a sacrificial male-specific domain. Against the general background of what he calls "The Public Magician," Frazer defines two types of human gods. In line with the (now-defunct) strict separation between magic and religion, Frazer speaks of a being "of an order different from and superior to man," who becomes incarnate "in a human body, manifesting his superhuman power and knowledge by miracles wrought and prophecies uttered through the medium of the fleshly tabernacle in which he has deigned to take up his abode" (244). Beside this god-man originated in religious practices stands the magician-as-god, who "is nothing but a man who possesses in an unusually high degree powers which most of his fellows arrogate to themselves on a smaller scale" (244). While the inspired or religious type of god-man "derives his divinity from a deity who has stooped to hide his heavenly radiance behind a dull mask of earthly mould," the one given to magic "draws his extraordinary power from a certain physical sympathy with nature"; this other man, undoubtedly an idealized shaman, is not "merely the receptacle of a divine spirit," his "whole being, body and soul, is so delicately attuned to the harmony of the world that a touch of his hand or a turn of his head may send a thrill vibrating through the universal framework of things" (245). In return, this sort of human pitchfork or god-man "is acutely sensitive to such slight changes of environment as would leave ordinary mortals wholly unaffected." An evolutionistic revolving door might be all that separates Frazer's two prototypes. Like Borges's classic and romantic types, their mutual dependence lies in endless contention. If one tries to separate them from each other and from their respective answers to pantheism, a difference might emerge between a prophetic and a shamanistic kind of charisma. The prophet's charisma haunts the voice of Jekyll, as the magician's art hides beneath Griffin's hide. Both forms of male-specific elation are cultivated by the character of extreme romantic powers whom Borges calls "el otro Whitman." Coriolanus would enjoy having either man in combat. To split such manly adversaries apart may require the sacrificial slaying of a talking soul.

Words Spoken by a Parrot's Mask

> Estaban quietos y sin rabia. Antes que después. [*They were peaceable and without anger. Before the time afterwards.*]—Mario Vargas Llosa, *El hablador*

Up to this point, in our discussion of Benjamin, Borges, and Wells, the figure of the storyteller has been reached mainly by way of inference. Rather than assuming a direct role in any given story or argument, the narrator has made its presence felt in a manner quite different from the ways in which a character may appear in a plot. The storyteller has come into play either as a far-flung assumption or as a precipitate of the drama of actions and ideas. He first emerged in Benjamin's essay on mechanical reproduction as a violent parthenogenesis of the film apparatus which in its attempted unmasking of ritual aura under fascist rule projected a subliminal view of the primitive magician, a figure that Benjamin excludes from the portrait of the narrator as artisan in his essay on the storyteller. The kinship between Benjamin's notion of aura and the social assumption of cosmic violence through ritual seems implicit in his own contrast between mechanical reproduction and the ancestral procedures of magic, but the contrast fails at two decisive levels. First, it reveals how Benjamin's enhancement of technical violence in the film apparatus endows it with primitive effects and a certain superstitious aura. To assume that such effects are held at arm's length by Benjamin's ironic use of theory would not guarantee his release from the dialectical need to associate film with the artificial maintenance of enchantment in a world severed from magic. Second, the contrast between magician and surgeon foregrounds once and for all the insistent dualities on which the entire conception of aura and mechanical reproduction depends: it shows to what extent Benjamin's essayistic arguments unfold by wavering between a dialectical and a narrative assumption of opposites, as if he were following the dualistic protocol of a magician's routine.

The storyteller was then located in the itinerant consciousness of the *flâneur,* a figure whose keen awareness of thresholds is protected by aesthetic immunity against the ritual intrusion of myth into personal history. The possibility of just such an intrusion of past stories into a life suddenly driven by atavistic compulsions became a reality with Juan Dahlmann, a character possessed by the ethics of ancestral identity struggling to achieve literary shape. In Dahlmann and Erik Lönnrot, the *flâneur'*s mythology of thresholds and ritual aura finds a country in which a nationalistic and colonizing mythology has been forged. A latent, occluded form of patriotic violence replaces the blessings of involuntary memory and the aesthetic opportunism of *flânerie.* In Borges, violence is native, it springs from the nation's own birth. Violence becomes the only means by which the individual may remember his birth. The bases of political solidarity and violence are imbued with a myth about genealogical and individual origins in which enemies otherwise truly despised or insignificant become intimate adversaries and sacred executioners in the hero's romantic death. In this personalized fashion, tumultuous forms of political solidarity and class-based struggles are assimilated by an always implicit storyteller into his own labyrinth of extended and incestuous kinship.

In Borges's essays and stories the impingement of other minds and memories upon a single individual offers a paradoxical access to pantheism as a literary alternative to political solidarity. Instead of a seemingly passive receptiveness toward the general will, the individualist (exemplified by figures like Whitman) vibrates to the will and emotions of the unnumbered many. Such vibrations may be narrated as distinct events within an awesomely autonomous expressive consciousness. Although mythic, the poetic character of Whitman does not undergo sacrificial metamorphosis. Instead, the other Whitman gains immortality by avoiding the type of ordeal that would make him memorable through ritual death. This represents the highest conception of sublime classic continuity of which Borges seems capable, but there is a darker side inherent in the dualities that animate his sense of sublime pantheism. In figures like Funes, or in the idealist amalgamations made possible in Tlön, the pantheist sublime collapses in a manner similar to the catastrophe that befalls the unshakable and grotesque visibility of a man turned invisible. From Borges's perspective, in both Henry Jekyll and Griffin storytelling reaches a confessional point in which suicide and ritual murder face each other in a single figure of monstrous kinship. In civilized form, a primitive confessional ordeal with its aura of ritual murder and suicide may be replaced by the narratological fashion of authorial self-reference.

Mario Vargas Llosa's *El hablador* (*The Storyteller*)[13] situates the issues analyzed thus far in a perspective of explicit thematic value. Virtually every significant theme discussed in reference to Benjamin, Borges, and Wells plays a prominent role in the novel. *El hablador* is told in the voices of Saúl Zuratas and the anonymous narrator, voices that communicate in antiphonal counterpoint the distinct duties of storytelling in the tribal past and the cosmopolitan present. Although quite remote from each other in geographic, social, and political terms, the two storytellers meet in the reader's mind and in the act of reading. The tribal storyteller manages to relay a sort of polemical confession to his former novelist friend through means that are not constrained by ordinary obstacles within material and empirical existence.

The confessional value of what is exchanged is imaginary and in that sense hyper-real. It is also quite unequal. The reader learns far more about Saúl Zuratas's family history than he or she does about the narrator's mimeographed life as a world-weary member of the Peruvian elite. In fact, the narrator's life is masked by Saúl's story. Just as Zuratas has traded the life of a Jew (in Lima or Israel) for the nomadic existence of a Machiguenga storyteller in Peru's Amazonia, the narrator has trimmed down to its bare essentials his own profile as a celebrity in order to be adopted by his fictional creation of Saúl's new life. Here and there, the storyline reveals that the modern writer has little to confess about himself in exchange for what he manages to create of himself in the act of inventing the storyteller's life. However, novelistic invention should not imply that Saúl Zuratas is merely the narrator's fictional creation in the same obvious sense in which he represents a character created by Mario Vargas Llosa. Rather, invention aims at lending vividness to the novelist's attempt to transcend creative solipsism. At stake is the narrator's aptness not to surrender to the relative omnipotence of novelistic creation.

Such a Flaubert-like challenge is placed under the constraints of Machiguenga wisdom, according to which life must be lived either in *rabia* (anger) or in peacefulness. Life may also be seen as an affair that happens *antes* (before) and *después* (afterwards). The narrator's invention of Saúl's life among the Machiguengas belongs to *después;* the novelist narrates from a realm in which anger has been trained in politics and placed under the control of professional cynics and managers of irony, whether as media people or world-class novelists. It is the invented life (Saúl's) and not its invention (the novelist's) that belongs to *antes,* or to a realm in which, provided one is at peace with oneself, the spheres of *before* and *afterwards* may cross paths in a singular way. Living afterwards, the narrator has imagined and given expression to a way of assuming personal ancestry, as portrayed in Saúl's life. Zuratas assumes his new (Machiguenga) and former (Jewish) ancestors in a manner not available to the narrator (unless it is through Saúl's own story), who would then become the writer's own ancestor, mourned in the same act of being invented as the writer re-creates himself. Two individuals are thus transformed into a double measure of spoken time rehearsed in writing, by means of which someone is created and someone, as it were, *de-created.*

The novel begins and ends in Florence during the summer of 1985, from which point in time (*frame*) the plot builds up two alternating strands of narrative. One strand consists of a chronological account (*storyline*) of the narrator's friendship with Saúl Zuratas, two visits to the Peruvian rainforest, and other professional activities; the other amounts to a quilted and cyclic string (*storytelling*) involving narratives and events rendered in performance by a storyteller at the heart of an implicit group of listeners. The eight chapters fall into the following pattern:

frame	1				8
storyline		2	4	6	
storytelling			3	5	7

Setting aside for the moment the two framing chapters, the storyline can be reviewed in isolation before seeing how it interacts with the three storytelling chapters.

Learning about Saúl Zuratas's transformation from a young Jewish student of law and ethnography in Lima to a nomadic Indian in the rainforests of the Upper Urubamba River brings the narrator into contact with two different families. His friend is the son of an East European refugee and a young Creole mother from Talara, where the family lived until Salomón moved his grocery business into the heart of Lima's

Jewish community. Before dying of cancer after two years in Lima, the mother became her son's loving playmate. They both felt like pariahs: she was a simple, almost illiterate woman in the midst of proud Jewish burghers, while her son was a new convert to his father's faith, but also "the ugliest lad in the world," with a huge, dark purple birthmark covering half his face (9/11). Besides Saúl's ethnic relatives, the narrator becomes acquainted with another family, the Schneils, to whom he never speaks of Zuratas's existence, even though the couple provides him with the one precious clue concerning the presence of a storyteller (*hablador*) among the Machiguengas who might be his lost friend. The Schneils are linguists trained at the University of Oklahoma who decided to spend their lives bringing small tribal communities into the Protestant fold by turning their nomadic ways into sedentary existence under biblical auspices and symbols. The couple's scientific work with the controversial Summer Institute of Linguistics includes the missionary goal of translating the Bible (from English?) into Machiguenga.

At first glance, the two Saúl-related families could not be more different. The Zuratas are a case of fractured assimilation under powerful recessive forces. Salomón's Judaism seems more lawful and cultic than tribal. In addition, because his Creole wife belongs to the wrong tribe, his only son is as natively odd as Hagar's Ishmael is to Israel, but not as fierce in his assumption of savagery: "And he will be a wild man; his hand will be against every man, and every man's hand against him; and he shall dwell in the presence of all his brethren" (Genesis 16:12). As a storyteller among savages, Saúl seems to fulfill only the first and last phrases of the scriptural prophecy, but the native brethren who gather round him are described at some point in the narrator's account as "an even more archaic group or fraction, hostile to the others, known by the name of Kogapakori . . . [who] went about stark-naked, though some of the men wore phallic sheaths made of bamboo, and attacked anyone who entered their territory, even those who were ethnically related" (79/80). In biblical terms, the Zuratas are patriarchal and Hebraic; their basic features relate to genealogy, to gender and ethnic marks of kinship. For instance, Saúl's birthmark will in due course appear as a token of mother-right, or as a moon-related spot in adversarial rapport with circumcision. Saúl's transformation into an *hablador* seems legitimized by the way in which his facial excrescence (or *lunar*) corresponds to the angry aspect of Kashiri, the male moon of the Machiguengas in whose mythic face the birth of sexual difference is endlessly replayed.[14]

The Schneils represent the Christian Bible and the modern utopia of

Adam and Eve transformed into a progressive Protestant marriage. Their religion is meant to have no nationality; it occupies a single country stretching across the pages of a translated book. Whatever flaws the narrator might perceive in the Schneils' mission and attitudes are trivial when compared with their role as witnesses to the storyteller and as unwitting and inwardly resentful apostles of his word. The Schneils do not know that the storyteller is a Jew, an ignorance for which they can hardly be blamed. In contradiction to Machiguenga culture, they deny that there should be anything religious about the man; they insist that he is just an entertainer, an eccentric, a *serigórompi* (175/181). Thus, their description of Saúl unknowingly reveals only one half of a dual Christ figure to the urbane narrator, a myth enthusiast and unbeliever in awe of what his lost friend Saúl seems to have achieved in becoming a speaker of myths.

Contrary to what the Schneils' religious faith allows them to comprehend about the storyteller, the would-be novelist who listens to them has no choice but to believe passionately that entertainment *and* religion speak through the *hablador*, that a peculiar (both universal and Machiguenga) grace comes wrapped up in stories wholly indifferent to Christian dogma but in essence as sacred and legitimate as the stories in the Bible. The narrator believes that what is known as the sacred may be voiced by certain beings who belong to families, or who might have forsaken their own kinfolk only to adopt and increase their relatives elsewhere, among a different folk and a different ancestry and by means other than sexual reproduction.

In this respect there is a perspective from which the Schneils might seem to have conceptually killed a godly man whom they never knew, either as a Jew or as a weaver of sacred yarns. The narrator seems fixed on precisely that perspective, for he cannot dispel the charismatic enchantment of knowing that the *hablador*'s practical sacredness wears the mask of his old friend's stoic mirth as *Mascarita,* a blessed freak with a parrot perched on his shoulder. Faced with the Machiguenga storyteller, and when it comes to regarding Jesus as an actual Son of Man, the Schneils' Christian God appears suddenly non-Jewish and non-native. By the same token, the narrator's Jewish friend becomes sacred when restored to the double-layered ethnicity of Saúl's pagan gospel as a savage Machiguenga archi-Jew.

The Schneils are disqualified for the moment from recognizing any Christ value in the *hablador* (as Saúl is inwardly conceived by the narrator). One must say "for the moment" insofar as the Schneils may one day (in some fictional realm) become themselves readers of *El hablador,* in which case they would share the opportunity to test their brand of Christian belief against the story that the narrator (as would-be author) has written. Whether or not the narrator should be regarded as the fictional author of the novel is not as certain as it might seem, but there is evidence that an entity or person within the story knows how the chapters in the storyteller's own voice can communicate with those told in the narrator's voice or through his novelistic account. In any event, such an entity or individual in contact with both sides of the story could be identified in discursive terms with a gospel writer *and* its audience, or with someone for whom whatever is told within the Machiguengas' nomadic range must be understood as a single intertextual narrative in cognitive relationship with the rest of the story.

The Christological implications are intriguing. The Schneils cannot grasp the presence among the Machiguengas of a sacred emissary unless he is Christian and Protestant. On his part, the narrator, who may not believe in God, is possessed by the truthfulness exuded by someone who must have a sacred yet nontheistic—but rather Christological—effect on his brethren. In terms of some New Testament polemics, the Christological irony may provoke amusement. Even though they represent doctrinaire Christian values of a particular modern sort, in their inability to recognize the *hablador* as Jewish and operatively sacred the Schneils resemble the uncomprehending Jews who are the butt of scorn, particularly in the Fourth Gospel, because they are excluded from Christ's secret message as a Son of Man or as a redeemer from heaven. For instance:

> The dialogue with Nicodemus and its postscript connected with John the Baptist constitute a virtual *parody* of a revelation discourse. What is "revealed" is that Jesus is *incomprehensible,* even to "the teacher of Israel" who holds an initially positive belief in him—within the context of Jewish piety—and even to the Baptist who has been his primary human witness. . . . The forms of speech which would ordinarily provide warrants for a particular body of information or instruction here are used in such a way that they serve solely to emphasize Jesus' strangeness. (Meeks, "Man from Heaven," 57)

For the Schneils, Saúl is twice a stranger. If the *hablador* is indeed Zuratas, they are prevented from knowing this because the one possible source of the truth (the Machiguenga storyteller) would never tell them. However, what the Schneils tell the narrator about the nonreligious and merely entertaining *hablador* already bears proof of their ingrained doctrinal unwillingness to regard such a person as anything but a performer.

The narrator might presume that the Schneils' knowing about a Kafkaesque Jew in the role of a Machiguenga storyteller is certain to compound their view of the *serigórompi* in him. In other words, a grumpy and eccentric entertainer would thus turn into a dangerous impostor: the Schneils would see in Zuratas's Jewishness the same embedded socialism that Nietzsche fiercely denounced in the Christian adoption of Judaism as a religion of slaves. On his part, the narrator (though most likely an unbeliever) is possessed by his private knowledge of the Jewishness and religious functions of Saúl the *hablador*. The narrator is likely to agree with the Schneils' judgment that no one, including Saúl, could be an actual Christ (a judgment he spares them by withholding any information about his friend). But a further judgment is likewise thwarted: that which the Schneils would have to consider if they ever had to deal with the status of a Jewish *hablador* as a repeated instance of Jesus among Jews who are also Christians, for that is what the Machiguengas become listening to Saúl's peculiar syncretistic enactment of the *serigórompi*. The narrator deprives the Schneils of a life-view of the *hablador;* he withholds from the evangelists *an* (or *the*) *hablador,* the one that only he can recognize and desperately identify with. It is this autobiographic desire and fulfillment that the narrator regards as his own and perhaps the reader's unique gift of charisma (including the Schneils themselves but only as *El hablador*'s potential future readers). Whatever sacredness may exist in this set of narrative affinities, the home of the sacred would seem to lie in a biography shared by at least two individuals.

The gospel value of the *hablador*'s stories should be no greater than that attained by a mere string of myths (or tales) in a storyteller's repertoire. But it is crucial to note that Saúl and the narrator are the only two individuals within the plot who can act as witnesses to the stories' proclamation of the *hablador*'s personal history as an example of ethical and religious wisdom. In their case, the notion of *gospel* comes down to the (secret) knowledge possessed by two men: that a story otherwise aimed at anyone has intricate sources in the biography of a single but dual individual, and that these sources resemble those from which religious charismatic personalities are typically born.

Beyond their considerable differences, the Schneils and the Zuratas are admirable nuclear families in their own respective styles. Both couples have produced children who they sent to universities, both perform their secular and religious duties with conviction and modest pride. Above all these two sets of parents seem incapable of turning their backs on their children or making them feel ashamed of themselves. A sense of loss in one of the families defines their greatest difference. Within the space of five years, the Zuratas have been reduced to one parent and then to none. Saúl serves as a courageous and sad reminder that a man may be an orphan twice. Also, to the extent that parents may be nurtured by their grown children, Saúl faces the possibility of further loneliness in a strict genealogical sense, for he avoids women due to his ugliness and may remain forever celibate. No one will ever know if Saúl would have found a wife in Peru or Israel, but the three chapters in the storyteller's own voice leave no doubt as to the fateful nature of his celibacy.

The state of remaining unattached to a woman and a place goes hand-in-hand with the *hablador*'s moral teachings to the Machiguengas about mothers not killing their imperfect offspring, as their ancestral sense of purity has always demanded of them. For him and for Saúl, the question goes beyond the elimination of flawed children; what is most deplorable is that mothers should be charged with killing their own children. It cannot be established whether or not Saúl adopts Gregor Samsa as his fictional hero before or after losing his mother, but Kafka's story about a young man who wakes up one morning changed into an insect and who becomes an outcast in his own house provides the definitive link between Saúl and the *hablador*. As Saúl migrates into the *hablador*'s body, he carries with him a complex story concerning the union between physical shame (compounded by the loss of the mother) and the spiritual pride of an eternal son who renounces the companionship of mothering. It is as if for Saúl mourning his mother meant honoring incestuous love in *not* being (re)born as the son (or daughter) he might have with any given woman. Step by step, the *hablador*'s stories reveal that he identifies with the surviving offspring as well as with those who might be killed, and that he does so out of a parallel sense of identification with the mother who may give birth but also might have to kill her children, a woman whom he renounces as his reproductive companion. It is not Oedipus but rather his own engendering (in male or female shape) that the myths on the *hablador*'s lips welcome into a savage range. But before looking into the mythic evidence, it should be added that Saúl's complex assumption of celibacy is copied in the narrator's own cryptic identity as a bachelor. His is a case of marriage unmentioned, of celibacy by inference: if he has a wife, the writer never mentions her, and she is neither in Florence nor in Lima. It is as if the novelist's ironic surrogate had shed all traces of marriage and fatherhood.

Celibacy seems to support the transfiguration of the incest taboo in and around Saúl's metamorphosis into the *hablador*. Rather than being reduced to a specific reproductive or sexual prohibition, the incest taboo represents a set of relationships bearing on how social and material existence becomes sexed, as evidenced in how genders clash and fuse with each other in the cosmological myths of the Machiguengas. It is in the telling of such stories that the status of an unmarried man outside biological lines of kinship may attain adequate symbolic thickness as a peculiar supplement to the diffuse sense of nomadic genealogy prevalent among the scattered Machiguenga, whose single name for males is *Tasurinchi*. Visiting, as he must constantly do, isolated men and male family heads, all of whom answer to this one name only (modified by a reference to the place where they live but may soon abandon), the *hablador*'s own identity will in the end be borrowed from an extended and complex notion of taboo affecting a host of improper unions and behaviors—hence its polemical character. Three meetings between the narrator and Saúl dramatize the polemic. Besides the ebb and flow of their passionate arguments, the friends exchange gifts as signs of their unique bond, but also as tokens of the adversarial roles they occupy within the affairs of storytelling.

Saúl's knowledge of the Machiguengas is first revealed to the narrator following a threshold incident. As the two enter a billiard parlor, Mascarita's face attracts the attention of a drunk who blocks their passage and calls Saúl a monster. A few days after the ensuing scuffle between the narrator and the drunk, Mascarita sends his "pal" a gift and a letter; on a small piece of bone "shaped like a diamond" is engraved a geometric design showing "two parallel mazes made up of bars of different sizes, separated by identical distances, the larger ones seemingly nestled inside the smaller ones" (17/14). The letter explains the cosmological and ethical implications of the carvings, an explanation that is then expanded by Saúl in conversation with his friend. The sequence of a text's being followed by its verbal account is as meaningful as the matter it explains. Letter and commentary share a tone of mock solemnity attuned to a deeper sense of respect for what is being disclosed. Given indirectly in the narrator's voice, the speech suggests a performance, with Mascarita "sitting on a trunk with his parrot on his shoulder," while the other lies in bed listening. Only after reading well into the novel can the reader recognize the scene as the *hablador*'s first rehearsal of the longer performances that he will give among the Machiguengas and, on one occasion, in front of a bored and benumbed Edwin Schneil, but never again before his friend the narrator, since the *hablador* will always perform only within his friend's storytelling imagination.

What Mascarita explains on this occasion he later expands in *hablador* speech, or in myths which recurrently fit within what should be regarded as an inaugural scene in the transmission of wisdom. In the middle of a mountain storm, Morenanchiite, lord of thunder, passes on to a tiger a revelation that is then handed down to a shaman while in a trance induced by the hallucinogen *ayahuasca*. The message is simple: violent emotions must be held in check, for there is "a fatal correspondence between the spirit of man and the spirits of Nature, and any violent disturbance in the former causes some catastrophe in the latter" (18/16). The warning from above has been given to Saúl by a native wise man from the Alto Picha, the same man from whom he learned Machiguenga lore during an early visit to the Upper Urubamba around 1956. The connection between Mascarita and this *seripigari* (wise shaman) has a lot to do with his own depiction as an eccentric or *serigórompi*; it constitutes a variation on the Gregor Samsa motif and it affects the biographic stamp that Saúl puts on the *hablador* figure as Mascarita. In a subtle way that could be easily mistaken for an outright case of Oedipal rivalry, the Kafkaesque outcast modifies the role of indigenous wise man as an archaic counterpart of the lawgiver, lending to it precisely the seemingly casual anecdotal character that the Schneils mistake for that of a simple showman. In such hybrid form, Mascarita's stories carry with them ethical teachings based on his own transformation from outcast into itinerant tribesman. These stories teach of the need for the Machiguengas and Kogapakori to change their customs regarding the elimination of imperfect offspring, like Saúl and a certain parrot born with uneven legs and named Gregor Samsa. The teachings are worked into the stories of Saúl's development as *hablador* at the same time that they draw parallels between his growth in that role and the biblical stories of Moses and the parables of Jesus. Indeed, the *serigórompi* turns into quite an eccentric. Rather than being unhinged from ancestral wisdom, he transforms it in ways hitherto unknown to any *seripigari* or wise man. It is clear that Mascarita-Gregor Samsa (or parrot-man) stands in relation to native shamanistic wisdom in the same critical fashion in which some prophetic figures from the Hebrew scriptures (as well as Jesus in the Gospels) do in proclaiming changes in the religious traditions of their people.

Saúl's mission among the Machiguengas opens the way for an exchange of iconographic and mythic motifs between savage beliefs and Judeo-Christian religious lore. The exchange differs radically from the one-sided indoctrination sponsored by the Schneils and other missionaries; it also alters the standard use value of the single literary tool carried by Saúl into the wild forest. Saúl's appropriation of Kafka's *Metamorphosis* turns the story into scripture, but only in the sense in which scripture may be performed as if made up of clusters of stories otherwise known as myths. This implies a reversal of orthodox hierarchies between religious and literary stories. It turns out that changing the outcome of Kafka's story involves finding elements of it embedded in biblical passages, and that such passages may be transformed into Machiguenga wisdom because, in terms of myth, the Bible is aboriginally Kafka's as it is ultimately Machiguenga. Transformations feed into each other within and beyond the space of Saúl's biography. Changing Gregor Samsa's grotesque banishment into a saga of personal success based on the teaching of new kinds of wisdom—such as not killing certain children— may correspond to understanding biblical passages as if they should accommodate a sort of *Kafka sauvage,* as a double displacement of the *Metamorphosis* into both Machiguenga and Judeo-Christian wisdom. The result would be a Machiguenga Bible, but not in the sense in which missionaries may have translated it into that language.

Frequently, having the answer to an enigma does nothing to resolve its fascination. Readers of *El hablador* have sufficient proof that Saúl is the *hablador,* but the fascination lingers when one thinks that he might also be the only *hablador* ever. Another way to preserve our fascination is to assume that, on becoming an *hablador,* each Machiguenga male anticipates and replicates being like Saúl, a man who, besides faithfully acting like any *hablador* would, brings to the task an irreducible element of biographic difference from any other such individual. A function such as the storyteller's—with its reliance on stereotypic performance—may remain relatively unchanged, but the person who adapts to the task should bring to it traces of individual difference.

The way in which Saúl behaves as the *hablador* becomes no less interesting if he is regarded as just another storyteller among many. Yet, the whole point about the way in which the novelist portrays him lies in the aberrant appearance and role which Saúl must assume as a man who tries to narrate into being a prohibition against Machiguenga infanticide. Saúl resembles Don Quixote in his relationship with the practice and taboo involving infanticide. Just as Don Quixote loses narrative purpose if deprived of his mad beliefs in the realm of chivalry, Saúl would lose a similar narrative thrust if he were to drop his opposition against a cruel practice that might in the end prove adaptive. Whether or not the Machiguenga do well in eliminating the unfit is not the point: the point is that their practice not only explains the very existence of Saúl among them but also lifts into special providence his prior common existence as a weird Peruvian child with an ugly face, but otherwise no more remarkable than many others. Not killing imperfect children may result in the existence of Saúl—the *hablador* who first spoke against the infanticide—among them. As he persuades the Machiguengas not to continue this awful practice, Saúl stands before them as if they had already spared him such a fate in the past.

Thus Saúl tells a story in which the *hablador* saves a newborn parrot from the mother who wishes to kill it, and since he is *Mascarita* in the parrot's tongue as well as being similar to the child that the parrot was when he saved it, one may conclude that Saúl tells a myth whose personal relevance has him saving himself from a mother unlike the one who gave him birth, but who must also be like all mothers, if the myth is to have the effect of creating a taboo. Storytelling tinkers with redundancies: the *hablador*'s best lesson is himself. Ethical law and biographic truth prove inalienable. Assuming this to be the case, Saúl's law of life (or his *bionomy*) might be stated as follows. *Saúl Zuratas speaks the* hablador's *truth when he renders inalienable two different kinds of avoidance: the one that mothers should observe against killing flawed babies, and the one that a son must practice against lying with his own mother*. Saúl's own survival as a flawed individual (saved by a caring mother and legitimized by his own teaching of the ethical norm that would save all others like him) transforms itself into the storyteller's seemingly fateful but in fact group-prescribed avoidance of all mothers as wives.

A further *bionomical* factor emerges from the *hablador*'s teachings. At least in Saúl's case, the Machiguenga storyteller is the mask of the male moon, Kashiri, but in earthly compliance with the avoidance of male-female union, just as Kashiri's astral self embodies the absolute cosmogonic excess of an opposite reproductive tendency: the relentless, baneful, and sumptuously egotistical acquisition of females.

A quick review of Kashiri's exploits in Machiguenga myth needs to be coordinated with some passages in the *hablador*'s nomadic itinerary. A "strong, serene youth," Kashiri is bored in the upper skies of Inkite and decides to come down to earth in search of a wife. The moon is about to become the sun's father by a Machiguenga woman. Upon meeting a female with the facial paint of an unmarried girl, Kashiri teaches her how to plant, harvest, and eat cassava and plantain, brings to her father an armload of game and fish, and then clears and sows a field for him to obtain the crops that his future family will need. The father offers him the bride, but everything must wait until the girl reaches menarche and undergoes the necessary ablutions before the equivalent of marriage. The sun is born from a model union in which the proper terms of exchange and husbandry have been observed, but the marriage is spoiled by another woman's envy, whose actions will mark the moon's face forever. In fact, two different versions are offered on how the moon became stained and diminished by an angry female. In one version, Kashiri's face is smeared with the woman's excrement; in the other, he throws mud at a girl in order to make her pregnant and when she dies in labor he is asked to eat her corpse, which he manages to do up to her stomach, whereupon, with the baby sun twinkling in the open belly, Kashiri pulls him out and flies up to heaven carrying on his shoulder the remains of his wife and leaving the gift-baby to the Machiguengas. Moonlight is weak, Kashiri's face has stains on it; his offspring, the sun, stops moving as punishment against those who tricked his father, but is persuaded to resume moving, walking with the ever-wandering Machiguengas. When asked, a *seripigari* says that "the moon is only half a man" (113/116); it is thus obvious that Kashiri's actions as a hypermale get him involved in the business of demarcating sexual and reproductive functions across matrimonial lines. It also seems as if, with all its disturbing and necessary maleness, the moon provides a mirror for a chimerical view of a would-be mother and menstruating male (and also for the image of a parthenogenic and necrophagous act of mothering the unblemished male character of a son, the sun).

The *hablador's* personal saga or ontogenesis is tied to the complex role played by the moon in Machiguenga reproductive affairs and in the rhythms of material existence. His own nomadism along with the ever-moving Machiguenga marks perhaps a strained avoidance of incestuousness. He tries not to be too much like Kashiri, not to be his own incestuous replicant. Under the sign of the moon, most episodes in Saúl's saga deal with having a wife and with the perils and consequences of being born of woman.

On his first narrated visit to a Tasurinchi, the man's pregnant wife treats the *hablador* as if he were invisible. The woman is feared to be a witch and is blamed for giving birth to dead babies. The figure of the dangerous mother (or odd wife) returns on the visit that opens the second group of stories (chapter 5). Another Tasurinchi has stolen (or traded for) an alien wife who arouses envy among the other women in his home. He suffers the humorously grotesque predicament of carrying around a huge swollen penis after being stung by a petty devil in the form of a wasp. It is from this man that the *hablador* hears of Kashiri's exploits in finding a mother for the sun. There is a resemblance between the men, for the swollen penis is carried perched on the man's shoulder, the *hablador* says, "the way I do with my little parrot." The talking penis looks at the man who owns it and, instead of "Mascarita!," it says "One-Eye—Little One-Eye!" (108/111). Like Saúl's father, this man has taken a wife alien to his group. The ordeal of being stung and burdened with useless maleness has taught the Tasurinchi with a swollen penis that "in some of my souls there's a capricious mother" (109/111). Hence his attempt to put the greatest distance between himself and all mothers from his own group by marrying a Yaminahua woman. The *hablador* knows quite well the protocols of exogamy, only that in his case the outsider and ultimate reject is always himself. On one definitive occasion, a Tasurinchi offers him a choice between two of his women, either a prepubescent girl or an old and well-tested mother. Before he has a chance to decide whether or not he wants to settle down and which woman he would take, the older one commits suicide in order to spare herself the blame for having deprived everyone of the wandering *hablador*. It seems obvious that in his case (and in Saúl's) exogamy and celibacy join hands under the hidden force of the incest taboo.

On his way to another visit, the *hablador* falls into a muddy ravine and loses his parrot. The journey that follows represents one of two prominent Gregor Samsa ordeals experienced by Mascarita. He is pinned on the back of an alligator drifting down the Kamabiría, the river of the dead, from which he is lifted into the upper regions clinging to the neck of a stork, until he brings her (the *garza*) into a lower path by squeezing one of her wings, and falls through the branches into the forest's floor, where he awakens at the voice of a *seripigari*. The shamanistic flight and the birth struggle clinging to the stork are elements of metamorphosis which return when the *hablador* later tells Kafka's story in Machiguenga idioms to another *seripigari*. The *lagarto* (alligator) turns into a *lagartija* (lizard), and the one who is pinned on its back and needs to fly like a shaman becomes an upside-down insect struggling to regain its feet. When it does, its broken wing evokes the earlier squeezing of the stork's wing and her pained release of the *hablador*'s burden. Being thus born changes into being swallowed by the *lagartija* and beholding from within her green eyes a domestic world and indifferent parents. Each of the stories is meant to draw a response from a *seripigari* and another one from the listeners presently addressed by the *hablador*. The story about flying to heaven and back elicits a lesson on the perils of flying while in rage or in fear. The shaman cautions against losing control in the midst of an adventure by telling the story of Kachiborérine, the comet with a flaming cane in his anus, whose exile in the skies seems like a smaller replica of Kashiri's own fate. The teachings of this shaman will prove useful later on, as the *hablador* recalls the story of learning the language of fireflies, or the story of those females whom the sun gave to his father, Kashiri, so the moon could spend all his time in the sky like a "macho insaciable" mounting his wives, as he used to do during his mad days on earth. However, the story about Gregor-Tasurinchi turning into an insect does not draw a learned response from the other *seripigari*. The wisdom narrative chain based on countering one story with another seems to snap, as though the *hablador* wanted his present listeners to repair it by supplying the missing link, the one connecting Gregor Samsa to infanticide—and incest.

It seems as if the type of wisdom at work here is by nature sequential, and that at certain points along its transmission it takes stock of itself by issuing a sentence (or sentences) in self-defense, making reference to what should make such wisdom appealing. A sentence such as: "Before, they were all something different from what they are now. Something happened to all of them that you could tell a story about. Would you like to know their stories? So would I" (188/198). A didactic sequence may pivot on such a sentence, carrying the theme of wisdom's possible decay and the need to repair it:

(a) "It is bad that wisdom should be getting lost. Before, there were any number of seripigaris. . . . There was always a se-ripigari close by. Smoking, drinking brew, thinking, talking with the saankarites in the worlds up above. . . . But now there are few of them and some of them shouldn't call themselves seripigaris. Can they counsel you? Their wisdom has dried up on them like a worm-eaten root, it seems" (183/189).

(b) The *hablador*'s words are followed by an account of his meeting with the wisest *seripigari* that he has ever known, whom he praises: "It's as though you'd been living since before we started walking, and you'd seen everything and tried everything" (184/190).

(c) The *seripigari*'s teachings boil down to the virtue of being patient, based on the rule to "Eat what's permitted and respect the taboos" (185/191).

(d) Accordingly, he tells the story of a hunter who breaks the taboo against killing deer; the hunter's wife fears that in killing and eating these animals they will be killing and eating their own relatives and ancestors; the hunter ends up turning into a deer; all of this happens at night, under Kashiri, "the resentful, the stained one," who creates an environment in which cannibalism represents the collapse of difference feared in the incest taboo (185–89/191–96).

(e) Then comes a question: since all beings were formerly someone else, does the *hablador* want to change into a *seripigari*? If he does, he would have to pass many tests, become pure, undergo trances, "and, above all, suffer"; but the *hablador* is already too old for such pains, so he should then be off, walking and talking and trying not to "disturb the order of the world" (190/196).

(f) On the *hablador*'s request, the *seripigari* explains how the men who walk came to paint their bodies with annatto; he tells the story of Inaenka, the evil woman who destroys the flesh, and of her son, "the child who walks" (190–95/197–202).

(g) The *hablador* responds with the story of Gregor-Tasurinchi turning into an insect and being ignored by his parents, and requests its meaning from the *seripigari*, who tells him to leave the strange story alone lest it may happen again, like things do when they are remembered (196–200/203–7).

(h) But the *hablador* does not comply; instead, he confronts what the wise man would rather avoid. He begins by telling his audience: "I wasn't the way all of you see me now" (200/207), and then spends the rest of his performance explaining how his listeners *ought* to account for the fact that he has survived the facial stigma that should have forced his mother to kill him. He does it in a way that transcends the wisdom of the *seripigari*; he weaves together his own personal story, the Bible, and the Gospels until reaching a moving etiological account of how he saved his parrot from dying upon its mother's rejection (201–24/209–34).

Besides being overtly given to his listeners, the *hablador*'s ethical amendment and supplement to the wisdom of the *seripigari* is embedded within a linkage in the above sequence. The amendment is not limited to supplementing the absence of the shaman's response to Gregor-Tasurinchi's story. Instead, it shuffles together the parrot's story of deliverance from the lethal mother and the myth of Inaenka's son's defeat of her, the evil mother among the several ones that are attributed to him in myth.

Once again, two stories are made concurrent. Inaenka and the parrot are both lame, so the evil mother in one story suffers from the same defect that makes the female parrot in the other one reject and want to kill her son. Mothers resemble their sons by virtue of their resembling each other; their power seems to lie in such resemblance, as mediated by the Moon and his/her surrogates. This implies that the moon's gender duplicity is modified according to reproductive ranks: the moon is female only in the mother's role and male only in connection to a *mother's* son (not a *father's* son). Even though Kashiri is regarded as the sun's father, in the novel's text he lacks a father, which is precisely the role in which the moon constantly threatens reproductive equilibrium and the affairs of subsistence. Kashiri conspires with Inaenka to bring harm into people's faces:

> During the night, dazed by the false light of Kashiri, the stained one, he fell asleep. Inaenka limped to his side. Very carefully, she removed his two stones and threw them into the river. After that, she was able to sprinkle water on him from her great blister of a face, and gloated as the seripigari's body boiled, swelled with innumerable blisters, and started peeling and bursting. (192/199)

In alliance with the moon, the evil mother ruins a man of wisdom and authority. But the unmanning might be taken as performed by both a son upon his father and by a mother upon a passive male. In both cases, the moon-allied mother impersonates an Oedipal male: the son who castrates and the male who remains in intimate bondage to a dominant female. Moreover, the sprinkling of the shaman's face with the liquid from Inaenka's facial blister could be seen as a nefarious way of making him pregnant (someone mother-harmed, mother-harmful), as though his inheriting a ruinous blemish from the mother were akin to being made pregnant by her. However, Inaenka's son is saved from resembling her (and Kashiri) in their evil ways, though the child will end up resembling Kashiri (and the *hablador*) in the redness of his new face. The child is saved with the help of a small bird who tells him to eat the achiote plant, in order to make himself look different and not be recognized by the mother; and then the bird tells him to lead Inaenka to a place "where what's imperfect becomes perfect, where monsters become men," and where she will get good legs like other women have (193/200). The transfiguration of the son into "a red boy, clay-red, annatto red" (carried at the expense of an evil mother who will remain limping and with a boiling face) is a Gregor Samsa exploit in Machiguenga style. It is also an act of specular mimicry involving mother-son incest; it both avoids and confirms incest through etiological resemblance, just as the parrot's story binds a son who might have been destroyed to another who never encountered that danger but suffered the social punishment of surviving it. The two sons are bound within the mask that parrots its own name in a new Machiguenga spelling as it repeats the word: "Mas-ca-ri-ta" (224/234).

The idioms of taboo thrive in redundancies; they repeat the obvious or the already unquestionable as though it were brand new. A taboo disowns the improper by properly repeating it. A minimal but decisive gap opens between such utterances and what they utter, a space of relative autonomy between the person who speaks and the spoken objects. The first *hablador* proved the point by demonstrating what happens when no such gap exists. Pachakamue was breathed out by the first Tasurinchi, together with sister Pareni; every time he spoke, he unintentionally gave birth to whatever he mentioned: animals, trees, rocks, and persons. Once uttered, each human being became as though named elsewhere in the shape of other objects and animals. The sister's children became monkeys upon a laughing reference to them. A niece purifying herself of her first blood ran into the forest like the sachavaca did in Pachakamue's words to her. Yagontoro turned into Yagontoro: he made Pachakamue drunk, cut his head off and buried it, but he forgot the tongue and the talking head tracked him down. From beneath the ground it said what Yagontoro was, and the brother-in-law fell on insect legs, and instead of being a man who walks, he went on crawling like a yagontoro. Linguists (perhaps the Schneils themselves) could see in this referential Eden a fable on deictic craving and its fulfillment as a parody of what the incest taboo would later on forbid: words holding endogenous mastery over an entire realm of pristine designation; things shifting their nature upon being pointed at or named by pristine voices; a feast of creative noises before the establishment of taboo sounds and a proper referential nexus, a sort of incestuous marriage between words and things.

1958/1985
*Does my ex-friend, ex-Jew, ex-white man, and ex-Westerner, Saúl Zuratas, walk
with them, taking those short steps with the whole foot planted flat on the ground,
like palmipeds, so typical of all the Amazonian tribes?*—Mario Vargas Llosa, The
Storyteller

An exorcist in reverse, the narrator comes to Florence to write a prose
elegy in memory of a living ex-modern. As a novel, *The Storyteller* would
rather be "ex" than "post"modernist. Like the totalitarian dread dys-
topically reversed in Orwell's *1984*, the summer months of July and
August of 1958 in Amazonia and Lima and July of 1985 in Florence face
each other as if from across a writing desk, or as though the desk were to
suddenly end at the edge of a circle formed around the speaking figure of
a primitive storyteller. The text of the novel shows a break in its texture
and a self-conscious mending of it. The text's composition presumes a
broken dialogue between the storyteller (as Saúl) and the writer as
narrator. They are seated in a little café in Lima as they meet and argue
for the last time in August 1958; but the scene is not only viewed from a
table at the Caffee Strozzi in July 1985, it is brought to the reader without warning—as Saúl aims a question at the narrator, as if he had
been either reading the latter's mind or the text that is (being) written in
the future. The mirror image of 1958/1985 is not only a sign of specular
bonding between the two men, it offers the only, but sufficient, sign
of apocalyptic numerology in the text—Saúl's passionate defense of Machiguenga autonomy and his execrations against missionary work are
gently mocked by the narrator as a "tantrum" that could provoke an
"apocalypse" according to native notions of cosmic order.

Skilled celibates become truly exotic among a growing postmodern
tribe of ex-husbands and wives. The narrator locates his lost friend by
extracting a hesitant confession from a couple securely married: Saúl
floats above the Schneils' words like a foundling in the bulrushes. Edwin
Schneil is fortunate enough to have witnessed two performances by a
storyteller. The first one was conducted by a man who might have been
rather old or middle-aged; he spoke among other things about a *seripigari* who trained a neophyte in the art of shamanistic trance (the
reader knows that another sorcerer—or perhaps this same one—taught
Saúl the ways and beliefs of the Machiguengas). Before Schneil goes on
to talk about the other storyteller, the narrator has a vision of the
hablador: he is under Kashiri's light, or rather, both are, the seer and the
seen. The storyteller appears with a "skin somewhere between copper

and greenish," decorated "with lines and circles," and with "claws and fangs of wild beasts"; he seems like a man who is always "walking amid the bushes and the tree trunks, barely visible in the dense undergrowth, walking, walking, after speaking for ten hours, toward his next audience." The narrator wonders: How did this man start? Has he inherited his occupation? Was he chosen for it, or was it "something forced upon him by others?" (173/179).

It is inaccurate to say that the narrator finds only Saúl in such a man. What he finds is a trio: one storyteller who was heard by all his people, another who is imagined, and a third one whose talk was endured for a couple of hours by Edwin Schneil (before sleep prevented him from listening to the rest of some ten hours of performance). This ultimate and immoderate storyteller is an albino who consents to the missionary's presence in the audience only out of respect for the laws of kinship honored by his hosts. The albino's recital must have included a good deal if not all of chapters 3, 5, and 7 as found in the novel. Particularly, the recital must have included the latter parts (those beyond Gregor-Tasurinchi's tale) and extended into the Bible and Gospels. But by then, on his own confession, Edwin Schneil was unfit to listen, let alone to comprehend, any such *midrashim* creeping into Machiguenga wisdom.

The lessons of the albino (or the gringolike man with the huge birthmark and red head) can be placed in relation to at least three storytelling traditions besides the ones cited in the novel (such as the jongleurs and troubadours). The life of Saúl transfigured corresponds just as well to the Aesopic fable and two genres quite common in late antiquity, gospel and aretalogy. In terms of the latter, the Saúl figure represents the holy man type. Peter Brown has summarized the office as follows:

> What is decisive, and puzzling, about the long term rise of the holy man is the manner in which, in so many ways, the holy man was thought of as having taken into his person skills that had previously been preserved by society at large. The word of the holy man was supposed to replace the prophylactic spell to which anyone could have had access; his blessing made amulets unnecessary; he did in a village what had previously been done through the collective wisdom of the community. He was a ruthless professional; and, as is so often the case, his rise was a victory of men over women, who had been the previous guardians of the diffuse occult traditions of their neighborhood. The blessing of the holy man, and not an amulet

prepared by a wise woman, was what was now supposed to protect you from the effects of a green lizard that had fallen into your soup. If "the natural death of paganism" is to become something more than a rhetorical phrase, its roots must be sought in the nooks and crannies of late Roman village life. (Brown, "Holy Man," 100)

Or they may be found, perhaps even now, along the paths travelled by the wild Kogapakori, and also—ready to surface again—in the Christian settlements where many of these nomads would have been brought to live. Even though the storyteller is not a ruthless professional, he is quite thorough and deft at the art of embroidering upon green lizards in your soup. After all, he was once born in reverse by being swallowed into the green spectral world of a homely *lagartija*.

The gospel connection may be narrowed to the epistemic role of speaking in riddles or being enigmatic. Although the storyteller does not exclude anyone from learning or from finding his stories both entertaining and useful, Saúl's life and his transformation into a most remarkable Machiguenga contain some teasing enigmas. The gospel teaching that emerges from having Saúl secretly inside a native storyteller summons a transnational readership to listen to live performances of local wisdom before they vanish into books. As Saúl the gospel writer, one of the narrator's functions consists in relocating magic across continents, as when he calls the photographer who dared to take pictures of the storyteller "Gabrielle Malfatti," and then has him dying of fever. Malfatti carries Saúl's heraldic signature, who in being compared to an "archangel" and in being himself "badly made" is thus registered in the dead photographer's name. Above all, the novel asks the reader to judge how the narrator manages his own novelistic irony, and what exactly are the implications—in terms of novelistic decorum—of the narrator's professing skepticism about Saúl's successful transformation into a storyteller and into the author of the chapters in which his transformation is represented as a direct voice without apparent scriptural mediation. If it is true that most gospels may invite misunderstanding as they try to sort out those in the know from those who are destined to remain ignorant, reading *The Storyteller* could very well amount to a lesson in how such gospels are written.

A related narrative tradition brings us to the exemplary figure of Aesop. Relying on the work of Gregory Nagy (*Achaeans*, 22–316), it is possible to establish important parallels between the Machiguenga storyteller as portrayed by Vargas Llosa and the most famous among traditional fabulists. Nagy's precisely rendered arguments can be summarized as follows.

First, in Indo-European society and in archaic Greece, the social role of poetry counterbalanced the actions of praise and blame. For instance, when, disguised as a beggar, Odysseus runs into another beggar (at his house threshold) in the person of ravenous Iros, the words exchanged fit into a diction couched in set patterns taken from the poetry of praise and its own tendency to incorporate blame as one of its foils. In the *Odyssey,* praise's norm is borne by *aînos,* a discourse celebrating someone and aimed at a reward (222–35).

Second, Homeric diction provides evidence that *aînos* went beyond praise for a patron and could designate *an allusive tale containing an ulterior purpose,* thus applying "to the general narrative device of animal fables" (237). Moreover, the code of *aînos* could have a message for those in the know (*phronéontes*) and thus "a built-in ideology of exclusiveness," likely to be misunderstood or garbled. Therefore, *aînos*-type discourse is enigmatic, it is related to the riddle (*aínigma*), and it binds listeners through the attendant exclusion of others (238–40).

Third, Aesop's *Life* (the *Aesopica*) provides the necessary context in which to understand the always ambiguous discourse of each fable, the formal name for which is *aînos.* The narrative of Aesop's death at Delphi puts him in the role of scapegoat: "like some primordial *pharmakós,* Aesop is unjustly accused and executed by the Delphians" (281). The entire affair is told weaving praise and blame together in what appears to be a ritual program. With "each telling of each *aînos,* the narrative reinforces the ad hoc application of Aesop's words to the Delphians as objects of blame. Without its framing narrative, of course, the ad hoc moral of any given *aînos* could be lost" (282). The presence of blame in Aesop's *Life* reveals its deeply archaic content. The sequence of plot events reverses if one pays proper attention to the *aînos* factor. While myth has the death of Aesop as the *effect* of his blame of Delphian institutions, the latter would have his death as the *cause* of their own existence (284). Hence, Aesop dies as a "poet" as he originates his own hero cult sponsored by the very institutions that he blamed (and created) with his sacrificial death (286–87).

Fourth, sacrificial aspects in Aesop are related to Apollo's anger (*mênis*) against him. Aesop's "essence as a poet is defined not only by the Muses but also by their leader, Apollo himself" (290). Between poet and god, there exists a relationship similar to the one binding Hesiod, Homer, and the Muses; behind it, hero and poet share the epic warrior's rapport with Apollo as his ritual double or *therápōn,* an archaic term for *alter ego* or *ritual substitute* (292). The morphology of the cult hero is present in the *Life of Hesiod* and in the figure of Homer: *Hēsíodos* is "he who emits the Voice," and *Hómeros* is "he who fits [the Song] together," like an artisan or carpenter (296). In poetic diction, the names *Hesiod* and *Homer* identify the poet with the Muses; the poet is their *therápōn* in the archaic ritual dimension of the sacrificial cult hero (297).

Fifth, as the epic warrior did in losing his identity to the god who took his life, the poet in Aesop dies a hero's death and becomes a cultic figure through the same *therápōn*-mediated process: "The poet becomes a hero because he forfeits his life and identity to Apollo as a leader of the Muses. . . . In such a hero cult, god and hero are to be institutionalized as the respectively dominant and recessive members of an eternal symbiotic relationship" (307).

Finally, Aesop is a storyteller-poet whose stories or fables are enigmatic and not well understood unless his life, the *Aesopica,* is also considered. Aesop serves as primordial *pharmakós* in the foundation of the very institutions he blamed; he remains in ambiguous *therapeutic* rapport with a great God (who feels anger toward him) and with his retinue of female aids. Aesop is the poet as cult hero and sacrificial object. He is also theriomorphic, for he made his stories with animals who had *phōné,* the power of speech that he himself received as a gift from the Muses. By "having no *phōné,* he [Aesop] had been excluded from the community of both gods and men" (315). However, Aesop "actually remains a theriomorphic figure throughout his *Life.* . . . In the end Aesop transcends the condition of both animals and men. The gaps that are bridged in his *aînoi* between animals and men and gods are bridged in the course of his *Life.*" (315–16).

As a name, "Aesop" might mean "having the looks of baseness" (*aîskhos,* baseness). He is insulted as a *dog-head,* his kinship with the animals in the fables is eternally portrayed on his face. If *Hesiod* means *the one who emits the Word,* and if *Aesop* bears analogous word powers in close association with the animals to whom he gives speech, it seems that these two storytellers would not look like aliens or strangers if they ever wandered across the forests of the Upper Urubamba, where, at the bend of some sheltered path, they could always run into the talking pair made up by a masked storyteller and his parrot.

Word Is Territory

Unlike the case of the nouns and labels *Homer, Hesiod,* and *Aesop* in their own narrative settings and traditions, the Machiguenga word for *hablador* cannot be breached (or broken into) as it exists in Vargas Llosa's novel. All one reads (and tries to hear) is a "crepitación sonora" [an odd crackling sound] (83/85) that occurs when Machiguenga is being heard on tape. There is also that "remedando la crepitación" [mimicking the crackling] (168/173) that would be heard as Edwin Schneil tries to repeat the word *speaker* in Machiguenga. The text observes a sort of cult irony in not *playing* or *performing* the word while stating that those native to it let it escape from their lips quite handily. In the end, the unvoiced word is textually masked within the name and label *Mascarita.* However, could the word itself be found in the notion of *crepitar?* The verb crackles often enough in the text: "Every so often a silent shadow passed by, and the Schneils crackled back"; "Another silent shadow passed by and crackled, and the Schneils crackled back" (170/175; 173/178). Things "crackle" when the storyteller is in the air, or on the ground. One can almost hear it (the sound if not the man, "Aesop" if not the dog-faced man). But there is always a break in the voice; what is heard is simply writing:

> *QUEBRAR* 'romper,' [*to break*] 1335; before 'estallar' [*to explode*], 'reventar' [*to burst*]. . . . Deriv. *Quebrada* 'an opening between boulders' . . . *quebradero* [*braker;* sic. *quebradero de cabeza,* 'headache, worry']. *Quebradizo* 'brittle, fragile, sickly.' *Quebrado* . . . 'broken, weakened, bankrupt' [*rolling ground,* color: brown sugar, mixed race; arithmetic: common fraction] . . . *Quebrantar* . . . *quebrantado* . . . *quebrantamiento* . . . *quebranto* . . . 'broken, fracture, rupture, violation, burglary, exhaustion, desecration, affliction, loss, damage' . . . *Requebrado,* 'torn apart by passionate love . . . one in love who speaks with *quiebros* in his voice' . . . *requebrarse,* 'to speak in such a fashion' . . . *requebrar* . . . *requiebro,* gallantry . . . *Crepitar* . . . Lat. *crepitare* . . . *crepitación; crepitante. Increpar* [*to chide, rebuke*] . . . , etc. (Corominas, *Breve diccionario,* 485; supplemented with translations)

Voices and stories crackle and break. In some sources, the Latin *crepitum* and its cognates are taken all the way back to a host of Sanskrit words beginning with *kr-* and relating to a broad range of "breaking" sounds of the type just reviewed in Spanish. It comes as no surprise that among such noises, if not among the ones made by parrots, there should seem to persist forms of crying in which the mimicry of humans and birds break into a shared dirge to loneliness.

Part

Two

Pastoral

and

Dark

Romance

Talking Heads:

The Archaeology

of Personal

Voice in

Of something felt, like something here;
Of something done, I know not where;
Such as no language may declare.
—Alfred, Lord Tennyson, "The Two Voices"

Cortázar's

"Cefalea"

Commenting on the narrative voice in "Cefalea,"[1] Cortázar once said: "I imagined the couple a bit like the couple in "House Taken Over," but in a more confusing manner even, because one cannot tell if there are two men or two women, or a man and a woman; or if they are husband and wife, or brother and sister. It is never said *'uno de nosotros'* [*one of us* (masc.)] or *'una de nosotras'* [*one of us* (fem.)]. The whole thing remains deliberately confused" (Picon-Garfield, *Cortázar,* 96). The deliberate confusion to which Cortázar alludes as interpreter of his own fiction is voiced by another reader of "Cefalea": "Members of a group of alienated maniacs (some of whom narrate the story) live inside a country house . . . and are subjected to a strange therapy that consists of breeding mancuspias . . . and who compile notes in periodic and minute detail (in the form of a clinical diary) about the symptomatologic process of their respective illnesses, for the purpose of incorporating them in the medical archives" (Planells, *Cortázar,* 44). It may not come as a surprise if readers should populate (or depopulate) "Cefalea" lifted on the wings of their own fancy, for the story depicts a primitive struggle between the thrills of animation and impersonation—of putting in motion voices and bodies—and the sorrows brought about by the presence of other minds and the desire to remain autonomous from them. In "Cefalea" the boundaries between minds (as between persons) are blurred if not totally erased; its demographics involve both an indefinite individual and a plural number of verbal couplings between persons who may not exist. The story provides a forensic study of communal alienation among a group of true believers whose solipsistic madness offers a parody of the heroic and visionary isolation endured by some great artists and religious founders.

Most of Cortázar's short fiction generates readings along the lines of the author's management of fantasy and the adversarial entrapments of the uncanny, perhaps best seen in line with Freud's own reformulation of the romantic dark sublime as the *unheimlich* in his essay "The Uncanny" (*Works,* 17:219–52). His work became known internationally just as the reading strategies issuing from structuralism gained their own prominence and led—in the work of Todorov (1970)—to a widely influential definition of the *fantastic.* Beyond surrealism and the stern suspicions against consensual expectations and common wisdom raised by existentialists and *nouveaux romanciers* alike, the *fantastic* offered at once a clearinghouse for nonpolitical sophistication and a Shangri-la in which to accommodate mild forms of cynicism and routinized awe. It might have been the fantastic that Claude Lévi-Strauss had in mind when he wrote in *Tristes tropiques* against travel books and the onset of universal monoculture with its negative impact upon ethnic singularity: "Mankind has opted for monoculture; it is in the process of creating a mass civilization, as beetroot is grown in the mass. Henceforth, man's daily bill of fare will consist only of this one item" (38). By contrast, his view of the neolithic age stresses the particularism of small isolated communities in what Rousseau called the state of nature:

> In that mythic age, man was no freer than he is today, but only his humanness made him a slave. Since his control over nature remained very limited, he was protected—and to some extent released from bondage—by a cushioning of dreams. As these dreams were gradually transformed into knowledge, man's power increased and became a great source of pride; but this power, which gears us, as it were, to the universe, is surely little more than our subjective awareness of a progressive welding together of humanity and the physical universe, whose great deterministic laws, instead of remaining remote and awe-inspiring, now use thought itself as an intermediary medium and are colonizing us on behalf of a salient world of which we have become the agents. (391)

The lofty conservatism reflected in these moral pictures can be related to the literary cult of fantasy. First, by deploring travel books as a commercial or frivolous recognition of exotic strangeness, Lévi-Strauss's criticism of mobile civilized behavior is indirectly alluding to the instant voyage, to the sudden fall into parallel but unfamiliar landscapes from different ages so common in the literature of fantasy. Also, regardless of what his view of such literature might be, Lévi-Strauss is suggesting by implication that a psychological reading of fantasy falls short of the ultimate context of the uncanny, of the *unhomely* or *unheimliche,* as established by Freud. The individual's illusions of omnipotence are shattered under ethnographic analysis as personal psychology and subjective fantasies lapse into "archaic" orders of behavior prevalent among savages. The urge to return through fantasy to what Lévi-Strauss calls *la pensée sauvage* corresponds to specific social practices examined through ethnographic activity in which the precedence of group concerns over individual interests seems to prevail among so-called primitives. It is not so much primitive as cohesive behavior and beliefs that Lévi-Strauss might identify as the main social force behind a civilized feeling for the uncanny.

A further insight into the literature of fantasy may be found in the anthropologist's notion of determinism as "the progressive welding together of humanity and the physical universe," for it is precisely such welding that finds local expression in those plot twists through which a character, by suddenly entering the realm of fantasy, would have been released from routine existence and thrown into an order of reality characterized by a mixture of the familiar and the alien. The passage between ordinary reality and fantasy falls in between two dominant modes of deterministic explanation: the older, hieratic or demonic view expressed by religious or magical wisdom, and the newer, still mysterious and transcendent view of scientific speculation. The appeal of the *fantastic* may lie in the sublime or uncanny feeling that may arise from witnessing how the two orders of explanation—the magical and the scientific—resemble each other across a vast gap in the evolution of knowledge. As present in Cortázar, *lo fantástico* preserves the effect of enchantment (*zauberung*) from the boredom of rationality.

Contrary to the ethnographic nostalgia for particular idioms and breeds of culture expressed by Lévi-Strauss, the literary cult of fantasy can afford to disengage itself from most local nuances of meaning; its vernaculars are conceptual rather than philological. Accordingly, the *fantastic* achieves international vogue hand-in-hand with another structuralist tendency, the one that would create a single network of semiotic strategies (or *readings*) situated above any given language or region. However, rather than replacing the transnational *fantastic* with a cozy enclave of local stereotypes (similar to the *borghetto* where Freud once entered the mazelike reiterations of the *unheimliche*), one may attempt a harder linguistic and anthropological view of how fiction behaves in stories like "Cefalea."

Chronicle and Nosology

Events narrated in "Cefalea" share one peculiar disquieting trait: they might never have taken place. The narrative voice is wholly naïve; it sounds as if it does not know how to lie, or as if it were unaware that lying exists. By the same token, the voice refers to place, time, and character as if they could not reflect how events and people may impact on a single individual who might not just as well be another one. In "Cefalea," narration designates too much; it mentions things and causes as if they were prescribed by an unknown external entity and yet haunted by self-reference.

Myths adapt to the world in the active attempt of giving it storied shape, but in "Cefalea" such a cosmic myth activity seems to have already ended by the time narration begins. Hence, the plot unfolds most obviously as a chronicle of daily routine in which actions follow a strict agenda. People care for animals, feed and bathe them, anticipate their reproductive schedules, and seem inured even to the fact that—as *mancuspias*—these animals are simply unheard of. The name is a lure but also a term of exclusion. The reader cannot but feel at odds with people who gather around a name that should be mysterious but is not, that should be totemic but remains simply commercial. Obviously, an unexplained protocol supports the use of the name *mancuspias* in the narrator's deadpan testimony. As it is brought undocumented into the reader's world, *mancuspias* becomes an event in need of its own myth. Such counterpoint between the explicit and the cryptic turns mancuspias into more than just animals or animal-like beings; it makes them *zoematic* (see Lévi-Strauss, *The Jealous Potter*, 97–108), which amounts to saying that a whole possible world could lodge—human furnishings and all—in the *mancuspias'* projected attributes, doing so with unspecified propositional authority.

A second line of development in the plot of "Cefalea" cuts through the chronicle of events with the force of superstition, identified here as any type of assertion situated beyond possible corroboration. As a token of superstition, the word *mancuspias* becomes a nominative fault, a symptom of lexical disturbance. It is then that medical jargon as nosography may enter the picture as a description of illnesses. From the very beginning nosography exists as a cognitive mediator (very much like the sacred) between the various references to persons in the text. Persons in "Cefalea" are said not only to care for their livestock but also for each other. In fact, all that the reader learns about the presence of human existence in the story leads, one way or the other, back to a so-called "Mentor" in the description of pain, anguish, and remedy. Setting aside for the moment any reference to the symptoms of migraine attacks, the expression of illness and temporary cure in "Cefalea" may be set within some general remarks made by Michel Foucault on the modern evolution of medical knowledge.

In *The Birth of the Clinic,* Michel Foucault refers to nosological analysis in the eighteenth century as involving, not "the encounter between doctor and patient," nor "the confrontation of a body of knowledge and a perception," but rather "the systematic intersection of two series of information, each homogeneous but alien to each other—two series that embrace an infinite set of separate events, but whose intersection reveals, in its isolable dependence, the *individual fact*" (30). Foucault sees in such a convergence between symptom and regulated significance a "sagittal figure of knowledge" (30). In his description, early clinical knowledge resembles ethnographic activity; thus medical consciousness "lives at an immediate level in the order of 'savage' observations," while nosographic discourse gathers itself at a higher level, "where it recognizes the constitutions, confronts them, and, turning back upon the spontaneous forms, dogmatically pronounces its judgement and its knowledge. It becomes centralized in structure" (30). At a latter stage (though already under the influence of Étienne Condillac), the phenomenon of disease reaches a sort of stand-off face-to-face with medical description; the "exhaustive presence of the disease in its symptoms" corresponds in Foucault's account to "the unobstructed transparency of the pathological being with the syntax of a descriptive language," and it results in "a fundamental isomorphism of the structure of the disease and of the verbal form that circumscribes it" (95). In Foucault's words, medical description becomes "a seizure of being" ("une prise d'être"), and the being or patient in question "does not appear in symptomatic and therefore essential manifestations without offering itself to the mastery of a language that is the very speech of things" (95). The talking cure that homeopathic medicine offers to migraine affliction in "Cefalea" rests on a similar seizure of symptoms in the jargon of pharmacological lore. The differences between the discourse of homeopathy in Cortázar's story and the deployment of medical rationality described by Foucault lie in the vernacular idioms and homespun prescriptions by which the doctrines of the Homeopathic Mentor penetrate the isolated rural enclave in which, at least at the level of narrative reference, migrainous folk live in "Cefalea."

The social milieu barely glimpsed through the narrative voice evokes the skeletal remains of a rural *Gemeinshaft*. As a story of survival, "Cefalea" may refer to the imaginary remnants of some vanished mode of agrarian communism. The doctrines of the *Mentor* have entered an isolated community of believers; analogies with sectarian millenarianism or with certain forms of marginalized religious enthusiasm seem justified as one begins to understand the teachings and symbolic bondage left behind by an absent leader, perhaps best identified as a *homeocrator*. Modifying Max Weber's understanding of *acosmic* existence (Weber, *Economy and Society*, 2:633; Mitzman, *The Iron Cage*, 289–91), the life of a homeopathic community of this sort could indeed resemble the precarious maintenance of sororal and brotherly ties in the midst of some groups that have felt themselves abandoned by the higher cosmic wisdom of a universal Church. An aura of Protestant evangelism permeates the covenant between labor and reading (or material routine and doctrine) among lost souls dwelling in the pampas (as they might in central Asia), in distant touch with a metropolis teeming with immigrants from Europe. Once again, Weber's notion of *acosmic love* may apply, insofar as social existence in "Cefalea" answers to a demand for heroic transcendence while being besieged by animal forces. Acosmic love would replace the ascetic demands of priestly dominance (the Mentor's hypochondrial discipline) with the mysticism of erotic cant present in the patients' sentimental adherence to a homeopathic language full of feminine drugs and male symptoms. In the story, the contours of enthusiastic religiosity—and a possible exchange between the mystical and the erotic—would appear as a faded picture of life amid a fossil cult (perhaps already reduced to two individuals), which has been replaced by a gospel of house remedies and by the commercial folklore printed in homeopathic publications.

Heimat *in the House of Grammar: The Uncanny*

No earnest approach to "Cefalea" can avoid careful scrutiny of how deictic personal pronouns behave in the narrative. Precisely because everything in the story begins and ends with the way in which pronouns shift, however, the need arises to ground what will prove to be the autistic signs of grammar on some theme of human value set beyond the play of syntax. In *To Take Place: Toward Theory in Ritual,* Jonathan Z. Smith discusses traditional themes of return to home (the Greek *nostos*) and homesickness (the German *Heimweh*) (29–32). Home, he points out, often designates a site of reverie; home "is best understood as the place-where-I-live," rather than as the site of birth. Home represents "the place where memories are 'housed'" (29). Smith then identifies as "present-day humanistic geographers" those whose view of *place,* in a geographic sense, seems to exclude the traditional view of locality as a creator of "Man and his culture as well as his character, rather than the other way around." "*Topos* or *physis*," adds Smith, "is what shapes, what gives form and content to *nomos* and *ethos*"; traditional place is "not the creation of personality; it is what forms or imprints personality" (30–31).

A good deal of what Lévi-Strauss means by the neolithic ecology of human communities and their local habitats is contained in the traditional precedence of home over the uniqueness of individual character discussed by Smith. In "Cefalea," the interplay between deictic designation through personal pronouns and the places that may exist in and around such deixis produces an ultimate lack of distinction between, on the one hand, the autonomous realm of grammatical person-shift, and on the other, the placement of each shifting personal speech act in space. It is as if, instead of being thrown out of Paradise, humans had been expelled from a sort of pronoun shelter, or hurled into a space of nakedness where they became undressed once pronouns ceased to offer them grammatical anonymity. In other words, characters in "Cefalea" always hide within a grammatical shift, each person in question always belongs to an indefinite roster of individuals hidden by the narrative voice's use of deictic self-reference. Hiding persons behind shifting pronouns eventually breaks out in other representational forms, or in actual human shape. In "Cefalea," however, the garments of pronouns are never torn open. Except for two individuals named "Leonor" and "Chango," human presence in the story remains clutched in deictic shift. Hence, in order to locate humans in a space other than that of grammar one has to search for their presumed signs in a sort of mimicry, as if reflected in a defensive looking glass on a shield that mirrors the threat of identification felt by someone who wants to remain unknown. Characters resist portrayal outside their own talking heads, which are little else than sounding boards for the Homeopathic Mentor's prescriptions on how each person should resemble migraine symptoms and remedies.

As a result of such dependence on doctrinal scripts, the characters' speech acts collapse into each other through a kind of indexing furor. In

"Cefalea," character is identical to itself because each of the characters involved lacks the support offered by the self-referential deictics *I* and *myself;* these designations are unavailable, they are occluded by other pronoun forms in which the individual may always *shift* as someone else—*someone I might not be* (taking *I* as a mask for a third person neither *he/she* nor *I* ever manages to *voice*). An extended quotation from the beginning of the story should help to grasp the occlusions and instabilities at work in its syntax. In the literal and somewhat awkward translation that follows, personal pronouns are underlined when their required appearance in English syntax corresponds to the embeddedness in Spanish of the grammatical mark of person in the conjugated verb— as when, in saying "*cuidamos*" [*nosotros*] the pronoun *we* is implied but not actually stated. The story begins:

> *We* care [*Cuidamos*] for the mancuspias until rather late, now with the summer heat they become capricious and whimsical, the more undeveloped among them require special food and *we* bring them malted oats in large porcelain dishes; the larger ones are already shedding the hair off their backs, so it becomes necessary to place them separate, to tie a blanket for shelter and to look out so they cannot get together at night with the mancuspias that sleep in cages and get their food every eight hours.
>
> *We* do not [*No nos*] feel [*sentimos*] well. It has been happening since the morning, perhaps caused by the hot wind that blew at dawn, before the birth of this tarry sun that blasted the house the whole day. It burdens us to care for the sick animals—this is done at eleven—and to go over the brood after the siesta. It seems to us ever more painful to walk, to follow the routine; *we* suspect [*sospechamos*] that a single unattended night would be dismal for the mancuspias, the irreparable ruin of our life. *We* go about [*Andamos*] then without reflection, fulfilling one after the other acts staggered by habit, hardly stopping to eat (there are pieces of bread on the table and on top of the mantelpiece in the living room) or to look at each other in the mirror that duplicates the bedroom. At night *we* fall [*caemos*] suddenly in bed, and the tendency to brush our teeth before going to sleep gives way to fatigue, it hardly lingers in a gesture that replaces it, aiming toward the lamp or the remedies. Outside, one hears the adult mancuspias going and going in circles.
>
> *We* do not feel well. One of us [*Uno de nosotros*] is *Aconitum*, that means having to take medicine with aconitum in large dilutions if,

for example, fear causes vertigo. *Aconitum is a violent storm that goes away swiftly.* What other way is there to describe the counterattack of an anxiety that is born out of any insignificance, out of nothing? A woman suddenly comes face-to-face with a dog and begins to feel violently dizzy. Then, aconitum, and soon afterwards all that is left is sweet dizziness, with a tendency towards going backwards (this happened to us, but it was a case of *Bryonia,* the same as feeling that *we* were sinking [*nos hundíamos*] with or through the bed.

The other [*El otro*], in turn, is markedly *Nux Vomica.* After taking the malted oats to the mancuspias, perhaps due to bending over too much while filling up the bowl, [the other] feels rushed as if the brain were turning, not that all swirls around—as in vertigo—but vision itself turning, inside him consciousness turns like a gyroscope on its ring, and outside all stands tremendously still, only that fleeing and ungraspable. *We* have wondered [*Hemos pensado*] if it might not be instead a *Phosphorus* picture, because the perfume of flowers frightens *him* [*lo aterra*] (or the one from small mancuspias, faintly smelling of lilac) and coincides physically with a phosphoric picture: being tall [*alto* (masc.)], slim [*delgado* (masc.)], desiring cold drinks, ice cream, and salt. (69–71)

In these opening paragraphs, the narrative voice refers to itself as *we,* but not until the second sentence in the third paragraph does *we* appear as *nosotros;* until that point, the sign for the first person-plural subject has remained bound in verb form (either reflexive or transitive), as in "*Nos* cuesta," "*Nos* parece," "cepillar*nos*," "deteniéndo*nos*," "mirar*nos*," [emphasis added]; or as "Andamos," "caemos," in nonreflexive form. Very seldom in "Cefalea" does *nosotros* itself appear as the pronoun for the active person, *we.* Most often, *nosotros* leans on (or shifts with) the third person sign for "the other" as *otro/otra;* or else it hinges on the "one of us" pronominal caveat expressed by *uno* or *una de.* Also, none of the other deictics for the personal subject—*yo, tú, él, ella*—appear, except for *él,* functioning as the object of the preposition, and *ellas,* applying to mancuspias. Thus, by itself, *nosotros* cannot be said to *act.* Without the company of *one of us,* the *we* in *nosotros* remains object-bound, as in "para cumplir nosotros mismos" [in order for us to comply with] or "a nosotros nos han mirado" [they have looked at us]. In the only other instance where *nosotros* appears by itself, it serves as the object of the verb: "Y nosotros aquí, rodeados de médanos" [And we, here, surrounded by dunes] (75). In particular, pronouns with performative-dialogic value (such as *I* and *you*) do not appear in a story whose voices decoy themselves in choral dress, but remain outside the stage of dialogue. In a rather eerie and ultimately pathetic way, the voices of *we* harbor a shifting, identical *I*. *We* bears *I* masked and unheard, as if tabooed; *I* is antiphonal yet mute, it is the hidden actor in a stichomythia whose alternating persons revert voice to the ancestral *persona* of the ritual mask.

The dialogic nexus has perished in "Cefalea." The reciprocal slots for *I* (the person designated in the instance of locutionary discourse containing *I*) and for *you* (the person to whom such an utterance containing *you* is addressed) do not appear in the written armature of discourse, unless it is at a level deeply ingrained in the text's prephonetic or archescriptural layers. Locating such a level of voice enactment would require rewriting the story, producing a kind of "Cefalea Unbound." Nevertheless, the *I-you* couple leads an intense discursive life right on the surface of representation.

We (as *nosotros*) first appears in the second sentence of the third paragraph, but it does so as "one of us" (*uno de nosotros*). An immediate shift takes place from the "one-of-us" third person within *we* to what should be called its nosographic instance—its medical picture. An individual comes into play as a sort of *symptheme,* as in *"Aconitum is a violent storm that goes away swiftly,"* so that, to the inlaid "one-of-us" person within *we* must be added the individual who that same person becomes while in association with a peculiar picture of symptoms—a picture in which the optic disturbances of migraine merge with the effects caused by the drug-remedy, *Aconitum* or wolfsbane. Thus a nucleus for *we* comes into play, made up of *one-of-us* coupled with *the other* and reflecting yet another person, the *Aconitum* actor. If such an actor were allowed to utter an illocutionary phrase in "Cefalea," it could begin as "I, *Aconitum*," or even as "*Aconitum* and I"; however, such allocutions on behalf of *I* or *you* would run into a double embarrassment at the levels of grammar and reference. Simply stated, "Cefalea" does not tolerate allocutions (or perlocutions) of any kind involving *I* and *you*; it also pulls the rug from under the *he* and *she* that the ungendered *you* and *I* would reflect when attached to persons in the gendered realm of social existence. If "Cefalea" were to express *I*'s and *you*'s, then *Aconitum* would be voiced in reference to the (gendered) *he* or *she* subscribed to by whoever utters either of the first two deictic persons. However, to the discursive removal of these "persons" one must add two attendant factors: anyone may become *Aconitum* at a particular time, and at no time in the story is anyone (as *he* or *she*) explicitly gendered, in being *Aconitum,* while remaining linked to a gendered *I* or *you* reference. In other words, the common assumption that individual *I's* and *you's* may in the end be underwritten by a gender other than the grammatical one (or by *sexed* gender) does not hold within the internal logic of "Cefalea." The fact that individual human minds must adopt gender roles (at times combined) from within bodies of a given sex is not registered in the story's deictic census. It happens the other way around: minds are hosted within ungendered pronouns by which they recombine their gendered sexes, which belong to bodies from which they feel severed. The characters of "Cefalea" are former males and/or females, presently shifting in gender fashion.

In Cortázar's acknowledged source and inspiration for the story—Dr. Margaret L. Tyler's "Síntomas orientadores hacia los remedios más comunes del vértigo y cefaleas"—one finds two nosographic formulas concerning *Aconitum.* The first one, dealing with vertigo, has been reproduced by Cortázar: "Una mujer se enfrenta repentinamente con un perro y comienza a sentirse violentamente mareada" (71). The other, which concerns migraines, presents one of several crucial aspects of gender inscription in the homeopathic material used by Cortázar in his fiction.

Tyler's homeopathic repertoire adheres to the protocols of gender in Spanish grammar, but not without causing a certain comic and even ontological friction, an effect of naïve surrealism that might have moved Cortázar into calling these uninvented afflictions and corresponding remedies an "admirable poem." *Aconitum* is masculine in Spanish, yet homeopathic women may host and even become the drug if—as men would be well advised to do—they take the remedy in the prescribed pharmacological dose. Aggressive and disturbed masculinity marks the standard grammatical designation for *Aconitum* in Tyler's formula; it is "repentino: salvaje: peor por vientos fríos" ("sudden [masc.]: savage: worse on account of cold winds"), before it tapers off to: "inquietud, angustia, miedo" ("restlessness, anguish, fear" [45]). Nevertheless, such descriptions of the environment of sensation (where drug meets the intensities of migraine attacks) must fit both males and females. The tendency to regard the epithets of fury as male-specific brings into the realm of homeopathic discourse valences of gendered personhood based on expectations that simply do not hold true within the paranormal realm of homeopathic imagery. Just as Cortázar puts phrases from Tyler's text into his fiction, Tyler blends her own descriptions with quotations from unnamed sources so that, as in the case of *Aconitum*'s stormy passage, the utterance would seem to come from a living patient's report. Besides quotation marks, the use of italics adds special significance to the authority of the citations. In each case, reported speech plays a constative-prescriptive function: what has been experienced before is recorded so that it may be experienced again; repetition acts in this context as a guarantee of remedy and as proof of the doctrinal covenant that binds doctor, patient, drug, and illness.

The drug *Pulsatilla* offers an even more interesting example of gender play in both Tyler's account and Cortázar's story. In going through her list, one soon realizes that Tyler's references imply (and would tend to agree in gender with) four kinds of subject: (1) any among several drugs (always feminine as *droga*); (2) the name of the specific drug in question (either feminine or masculine); (3) the symptoms (held under the aegis of three implied feminine nouns: *cefalea, migraña*, or *jaqueca*); and (4) the patient (masculine, in line with traditional usage in Spanish). As such, *Pulsatilla* represents both a typical and an atypical case. The effects of this drug blend and interact with symptoms of migraine and lead to designations such as "llorón" (a crier [masc.]) or "nadie puede verlo" (no one can see him). But then *Pulsatilla* involves the only instance in Tyler's text where a feminine reference applies to *both* the drug's name and a patient under the drug's effects who becomes identified with the feminine: "typically, *Pulsatilla* is voluble, crying [*llorona* (fem.)], demanding, irritable" (40). Of the four adjectives used, only one, *llorona*, happens to register gender, so in the case of this one adjective directly involved with the drug's feminine name, the name's gender replaces the universal masculine that conventionally labels every patient. What is remarkable is not that patients may count as both masculine and feminine, but that they may *not* have to count as *one gender only*, once freed from the peculiar universal masculine. This statement may be modified by claiming that the conventional masculine reference quite "naturally" includes females under its designation, while the corresponding and uncommon feminine reference implies that either kind of sexed individual could opt to be known as female. Tyler's phrase offers the best example of coupling/uncoupling in "Cefalea": "Uno de nosotros ha tenido con intermitencias una fase *Pulsatilla*, vale decir que tiende a mostrarse voluble, llorona" (77–78).

More so than in Tyler's text, the feminine adjective creates in "Cefalea" an accident of the particular. It does so not by confirming that female humans are designated in the text, or by replacing the usual generic masculine with its feminine counterpart, but by establishing that such a feminine designation might also be adopted by a specific individual, who would not necessarily belong to the female sex while identifying with it. The phrase also implies that individuals sexed female may indeed decide to gender themselves as feminine or as masculine. The notion of cross-gendering the sexes comes into play through subtle antithetical inscriptions, adding a suggestion of specular play and mimicry to the grammar of personal pronouns.

In the passage in question, the text binds together the drug emblem *Pulsatilla* with that of *Petroleum*, as if they were confronting mirrors: "*Petroleum* affects the other, a state in which everything—objects, voices, memories—go over him [*él*, one of two instances of the pronoun in the text], numbing and making him stiff ["entumeciéndolo y envarándolo"]. There is no shock, hardly a parallel and tolerable suffering. Afterwards, at times, sleep comes" (78). Taken as a block of signification similar to the notion of *lexia* (see Barthes, *S/Z*, 13–14), the *Pulsatilla-Petroleum* cluster represents the core of an untold story, of which some cardinal surface signs are given—a minimal and negative stereography of sex ("a parallel and tolerable suffering") followed by oblivious rest. It should be noted that the entire passage operates under the dual subject *uno de nosotros . . . el otro*, dual in the sense that it may involve two different individuals, or a single one who imagines another in ever-present counterpoint with him or her. It is the status of the designation *her*, however, that appears unregistered at the level of deixis, while being registered at the level of reference or denotation, or in the adjective *llorona*.

The untold narrative carried within the *Pulsatilla-Petroleum* cluster belongs to an imaginary space from which individual consciousness in "Cefalea" seems altogether barred. The allegorical couple behaves as a signature, as if its presumed members were two pharmacy labels, two prescriptions acting as voices: one crying as female, while the other suffers tumescence and stiffness. The canon of sympathetic remedies offered by homeopathy confines its users within a prison already sealed off by the encumbering symptoms of migraine, to which each drug adds a crystal wall of echoes and redundant visions. And yet, beyond such enclosure, words like *Pulsatilla* may be emblems of natural piety or objects of poetic revery, as in the case of a (pulsating) flower whose petals tremble in the breeze before being gathered by a master of drugs and poisons (or as in the case of *Aconitum*—"the invincible one"—from which an epic simile might emerge: "invincible, resembling a storm that arrives swiftly, *Aconitum*"). The space of specularity and mimicry consists of latent extravagances such as these; to call upon them fulfills a role implicit in the inner logic of allegorical expression at work in "Cefalea," as imprisoned storylines and personal myths try to break away from the minimalist labyrinth of grammar and the apothecary's manual.

The way in which deictic shifters behave in the text suggests a persistent dualism between the *one* and the *other*. Behind any given *one* (as a sign of person) stands the *One*, the largest Other, who splits further into *itself* and the *other*. Rather than as an indefinite number of possible individuals, the pronoun *we* seems to operate in the story as a repeated instance within an indefinite series of *one*/*other* couplings held together in whirling specular bonding. When marked by gender, deictic shifters become a chiasmus of four sites occupied by confronting couples of masculine and feminine pronoun effects. Deixis gives to sex in "Cefalea" a semiotic playground in which to engender itself in autistic rituals. But behind such unhinged joy and unreproductive mobility (found in the house of grammar) a more archaic dwelling exists: a *Heimat*, an ancient well of dreams and laws in which the stereotypes of reproductive behavior, sexed difference, and tokens from old biologies hold court and bring with them uncanny reiterations of phobias made visible.

While deixis allows the One (the largest Other) not to fade out within the free play of its ubiquitous replicas, the archaic agenda of *Heimat* calls for identicalness to transcend itself and become resemblance. The two notions—to be *identical* and to *resemble*—could not represent more antithetical modes of being than they do in "Cefalea." For identicalness collapses into the split oneness of *one* and (the) *other*, while resemblance searches, perhaps in vain, for a real *other*—other than the otherness programmed in (the) One's specular recognition of (itself as) the other. Here, the identical is jammed into duality. Resemblance implies action beyond speech act; it requires a free space for affinities to take hold in distinct bodies, distinctly and singularly felt through their enactment— from two sites of mutual resemblance—of two reciprocal lives animated by the tutelage of choice.

Cephalalgia and Its Discontents

Most analytical readings of "Cefalea" exercise condescension toward the drama of consciousness and neurological pain reflected in the story; they see it through the bifocal perspective of allegory and irony (see Aronne-Amestoy, *Utopía*, 128–31). Indeed, the application of these tropes seems hard to avoid, for how is one to surmise from the story a broader view on existence if not by moving outside the doctrinal world-picture of homeopathy? Irony surrounds the canopy of nosographic didacticism; references to pain as well as the progressive collapse of remedial certainties suggest a fable of alienation. In "Cefalea," individual existence lies in ruins, the self drains out, loses its words for life and the ability to refer with force to its own bodily and worldly existence. Hence, irony should point in the direction of a controlling antithesis in "Cefalea," but not toward the traditional one between mind and body, or soul and flesh, but rather toward the one antithesis tearing apart the corporeal self from its sheltering and encumbering habitat. What some would call the *lining* of selfhood in the environment of social intercourse alienates itself as a fault line, a chaotic fringe marking the inner range of individual participation in society (see Kristeva, *Powers of Horror*, 64). But that same lining would also mark the outer rim where social existence welds itself to higher and perhaps random beliefs, such as those that may inform religious practices, political behavior, and the folklore of routine existence. In tracing the fault lines between embodied knowledge and the intricate tissue of social relations, irony should be able to find in the text of "Cefalea" concrete evidence of where and how fictional discourse becomes bound within its own prescriptions, habits, and peculiar modes of appropriation and foreclosure.

However, irony should not engage in such a scrutiny of boundaries and fractures without making explicit its own assumptions, biases, and management of rationality. Thus far, the present analysis has chosen to decode the infrastructure of grammatical voices that continue to shift within the relative paucity of the personal pronoun *we*, specularly broken into a dyad of two individual tokens marked as *one* (foreclosing *I*) and *other* (in parallel foreclosure of *you*). As the world of represented existence in "Cefalea" crumbles under the pressure of fear and delirium, the dispositions of grammar remain intact; its hallucinatory outer reaches and innermost solipsisms continue to reiterate meanings in contract with grammar. In such a specific context, grammar and representation come together to suggest, but never actually propose, a simple question: Why not *nosotras*? Why is the feminine *we* absent from the shifting repertoire of voices in the story? The answer might organize itself around the one breach of grammar that haunts the almost twenty instances in which variations of *one of us* never render *we* in the feminine. Were *nosotras* to appear either by itself or as *una de nosotras,* an ensemble of at least two individuals gendered feminine would voice itself into being. This would imply at least two things: (1) that the voice conveying fiction in the text has agreed to adopt a partial or total designation of what it professes to represent as a group of individuals gendered feminine, and (2) that such a group under such a voiced phrase may be composed of more than two individuals. This would further imply that *nosotras* motivates plurality in "Cefalea," while *nosotros* motivates the generative dualism of *one* and the *other*—plus an ultimate reference to a universal token of identity situated beyond the concrete disclosure of sexual difference. The absence of the grammatical *una de nosotras* from the text's cast of enunciated voices suggests the equally absent and ungrammatical *uno de nosotras* (*one* [masc.] *of us* [fem.]). To assess the full significance of the *unvoiced* masculine singular (*uno*) ungrammatically lodged in the compact feminine (*nosotras*), analytic irony may commit the impertinence of searching for voice where none should be expected, or among the mancuspias. Irony should call for a mancuspia-utterance in self-reference.

All that remains in relative occlusion within the perimeter of human voice in "Cefalea" comes out of hiding among the mancuspias, which include mothers ("las mancuspias madres" [74]), fledglings ("pichones" [73]), males ("los machos" [77], adults and young ones, those who grow fast and those who lag behind. They eat, breed, and in the end fight with each other out of hunger. Mancuspias perform under their feminine name and also under the (unstated but tacit) illocutionary utterance, "we, mancuspias." It is fitting to place the word in a phrase, since it entered Cortázar's existence as a teasing syntactic element, a sort of minimal mytheme. A certain professor would refer to "mancuspia hot weather," or to a "mancuspia kind of hunger" (Picon-Garfield, 96). Thus, in the professor's speech, a word acting as a sort of occlusive genitive—an idiolect expressing a singular female magnitude of swollen significance—took the place of a small roster of nouns and genitive phrases that in vernacular Spanish may include from moderate to blunt vulgarisms pertaining to size or intensity. In fact, such vulgarities might well constitute signatures of regional wit, expressive tags of the way in which strong feelings might be said to color the speech habits of a distinct area in a language's cultural map. In describing his adoption of *mancuspia* from Ireneo Fernando Cruz's vocabulary, Cortázar regards the word as a lexical token that can be made to play the role of a noun. He sees characters in "Cefalea" fighting their migraine attacks as these become embodied in animal shape; then he sees the animals as mancuspias and gives them the name, transforming the word into a substantive (Picon-Garfield, 96). In its new *zoematic* context, the word always operates in the plural; a former universal singular (meaning "like" or "pertaining to") becomes a proper noun, a species-label, a generic brand (not unlike the universal masculine *nosotros*) designating action and effect. In the realm of narrated phenomena, the animal mancuspias behave like speech acts; the all-inclusive genitive from which they derive never returns to its former singular form; the noun *mancuspia* has become sheer plural-effect, a species made up of place-effects, moment-effects, always brought into being by a local effect (not unlike the occluded feminine *nosotras*).

Mancuspias function like voices without a voice. As objects of reference, they are the object of talk (they suggest animal speech even in humans). In not being able to speak, they resemble the talking head that articulates writing and reading within the story's narrative voice. The sham telepathy of a constant talk back and forth between writing and reading occupies the place of speech within this peculiar narrative voice. Inside the register of either written or spoken voice-effects, mancuspias function like percepts lodged in the inner lining of propositions bearing on objects that cannot be severed from their own status as words. Such objects lack an *elsewhere* other than the one found in cognate propositions bearing on mancuspias. Upon reading Tyler's nosography, Cortázar added these animals to the folklore of homeopathy; they embodied for him a further projection of optical disturbance in migraine.

One may consult Oliver Sacks's historical survey of this phenomenal illness, *Migraine: Understanding a Common Disorder,* in search of an appropriate context. One example from among the many discussed by Sacks should suffice in demonstrating how the mancuspia-event takes place in what he calls the classical migraine aura. In becoming a word or being voiced, *mancuspias* borrows its makeup from the phonemic register, but in the realm of migraine aura a mancuspia-event would first come into representational view as a *phosphenic* incident. Amending what has been previously called "the inner lining of propositions," one may now refer simply to the eyelid's inner surface as the screenlike support on which phosphenes (radiant events in the field of vision) arise after pressure is applied on the eyeball. What happens in episodes of migraine aura happens without the eyelid screen, it takes place in the spectral environment of sight. The patient perceives phosphenes and then constructs propositions about them. Sacks mentions one such patient who described "small white skunks with erect tails, moving in procession across one quadrant of the visual field" (60). If informed of such a report,

Professor Ireneo Fernando Cruz might not have hesitated in calling it a mancuspia-like portent. An element of detached humor creeps into the reception of pictures that report on mancuspia-like events. Reversing the angle of reception, one can point at skunklike phosphenes and, with the same cognitive gesture, one may detach from the phonemic ensemble of such a report the particle of resemblance (*-like*), leaving all by itself the *zoematic* kernel (*skunks*). The gesture would leave standing a fantasied product in place of a former hallucinatory referent: a skunklike migrainous phosphene would have become *mancuspious*.

In attempting a description of the semiotic production of mancuspias as fantasy kernels, irony has presently reached the near side of the protocol observed by literary fantasy in "Cefalea." A certain degree of frivolity seems inherent in the act of replacing (within the report of an actual hallucination) a disturbing image with one brought from a different, essentially ironic sector of percipient existence. As congruent images, mancuspia-events place products of hallucination within fictional synchrony; they help to sustain a storyline like a constellation of signs held in virtual suspension before the reader's eyes. On the side of migraine aura, the same picture of constellated instances appears before the eye of the nosographer, as he or she rounds off the analysis of a reported event. In both cases, synchrony binds the picture together; products originating in phosphenic or phonemic activity manifest (in hallucination and fiction) an autonomous world of present sensations lacking a past. In this sense, such optic disturbances do not resemble fantasies.

Rather than any fantasies at large, events in migraine aura and in Cortázar's mancuspia-fictions resemble extant theories on the origins of fantasy in the archaic phases of the psyche. In *Life and Death in Psycho-Analysis*, Jean Laplanche has offered a rigorous account of how Freud speculated on the genesis of the so-called *object relation* by situating the notion of a *primal hallucination* as the impact zone (or event) between internal needs and external excitations experienced by the infant child (8ff.). Hallucinated instances of pleasure and discomfort might have punctuated the child's existence between moments of need and satisfaction. The active presence of a time lapse or a space of deferral between such hallucinatory episodes lends to them and to their surrounding contingencies a strong diachronic texture. As proto-fantasies, these archaic hallucinations seem time-bound and temporally factored, inseparable from the unending contiguousness of desire, demand, and pleasure.

According to Laplanche, it is from this minimal plot involving need and satisfaction and marked by episodes of cleaved sentience that Freud's understanding of fantasy evolved (97–102). In Freud's view, fantasies extend any present situation along the curved lines of the enveloping past issuing from memory. Fantasies envelop the individuals from whom they issue within forms of celebration and mourning; their vague and omnipotent *presentness* manifests the unresolved manner in which the past refuses to perish without taking with it the individual itself as a kind of memorial. In the end, fantasies reflect (by all at once projecting and obscuring it) a relation with past and future deaths; they manifest how individuals attain transmissible form only in *pastness*.

The voice of character in "Cefalea" expresses its own past and buried memories through a narrative mode that places such vestiges beyond the reach of reading. Voice travels through mindful spaces where its echoes remain chambered in the premature niche of an empty skull. The past of character lies dissolved in present pastness, it comes recorded and un-sung in a testimonial talk held by voices already dead. In the archaeology of such voices lies (in fossil form) names of distant flowers, of remote landscapes and breezes, of petals that once drummed in the wind, of urns once filled with unseen gifts and now hollowed by figures dwelling inside a drugged head.

Severed Versions

of Pastoral:

"Bestiario,"

"Final del juego,"

and "Las

armas secretas"

. . . It next will be right
  To describe each particular batch:
Distinguishing those that have feathers, and bite,
  From those that have whiskers, and scratch.
—*Lewis Carroll*

The following sequence of interpretations deals with the title stories of three of Cortázar's best-known collections of short fiction. The analysis will focus on themes of harmony and discord made conventional in pastoral literature, but it will also address questions raised from a psychoanalytic and ethnographic perspective. Moving against the grain of William Empson's synthetic notion of pastoral as the "process of putting the complex into the simple" (*Pastoral,* 23), the readings attempt to generate deep involvement with complex meanings in stories read intertextually. Obviously, if read in isolation from each other, the stories could prove as simple or as complex as the reader's involvement would determine, just as a certain thematic simplicity could quite possibly emerge from mapping a fictional world common to all of them. Where complexity may come into play is in furnishing such a fictional world with certain speculative though not arbitrary themes, such as those emerging from a counterpoint relation between pastoral and ethnography. The overarching norm requiring human beings and styles of conduct to coalesce in harmony against a background of threatening discord ranks high among pastoral values; here lies the strongest element making pastoral a climate of being rather than just a style or genre. Hence, rather than being transformed into pastorals along essentialist lines, the stories gathered here should resurface as interdependent yet autonomous components of an ontological landscape linked with the ideal world of pastoral, from which it may then become severed.

The Fractured Landscape

The importance of the ontological view gains pertinence as pastoral themes are brought side-by-side with the standard features of the *fantastic*. As already seen in the case of "Cefalea," the received notion of *lo fantástico* can lead to a rigid, dualistic understanding of humdrum as opposed to intruding realities of an uncanny nature. Typically, either the social or the personal existence as established in the disenchanted world of routine and present reality will suddenly overlap, in unexplained synchronic fashion, with another realm inherently at odds with (or impossible to fit within) the social and psychological norms first established as routine and presently real. The unexplained overlap of two realms, or the shift from the already known to the known by other means but otherwise unknown may define *lo fantástico*.

In ontological terms, the onset of fantasy in Cortázar's fiction may attract readers on the grounds of a prior segregation of familiar routines to the status of "stool-pigeon" realities. Just as it shifts into fantasy, the real may demand explanation precisely because it has been established as a set of peculiarly boring routines. Rather than trying to account for the element of fantasy as something detached or unusual, the interpreter may decide to search for it as an ongoing and ordinary element in the personal pursuit of the real. Moving away from semiology, the interpreter would engage in a hermeneutics of the stubbornly sublime, in which the routinely real established by the story circles back upon itself, bringing with it a share of the interpreter's own fantasies. Therefore, instead of trying an objective survey of the boundaries that presumably separate reality from fantasy, the interpreter could trace (nonobjectively and quite self-consciously) whatever might paradoxically bind together introspection and a certain divestment of self-interest in the life of a real person, of a social being in salient ways similar to the interpreter itself.

Adhering to a presumably objective program even in terms of psychoanalytic criticism, the semiology of narrative avoids an introspective approach to storytelling, perhaps out of the fear that the critical mind might sink into a kind of autoleptic bondage to fiction. But the risk of misprision would seem justified if one considers how, in stories like "Las armas secretas," the personal self implicit in the main characters escapes recognition (of any significant sort) unless its own construction comes as the result of further fictional mediations provided by the interpreter itself. In other words, a story haunted by signs of pathological disturbance and symptoms of frigidity and paranoia (caused by rape trauma) nevertheless lacks a genuine psychological character, unless it is surmised and to a large extent invented by the interpreter. However, the story continues to lack an object of genuine clinical status even when the literary interpreter uses shorthand terms like *psychosis* in order to explain the characters' aberrant conduct. As a creation of *lo fantástico,* the story hinges on the fascination that comes from rejecting the ontology of emotional illness, or from preventing an ontological fusion between the order of illness and the *mise-en-scène* of the fantastic. A particular discursive account of madness in the protagonist would bring about the type of coherence needed to maintain fusion between the intercepting orders of routine and disturbance, of analytic discourse and symptom. Unfortunately, such fusion depends on making madness a discursive object alienated from the specific mood and descriptiveness that the story communicates about it but never designates as being madness, judged as such from a detached and privileged viewpoint. As a set of analytic propositions, madness would turn into a negative of its own singular discursiveness, into an object of clinical research and social management. In the end, *lo fantástico* remains in complicity with the structures of rationality it tries to disturb, as long as it may not motivate the reader's own rehearsal of the type of introspection and analysis that the story forecloses with respect to its own characters and situations in order to insulate and sustain the pleasure of its reading.

Stories like "Continuidad de los parques," in which the pathological does not play any discernible role, end with a twist into the uncanny, and thereby reward the reader's implied moral condescension toward the central character, another comfortable reader. In general, the criticism of Cortázar's short fiction has produced a small library of smug and formulaic lessons against polite living, but such lessons rarely fail to imply a secure order of politeness embracing their authors. The *fantastic* has nurtured an orthodoxy. In fact, its stories could serve as examples of how the ontological fusion between the disciplines of the *real* (underlined as the dominant ontology) and the fascination of the *unreal* (underlined as the adversarial background of latent desires and fears) translates into a type of incoherence for which the reader must assume ultimate responsibility. Incoherence of an ontological kind exists as long as a particular event or outcome within a given story cannot find explanation for being (or for having occurred) without breaking the unstated but obvious rules that lend coherence to the dominant ontology on which the real world implied in the story transparently rests (see Pavel, *Fictional Worlds,* 138ff.). Once such rules are broken (once a man reading a novel can be accepted as the victim of the *same* murder of which he is about to read in the novel) incoherence (inside the dominant ontology) ceases to exist, and two different orders of being emerge side by side. Within the order belonging to the dominant ontology that provides the *real*, two murders take place, one real and the other fictional; while within the order belonging to the adversarial ontology that supplies the *unreal*, one murder-event represents all that is the case.

The analysis of delusional phenomena may begin by upholding ontological fusion between its own conceptual coherence and the one built into the disclosure of psychotic experience. But at no point could analysis afford to include within such fusion an attribution of transcendent origin to a phenomenon plainly at odds with its own sense of the real. The maintenance of fascination within the genre of *lo fantástico* operates otherwise. The genre sustains an imaginary fusion of the real and the unreal within a single ontological landscape whose fundamental incoherence it hides from view and upholds as a subversive or adversarial claim against ordinary reality. In order to highlight the unresolved contradiction between objective and subjective claims in this peculiar maintenance of fantasy, one may look into two of Cortázar's stories clearly marked by the intrusions of the unreal upon a fractured landscape held together by erotic desire.

Parks That Continue Ending in Silvia

Strict antithesis separates and holds face-to-face the central characters in "Continuidad de los parques" and "Silvia."[1] Both men inhabit a world of leisure set in the country, but besides such resemblance they seem like inverted images of each other. First, we have a wealthy landowner absorbed in the reading of romances, who lives in a transparent but limitless area in-between the ordeal of writing and the parasitic state of reading (that writing should amount to an ordeal might be the key heroic doctrine behind "Continuidad de los parques"). Second, we have a self-proclaimed writer enjoying the sweet melancholy brought on by the memory of a summer vacation in France and the vanishing image of a young woman (that a young woman ought to be the ultimate reward of reading seems obvious in "Silvia"). This writer is twice called "Fernando," but his repertoire of references to literary works and to other artists makes him seem like a parody of Julio Cortázar. Just as in "Silvia" the writer ("Julio Cortázar") seems to be portrayed as an alternate self and ironic signature, in "Continuidad de los parques" the reader is seen as if the author were playing him in a hidden cameo role, perceived only when the black-and-white allegory of a peculiar murder is pondered. Author and reader switch places: reading may become an ordeal, just as writing may turn into the impotent aftermath of reading too much and too hard. (The ideal reader of *lo fantástico* should always die at the end, as if in mimicry of some sexual release.)

The notion of "parks continuing" becomes pictorial and cinematic when the landscape imagined by the reader of romances comes to life, but not inside his own reading mind but surrounding him with a melodramatic version of the dark sublime. The metamorphosis (of a reader absorbed in contemplation into the victim of what his own absorption brings to life) evokes the fate of Narcissus. In both instances, attention must be paid to continuities and gaps between image and voice. With Narcissus, the image of a personal self hides in reflection; but voice, too, lies not so much hidden as withdrawn from the person absorbed in contemplation. Although customarily seen as a drama of sight lured and arrested by appearances, the Narcissus story might involve a drama of the voice entrapped, withheld in a purely visual landscape and thus lodged in places outside the reach of the self to whom such voice should belong. The story may suggest that, Narcissus's fixed self-reflection produces an echo without a voice, which is the reverse of Echo, whose voice sounds but is always borrowed. Applying this to the romance reader in "Continuidad de los parques," one may observe how unsung voices, rustles, and other aural phenomena are activated by his absorption into reading. The story of a reader murdered by an absorbing story can be reread as a catastrophe of self-enforced muteness involving a perverse witness or voyeur inside whom swallowed voices resolve themselves into echoes, and echoes into persons and sites in which a yearning for self-punishment switches into a desire to murder.

Without necessarily shifting away from the parable of a reader who falls prey to his own escapist fantasies, our perspective can then focus on the implied effects of a primal scene. At this point, however, the question of the *real* returns, underlining a term that should represent the very opposite of something received, of something already established or merely given. For the *real* should represent an entity in the act of being constructed, rather than one already deconstructed by boredom. The *real* may thus emerge as a contractual affair brought to light by the interpreter's own desires to see it become like reading for the sake of perversity (here lies Poe's true mark in his translator Cortázar). Rather than being the point where fantasy or the uncanny impact upon boredom, the *real* shifts in order to disclose a different, more personal glimpse of the unseen and fascinating. Forced into view, fantasied products arrange themselves on a screen made up of sight and sound effects. Thus, in "Continuidad de los parques," the two lovers whose clandestine affair in the forest the reader has been spying (and abetting through breathless reading) are transformed from being purveyors of delicious romance and death into a remodeled version of the parental couple. The reader desires these models and molds of passion as much as he desires their punishment, but his desire is bound to a masochistic contract according to which their punishment would be indistinct from his own.

Severance of sight from sound (of image from voice) would have been the result of a specific trauma behind the masochism informing the pleasures of the man depicted in "Continuidad de los parques." The desired effect of such masochist's contract would legitimize the man's and the reader's clandestine spying on lovemaking. Instead of killing the postparental couple, as any grown child may wish to do, a sort of reader's vengeance unfolds with the spy's own death at its center, in the company of his intimate accomplice, the reader. A pleasure chain links the story's inside and outside readers, just as a conceptual link binds the notion of reading one's own murder to the notion of staging one's punishing suicide. Masochistic desire supports the egoist's investment in the pleasures of being ruled (and killed) by the parental couple, the deposed monarchs and inventors of love, a sentiment quite hard to conceive outside its fantasied origins in a minimal pair-bonding nurtured inside the infant environment of a family.[2]

The relative value of calling on the notion of a masochistic contract transcends the psychoanalytic view; it implies not taking the real for granted and seeing it as inherently informed by the operative logic of contracts. With its perverse recourse to symbolism and ritual, the egoism of the masochist type rubs into view the contractual grain that makes up the surface of social interaction in general. In "Silvia," the signs of agreement made, enjoyed, and broken occupy the foreground of the writer's self-portrait in melancholy. Antithetical aspects concerning recollection (nurtured by writing in "Silvia") and the instant effects of memory (created by reading in "Continuidad de los parques") can be reviewed within a specific analytic situation touching on the question of memory and authority.

The prevailing view of the unconscious obtained in the wake of Freud's heroic act of self-analysis focuses on the broken companionship between authorial knowledge and the voices of the past. With the publication of

The Interpretation of Dreams, analytic authorship emerged from the struggle to possess and re-create memory with the ultimate aim of divorcing it. Analytic retrieval engages the past with ironic suspicion; it perceives in traces of personal ontogenesis a sort of allegory, an incestuous affair involving the inlaid voices of memory (Mother) and time (Father). In a manner that should become transparent upon reading the short blueprint of innocent betrayal sketched in "Family Romances" (*Works*, 9:236–41), the child's own portrait becomes the reverse image of the mature analyst, as the real parents of childhood migrate into fantasy and become an exalted couple of noble origin or royal blood. In their fantasies of being especially chosen, children forsake whatever autonomy they might enjoy (and fear) in their parents in favor of a vivid access to parenthood itself: in fantasy, children not only bind themselves to parental images, but may indeed *become* their own parents. As a result, imaginary voices, attitudes, and semblances overlap incestuously. Moved by self-love, memory betroths time like a royal sister would her kingly brother. The analyst will endeavor to sever such ties upon finding them still intact in the fantasy life of the adult neurotic. The task of analysis should proceed as a divestment of such sheltering illusions: the analyst is shaped as he or she learns how to overcome the incestuous protection of the past, perhaps most actively preserved in fantasies. But it might be that the analyst derives authorial voice precisely from large residues of such incestuousness, from powerful acts of imaginative and fantastic transgression into other lives as if they were extensions of one's own.

The ancestry of authorial voice includes murder. In a manner peculiar to Freud's sense of trauma, voices within any given imaginary community persist in dire need of being stylized by ritual, perhaps owing to their complicity in the awful noise of some forgotten and cruel event. While voice disguises murder and thus preserves it whole but muted, written signs try to digest it, to break down and bury murder beneath scripture. As if haunted by or presupposing self-consciousness, writing cannot escape self-betrayal; it drives itself into confusing the slain body with the fragmented (and distributable) corpse of murder: murder scattered in the propitiatory signs of its own aftermath, murder calling on murder calling on suicide. As argued in *Moses and Monotheism* (1939), writing partakes of murder by facilitating distortion: it re-creates the site for "striking omissions" and "disturbing contradictions," and it opens the way for the "signs of things the communication of which was never intended" (*Works*, 23:43). Like murder, writing cannot alter the object it attempts to destroy without creating the need to get rid of traces that no longer seem distinct from one's own guilty imprint, that do not seem to have originated in a separate or alien body. In Freud's understanding, the compulsion to repeat finds in writing an ideal vehicle to alter the past in order to better preserve it. The deeper truth behind the discovery that a particular fragment of writing has altered a previous script lies in the further discovery that most writing articulates a need to suggest disfigurement, that written signs may occupy a place previously held by older written signs. Freud's intimate authorship of murder cannot erase from itself the signature of suicide.

Since incest and murder represent the unsevered minimal pair in Freud's master plot, they constitute the Oedipal kernel at the heart of the stories that he found most memorable. The Oedipal example brings the notion of murder into inextricable kinship with modes of symbolic suicide. Our revision of "Continuidad de los parques" in terms of masochism represents a variant of the Oedipal scene, in which the tragic aftermath of murder and the horror of self-recognition find contractual stability in the cool and perverse drama of dying, step by step, a liturgical death. In the case of "Silvia," the writer has created a more complex world of symbolic mediations with no explicit relationship to violence. The contractual elements that should enter into the making of the *real* in "Silvia" hinge on two interlocked figures descended from the Victorian world and the writings and life of Lewis Carroll: the orphan and the bachelor (see Gordon, "The Alice Books," 101–17).

To a great extent, "Silvia" is a story about the erotic sources of light. Outright lunacy animates the epiphanies of the young Silvia facing Fernando, but the effects of the moon cannot be credited with bringing the glare of the girl's eroticism to the writer; these effects are unveiled only at the very end, as they are wrapped in the answer that a witty girl gives to a riddle she has heard but whose actual form the reader may only surmise: "It is the moon. . . . What a dull riddle, man," Graciela tells Fernando, leaving the reader guessing at the riddle's unvoiced and teasing phrase. The reader should be able to guess that the whole of "Silvia" encompasses both the riddle itself and its narrative allegory.

Silvia's earliest presence among the children is framed and infused by fire. Night (*la noche*), just fallen, acts as sacred painter of its (*her*) own features; it (*she*) invents fire and daubs what resembles a canvas with animated hues: "la noche inventó el fuego del asado hasta entonces poco visible entre los árboles, se embadurnó con reflejos dorados y cambiantes que teñían el tronco de los árboles y alejaban los límites del jardín" [night invented the roasting fire until then hardly visible among the trees, it daubed itself with golden and shifting glares that tinged the trunks of the trees and pushed away the limits of the garden, (83)]. Similar passages—with the counterpoint suggestion of naïve as opposed to ironic meta-morphosis—recall the value of antithesis as a figure of specular exchange lodged between the previously analyzed stories. At the opening of "Continuidad de los parques," the still canvas of the park at dusk gains visual animation in the unfolding of a kind of reading unpunctuated by the self-conscious effects of writing, an activity of which the reader of romances seems blissfully ignorant. In contrast, "Silvia" moves forth punctuating its plot not only with signs of self-conscious writing, but with references to the imprint of particular writers. The passage where Silvia first appears falls (as if within brackets) between the names of Philippe Sollers and Francis Ponge. As a figure, Silvia is ushered in attached to an author's name ("Sollers") in whose work she might never have managed to gain a similar entrance, and she settles briefly into view etched in the worded contours of an object signed by "Ponge." As a writer, Fernando recalls her kneeling by the fire, a vision that increases Silvia's neighboring but remote splendor, like that of a figure carved on a bas-relief: "her burnished thighs, thighs all at once lightened and heavily etched as in the style of Francis Ponge, . . . her calves remained in shadows, just as her torso and face, but her long hair shone when startled by each flaming wing, a hair also made of ancient gold; all of Silvia seemed toned in fire, in heavy bronze" [sus muslos bruñidos, unos muslos livianos y definidos al mismo tiempo como el estilo de Francis Ponge, . . . las pantorrillas quedaban en la sombra al igual que el torso y la cara, pero el pelo largo brillaba de pronto con los aletazos de las llamas, un pelo también de oro viejo, toda Silvia parecía entonada en fuego, en bronce espeso, (83)]. The scene of epiphany represents light as the source of energy and illustration, alluring light inviting fusion as the primal element of being.

Three photographs of a girl illustrate "Silvia." In the first, the girl appears suspended, like a premature woman, in the act of eloping through a window by a rope ladder. In the second, she is holding a doll, posing in strange surrogacy to her own indifferent, provoking image; her eyes are in line with a lost point removed from light, a point in space fixed by her and which no viewer could ever occupy in answer to her glance. In the third, she is seated cross-legged on the ground with an open book on her lap, her figure hemmed in by two younger girls, her face tilted in laden pensiveness against the head of the girl on her right. Next to fire, light exists in "Silvia" in the singular nonmetaphoric way that Roland Barthes assigns to the photograph: "For the *noeme* 'That-has-been' was possible only on the day when a specific circumstance (the discovery that silver halogens were sensitive to light) made it possible to recover and print directly the luminous rays emitted by a variously lighted object. The photograph is literally an emanation of the referent. From a real body, which was there, proceed radiations which ultimately touch me, who am here" (*Camara Lucida*, 80). Photographed (and, only in that manner, *not yet vanished*) childhood holds its own against adolescence in the worshipping light of Lewis Carroll's fascination with female dream-children. The small photographic album included in "Silvia" bears the structural function of a passport picture for time travel. Moving in time, the bachelor writer discovers that *any* childhood (not just a Victorian one) may deny entrance to those who are not (or do not feel like) orphans, but that orphanhood may not survive childhood.

Just as the reader-protagonist of "Continuidad de los parques" seeks entrance into the primal scene, the writer (who unavoidably reads himself in answering the riddle of "Silvia") tries to enter the magic circle where the children's curious trial-by-fancy almost lays within his grasp the flesh of a forbidden gift. Silvia's epiphany brings her next to Fernando, but her sight is as powerful as the transparent wall that separates them. Her body can only be touched by a gaze shared with someone else, with a real girl and intellectually premature woman, Graciela. The children and the writer share the gaze so that they may (unequally) partake of Silvia's presence. The gaze includes being touched (nursed, wiped) by Silvia, but only when she is being looked at by the man who holds the gaze that she does not possess, for Silvia never answers the gaze, never looks back at the man who witnesses, remembers, and writes. The children play a dominant role as judges and witnesses in the writer's curious affair with *their* Silvia. They differ from *his* gaze in that they should be touched as much as they like to touch, while the gaze touches only as if by proxy: it observes a taboo against touching with anything but the eyes. Little Graciela breaks the spell of this implicit taboo; she embodies the nearest chance of Silvia's being touched by the gazing author. Graciela's adhesiveness has license to anoint the writer; she comes to his lap, drops her sticky ammunitions, wipes her hands on his neck, and sits indelibly on his legs ("se sentó imborrable en mis piernas"). Graciela (the womanchild) acts as a skin alter ego of Sylvia's being an object forbidden to the laying of hands, an object protected by the taboo bestowed on it by the touch of sight.

Between Graciela's unforbidden touch and Silvia's tabooed flesh a secret awaits answer. Seduction persists as childhood survives; it is a child who is always charmed—vulnerably seduced in the actual child, sinisterly imprisoned in the imaginary child inside the seducer's soul. The writer in "Silvia" looks at children who act like bachelors at play, married only to their own seductiveness. They teach him not to feel like an orphan when he is exposed to their mastery of play, not to feel inferior to their world, a world he sees in gestures, words, and glances he can only ape like small lessons in performance. Fernando's situation borders on masochism: it depends on a contract, on a bond between acquiescence and reward.

Silvia's reward comes only in the erotic warmth of the story. The wounding taboo created by the gaze reveals a composite view of woman as mother, sister, daughter, niece, stranger, mirror-companion, orphan-muse. Either as a result of reading or writing, the *real* in "Silvia" projects the desire to abridge the companionship of love, not by trying to be the other, but by imagining it/her free.

Games Bearing Poisons and Gifts

Aversion between love and freedom represents a rich moral theme in "Final del juego," a story whose links with pastoral become more suggestive and complex in relation to "Los venenos."[3] The brief but fraternal friendship (broken by the dark epiphany of jealousy) between the unnamed narrator of "Los venenos" and his guest, the worldly Hugo, can be linked with the fate of Leticia, the chosen one among three sisters or cousins who, in "Final del juego," bring to life ornamented attitudes and allegorical statues in a game reminiscent of pastoral stereotypes. United into a single plot of awakening moral consciousness of guilt, love, and envy, the two stories evoke elements from the plot of Shakespeare's greatest pastoral mystery, *The Winter's Tale*. The narrator and Hugo bathe together and enjoy what—in the spirit of a narrative controlled from the vantage point of boyhood—amounts to a borrowed sense of superiority over girls in general. The narrative has the boys knowing that girls want them, and knowing also that which girls should want and do not have. However, as in the case of Shakespeare's Leontes and Polixenes, play-brothers learn from their shared sentimental education that a sense of giftedness and election must face the mirror of sacredness, as when Hermione (with "an art Lawful as eating") breaks from the numbness of her own statue and descends back to life conjured by the spirit of regained friendship.

In "Final del juego," Leticia performs a similar sacred trick. It comes at the instant of skillful candor when, while playing the allegory of sacred beauty and placing it on her own pedestal, she acts as a statue to her own absence, mimicking the fragile truth that performs within each inspired illusion. At a corresponding instant of revelation near the end of "Los venenos," the boy (whom the narrator remembers as himself) is betrayed by Hugo's departure, after being seduced by him into becoming his naïve alter ego, and learns something he has yet to understand: there is truth beyond (and quite besides) any particular fact or ensemble of habits that he might have known, enjoyed, or exploited until then. Pastoral values lend coherence to the notion that such mysterious yet incarnate truth (seemingly placed beyond particulars) can be formal and yet passionate, that it might help to support an entire world of illusion and performance—but also a personal world reduced to melancholy and a sense of loss.

In both stories, the pronoun *I* acts as a dual point of authorial reference; first person joins third person, but not in the same way as in "Cefalea." In "Final del juego," the couple "Holanda y yo" segregates itself from Leticia, the remaining and foregrounded symbolic sister.[4] The "Holanda and I" couple performs a role that reveals how games may turn into rituals. In a similar fashion, the couple "mi hermana y yo" in "Los venenos" marks the authorial voice's first point of self-reference; from then on, however, much of the story conspires to break the union "my sister and I" and to set the narrator apart from the rest of the cast. The respective focal points of authorial presence in the two stories differ according to the distinctiveness by which physical actions—while creating a sense of histrionic force—may or may not highlight resemblances among those who perform them, even to the extent of hiding one from view. "Los venenos" offers a clear view of children and adults weaving their roles together without loss of individual identity, except in the case of the Negri sisters, a threesome similar to the sororal trio of "Final del juego," albeit in marginal and uncharming fashion.

In pastoral terms, the game of Statues and Attitudes in "Final del juego" sets the virtue of grace in motion just as it fans and tries to control the fires of envy. Apparently, the game first took its present shape in order to hide Leticia's rigid figure within the three girls' combined actions, allowing her physical handicap to display itself disguised in stylized stillness. Careful reading of the story reveals how the implicit figure of Leticia leads a double life: one in motion and the other in rest. The girls move with the swiftness of nymphs:

> We ran, trying to get the speed to scramble up the low embankment
> of the right-of-way. . . . When we stooped down to touch the
> rails, . . . the heat of the stone roadbed flushed our faces, and facing
> into the wind from the river there was a damp heat against our
> cheeks and ears. We liked to bend our legs and squat down, rise,
> squat again, move from one kind of hot zone to the other, watching
> each other's faces to measure the perspiration. (137)

Nothing in such joy and frenzy excludes awkward Leticia from the other
two; the separate couple of "Holanda y yo" does not apply when the
three partake of a life in motion. But a different Leticia suffers exposure
when it comes to identifying her as the leader:

> Leticia was scragglier than we were, and even worse, that kind of
> skinniness you can see from a distance in the neck and ears. Maybe it
> was the stiffness of her back that made her look so thin, for instance
> she could hardly move her head from side to side, she was like a
> folded-up ironing board . . . with the wide part up, leaning closed
> against the wall. (138)

Possessed by motion, the three girls act as one; otherwise, the rigid body
of the one falls from grace.

Among some of the older known layers of pastoral, nymphs play the
role of dreaded divinities responsible for a specific form of rapture
known as nympholepsy (Borgeaud, *The Cult Pan*, 104–8). Inspiration
and madness of the sort ironically broached by Socrates in *Phaedrus*
reflect an equally archaic experience, not so much inspired as endured by
nymphs in sharing the Arcadian landscape with the primitive god Pan.
Typified by Echo and Syringe, nymphs undergo metamorphosis to
escape Pan's erotic hunger; they vanish into features of landscape forever
animated by their ultimate fate. Their bodily motion begins a life elsewhere: female movement leaves its former tracks, it follows a different
surface, it even creates surfaces unseen, resonant, unsoiled. The ecstasy
of nymphs seems to deny and replace all sexual union. They vanish by
leaving to their erotic pursuer an object or an effect for him to play with
or to enjoy—wherein they remain forever hiding but in bondage to a
form of intercourse in excess of carnal contact. Nymph ecstasy transfers
an element native to such rapture to the pursuing activity it provokes.
What ecstasy transfers to the pursuer is the urge to create a nymph-
specific activity that not even a god may in the end control or enjoy. Pan
plays Syringe with the syringe—by way of having failed to rape her. In

the nymph's former body, female ecstasy recovers a shape vulnerable to an assault by sex, a shape (now) only imaginable in her ecstasy. These remarks might lead to a deeper understanding of female elation in the chaste offerings of statues and emblematic poses enacted by the three girls in "Final del juego."

The girls display forms of self-fascination. In specular terms, what they offer Ariel (as a passenger on the train that flies by) is meant as a charmed circle of poses that mirror each other before and after luring him into communing with them. Ecstasy would not exist as a phenomenon of formal climax on display without Leticia's passion and its transformation of the pathetic into the sublime. An element of affliction and the threat of ridicule absent in the other girls produce in Leticia the ability to simultaneously hide the truth of her rigid condition and give elated expression to the truth of artful display. Fueled by passion and moved by the pathetic resolve to renounce the game with one last gesture, Leticia fulfills with her own body the conditions for sublime expression listed by Longinus: "the ability to form grand conceptions," "the stimulus of powerful and inspired emotion," and "the total effect resulting from dignity and elevation" (Dorsch, *Criticism*, 108). However, tensions inherent in sublimity reach beyond poetic tone to disclose elements within the ontology of sentiment. The sororal game promotes envy among its participants and creates the chance to obtain a victim of ridicule, who represents both a gift to and from envy.

The higher sublimity of Leticia's last pose contains a synthesis of the previously separate modes of Attitudes and Statues. It might also stand as a last gesture in the surpassing of ridicule by candor:

> The game came out Statues, and we chose lovely things that would go well with the jewels, lots of peacock feathers to set in the hair, and a fur that from the distance looked like a silver fox, and a pink veil that she put on like a turban. We saw that she was thinking, trying the Statue out, but without moving, and when the train appeared on the curve she placed herself at the foot of the incline with all the jewels sparkling in the sun. She lifted her arms as if she were going to do an Attitude instead of a Statue, her hands pointed at the sky with her head thrown back (the only direction she could, poor thing) and bent her body backwards so far it scared us. (148)

Envy negotiates the stereotypes of sentiment listed when defining the rules for Attitudes: "For Envy you could show your teeth, make fists and hold them in a position so as to seem cringing. For Charity the ideal was an angelic face, eyes turned up to the sky, while the hands offered something—a rag, a ball, a branch of willow—to a poor invisible orphan. Shame and Fear were easy to do; Spite and Jealousy required a more conscientious study" (139). Against this background, Statues represent a higher order of performance in at least two ways involving reciprocity as a stimulant and antidote to envy. They are meant to produce in return either a better or a worse offering.

> The Statues were determined, almost all of them, by the choice of ornaments, and here absolute liberty reigned. So that a statue would come out of it, one had to think carefully of every detail in the costume. It was a rule of the game that the one chosen could not take part in the selection; the two remaining argued out the business at hand and then fitted the ornaments on. The winner had to invent her statue taking into account what they'd dressed her in, and in this way the game was much more complicated and exciting because sometimes there were counterplots, and the victim would find herself rigged out in adornments which were completely hopeless; so it was up to her to be quick then in composing a good statue. Usually when the game called for Attitudes, the winner came up pretty well outfitted, but there were times when the Statues were horrible failures. (139)

Symbolic elements of rebirth and death (and of birth in deformity) inform the perilous reciprocity to which the actress commits herself under the judging eyes of the other actresses. Statues bring about the question of difference; even though they bind the sisters in a common task, Statues owe their distinction either to acts of discrimination, or to the norm that requires being singled out and put on the spot—left in the peculiar loneliness of not seeing while being seen.

The ontology of sentiment reaches a paradoxical climax when the challenge of offering encouragement and stimulating envy is translated into allegorical gestures. The paradox lies at the origin of the game itself, a game at first glance similar to any other game, but on closer inspection quite unique. Similar in being made for all participants, unique in having been devised above all to fit Leticia's awkward body, allowing it the garments of symbolic gesture. More than anyone else could or would have the need to do, Leticia hides in performance, her defects turned into grace, her handicap triumphant. The paradox runs deeper when one considers that the game does not need to have originated for either the overt or hidden purpose of allowing Leticia a favorable form of play.

However, her abnormality (favorably and unfavorably acknowledged) makes it impossible to rethink the game's origins outside the tacit program of enshrining Leticia's transformed figure. Then, each time that any of the girls (including Leticia) perform an Attitude or a Statue, Leticia-as-triumph-over-predicament is embodied in the performance. The game resembles the allegory of a unique person named Leticia, at the same time that another strand of allegory brings into being the figure of *someone* not unlike Leticia, but precisely by virtue of not being her—even when Leticia herself stands in place of that someone. This type of allegorical intricacy concerning the identity of persons, the preeminence of role over individual autonomy and of binding reciprocity over the narcissistic bases of love, finds resolution when the choice of the beautiful over the unremarkable turns into the choice of truth as inseparable from death.

The notion of symbolic death permeates "Final del juego." Transience and permanence exchange perspectives between the fixed site from where the girls perform and their fleeting audience on the train; the river that runs beyond the tracks offers another latent image of flux against unchanging appearances. But the main theme (as in "Los venenos") is the question of choice, or the act of electing, of choosing someone as an affirmation of permanence over mutability. Analogies can be pressed home by way of Freud's elegant interpretation of the allegory of choice confronting death in "The Theme of the Three Caskets" (*Works*, 12:290–301). The key elements in Freud's essay come down to a sequence of findings: that *someone* has no other choice but to choose; that the choice is made by a male figure at certain points along the ages of man; that choosing from among three caskets amounts to choosing *one* woman; that the choice of (a) woman represents not choosing her, but rather being chosen by her; and that this peculiar reversal of fortunes in the act of judging comes from the mythological wisdom that would have three women being in the end only one—the bringer of death's embrace. The conclusion to Freud's essay applies unchanged to Ariel's choice of Leticia over her playmates: "The free choice between the three sisters is, properly speaking, no free choice, for it must necessarily fall on the third" (12:300). Although the necessary elements of uncanny force associated with the third choice do not exist in the case of Leticia, her special nature as the game's central object seems redundantly obvious: she links death's figure(s) with the powers of metamorphosis; the game dwells on changing and preserving her, on doing away with her just as she does away with herself in the final pose.

In his brief historical survey, Freud regards the creation of the Moerae (Moirai, the Hours) as "a recognition which warns man that he too is a part of nature and therefore subject to the immutable law of death" (12:299). The harshness of such recognition leads to changing the Greek goddess of Death (who stood behind the Moerae) into aspects of the goddess of Love. This would explain how "the third of the sisters is no longer Death"; she becomes "the fairest, best, most desirable and the most lovable among women" (12:299). The text of "Final del juego" makes it clear that being third binds together Ariel and Leticia: he travels by the third window ("In the third window we saw a boy with blond curly hair and light eyes," 141), and when he visits the girls he refers to the absent sister as "the third one" (146). In Freud's view, Leticia must be the absent sister because, in choosing the third one, what is chosen is a form of absence. This means that, in spotting her from the train, Ariel beholds Leticia at the same time that he is being chosen by a figure other than her (but other in sameness, which represents the uncanny double-ness of death).

Leticia's name (*Letitia Uberrima,* "Abundant Pleasure" [Wind, 118]) offers the clearest clue of a link between Ariel's choice, the allegory of the three Graces, and the Judgment of Paris. Just as Freud's interpretation uncovers dark finality and a collapse of difference in man's last choice, the rich allegorical tradition on this subject (to which his own essay belongs) centers on the cosmic harmony revealed in the whirling symmetries composed by the pastoral group of Verdure, Gladness, and Splendor. The text of "Final del juego" does not support any detailed connection with this tradition, but it nevertheless suggests themes that the tradition has elevated to the status of mysteries (see Harrison, *Prologmena,* 286–300). Unbroken, the circle composed by the three Graces links the actions of giving, accepting, and returning (Wind, 38).

The notion of a gift offered, accepted, and in return enhanced serves as a thematic bridge between the situation of Ariel and the girls and that of the central cast in "Los venenos." In the latter, the gift of a peacock feather may be a symbol of passage between two moral realms. In one realm, envy and loyalty to existing roles (in and around kinship) pro-mote adhesiveness among children near adolescence; in the other, envy turns into jealousy and creates divisiveness between two members of the group—the narrator, who neither gives nor receives the gift, and Hugo, who in a crucial sense must give it to someone else. The same ontology of sentiment that in "Final del juego" joins in antithesis personal inter-ests with transpersonal allegorical values, might be seen reflected in "Los venenos" as a drama of four characters who ultimately blend into two. But, the resulting two individuals could not be said to represent characters; instead, they should be seen as couplings holding together the related but conflicting roles of author and actor. The question of gender is at the core of the coupling role, since the two named persons involved from each story would be Leticia and Hugo.

In both stories, the implicit role of author coincides with the act of narrating without being limited to this somewhat abstract function, which in "Final del juego" belongs to a female and in "Los venenos" to a male. Both storytellers associate with a sister or sisterly companion; but while the union between "Holanda y yo" holds firm through the end, in "Los venenos" the unnamed narrator loses control of his sister and falls victim to her ridicule when both of them suffer (in different but parallel ways) Hugo's rejection in favor of Lila. All in all, the two storytellers are a disembodied mode of authorial presence. What makes them most resemble each other goes beyond their lack of stated proper name: they represent the same predicament in that they both miss not being, respectively, like Leticia and Hugo.

Next to the unnamed narrators stand their respective performing selves. In each case, unnamed authorial presence relocates specularly in the person of named characters, who are less authors than actors in whom the ability to perform with distinctive appeal bears the mark of an illness (near invalidism in Leticia, pleurisy in Hugo). Thus, possessing a name, reading a lot, and knowing how to take over the center of play might be seen as emergent embodiments of the unnamed author's figurative projection on the figure of a chosen other. Simultaneously, the named other involves a pathetic existence redeemed by style and appropriated by the storyteller with a mixture of love, envy, and pity. If not a theory, at least a certain profile of authorial love is drawn in this coupling with a singular person and its chosen name. It would seem as if the author could not properly register feelings of vanity and envy unless and until they are reflected in a person whose performance and possessions the authority of narration can then love and hate. Writing and love merge in Leticia's final letter to Ariel (set beyond the reader's eyes) and also at the moment when the unnamed narrator of "Los venenos" peers into Hugo's Botany and discovers the peacock feather (emblem of ancestral writing as well as vanity and love) that he will share with Hugo until it becomes a gift of love to Lila.

With the gift, love falls apart and the lover turns to writing stories about poisons. Love becomes disassembled. The emblematic feather and the brilliant friend who offers it to another become tokens of betrayal for a loving and envious artistic self that cannot operate without imagining itself hauntingly imperiled in others. Hugo's gift to Lila is doubly painful, since it replaces the narrator as both the one who should have given it to her and the one who should have received it from Hugo. The narcissistic expectation of receiving the feather from Hugo cannot be uncoupled from the specular wound of seeing it awarded to Lila. Perhaps love for her dates from this moment: who comes first, the lover or the gift? Love affects the sister too; from being a mere appendage to her brother, she becomes both the passionate lover who repeatedly writes and erases Hugo's name and the laughing cynic who makes fun of her brother's ignorance of Hugo's real love.

As a rehearsal of love's domestic perils and the quickening of familiar spirits, these two stories by Cortázar seem to take for granted that a sort of formal envy (mediated by play and the renewal of risk through performance) may have kept traditional families and neighbors alive to each other. The stories go on to portray the individuation of envy as jealousy and the emergence of guilt within the inner circle of a few who, in spite of this sentiment, might claim to be happier than most because the storyteller's memory discovers in the group a style of sadness (and joy) that only art may know how to represent and childhood to spontaneously experience. When, near the end of *The Winter's Tale*, Leontes asks Hermione and Polixenes for pardon, his phrase alludes to jealousy's semblance in sacred awe:

> . . . both your pardons,
> that e'er I put between your holy looks
> my ill suspicion.
> (5.3.147–49)

By "holy" is meant that which should never have inspired jealousy, and yet it is hard to imagine how Leontes might have become so unholily enraged without experiencing the illusion of holiness in the woman he could not love without hate. In the stories just examined, Cortázar explores the sentimental range of love and jealousy; in "Bestiario," he places these sentiments closer to myth.

The Elementary Structures of Domestic Feeling

If the family figures mourning, the economy of the dead, the law of the oikos *(tomb), if the house, the place where death guards itself against itself, forms a theater or funeral rite . . . if the woman assures the representation of this, it falls to the married woman to manage, strictly, a corpse.—Jacques Derrida,* Glas

Although not mentioned until now in reference to these stories, myth can play a proper mediating role between symbolic elements in "Los venenos" (not yet explored) and a specific ethnographic reading of symbolic kinship and incest in "Bestiario." A sudden strangeness in matters of kinship comes to the foreground when family affairs in both stories are placed in a well-delineated context of defamiliarization, in which ancestral themes of pastoral coevalness with nature shift ground under pressure from even older laws of shared existence and affiliation. At the same time, the question of surrealist elements in Cortázar's fiction changes focus, requiring a response whereby ethnography itself adopts a specific perspective:

> The ethnographic label suggests a characteristic attitude of partici-
> pant observation among the artifacts of a defamiliarized cultural
> reality. The surrealists were intensely interested in exotic worlds,
> among which they included a certain Paris. Their attitude, while
> comparable to that of the fieldworker who strives to render the
> unfamiliar comprehensive, tended to work in the reverse sense,
> making the familiar strange. The contrast is in fact generated by a
> continuous play of the familiar and the strange, of which ethnogra-
> phy and surrealism are two elements. (Clifford, *Predicament of
> Culture,* 121)

Even though the surrealist climate in Cortázar's fiction resides mostly in Paris, the stories he places elsewhere partake of the same alternative world, one endowed with a sort of alien and remote formality and a sense of structural uncanniness.

The ethnographic view may focus on elements present in the social rituals of reproduction and death.[5] For instance, the ant-poisoning machine in "Los venenos" may reflect elements of marriage symbolism, children making, and death. However, the machine's symbolic aspects should emerge from the prior reduction of the story to the contours of a kernel-myth—as if it were a story about sister-marriage and the complex role of a brother-type donor in the affair.

In myth and folktale, the machine would take the shape of a beast (dragon, anteater) playing a key role among or against contending suitors in marriage. But in "Los venenos," the poison machine suggests charm and complex beauty: it evokes a strange domestic animal with the talent to annihilate pests. As such, the object soon creates its own practical habitat: it confirms a division of labor between men and women, creates the need to learn prescriptions and warnings from a manual, and segregates the narrator's sister to a singular position as the one potential victim of its poison: "At lunch time, mother read to us from the instruction manual, and each time she reached the part about the poison we all looked at my sister" [A la hora del almuerzo mamá nos leyó el manual de instrucciones, y cada vez que llegaba a las partes del veneno todos la mirábamos a mi hermana (25)]. The machine encodes the sister according to meanings of decorum and protection; she is the family's most treasured possession. The poison may link the storyteller's sister with the other young female in the story (Lila), who seems to fit into a matrimonial logic as both the brother's prize and in contention with his friend, rival, and alter ego, the guest-resident Hugo. The marriage myth would attempt to differentiate the kinship term *sister* in reference to an existing sister ("mi hermana") and to another young female (Lila) whose status as sister remains intriguing with respect to the matrimonial slot *sister*. Thus, any given kinship term may represent an element of classification looking in at least two directions at once.

Beyond her overt role as Hugo's choice, Lila occupies a strong exogamous position of sister-other-than-my-sister by virtue of the color and flower encoding that links her with the *violet* character and other attributes of the two highly enhanced objects in the narrative, the poison in the machine and the peacock feather. Since the feather belongs neither to the sister nor to her brother but to Hugo, however, its mode of entering into symbolic interaction with the machine requires close attention. The feather fascinates the storytelling brother:

> It resembled the spots that gather on the surface of puddles, but it could not be so compared; it was much more beautiful, being of a brilliant green, like those bugs that live on damask trees and have two long antennae with a hairy little ball on each end. In the middle of the broadest and greenest part, a blue and violet eye opened, all bespattered, such as I had never seen. (34)

The brother who speaks can neither give nor receive the feather; he rejects the thought of stealing it, although in one sense he already has stolen it as a token of elective affinity with Hugo denied to others until the end, when Hugo leaves the gift-feather in Lila's custody. Denied the actual feather by someone who might have been his sister's suitor (but who has instead become a donor of nuptial prestige to Lila), the speaking brother comes into strange possession of the poison. In his imagination, the poison spreads in the form of an inward vision, a microcosm similar to the visionary episodes experienced by Isabel in "Bestiario":

> I liked to lie face down and smell the earth, to feel it underneath me, hot with the smell of summer. . . . I thought of many things, but above all of the ants; now that I had seen what ant-nests were like, I would remain thinking of the galleries which crisscrossed everywhere and that no one ever saw. Just like the veins on my legs, which could hardly be made out under the skin, but were filled with ants and mysteries that came and went. If one were to eat a little poison, it would really be like the smoke from the machine, poison traveling through the body's veins like the smoke inside the earth, there would be not much difference. (32)

In a symbolic space (next to the telluric and endogenous body imagined by the brother) tokens might circulate in mazelike fashion, going from feather to poison and back, and then from violet to Lila, from bride to machine, from poison to sister, from sister to bride, from poison to gift. Another circulation could be organized around the speaking brother's boldest experiment with the gifts of husbandry: his planting of a jasmine for a future bride (Lila), who in terms of the matrimonial logic examined here would have to be classified as a nonsister to a brother-type (the storyteller). On his part, Hugo (the nonspeaking, nonstorytelling brother) would classify as a brother-type lacking a sister in reference to the kinship category *sister*, from which he would obtain a bride without having one of his own to offer in return. This would imply that Hugo belongs to an exogamous (and the narrator to an endogamous) position with respect to the category *sister*.

In summing up the fictional ethnography, it may be proposed that the position of brother (as a wife-giver) appears threatened by sheer avoidance. The narrator prefers to be parentlike (not even to the exclusion of being motherlike) in his reveries of becoming an earth-body, through which the poison might circulate until regaining a life-giving property denied and affirmed by its own mutable beauty. It should be added that the machine's transformation of violet (intense Lila) into deadly poison relates within the color code to the suggestion of brilliant colors, painting, and the arch-signatures of nature on the peacock feather. The sister ("mi hermana") fulfills the colored notations generated by Hugo, the owner of the feather, when she repeatedly writes his name on a black-board using colored chalks. Instead of resembling a brother who would give away a sister as bride within some matrilineal system, the storyteller looks like a man who would marry his own sister. His companionship with the one he treasures and at times detests includes at least one echo of the brother-sister situation in "Casa tomada" (*Bestiario,* 9–18), a story well recognized by critics as an allegory of domestic incest. "My sister would read *Billiken,*" says the narrator of "Los venenos," "while I classi-fied my stamps in the enclosed yard" (26); the sister in "Casa tomada" knits and unknits colored yarns while her brother studies his stamp collection. The improbable sister that a brother would marry cannot be found in just one person, but rather in two (the sister and Lila); likewise, the same brother would have to be found not in one male individual but in two, one (the narrator) who could give away a bride but does not, and one (Hugo) who gives a gift to a bride but leaves the scene (perhaps) forever. The kernel-myth couples two couples, one lacking names ("mi hermana y yo") and another named by desire as *Lila and Hugo.* A biography of Cortázar's stories would have to include his *petite histoire* about the role played by a girl-type like Lila in his own childhood experiences with platonic love (see Picon-Garfield, 103–4).

Obviously, a construct such as the kernel-myth just sketched lacks genuine empirical grounds, it does not possess the extended social resonance that it would have in an actual ethnographic setting. The human community in which such a storied artifact would possess both material and symbolic significance does not exist in "Los venenos." Instead, the fragments of domestic trivia and symbols gathered in the story lend themselves to the not so arbitrary task of identifying within them remnants of social practices now vanished. A *collectible* memory (as opposed to a *collective* one) rises from such a view of fictions in associa-tion with myth and folktale.

At a distance of half a century, the surrealists might be regarded as collectors or museum curators roaming at large through streets and neglected alleys in which, as self-conscious *flâneurs,* they managed to recognize objectified fragments of archaic consciousness. Such a surface archaeology can easily (perhaps all too easily) compare with Jung's search for evidence of archetypes and tokens of collective memory, creating a kind of anthropological cabinet. Interpretations of *lo fantástico* often depend on such archetypes, in which they see signs of sublime or occult alterity, instead of bits of doctrinal knowledge or shreds from the allegorical recycling of myth (see Hernández del Castillo, *Cortázar's Mythopoesis,* passim). The card-index of a pluralistic contemporary my-thography replaces in such readings a carefully staged juxtaposition between fictional worlds and ontological landscapes, or between the conventions peculiar to a literary genre and the products of ethno-graphic research.

One may not entirely eschew the role of archetypes in order to under-stand the kind of alterity at work in *lo fantástico,* particularly upon recognizing, as one perhaps should, that fantasy products derive their continuing prominence from stereotypical and redundant features in cognitive experience. This fundamentally conservative aspect of fantasy usually becomes an excluded term in understanding Cortázar's stories. So excluded, it tends to keep plots suspended in the kind of dualistic recognition identified by Lacan with the Imaginary (*Écrits,* 89–101). To break away from the Imaginary's dual structures would seem to require relinquishing objects of interpretation on whose exposure the whole character of fantasy depends: fantasy is nothing if not fantasies. Arche-types fit a possible description of such objects: they are Janus-like. As commonly described, archetypes have a face that looks toward the ever-lasting but deferred immediacy that some significant objects are said to enjoy in the archaic transitional status explored by Melanie Klein and D. W. Winnicott (Grosskurth, *Melanie Klein,* 397–98). Simultaneously, archetypes face a horizon of indefinite transcendence, implicit in their definition as imperishable clusters of meaning and psychic force; such an aspect of force implies a charismatic notion of meaning in archetypal interpretation. The two perspectives fit within Lacan's combined notion of the Imaginary and the Symbolic, but without facing the more prob-lematic one of the Real. It would be within the Real that the conservative function of fantasy, as an excluded term in the dual structure of *lo fantástico,* could reappear in association with ethnographic knowledge. Ethnography contributes a specific context in which to control the abuse of fantasy that Nicolas Abraham and Maria Torok call "panfantasism," in attempting to restrict their own view of fantasy:

> If one agrees to use the term "reality" (in its metapsychological sense) for everything that acts on the psychic system so as to bring about a topographical alteration—whether through "endogenous" or "exogenous" constraint—one can reserve the term "fantasy" for any representation, belief, or body state working to the opposite

effect, that is, toward maintenance of the topographical *status quo.* Such a definition refers neither to content nor to formal characteristics but solely to the notion of fantasy—a conservative, preservative function, no matter how innovative in spirit it may be, how broad its field of action and how great its hidden compliance with wishes. . . . Fantasy is in essence narcissistic: rather than make an attack on the individual, it attempts to transform the world. The fact that it is often unconscious indicates, not that it is irrelevant, but that its frame of reference is a *secretly maintained* topography. (quoted in Lebovici and Widlocher, *Psychoanalysis in France,* 3–4)

Such a "secretly maintained topography" should be familiar to readers of *lo fantástico;* it is present in that zone of the story that surfaces (or overlaps) in sudden continuity with key elements of the plot, but that clearly belongs elsewhere, as it latches onto the character's individual experience without ever wholly revealing its own sources.

Ethnography brings into play social practices and beliefs which may be easily confused with fantasy and delusional states of an individual sort, rather than properly understood as elements of a contingent social reality in existence *elsewhere*—in the actual ethnographic setting where such practices and beliefs may operate as components of material and ideational existence. With a careful sense of how unsegregated (nonindividual) fantasies may function among other groups explored ethnographically, the interpreter can relocate the nexus between the narrative orders of fascination (the Imaginary) and interpersonal norms (the Symbolic). Besides an archetypal foreground or primitivist scenario in which desire and fantasy objects may lock into each other, such an ethnographic setting may signify the very opposite: loss, lack, unfulfillment, or the foreclosure of the Real as an element of individual (as opposed to group) existence in the reading of *lo fantástico.* By the same token, as successful as it may be in reworking fantasies and attributing origins to them, the psychoanalytic reading usually gives a formulaic and individual-specific account of social realities occluded by fantasy. Since the genre of *lo fantástico* offers an even more token glimpse of them, it might be better to supply the undeveloped social realities of a given story with what might be called the ethnographic Real.

Along these lines, the interpretation of "Bestiario" lends itself to two kinds of foregrounding, the archetypal and the ethnographic. Each looks at the phenomenon of incest from a different angle and with different results motivated by sensibilities seemingly at odds with each other. A preference for archetypes tends to see in incest a sign of mystery, a blend in which shame, resentment, and sheer desire join with a certain sense of being exempt from ordinary feelings and habits of the heart. Next to this mixture of dark sentiment and latent sublimity, any archetypal view of incest must also consider how Jung's masterwork, *Mysterium Coniunctionis* (1963), demonstrates the thematic and structural incestuousness of thought itself, of the psyche's rise into consciousness as it absorbs (as alchemy pretends to do) the basest of matters in pursuit of the most ethereal (it is in alchemy that brother-sister incest plays a crucial symbolic role emblematic of archetypal fusion). In this regard, incest would seem to represent an ultimate point of reference in the arcane universe of connections brought into view by archetypal interpretation. On the other hand, any ethnography of incest sensitive to complex manifestations of symbolic meaning should recognize degrees of interconnection among different instances of marked or forbidden behavior, in which the incest prohibition cuts across and wires together sectors of ordinary existence.

Incest beliefs may involve "various forms of adultery between allies or illicit sexual relations between unrelated individuals, but also those that involve menstruation, sexual relations with prepubescent girls, with women during their periods, with women who are nursing, all of which involve the relations among the humors (sperm, blood, milk) and the functions of the body (Héretier, Izard and Smith, *Between Belief and Transgression*, 155). With this in mind, one may posit two different ethnographies of incest applicable to "Bestiario": one wherein the cast of characters (centered on the figure of Isabel) provides the domestic setting for a contemporary ethnography of family incestuousness in which extended ties of kinship have been reduced to a few surviving elements; and another wherein the same situation is set against a kinship background regulated by norms of descent bordering on incestuousness but rigidly established to avoid it. Ultimately, both types of ethnographies could merge.

Before applying the ethnographic model, the archetypal view may be studied in terms of an inherent internal predicament. The appeal of archetypes stems from their unrestrained faculty to naturalize and empower diffuse meanings under one main function or name. Accordingly, literary characters may become infused with an archetypal significance that both enhances their respective individual identities and uplifts their value as extraordinary types. Rather than opening a gap between ordinary persons and their recognition as symbolic or allegorical types, such an interpretation asserts a continuous passage back and forth between two orders of being, in a manner that resembles (naïvely or by way of some stated doctrine) a basic faith in the force of charisma. Archetypal characters and situations claim a sort of preeminence analogous to that found in charismatic ensembles and individuals. However, a view quite different from this one may equally obtain in the use of archetypes for interpretation. Characters and situations may have the same force as in the first case, but at the expense of their ordinary identity, or at least at odds with it. As long as it represents a mere shift of emphasis, such a questioning of identity need not bother the essentialist or charismatic view of archetypes. But it can create a larger issue, one that should disturb archetypal interpretation in demonstrating its inherent lack of an autonomous object of analysis within any given narrative. This second view would demonstrate how an archetypal reading amounts to a case of suppressed intertextual reference, and how such a reading, when best achieved, should lead to an ontology of fictional persons in which no single individual could be marked by reference (such as a personal name implying his or her discrete existence) without undoing the textured ubiquity of the archetype.

Archetypes may be used to rescue personal fate from randomness and from imprisonment in triviality and sublunar sentiment. Two different critical versions of "Bestiario," each with its own brand of appeal, may illustrate the context of sentimental inference resolved by the essentialist view of archetypes. First, there is the interpretation of Armando Pereira in *Deseo y escritura* where, in the style of a modern gothic romance, Isabel is lured into spending another summer with the Funes family in the *estancia* of Los Horneros, where a lurid drama of stagnant passions awaits resolution.[6] A sister named Rema lives flanked by the indifference of her withdrawn brother Luis and the incestuous desires of her younger brother, el Nene, desires that find blatant and mysterious expression in the form of a tiger agreed by all to be at large in the house. The beast may represent "the image of el Nene when he contemplates Rema's body from the vantage point of a nameless desire, older than any language, which takes hold of his own body and devours it" (23). Besieged by el Nene's cannibal lust, Rema brings an offering ("ofrenda") into the Funes home in the person of the pubescent virgin Isabel, who will serve as "the sacrificial object" in a rite of expiation avoided by Rema, for whom it would represent an act of self-punishment and symbolic death (24). The perverse offering belongs to the same style of melodrama that engulfs the reader depicted in "Continuidad de los parques." Rema's gesture in begging Isabel to enter el Nene's bedroom with a jar of lemonade, "makes of the small Isabel a vicarious body that shall suffer in the skin, within the flesh, the effects of a desire that never concerns her. Victim of a subtle and perverse game that reaches beyond her, Isabel will carry, like the offering itself of her own body, the jar of lemonade to Nene's bedroom" (25).

Although Pereira's soap opera reading leaves unresolved the exact nature of el Nene's fall, it may easily solve the minor mystery of not knowing how to dispose of an incestuous body. In so doing, however, this passionate reading would have to deal with the story's major embarrassment, the tiger. It must also revise its own construction of a tiger fearfully different from the one occasionally mentioned in "Bestiario." Pereira's tiger should frighten and fascinate not because it is a real tiger living among the Funes, but because it embodies incest in a language overwrought with ambivalent feelings. The interpreter's version of "incest" underlines the creepy awesomeness of committing it at the expense of the routine norms and habits that forbid it. Thus the effervescent charm of incest displaces the ingrained taboo in which it is recognized as a transgression against the order of kinship and reproduction.

The melodramatic version of "Bestiario" relies on two different accommodations to the notion of incest as distinct from plain sexual abuse. In one, the inspired interpreter commits the equivalent of sentimental incest with the story as he applies himself upon its imaginary surfaces with great specular intensity. In the other, the incest taboo continues to support the major melodramatic assumption that crime is mysterious and elusively primal, rather than clumsy and devoid of charisma. As an object of propositional reference, the tiger centers both accommodations to the arcane and primitive: the one aping transgression with profuse language, the other signifying prohibition in charismatic terms. Hence, the tiger references commit readers of "Bestiario" to assumptions and anecdotes typical of the manner in which abstract prohibitions such as the incest taboo are believed to find reflection in actual feelings and acts. It seems that the tiger references can support the notion of taboo not with the sultry purpleness of melodrama, but as tokens of signification in which "the tiger" is falsely endowed with a story no one may know, and truthfully resonant with many others it cannot disclose in its present referential shape. In fact, "el tigre" always lacks an actual description. "Bestiario" *shows* the beast only as it is *reported* (or witnessed in the form of reports); it is never actually narrated in the act of being *seen,* or as it might have been seen. Readers of the tiger-beast in "Bestiario" take up a description not offered by the text but rather provoked by it.

Since the tiger burns brightly in the plot just beyond ordinary description, it should resemble archetypes. The surface of sentimental inference in "Bestiario" gives tacit support to the cooler mysteries of the archetypal view. In a second version of the story, Daniel R. Reddy draws a picture of Isabel's ordeal as a saga of symbolic initiation laid over a drama of psychic birth into wounded but wiser adolescence. In this view, the strongly linked figures of Rema and Isabel join the archetype of the Magna Mater activated in figures like the praying mantis. As females they must come to terms with their own incestuousness in dealing with the prosaic urging of the incestuous el Nene:

> Isabel seems to have no conscious understanding of her reasons for feeling such emotional attachment for Rema and hatred of el Nene, but her unconscious involvement in the conflict is made manifest in a number of ways, especially in her mental association of el Nene with a captive mantis which we are told "Isabel hubiera querido decapitar al mamboretá, darle un tijeretazo y ver qué pasaba [Isabel would have liked to cut the mantis' head off, a good snip with the scissors, and see what would happen]." We are reminded that the mantis is one of the insects whose females destroy the male by devouring him after they mate. Isabel also calls the mantis "bicho," a term which in some areas of Spanish America refers to the phallus. . . . [Isabel's] desire to destroy the mantis foreshadows her tricking of el Nene into the room with the tiger. . . . In a sense Isabel is representative of the mythic hero construct and has been involved in a rite of passage in which she has confronted the figurative dragon (el Nene) in her "Road of Trials" and has emerged victorious. . . . Rema represents the protective "Mother Goddess," corresponding to one aspect of the Magna Mater archetype. ("Through the Looking Glass," 126–27)

Proponents of archetypal analysis may want to improve or radically alter the basic elements of this construct, but they would likely do so while increasing, in detail and prominence, references of potential intertextual value more or less held under control in Reedy's restrained account. For instance, the phallic character of the mantis might work against any notion of a symbolic castration of the male that does not include the inextricable issue of a female empowered with a phallus. Setting aside the respective Freudian and Jungian theories on the phallic female, one may regard the mantis-mediated castration of el Nene as the first step in the binding together of individual identities into an archetypal ensemble intolerant of individuation or autonomous selfhood. Girl and young man would be bound forever at the center of the castration and phallic scene, much like the perpetrator and victim in a case of actual or imagined sexual abuse would tend to remain bound together in motivated fantasy. Rather than being analogous to Jung's interpretations in books like *Symbols of Transformation* (in which the psychic life of an individual comes under close comparative scrutiny with archaic religious myths), archetypal interpretations of stories like "Bestiario" differ remarkably from Jung's analyses in their lack of anything resembling a patient's life or writings. If Jung's ultimate goal lies in describing Mrs. Miller's rich fantasies in order to (among other things) outline a theory of psychic differentiation from primal incestuousness, archetypal views of "Bestiario" might in fact work toward the opposite goal, that of denying that Isabel or any character could ever possess meaning outside the narrated situations in which the force of archetypes has taken hold. For the author of *Symbols of Transformation,* an actual patient existed, differentiated from her own writings and Jung's account of her psychic ordeal; for the analyst of archetypes in "Bestiario," it is not simply a question of there being no Isabel outside the story, but rather of there being no authentic references to her unless they are archetypally empowered by being firmly interlocked with key elements of plot and character in the story.

It follows that the richer such archetypal character constructs become, the more their details should demonstrate the intransferable nature of the characters constructed as interlocking types. Unless at bottom frivolous, appeals to archetypes cannot regard their chosen literary plots with indifference; plots should communicate to the archetypist exigencies not otherwise released (and in all likelihood denied) to those not persuaded by the theory. Even the most casual reading of Jung should make clear the momentous transference of energies he perceived in identifying the presence of archetypes. It so happens that "Bestiario" could lead to just such a transfer, or to a deepening of its own archetypes through intertextual supplement. Lack of evidence for Cortázar ever having read Roger Caillois's "La mante religieuse" (*Le Mythe et l'homme*, 35–83) should not deter archetypal analysis; rather, it should come as proof of the theory's view of psychic structures reorganizing themselves above and below individual mediation until reaching a point of coalescence in a given archetype. The relative nexus between essay and story should be held reversible, on archetypal grounds: Caillois wrote something in typological kinship with "Bestiario."

"La mante religieuse" makes blind reference to the archetype, phrasing it in a different key: "La mante se présente comme une sorte d'idéogramme objectif réalisant matériellement dans le monde extérieur les virtualités les plus tendancieuses de l'affectivité" [The mantis comes forth as a kind of objective ideogram materially achieving upon the external world the most biased among the potentials of affectivity] (80). With Bergson rather than Jung in mind, Caillois strives to frame his mythographic portrait of the praying mantis in materialist terms. Yet he perceives in the "ideogram" figures of accumulated lore (like the mantis) becoming *windows,* ensembles built by psychic forces and habits of the mind with no other terminal reference than themselves, figures expressive of how organisms imprint on a continuum of matter their transient singularity.

In a mutual exchange of archetypal elements, "La mante religieuse" and "Bestiario"[7] would share the following elements of myth and folklore. First, as a figure of prophetic wisdom and *mantic* powers, the insect is predominantly though not exclusively female: a seer, goddess, or daemon. Caillois refers to "the name of *mantis,* prophetess, that the ancients gave the animal" (37); and inscribed in his title one finds a pun on the notion of a *female religious lover.* Isabel's nocturnal visions are homologous with mantic receptivity toward forces unseen by others; at the "hora de las caras," her vision captures faces and serves as a theater where other characters merge in transmographic and partial form. But, above all, Rema's hands and fingers have what Lacan (*Concepts of Psycho-Analysis,* 73ff.) would call a *scopic* rapport with Isabel's visual experiences, suggesting a magical transfer between tactile and ocular talents: "[A]nd also Rema's soft hands—she saw them coming out of the darkness, she had her eyes open and instead of Nino's face—zap! [*zas!*]—Rema's hands" ("Bestiario," 78).

Second, the mantis protects and guides lost children: "The little beast [*la bestiole*] is considered so divine that, upon being questioned by children who have lost their way, she shows them the right path extending the finger" (37–38). Caillois traces the mantis's folklore back to religious beliefs widely scattered among native food gatherers and pastoralists in southern Africa, who worshipped the insect as a daemon of the hunt and believed that the small finger was the mantis's youngest daughter. Isabel squeezes Rema's fingers twice in what amounts to the strongest gesture of female bonding in the plot, in sharp contrast with el

Nene's similar gesture of harassment. The two females form a triad with the child Nino, who plays the hunter; the three figures would fall within the role of benefactress played by the mantis, a role exclusively assigned by Jungian allegorists to the dominant archetype of the Magna Mater.

Third, the praying mantis is better known as a spectacular mirror of sexual perversion. The surrealists—Paul Eluard in particular—engaged in a virtual cult of the insect's mating dance (Rubin, *Dada,* 220; Pressly, "Praying Mantis," 600–615). Caillois devotes much space to illustrate the merging of "la volupté sexuelle et la volupté nutritive" (51) in the female mantis, her return to "un cannibalisme sexuel primitif" (54), and the rapport between these features and "sexual desire as a kind of protoplasmic hunger" (57). The theme of erotic hunger introduces a young female protagonist into Caillois's essay: first, giving the *love bite* ("la morsure d'amour"), like "those women who sketch [*esquissent*] the behavior of the praying mantis, and above all, certain idiot girls and females from savage races" (57); and second, concerning the taboo of virginity, as the *Giftmädchen* or poisoned maiden ("pucelle venimeuse"), whose love bite or maiden blood would kill her groom (57, 64–65).

Fourth, these elements in Caillois's mythography are less alien to "Bestiario" than it might seem, particularly if earnest attention is paid to the story's archetypal texture. As if holding a kaleidoscope, three important interpretations influence the plot as seen from Isabel's viewpoint. *She is the catalyst of change in Los Horneros;* on her, the stagnant, ingrown relations among the Funes reflect themselves and break into the open. As an *actant,* she can compare with Mauss's notion of turbulence in primitive gift-exchange; the same disturbance of interpersonal relations obtains when her role as intruder is viewed in actantial fashion, falling in between each character. Also, due either to her own nascent sexual feelings or, as some would have it, to a perverse or desperate intent on Rema's part, *Isabel is a girl-offering to el Nene.* In fact, the noise of his agony at the end could have, among several interpretations, the one that Caillois might have adduced from folklore: the young man dies the horrible death of those who do not properly manage their way around the taboo of virginity. Rema, acting as a terrible Queen or Witch-Mother, would send her daughter—bearing the poison of *aconitum ferox*—into a nuptial night with someone she wants destroyed; poison (*Gift, Giftmädchen*) being among Mauss's privileged etymologies for the hidden threats contained in gift-giving (Caillois, 64–65). Finally, *Isabel bites.* El Nene's mouth shows up in her visions with iconic intensity, by turns cruelly appealing, voracious, and grotesquely cloacal, as if representing the body's navel, revealed to Isabel like a point of linkage between her visions and the pull of anamorphosis. In prelude to the crisis when el Nene beats Nino in a sadistic display in front of Rema, and just before she kicks the ball that shatters the window glass and brings the punishment of the child, Isabel bites off a terebinth leaf and spits it out in disgust.

According to this evidence, Caillois's "La mante religieuse" reinforces the essentialist or charismatic view of archetypes by simply adding a wealth of fascinating lore to the minimal but highly enhanced intervention of the praying mantis in the plot of "Bestiario." His essay shows how archetypists might risk frivolity by having to sit on the Pandora's box they themselves have opened. The mirror of intertextuality blocks their path to the collective unconscious. In this case, an unquestionably male *mamboretá* would not escape being foreshadowed in the flurry and fury of female prestige that folk traditions (sufficiently ancient to claim entry as archetypes) have bestowed on a certain species of uncanny insects.

Whether or not it was read by Cortázar and inscribed in the text of "Bestiario" by the sheer migratory force of archetypes, "La mante religieuse" contains a reference that only a devoted reader of the story would appreciate. When Caillois mentions that a fanciful writer has called the praying mantis the *feline among insects* ("le félin des insectes"), one might hear archetypes in "Bestiario" quaking with joy at how brightly paper tigers might burn.

Structuralism can be fulfilled only if it places itself in opposition to something other—*and marries it.—James A. Boon,* Other Tribes, Other Scribes

If structuralist anthropology can indeed find fulfillment only in contractual reproductive linkage with something other, the fictional mode of *lo fantástico* might do likewise. Hence, in this section an attempt is made to understand some salient features of "Bestiario" in terms of the structures of kinship. When "Los venenos" was examined according to marriage symbols of wife-giving and the brother/sister dyad, attention could not focus on any overt theme or disturbing sign of incestuousness as it may now do with respect to "Bestiario." Moreover, the few essentials of kinship known about the Funes family refer at least to one generation of marriage-related events situated vertically above the one child in the plot (Nino). References and conjectures involving the Funes' current household head (Luis) and his absent wife may serve as a focal point to construct a view of kinship as it might have existed had the family belonged to a network of groups bound by strict rules in the reciprocal exchange of spouses between interrelated couples and lines of descent.

In kinship terms, what is left of the Funes family includes three parallel siblings and a child: an older brother (Luis) and his son (Nino), a younger brother-uncle (el Nene), and a sister-aunt (Rema). Assuming that Nino descends from a female who at some point was his father's lawful wife, one may assume that either death, flight from home, rejection by her husband, or a mere matrimonial split would have to account for the absence of the child's uterine parent from the family residence. By the same token, the absence of Nino's father from home would have underscored the custodial importance of the two individuals closest to such a uterine base: Rema and el Nene, presumably womb-siblings to Luis. In fact, although not absent from the Funes house, Nino's father performs at the formal periphery of the child's world; his authority over Nino applies less to the child's actions as unsheltered by play than to the shelter itself that play may always provide. If Luis's title as Nino's father were to be dropped from the text, his gentle avunculate toward the child would lose all traces of the strong patrilineal blood relation already attenuated by the father's present attitude of distant custody. In other words, a more complex structure in kinship affairs might have placed Luis in a father-position indifferent to the synthesis of feelings and moral claims present within the so-called nuclear family, feelings and moral claims not much in evidence in the behavior of Luis toward Nino in "Bestiario." Luis behaves toward Nino in ways reminiscent of the diminished role assigned to fathers in relation to their sons in some matrilineal systems, a role mediated by the custodial strength of the maternal uncle over his sister's son relative to the man (the nonmatrilinear parent) whom his sister should marry. But since Rema has married no one that we know of, and since Luis's wife is both missing and obviously not el Nene's sister, the matrilineal nexus seems wholly absent in Nino's and el Nene's case—uncannily absent.

A worthwhile account of kinship tensions in "Bestiario" should reach beyond references to incest and be able to give contextual value to some missing links. Hence, the Freudian view of the mother's absence and of her fantasy makeup (absent mother = Rema) should be set aside in favor of a more comprehensive view of the kinship network. The absence of the father's wife should link with the active role of his sister, just as the latter's motherly role as aunt to his son should link with her own lack of husband and child, and with the parallel lack of wife and issue affecting her other brother, her nephew's would-be matrilinear uncle. Luis has a missing wife just as he has an active sister (in Rema) who plays the absent role of mother, but who is also an unmarried sister that would otherwise have her own husband and child, and who is pestered by a brother (el Nene) who resembles her in being equally deprived of spouse and uterine descent. Custodial rivalry between a brother and a sister (both of whom lack children to offer in marriage) represents the beginning of an ethnographic fantasy not content with "incest" as a single answer to a conflict marked by gaps and riddled with fictional ambiguity. The issue of sibling rivalry—not incest—might be the answer found in "Bestiario" by the expectations of one looking at the plot from within a so-called archaic system of kinship exchange whose mode of absence from the story might be regarded as relative rather than absolute, and as such as both fantastic and real within currently or formerly established social practices.

To recognize the viewpoint of such an ancestral witness to the story, one can look at the Funes siblings from the perspective of social groups bound by rules of kinship based on the exchange of sisters in bilateral cross-cousin marriage. Parallel to the standard view of incest in "Bestiario" in which Rema and el Nene are locked in a struggle between autonomy and bondage, the cross-cousin network of virtual and strictly prescribed marriages would hold the brother-sister pair in fixed positions with respect to how (or with whom) their children may marry. Following James Boon's account of the system in *Other Tribes, Other Scribes* (94–97), one would have each of the Funes siblings marrying "the child of his mother's brother *and* father's sister" (95). Thus Luis's unknown wife would have been the daughter of his *paternal* aunt and *maternal* uncle; Rema would have to marry a brother of that same unknown wife; el Nene (excluded from marrying her) would marry a sister of that same missing woman *and* of Rema's husband; and Nino's future wife (by rule, the daughter of his maternal uncle and paternal aunt) would be Rema's daughter (but never el Nene's) by the brother of Nino's missing mother.

Beyond such trivial but necessary links, a fundamental nucleus of transpersonal identity—an atom composed of two paired and inalienable persons and utterances—serves as the base for the entire system, in a manner that resembles and articulates the deictic marriage of anonymous pronoun voices never resolved in the fictional world of "Cefalea." Instead of *one of us . . . the other*, the filial and female prenuptial utterance implied in the atom of kinship would run: *I am your mother's brother's daughter in being your father's sister's daughter.* In avoiding (at such close range) brother-sister incest, the network of cross-cousin marriage may imply an absurd utterance involving a double-being, or someone who might say: *I am mother's brother's daughter in being father's sister's daughter,* signifying two children of parallel brother-sister incests, who join the two pairs of parental siblings by the navel cord of a single dual-child.

A less chimeric or monstered issue concerns el Nene. In his case, being the *paternal* uncle of Luis's children means that they could not marry his own children. In Rema's case, however, both brothers could marry their children to hers. As Boon puts it, since every spouse "is the child of someone categorized as both mother's brother *and* father's sister," the two actors of parental rule form a single entity, they "are undifferentiated, generalized" (95) through all lines of descent. And, one may add, they collapse the rules of difference to a point of maximum resemblance to incest and of elementary insistence on avoiding it.

El Nene's role as a token of perverse in-house incest must now be understood in a different light. The wife whom el Nene has not married is akin to Luis's own absent spouse. The children whom el Nene has not had impinge on Nino, the child obtained by el Nene's older brother, Luis. Also, the daughter whom el Nene might have produced could have married the son whom Rema has not begotten (or el Nene's nonexistent son could have married Rema's nonexistent daughter). At the same time, Nino could marry one of Rema's daughters, but never a daughter produced by el Nene. Thus, from the point of view of the one real child in the story (Nino), the *atom of kinship* in relation to which he may elect (or be given) a wife would be the one made up of Rema (Nino's *paternal* aunt), her husband (Nino's *maternal* uncle), and their children, rather than that made up of el Nene (Nino's *paternal* uncle) and his wife. Within this structural kinship view, the custodial role of Rema toward the other childlike presence in the story (exogamous Isabel) signifies her nurturing of the daughter she might have had, and whom Nino might have married (just as one of el Nene's sons might have). In the end, Isabel becomes most interesting in the symbolic role of a *missing* daughter next to an only child (Nino) by an *absent* mother (an imaginary wife, who is absent as Luis's spouse, but who is also turned into a tacit widow in Rema and, uncannily, into a sort of spectral virgin). In the transpersonal logic of myth, Rema's virginity *is* Isabel as the daughter of virgin-birth, and as the widow whose lost spouse seems to be marriage itself. Rema's complex role should be understood by regarding her link with Luis's missing wife as the *virginal widowhood* of one who has never married and who never will, unless by breaking ranks with the system of kinship in order to marry a brother who neither Luis nor el Nene seem fit to represent.

Returning to Boon's notion of exogamy between structuralism and some other entity, the question of incest between the anthropological view and what he calls "German philosophic-poetic Romanticism" promptly adds an endogamous twist to the affair of marrying "Bestiario" to a real ethnographic fantasy. In other words, *lo fantástico* might descend aesthetically from stories that were first written in the philosophical environment of German idealism and its romantic contexts. Then, in being read through a fantasy of kinship based on structuralist notions of exchange, "Bestiario" may provide structuralism with a home for the fleshless, uncharismatic networks it routinely constructs as elements of social design. In so doing, "Bestiario" may offer its own legacy of romantic storytelling as a lost sibling to structuralism's ingrown tendency to reduce social practices to immanent rules and designs of increasing abstractness. Marrying a stranger as one might a lost sibling is an affair in which *lo fantástico* could reaffirm its own siblinghood with German romanticism, by way of the fiction of Hoffmann and Kleist and Freud's "The Uncanny," married to the structuralist study of myth as a symbolic practice.

A Tiger Is Being Beaten

There once was a knight full of sorrow and doubt . . .
—*Heinrich Heine,* Lyrical Intermezzo

"Las armas secretas" belongs to the darkest zone in Cortázar's vision of the uncanny.[8] The plot involves the reenactment of rape and retribution, the return of the dead, and the destruction of ordinary innocence. It poses questions of trauma, defilement, and guilt. Can someone be raped or the rape be avenged only once? Can it be that the one raped but not killed is less a survivor than the rapist killed in punishment for the crime? By the compulsion to see the act repeated, does a certain view of rape endeavor to have the rapist raped by his own actions—just as rapists would have their victims guilty of their own rape? Should rape more so than incest induce suicide? These Ambrose Bierce-type questions might lack grounds or be dismissed as nonsense outside the story, but inside "Las armas secretas" they are begged in stubborn contract with fantasy.

Pierre is in love with and wants to make love to Michèle, who seems to avoid sexual intimacy with him. When the occasion comes for them to enjoy such intimacy, the encounter aborts: Pierre turns into a sadist, and Michèle rejects him in anger and pain. He leaves the scene as she phones her friends. Pierre's eventual return to the scene and the friends' arrival would coincide in a manner incongruent with the situation explained in this simple account. In fact, no simple account of "Las armas secretas" is possible, for Pierre is not only the frustrated lover of a resisting woman; he is also the German soldier who raped her in her own bedroom a few years earlier, and who was caught and put to death by members of the French resistance not far from the house. Besides being one with the body of the man who would rape, Pierre lies in the corpse of the executed rapist. Likewise, the German soldier dwells inside Pierre, who does *not* commit rape, but relives it as a psychic victim possessed by the soldier. The actual rape event remains untold, as does Pierre's execution. The simplest outcome of the plot lies untold in the reader's imagination of it: Pierre's death and the experience of dying violently. Sinister tensions and feelings of horror and moral dread are deprived of a retributive outlet if Pierre's death is missing. His death though remains untold and unsevered from the German soldier's prior crime and punishment.

Thus far one confronts a dual, receding structure always ending with a missing link: a rapist found in a soldier, a rapist-soldier found in a man who seems far from being a rapist or a Nazi soldier. This is the same man who dies the untold death that the soldier's own dying provides with an actual and antecedent story. Pierre's death is left without actual narration; it has been strictly framed within that of the soldier. It seems that once told, death may recur. In having the soldier's death as antecedent, Pierre's execution by the same people who killed the soldier belongs to the type of dying that copies another dying, and that, repeating itself in someone else's consciousness, suggests the reflexive fate of suicide.

Repeated retribution follows upon repeated rape. Rape in uniform, linked by proxy to a war machine of men who thought they could conquer the world as members of a superior brotherhood. The German Romantic plot may boil down to this: a youth who might have loved a pastoral lyric song by Heine and Schumann about "the fires of love awakened" in "the magic month of May," becomes a "Nazi" soldier who rapes a young Frenchwoman. The French side of the plot may be seen as follows: a young man can only become a Nazi warrior by dressing like one, perhaps for the sole purpose of committing rape with a double degree of perversion, but also as a fantasy of punishment on himself or suicide. The double plot unfolds from pastoral love to the ruins of rape, from green May to what feels in the end like the soil of dark November. Rape takes place in uniform or in disguise; innocence is perverted, ruined, killed again and again, as many times as it might take suicide to rehearse its own release from the impasse of perversion. (Thus, the notion of shifting from individuals to compulsive entities such as rape and suicide may define a key aspect of the uncanny in the mold of *lo fantástico.*)

What is being proposed is not that a delusional pervert named Pierre commits suicide dressed as a Nazi soldier who brags about Aryan supremacy and has (or believes he has) raped a woman. Interest does not lie in suggesting an actual event but in pondering the repetition of a compulsive event within another one claimed to have actually occurred in the plot. Further interest lies in the embarrassed thrill that follows enjoying the rape/murder plot while being unable to rationally consent to its uncanny suggestions. As in the case of Pierre's death, the plot does not need the missing part it leaves for the reader to find or to accept as given but not told. Just as Pierre must ultimately die, the return of the dead soldier to the scene of his crime and death must be held as real, precisely in order to undo the unrealness (to the very insistence of which the real itself owes its compulsory claim to exist).

In "Las armas secretas," the real exists by compulsion. Seen through the mechanisms of compulsiveness, events never take place sufficiently, not even through ceaseless reiteration. If Michèle is raped a second time, she would already have been raped a second time, even if for the first time ever: raped in the time that haunts Pierre's conscience as he tries to make love to her for the first time and fails, because the man who already raped her is about to rape her a second time. One only dies a first time, but when death comes to Pierre it also comes to one ready to die a second time, one who is both (the) soldier and Pierre. Without Pierre's death, the soldier does not return; without the soldier's death, Pierre does not die. In what might be called Pierre-specific compulsiveness, Michèle was not killed by her rapist, nor did she kill herself. Mention of Michèle's survival—or of her not surviving—might seem redundant and unfounded in light of the plot's need of her life as a traumatized victim of rape. Yet Michèle's life is as compulsory as the rapist's return and Pierre's death. In the plot, secret weapons are aimed at the undead, at life compulsively lived and thus repeated. The plot hinges on who holds the secret weapons and on whom they are aimed.

In war and peace, rape behaves repetitiously. By dint of its inherent cruelty and addictiveness, rape is vicious and repetitive; it is a spreading fault. Perversion structures rape as one among many forms of repetitive compulsion. Suicide (perverse or not) may show features of the same compulsion to repeat. Obvious fear of dying may not be the only factor involved in rehearsing suicide; one suicide often copies another, as it may copy and play with itself. Also, the chance to see one's own corpse slain might play a role in sadistic serial murder, a phenomenon often driven by self-hatred and a deferred need for self-destruction, for death by installments. Death refigured and disfigured, repossessed and repositioned, staged and reviewed. Sibling rivalry between love and hate. Love, confused and ruined, hating death the way only mothers can be hated (and feared).

The union of opposites, of man and woman, may have the form of a syllogistic copulation. More precisely, this syllogistic copulation unites two syllogisms into one single one and thus produces the ethical reign. . . . The copulation of these two "opposite movements" appeases nothing. There's no reconciliation. . . . The scene of the crime being opened between two laws (singularity/universality, woman/man), being read according to its two codes [sur ses deux tableaux], there is no murder that is not the (ethical) effect of the sexual opposition. Every crime is a sexual and family operation.—Jacques Derrida, Glas

The philosophical claim unearthed by Derrida in Hegel's arguments puts crime in a Freudian enclosure. But the reverse applies with greater force: exorbitant and beyond experiment, the highest arguments and fables of idealism can add to psychoanalytic insights (burdened as they are with the need to resist testing) a sovereign disdain toward the gossip of proof. Faced with an object of study lacking an actual patient such as "Las armas secretas," psychoanalysis might become half-Socrates half-midwife in searching for insights, as if the story contained fragments, hysteric kernels of a belated idealist birth. One is reminded of Lévi-Strauss's analysis of the "Sorcerer and His Magic" (*Structural Anthropology*, 161–80), where a woman's lengthy labor finds help in the shaman's enactment of a therapeutic myth proffered as if possessed by a case of doctrinal hysteria, since the myth involves his own disciplined symbolic appropriation of pregnancy and labor. Inducing idealist labor through psychoanalytic insight involves products of fantasy released in partial analytic shape and lacking any definite narrative outcome; the model comes not from obstetrics, but from the birth of hysteria.

Beginning with insights into perversion, elements in "Bestiario" and "Las armas secretas" would undergo specific modifications in light of

Freud's "A Child Is Being Beaten" (*Works*, 17:177–204). Freud's complex view of the sources of perversion includes the choice of parents as objects of sexual attachment, modulations of sadism and masochism, the presence of guilt, and the reenactment in fantasy of a scene in which the child either actively or vicariously takes part in an act of beating in the shifting roles of victim, punisher, and witness. In "Bestiario," with Isabel as protagonist, el Nene's beating of Nino would involve her in incestuous attachment to the father, an individual not wholly unrelated to Luis but by force fantasied in el Nene's perverse wishes and fears. Setting aside for the moment Isabel's strong involvement in the climactic scene of el Nene's punishment by the tiger, analytic insight would break direct contact with matters of perversion (as focused on Isabel) in order to review el Nene's perverse sexual need for Rema. Incestuously attached to his mother and embedded in her, el Nene becomes childlike and takes possession of the two beating fantasies, first the child's and then the tiger's. Linked to a specific chapter of analytic insight, Isabel and el Nene (on each side of sexual difference) would act as main points of reference for two different stories severed from their respective births and developments. The same can be said about the sibling-related and incest-based view of Pierre and Michèle in "Las armas secretas," a story invariably interpreted only at the more manifest level dominated by two men linked by rape to a subordinate, home-bound woman. Each story generates a fantasied rejection of sexual difference whenever the seemingly fragile option of reading either as if fractured by sex and gender remains unfulfilled. Whenever products of *lo fantástico* are not brought under psychoanalytic scrutiny, the issue of sexual difference is left exposed but ignored: fantasy is viewed but not projected in specific details. Fantasies lose an important claim to our attention when they are not narrated or projected in detail: fantasy is nothing if not narration.

The following set of assumptions testifies to the complex variations of plot elements involved in reading by projecting an alternate order of narrated fantasy. In Nene's case, incest becomes rape (and punishment by the tiger suicide) when the plot of "Bestiario" links in terms of sexual difference with "Las armas secretas." Likewise, rape (Pierre's or the soldier's) becomes incest (and a hidden suicide being killed by relatives) when the plot of "Las armas secretas" links in terms of domestic strife with "Bestiario." In other words, the intimacy of incest sought by el Nene in a mother turns into the alien but familiar crime of raping Rema; the compulsion to repeat or to restage rape that possesses Pierre turns into a sign of incest with a woman he always finds either at home or missing from it. Transfer of the death drive onto a punishing beast (which he symbolically resembles) becomes el Nene's form of suicide. In Pierre's case, the incestuous sibling's suicide (or that of a mother's son) becomes his own death at the hands of avenging parents. Rape would be punished in Nene's beastly suicide or tiger-death, as incest would in Pierre's killing by parents repeated (Michèle's parents, who exist far from home, and Roland and Babette, custodians who are never far from the house and always return to it as avengers).

A scandalizing question traverses the text. How, in sum, is a brother possible? How can one have two sons [fils]? How can one be the father of two phalli, erected one against the other? How can one have a brother? How can two beings of the same sex cohabit in one family? . . . Two males can, for example, belong to the same litter. But precisely because they are not brothers. Brothers are not possible in nature.

But not in culture either. So brotherhood must find accommodation between nature and culture. The figure of monstrosity: passing on to culture, brotherhood has to disappear violently. Two brothers going head to head can only kill themselves.—Jacques Derrida, Glas

In closing, we may reconsider the opening questions, now framed by the intertextual reading of "Las armas secretas." (1) In the criminal and guilt-ridden mind, twice-told parents are the ones who hold the secret weapons, weapons aimed at incestuous lovers receding back into childhood within a single family. (2) The same haunted mind sees females (whether as siblings or mothers) as tokens of homeliness and *unhomeliness*. As such, as a gendered product, femaleness stretches all the way from the oldest core of fantasied intimacy to the outer reaches of incestuous reference. All forms of self-involvement (incest and suicide included) are implicitly gendered female *by implied maleness only*. (3) On one side, home-brothers are the sons (or the split son) of mothers only. On the other side, such a minimal domestic brood of two males (or a single one) becomes in itself a dual father's affect, one half of whose lust is aimed at his own daughter. The locked together brother-types can only rape incestuously, and always across what represents less a gender gap than a gendered annexation of femaleness through incest. To such an Oedipal negotiation of incorporative incest corresponds what might be called the *excorporative* solution: the simultaneous embodiment and disembodiment of fear of homoerotic desire, transformed into urge and dread inspiring suicide. (4) Thus rape always appears to come from abroad, as if from outside the house, from brotherhood and war; and yet it all remains in the family. Thus Michèle will not come to Pierre's room, just as Isabel does (and as Rema does not) come to el Nene's room, and just as Pierre may not come to Michèle's bed, bearing with him rape's built-in repetitiveness.

Such analytic (and abstracting) answers should lead to a sequence of further propositions and questions in the form of a protonarrative and its commentary:

> Pierre hurts Michèle's little dog, just as el Nene hurts Nino, just as a tiger kills el Nene, just as Pierre dies a soldier's death. Could mother Rema be a soldier's widow—but by rape and by its punishment only? Could sister Rema be the widow, not to a dead soldier, but to a soldier turned alien by war's brotherhood? And could this son of warring brotherhood stage his own return, not as that of a husband gone to war, but as a brother ready to commit incest—yet incest as desperately *other* than rape?

> But, as "mothers," "daughters," and "sisters" are raped by a prodigal actor who comes home, there might not be incest, for this crime may happen only as the fantasies portrayed in *lo fantástico* fulfill their idealist range and send the family abroad, beyond its own realm. As if it were the orphan child of some savage and ancient kinship norm, fantasy comes to recognize in rape the only form left in which to ground the power once felt and enacted in nonroutine incest practices. Like rape, incest is always extramural yet homely.

In the end, a Freudian ending, it is whenever woman is raped that there is always incest: rape procreates incest, it repeats incest as if for the first time and as a *womanizing,* a woman-making act.

These bizarre offerings might represent Hegel's truth more than Freud's fantasies. In light of such truth and such fantasies, one may offer the following solutions to the compulsive crimes shown in *lo fantástico.*

> Suicide's own desire incestuously loves and hates a life that is bound to the wish to give itself an ending.
> Suicide's own driving urge confuses individual fate with parent-hood, and thus requires life itself to be orphaned.
> Suicidal compulsion tries to reach out for a missing corpse in the same way in which one searches for oneself as a lost child.
> Self-destruction (ruled by family fantasies, as insistently veiled and

exposed in *lo fantástico*) becomes a closing figure for the consciousness of orphanhood as a peculiar idealist response to social forlornness.

Issuing from a reflection on its own ending and closure, fantasy fades out as a wish-bound form of incestuously raping loneliness.

Part

Three

The

Confessional

Self

4

The Raven

and the

Writing Desk:

A Biographic

View of **Yo el**

Supremo

*The Hatter opened his eyes very wide on hearing
this; but all he said was "Why is a raven like a
writing-desk?"*
—*Lewis Carroll,* Alice's Adventures in Wonderland

> *—married with my uncle,*
> *My father's brother—but no more like my father*
> *Than I to Hercules. Within a month,*
> *Ere yet the salt of most unrighteous tears*
> *Had left the flushing in her galled eyes,*
> *She married . . .*
> —*William Shakespeare,* Hamlet *(1.2.151–56)*

If it were not for the tragedy he rushes into, Hamlet's childhood would be the longest in literature. Stepping on comic soil (Plautus's *Amphitryon*), Hercules's half-brother would not be Jupiter's son, like the hero, but a mere mortal—a mortal son of a mortal father who left his wife pregnant and went to war. The son had been but three months in his mother's womb when a strange, semidivine twin came to share it with him, younger than him by a haunting measure of hysteric time. But by the same divine powers that made Jupiter resemble the departed husband lying with Alcmena, the two half-brothers would both leave the mother's womb in a pinch, instead of the hero trailing the mere mortal not just within a month's span but across the loneliness of three. Being thus trailed by the greatest demigod in ancient myth should prove enough hard labor to extend tragedy into farce—and childhood into old age, within a comedy of errors.

Yo el Supremo enters *Hamlet* at the grave diggers scene, but through several other instances of mythic resonance, Roa Bastos's novel incorporates the saga of the raving prince into the making of a life always as fresh as a newborn babe and as brittle as an old skull or an ancient parchment. Prenatal childhood is bound in the nutshell of a lunar skull and recollected by a man lying on his deathbed, a man whose memories make him older than the telling of the first myth, a man haunted by and chasing after lives he has impounded in his womb-brain. Hamlet's is one of several lives (literary and historical) given farcical and grotesque shape within the Supreme's gestation as a cosmic person; they are lives seen on comic parade even as they express the tragic urge to speak of higher sorrows. No person in the novel escapes the fate of its protagonist; like the Supreme, everyone, even foreigners, become aspects of the Country. Paraguay lost, Paraguay regained; a country's biography growing like wild seed in the potted life of its bachelor founding father. An American Thebes, seeded with the bones of warriors and reduced tribes, burdens the personal myth of a tyrant with the chronicles of a tragic national history. Inseparable, at least in the text of the novel, the life of José Gaspar Rodríguez de Francia and the birth of his nation survive modes of storytelling and textual mediation in which notions of *life, birth,* and *nation* sink into levels of significance too archaic to sustain them whole. Not a single mortal coil, individual or communal, but the endless issuing of a coiled *biogram* gives tragic character and grotesque shape to the spiral textures of *Yo el Supremo.*

Hiding at Birth: Mortinatality

The undiscover'd country, from whose bourn
no traveller returns, puzzles the will. . . .
—*William Shakespeare,* Hamlet

I play dead. I open the door of my tomb a crack. I draw the tumulus open. It parts with a gritty granite sound. I open my eyes. I practice the simulacrum of my resurrection by raising myself up. Before me, He-who-is-sleepless. He-who-is-ageless. He-who-is-deathless. Keeping watch. Watching.—Augusto Roa Bastos, Yo el Supremo

So saida to Moyhammlet and marhaba to your Mount!
—*James Joyce,* Finnegans Wake

Hamlet returns to Denmark like an undelivered letter addressed to someone's death. At the grave site, he (*naked* in his letter of embassy to Claudius: "*I am set naked on your kingdom*") faces the royal jester's death's-head.[1] As skulls fly, Yorick's topmost insignia allows him paternal passage into prenatal comedy in the person of Tristram Shandy's uncle and hidden father, his name having been adopted as a rubric of the prebendary of York, Thomas Sterne. Rescued by comedy from at least two deaths, Yorick's would become "the most famous talking skull in literary history" (Macksey, 1,013; Monkman, passim). In line with such antecedents, one may knock twice on old Philology's door with the request to bury four skulls in one labeled *Yorick-Rorik-Roricus-Rodríguez*. *Yo* would of course be *I*, but an *I* named *Yo Rick*. The *rick*, as in a certain stick (*rodrigón*), would be driven into the ground to support a young plant, and by accident and secondary influence be linked to *Rodrigo*, and possibly to Gothic roots mixed with Latin and German words for setting straight, hoisting, stretching, ruling: *regere, rechen* (Corominas, *Diccionario crítico*, 4:51–52). *Yo* bears no name, while *Rick* pricks the air out of patronymic pride. These nonsensical trademarks would have passed for common bits of dialogue if Hamlet (nearing eighty) had survived (in Paraguay) wrapped in constant verbal scrimmage with a secretary-amanuensis-clown, in whose dark ink the princely life had been written in the sacrificial characters of archaic comedy.

Our search for old Hamlet in Asunción begins by resetting the *Mousetrap*, still as a conscience-catcher but more as a trap door through which Hamlet and his retinue would migrate to an undiscover'd country (the Supreme's Capricornial bourn) where a single actor plays ventriloquist with the entire cast. Sole conduit, *viator*, and perpetual Voice, *el Supremo Dictador* plays a game of *I* and *He*, a cat-and-mouse wheeling round a name in hiding, *José Gaspar Rodríguez de Francia* being in fact a biographical and historical attribution restricted in *Yo el Supremo* to the alternate text of footnotes and documentary asides in which histories and legends become unpacked and checkmated by research. Otherwise, what prevails is an endless seesaw mounted on immobility: "*I* am not always *I*. The only one who doesn't change is *HE*. . . . Only *HE* remains, not losing an iota of his form, of his dimension, but rather, growing, increasing by himself [*de sí propio*]."[2] Either reflecting Spanish (*YES*) or English (*ITS*), the Supreme's power-performative (his signature-utterance) suggests a possible reduction to a sigil—or to sigla—not unlike that of H. C. Earwicker to HCE in James Joyce's *Finnegans Wake*.[3] Like Joyce's tavernkeeper, the Supreme (besieged father of a nation's breed) hides (inside his own boundless headfulness) from rumors and gossip that regenerate monstrously *there*, within that supra- and infraterritorial "tropped head" (head-of-heads), "Headth of Hosth" (*FW*, 34.6, 317.32). In *Finnegans Wake*, the Hosting Head listens to all in a dream, while in *Yo el Supremo* it remains in perpetual wakefulness, auditioning the realm. These are father-heads, father-twins, a tribe of

One. Someone is buried alive in his own paradox of oblivious omniscience. The head has become a limb, but all limbs offer false ends; what they touch and feel is all there is (it can be known but never changed). The monarch of Head drifts incestuously, led by the hand of nocturnal daughters, the muses of dreamscape's feast of yarns: "(since in this scherzarade of one's thousand one nightinesses that sword of certainty which would indentifide the body never falls) to indendifine the indivi-duone" (*FW*, 51.4–6). In fact, *Finnegans Wake* offers an acrostic sign for that "someone imparticular" (602.7) whom it would find in the Supreme by embedding HCE in "HeCitEncy! Your words grates on my ares" (421.23), a phrase that Patiño's amanuensis-blistered ears would not hesitate in relaying to his own reading eyes as *HeSeatsEncy*.

The Supreme's text also evokes Shakespeare's wordplay. The script of *Yo* appears prompted by a double *eye:* an *I perjured* by its blind control of a *conjured I*. In the context of the Sonnets, perjury involves *eyes* caught in the egotistic blindness of personal pronouns through which treacherous praise and seductive insult coil themselves round a homoerotic lover and a dark female of awful powers. In *Yo el Supremo*, intimacy with *I* and *eyes* falls to perjury, particularly under the sway of deliriously debunked women-ladies, mothers, and would-be lovers who could represent (if they would but *speak*) the only persons ever to address the *Yo* of the Supreme as *tú*, except for the invisible *corrector,* whose meddling hand in the Supreme's private writings cannot be severed from his own, and from the voice of the accusing historiographic reader who addresses the Dictator's death at the end (see Krysinski, 48–52). The *tú* mode of address (involving the Supreme) belongs exclusively to a complex register of biographic self-absorption; it does not reflect independence from him; it neither belongs to a realm of performing voices nor to any dramatized, autonomous characters who would act beyond the Supreme's encompassing consciousness. The Supreme-being-of-narration constitutes a one-person-centered plot of conjured-up characters acting as third-person designations and embowered in a single mind. Thus references to *Yo* remain hitched to *he* and *him* designations, and to the *it* of authorial and authoritarian expression. A noncharacter (probably female) runs like a ghost through the fictional galleries of the text, the one character that might have called José Gaspar by his first name.

The absence of any genuine intimacy between two independent first persons makes banter, gossip, and punning the text's mood of *tuteo,* of tickling and itching address—of which there is plenty. Accordingly, in horseplay (and as a beer-drinking song from the mouth of a young

Scotsman), Hamlet's words may compete with a talking dog's lessons in mythology under the Supreme's roof. A dissertation on parthenogenesis may follow the humming of: "There's a divinity that shapes our ends, / Rough-hew them how we will." The quotation belongs to the comedy of the brothers John P. and William P. Robertson—"two green men with red hair"—who entered a virtually sealed-off Paraguay in search of trade. The "King of the Belgians" headed the list of subscribers to what became the brothers' *Letters;* his highness would get three sets of them (*Letters,* 1:xi). Just how far the business of being born out of one's own self may extend outside its cradle in myth represents the main correlative question that the Hamlet mytheme finds in *Yo el Supremo.* The dog's talk ("Hieroglyphic voice of the dog," 252/134) blends cosmogonic motifs (ranging from ancient Egyptian to Guaraní-Mby'a and Payé indigenous myths) about androgynal origins and the crossing of sexes in a single composite being that unites within itself the primal generations—much like the chimeric family does inside the dreamer's head in *Finnegans Wake.* Parthenogenesis rejects exclusive birth out of female bodies. First as a mother-pelican to his Paraguayan brood, but then as an insatiable pelican-tyrant who gobbles up his subjects after turning them into fishes, the Supreme will ultimately grasp his own image in native myth as that of twins who are born of themselves and manage to engender their own mother.[4] Just as Hamlet's saga extends the range of Oedipal feelings to include matricide, the Supreme's mythic genealogy places its small Hamlet-repertoire within an elaborate scheme representing the annulment of birth from a female. The Supreme has written:

> The only serious maternity is that of the man. The one real and possible maternity. I was able to be conceived without woman by the power of thought alone. Do people not credit me with two mothers, a false father, four false brothers, two birthdates? Does all this not prove beyond doubt that these many stories are without foundation? I have no family; if indeed I was really born, which has yet to be proven, since only what has been born can die. I was born of myself and *I* alone have made myself Double. (250/133)

But parthenogenesis can do more than reject exclusive birth from females; it can also make multiples of mother and child and turn the father into a bygone presence, a quarrelsome threat to the son's growth in consciousness.

Hamlet the avenger could regress to parthenogenesis and regard himself as both his own son and father, a mixed identity assumed by the

Supreme through his mythic birth as a child who plots the killing of fatherhood inside a microcosmic skull. Thus Hamlet's highest expression of melancholy would follow a different orbit:

> O God, I could be bounded in a nutshell
> and count myself a king of infinite space—
> were it not that I have bad dreams.
>
> (2.2.254–56)

From being imprisoned in a cosmic shell, the Hamlet figure may find itself being born inside a skull that could be Yorick's, and where detached fatherhood would be transformed through alchemy into an alloy of egotistic fear and hatred. Increasing in cosmic prestige, Hamlet would join a dynasty of mythmakers ruled by a single autocratic will. His melancholy wish to become *unbound* into infinity as an all-powerful being may then translate into an injunction against all forms of personal will, as in *Finnegans Wake*'s "Putting Allspace in a Notshall" (455.29) when it brings into play the oblivious will of sleep and death inherent in the dark infinity dreamed of by Hamlet. (A bit earlier [276.2], Joyce had found the missing link between Shakespeare's nutshell and the skull: "*Omnitudes in a knutshedell*" [Dutch: *schedel,* skull].) Thus the basic mytheme linking *Hamlet* and *Yo el Supremo* turns on the skull as an object of cosmogonic significance appropriated by a distant son reimagined inside the mind of his narrative and adversarial dying father (the old Supreme), who dictates the mythic script to himself in the person of an author compiling such messages of grandeur and obscure bondage to solipsism.

Everything centers on two institutional buildings linked by a skull. Young "Hamlet" has gone to Córdoba to study law and become a doctor in sacred theology under the ironfisted Franciscans (Chaves, 38–51). There, in "the crypt-cryptorium of the Gothic pagoda of Monserrat . . . students read in secret the books of the 'libertine' authors, sitting on skulls that had been robbed of their authority centuries before" (266/ 145). Imbued with *doctrinas nuevas,* the students might have treated with irreverence the story of old Polonius hiding in the Queen's closet and being killed by the intruding Prince, who is mistaken for a matricide by his own mother. Specular Polonius killed [as] a rat: "How now? A rat! Dead for a ducat, dead" (3.4.20–23). For it so happens that among the students at Monserrat there grew a legend involving a rat-slayer:

> Inside the church of the Company [Monserrat had been in Jesuit hands before their expulsion] (which he called the "Gothic Pa-

goda") there was a deep subterranean passage that ran through a good part of the city and came out at the other end of the building known as the Old Novitiate. That cellar containing numerous tombs of saintly and illustrious men also contained cells for the application of corporeal punishment. The students were in the habit of stealing into this catacomb to hold their revels and carouse. The scholarship student from Asunción acted as leader of these forays, preceding the others with a lantern. One night he induced one of his companions to accompany him. Frightened to death but urged on by his pride, as the lad confessed later, he started down the gloomy passageway. Halfway through it, a skull appeared amid the tombs, blocking their way. The companion stumbled over it and fell to the ground, half terrified to death. The impetuous roisterer then unsheathed his rapier and plunged it repeatedly into the eye sockets of the skull. The subterranean passage rang with the cry of a wounded animal. . . . With a kick of his foot the ringleader sent the skull flying into the wall, as a rat ran off amid the bits of bone scattered about on the ground. This episode won the Paraguayan pupil a somewhat sinister reputation, and made his influence on the others all the greater. (268/146; cf. Chaves, 43)

Josep Gaspar Francia—a name engraved on a stone at Córdoba and later erased by lightning (Chaves, 43)—reached Monserrat after having to demonstrate in court that he was not a mulatto. While there, we would learn of his mother's death and of his father's quick second marriage and separation. But these factors of adolescent resentment come in the wake of the mythic gestation of an earlier son-figure within the order of narration. Hamlet's adolescence is tied by a mythic thread to an older site of biographic emergence.

Government House in Asunción might have been erected as a Jesuit enclave, a fact denied by the Supreme: "The mistake regarding the origin of the House of Governors as a House of Spiritual Exercises arose from the fact that the edifice was constructed with materials that were listed in the general inventory of goods belonging to those expelled, under the rubric of Royal Confiscation" (191/83). Historians of Asunción have not failed to endow the place with omniscient powers:

Those who laid the foundations for that building, with purely spiritual goals in mind, no doubt had an admirable sense of its earthly placement. The large quadrilateral site on which it was erected offered four angles from which to observe the most important centers of activity in Asunción. From there, the pulse of civil, political, and ecclesiastical life could be taken and regulated. And the fate chosen for the building was so accurate as to be regarded by many as providential; since, as the passage of time would demonstrate, power could not have enjoyed a more strategic situation from which to spy, as from a motionless domain, the nascent energies of the people.[5]

If indeed built by Governor Morphi (known as "the Earless"), Government House would also lose its ears. The Supreme should smile at this view of a building whose body he regards as his own in compounded fashion. He has improved the House since receiving it from the colonial governors, but he has also knocked out two pillars and a wall panel to bring a surrogate meteorite into his cabinet. As part of an earlier lesson in writing, this fallen body has marked a zero point of origin:

> An aerolith falls from the sky of writing. The ovule of the point makes its mark in the place where it has fallen, where it has buried itself. Sudden embryo. It sprouts beneath the crust. Very small, it overflows itself. It designates its nothingness at the same time that it emerges from it. It materializes the hole of the zero. From the hole of the zero there comes forth sin-zerity. (162/60)

Buried but emergent at the oval-seminal point of black ink upon blank page, the meteorite has just started its mythic migration toward the center (and mystifications) of power.

The Supreme had seen the rock fall from the sky at the beginning of his perpetual rule. A saga of capture, transport, and passage ensued. The meteor would not budge from its landing site unless it was to follow the lead of a black slave and her child. Upon her death from a snakebite, her crawling son guided the caravan until the rock was sent by river to its final seat in Asunción. In the meantime, a hidden hand has inserted into the Supreme's papers a mocking version of his desire to possess the meteor as a talisman against chance: "(*Unknown hand:* Did you believe that you were thereby doing away with chance? . . . One aerolith does not make a sovereign. It is here [at Government House]; granted. But you are shut up here with it. Prisoner. Gouty rat poisoned by its own venom" (211/99–100). In a solipsistic sense impossible to rule out from the experience of reading the text, all hands that meddle into its layered composition might involve the Supreme's own inscriptive and expressive designs. The unknown hand that denounces as hopeless the cult of the aerolith as a talisman against the ravages of chance might be the same hand that has collaborated in its symbolic circumcision. For, circumcised, the aerolith has entered the House where the Supreme rules in presumed isolation from the effects of randomness: "I circumcised the aerolith. The metallic clipping provided enough material to manufacture ten rifles" (212/101). From its emergence at the point of scriptural impregnation, the rock has traveled, guided by mother and child, through circumcision and into a House in which the Supreme—across whose mind the tale unfolds—resides, surrounded by images of past fathers and rulers, and perhaps embodied there as an old man who is also the mother of his own chosen birth.

Rather than heroic cosmogony, a sort of prophetic *lithogony* (as the birth of voice and self from rock or stone) links the aerolith with another singular object in the narrative, the bezoar stone found inside the belly of a cow owned by Petrona Regalada, the Supreme's sister. When implanted at the seminal point where stylus and white paper meet, the aerolith predates personal memory; it takes effect at the point of marked commencement within a matrix severed from any spoken links between persons along generational lines. In contrast, the bezoar stone embodies memory-growth; it proceeds from St. Augustine's notion of memory as the soul's stomach. The bezoar stone represents memory's gastric child, a growth made of collective ruminations and prophecies: "Do you know what memory is [the Supreme asks]? The stomach of the soul. . . . A memory of cud-chewers. A ruminant's memory. Ingestive-digestive. Repetitive. Disfigurative. Sulliative" (95–96/5–6). At this point in the narrative, Patiño, the Supreme's amanuensis and cabinet shadow, has been ambiguously saddled with representing gossip and oral memory, so he has heard "those moos-that-were-words, like human words. Voices very far away, a bit hoarse as if from a cold, gurgling words. The remains of some unknown language that doesn't want to die completely." To which the Supreme answers by denying voice and memory to the loquacious talisman: "What language, may I ask, might that excremental ball petrified in the stomach of a cow remember?" (98/7–8). On her part, the Supreme's sister, herself a Gift-Stone (*Petrona Regalada*), taints the aerolith with the incestuous resemblance between her and its owner. She places ancestral likeness (on the father's side) before the Supreme, at the moment when he would want to lift the meteorite above all superstitions, like a talisman signifying his unsullied descent only from himself: "I see myself in her. A mirror-person, old França Velho [his hated Portuguese father] sends me back my image, dressed as a woman.

Beyond all ties of blood. What have I to do with blood relations?"
(100/9). Yet, the recognition of resemblance defeats all such denials in
the same way in which memory's brooding legacies undermine the
autonomy of male writing and mire it within a specific type of uterine
origination.

In the Supreme's mind, sister Petrona represents the worship of memory as the soul's stomach and womb. It would seem that, being born
from the Word as Christ did, and from a womb where no man's seed has
ever fallen, amounts to a myth sanitized by scriptural hygiene. The
involvement of Petrona in the traditional cult of Christ and the Virgin
offends her brother's sense of virile political rule:

> She is never without her bezoar stone. She keeps it hidden under-
> neath the niche of the Lord of Patience. More powerful than the
> image of the Bloodstained God. Talisman. Stair. Platform. Last
> step. The most resistant. It sustains her in the place of certainty.
> Place where there is no further need of any sort of help. Obsession
> has its foundation there. . . .
>
> The ruminant-stone has its own vigil light. Someday it will have
> its own niche. Perhaps, in time, its sanctuary.
>
> In the face of the bezoar stone of the person taken to be my sister,
> the meteorite still has—will it ever cease to have?—the flavor of the
> improbable. And what if the world itself were only a sort of bezoar?
> Hairy excremental material, petrified in the intestine of the cosmos.
> (101/10)

Circumcision would remove pollutions peculiar to mother-birth. Voices
and memories are pregnant with bloody ruminations from their origin
in a womb that ultimately cannot be strictly circumcised from the stomach. In a hopeless way, the bezoar stone (digestive, hungry, and loquacious with prenatal rumors and prophecies) might be labeled a
gasteroid; a stomach-clone next to the Supreme's self-cloning as the clean
meteorite of scriptural logos.

In this regard, one should recall how Odysseus entertains the Phaeacians with stories taken from a complex, epic word-hoard based on *gaster*
as: *stomach, beast, biological need, rhetorical figure* (Pucci, *Odysseus Polutropos,* 181). The word *gaster* (perhaps linked to the verb 'to devour')
might represent a synecdoche for the entire human condition. The
bezoar stone falls within such a synecdoche, which in ancient Greece
included *grass, green fodder,* and *grazing animals* (Pucci, 165, 177). The
Supreme's own ruminations take place in deferment of death, while

Odysseus's narrative performance delays his return home and forces him to build his fame before the Phaeacians as a hero driven by *gaster:* "The economy that promises pleasures and gain out of a somber relationship with death is called, in the *Odyssey,* that of *gaster*" (Pucci, 186). In *Yo el Supremo,* a similar economy keeps mourning away from a dying pelican-tyrant, while he feeds a brood of memories to his own spiced rebirth.

Government House serves as the shrine for a metallic, virile, cosmic body that has been circumcised and placed inside a one-man *Ka 'bah*—a seat of power *unmothered.* But it so happens that boy-Hamlet had seen a skull fly out of the trenches when Government House was being built and earthen embankments were being thrown against the rising river in fear of marauding Indians: "The skull sailed over the mounds. I caught it on the fly and put it under my altar boy's hood. Patch of red taking off into the darkness" (188/81). Presently, the Supreme's dictation will take the boy and his talking skull into *Hamlet*'s grave-diggers scene, working over a "droll story" that he and Patiño have heard translated by John Robertson during his English classes. Yorick's part assumes the role of his delving into Adam's gardening as a gentleman with arms buried in the first mother: "Was Adam a gentleman? . . . He was the first that ever bore arms, the skull answered in a clown's voice. . . . Haven't you read Holy Scripture? It says somewhere: Adam delved. How could he had delved if he didn't have arms?" (189/82). Hamlet's resting place has been found in the soil of the Supreme's fortress garden.

As the story unfolds in complexity, the reader loses touch with the scene of dictation (*fictation?*), and enters a microcosmic environment where the child plays alchemy by gaining nocturnal entrance into the skull: "a child still unborn incubating in the cube of a cranium. . . . lying hidden by my own will within the six walls of a cranium. The memories of the adult man that I had been weighed heavily on the child that was not yet" (263/142). The child in question should be regarded as an orphan or, better, as the embodiment of orphanhood split into tacit twinship. (The presence of twins and of self-creation as orphanhood in this scene will be illustrated further by looking into "Lucha hasta el alba," the short story chosen by Roa Bastos as his first attempt at the art of fiction). Here, the moon presides over the scene from her last quarter, and a "whore-nanny" presents her dried-up womb to the child for a rubbing. The child also gives a rubbing to what alchemists call the *caput mortuum* or *caput corvi,* "the head of the black Osiris or Ethiopian," the raven's head that stood in their craft for the *nigredo,* the state from which death and resurrection rise into an incorruptible age, the raven being also Christ's allegory (Jung, *Mysterium Coniunctionis,* 510–11). Hamlet's words to one of the skulls (preceding Yorick's) can be heard even here, as Adam and Christ try to rise again: "In other days he had a tongue, he could sing. . . . The gentleman's tongue is now in the power of milord the worm" (265/143–44; cf. *Hamlet* [5.1.74, 87]). Throughout the entire passage, an orphan is being made in a very dark place, the chamber of the lunar *albedo:* "Craters. Lunar globe. Ancient cranium. . . . White, disborn, not-finished. All white in the little milky shadow it casts about it in the darkness" (266, 272/144, 150). And "dark, feminine, corporeal, passive . . . *Aurora Consurgens* . . . universal receptacle . . . 'belly and womb of nature' . . . 'mediatrix of the whitening'" (Jung, 129–30). Two orphans take shape, one already fashioned by his father's hatred, the other being made inside alchemy's womb, emerging elsewhere, away from his mother: "I don't want to be engendered in a woman's womb. I want to be born in a man's thought. . . . [T]he skull was my mother-house. . . . Embryonic matter. . . . Darkness. Viscous matter. A cord burning in my mouth. Mouth sewn shut. Eyes sewn shut" (274/152). The philosopher's stone is called *orphan* by some alchemists because of its uniqueness; but the stone "'is first an old man, in the end a youth, because the *albedo* [pristine whiteness] comes at the beginning and the *rubedo* [redness] at the end'" (Jung, 10, 17). The orphan being made inside the skull says:

> Oldster's skull or a youngster's. Ageless. The metopic suture divides it into two halves. Childhood/Old Age. Now that I repose in my great age without having emerged from the infancy that I never had, I know that I must have a beginning without ceasing to be an end. (266/144–45)

A black point grows, an orphan crawls out of a raven's head, born unmothered. He crawls into "the shadow of the Paulist or Marian mulatto from the January River, the dark silhouette of the captain of militias astride the skull palpitating in the white tremor of its last contractions" (275/153). By contractions and coils (through earth, water, and air), the biography of the Supreme will renew this battle of orphans for father's brain and mother's womb.

Couplings and Cryptomania

But culture is not limited to what is eaten. . . . Culture is formed by hearing and sight, an old man's babble is as important as the genealogies of a Hesiod.—*Marcel Detienne,* The Creation of Mythology

The revelations, the group of words uttered by Muhammad as inspired by Allah, formed what was called a "recitation," qu'ran. . . . They were taken down in his lifetime on a variety of materials such as scraps of leather, flat camel-bones, potsherds, palm-fronds, and so forth.—*Maxime Rodinson,* Mohammed

Reeling and Writhing, of course, to begin with, and then the different branches of Arithmetic—Ambition, Distraction, Uglification and Derision. . . . Mystery, ancient and modern, with Seaography; then Drawling— the Drawling-master used to come once a week; he taught us Drawling, Stretching, and Fainting in Coils.—*Lewis Carroll,* Alice's Adventures in Wonderland

The circular unfolding of the Supreme's personal cosmogony requires some elucidation in reference to the composition of heroic and dynastic myth as well as sacred scripture, a task made difficult by the extraordinary complexity of the text's allusions and mystifications concerning authorial responsibility and efforts to either divert or destroy it. For instance, the narrative of parthenogenesis through alchemy just examined belongs to a layer of text that comes from the *private notebook.* This layer contains an assortment of genres of peculiar autobiographical significance, including perhaps two powerful accounts of strife with parental figures, the *logbook* and the *tutorial voice.*[6] However, the autobiographical fate of the *private notebook* runs counter to their original purpose as Great Books of the realm. They were given monumental shape inside a thousand folios of outsized ledger, broken into "Credit" and "Debit" columns, where the Supreme entered the negative and positive affairs of his government. In the last folio, this parallel monument to executive routine falls into disarray: "Real accounts are scarcely begun, there appear other unreal and cryptic ones. . . . In this way words, sentences, paragraphs, fragments are divided, continued, repeated, or inverted in the two columns, in an effort to strike an imaginary balance" (110/17). The *notebook* has turned into a monstrous prototype of *Yo el Supremo,* not only in its amalgamation of chronicle and invention, but by introducing autobiographical writing in belated form as a latent fever that breaks out in old age:

I think I recognize the handwriting, this paper. Once upon a time, in days long gone by, they represented for me the reality of what exists. By striking a flint spark above the sheet one could see infusoria still teeming in the ink. Parasitic fibrils. Annular, semilunar corpuscles of plasmodium. They finally formed the filigreed florets of malaria. The squib quivers with the shivers of swamp fever. Long live the ague!, the fever buzzes in my ears. The work of anopheles culicids. (142/45)

Infectious biography penetrates the self and debunks prior biographers of themselves on behalf of the Supreme's own enhancement. If it is true that the *notebook* entries "are addressed to no one," if they are not meant, like Rousseau's *Confessions,* to provide readers with Intimate Memoirs— "like those of illustrious whores or scholarly sodomites"—it might be because they are meant to improve individualist confessions as if from the rear, by coming into them from all the way back, from the origins of heroic saga and the intermingling of the divine ruler's fate with the recorded life of his theocratic realm—or as the prophet's voice would enter into his people's gestating future.

The *private notebook* surfaces now and then within the running *notes* (*apuntes*), which have been compared with a tape recording of the entire dialogue between the Dictator and Patiño: "The *Notes* are, in a way, the mode [of writing] that includes all the rest, because they represent the fundamental setting of communication, the one that perpetuates itself throughout the work, from the first page to the expulsion of the amanuensis" (49; my translation). Patiño's paradoxical nature rests on a salient feature he shares with other victims of satirical assault: he is a figure shackled to his attacker's means of ridicule and invective, but one not wholly deprived of the power to reflect at least some defining aspects of the attacking satirist. In the case of the amanuensis, satire is so violent and sustained as to betray, beyond the antidotes of applied self-irony, a large degree of self-contempt on the part of the Supreme himself. Satire locks up master and scribbler in a single authorial chamber. While not untypical, the binding satirical relationship between the two characters may lead to a split in the operative notion of *myth*. Patiño receives myth as *rumor,* as the constant renewal of chatter among people of all descriptions. While much aware of such humming beliefs, the Supreme nurtures a seemingly higher understanding of myth as a political tool capable—in the right anonymous hands—of exploiting and adapting to its own ends all previous expressions of common wisdom or mere superstition. For him, myth overlays with fresh paint a pyramid built by ancient hierocratic cunning in which the voices of even older beliefs are both engraved and buried. Voice and hieroglyphics, vision and penmanship, palimpsest and pristine conscience make up the Supreme's authorial agenda as he attempts to batter his fetishlike companion into accessorial submission.

An anecdote from the composition of the Qu'rān may serve as preface to a characterization of the Dictator and his amanuensis in the role of hieroglyphic doubles. Tradition tells how a secretary of the Prophet named 'Abdallah ibn Sa'd was copying down the sayings of the Qu'rān when, upon the Prophet's breaking off dictation, "the secretary continued aloud to the end of the sentence as he thought it should read, and Muhammad absentmindedly incorporated 'Abdallah's suggestion into the divine text" (Rodinson, *Mohammed*, 219). 'Abdallah fled to Mecca to spread the word of his inspired interpolation, and though the Prophet wanted him dead, he managed to outlast the editorial crisis and later held high office in the Muslim empire (Rodinson, 261). 'Abdallah's verbal forgery and written sham (in anticipation of Salman Rushdie's more recent adulterations and satirical apostasies) represent a circuitous affair; he dictated aloud to his own hand in the style of the Qu'rān, and hence tricked and doubled the Prophet, who stood behind the Qu'rān's dictating style. What 'Abdallah did not do was to dictate *in secret* to his own copying hand the message that voices (heard only by the Prophet) dictated to him (to 'Abdallah) only "through" the Prophet's own voice. The Prophet missed 'Abdallah's interpolating (*penning*) voice while concentrating on his own, and later found a voice other than his own in the written word taken down by the usurping scribe—a written word read to him, since according to Muslim tradition, the Prophet was illiterate. The orthodox assumption that such revealing voices had chosen the Prophet as their sole vehicle and point of first inward impact separates belief in receptive charisma (in this case, *baraka*) from the dutiful entry of doctrinal stuff into collective memory in the form of a Book held sacred by its users. In the end, proof of 'Abdallah's prophetic lapse being either a fraud or the result of secretarial rapture would come with the Prophet's unique ability to sustain his charismatic hold on his followers by the sheer force of his deeds underlying that of his revealed rhetoric.

This view of the secretarial/editorial affair puts it in parallel relation with the Supreme's debunking of Patiño as a corrupting mediator between the ruler's oral and written authority and its faithful transmission to posterity. Ceaseless and extravagant denunciations are hurled at the "trust-unworthy secretary," who cannot "secrete" what dictation tells him to put down on paper. (Compare Sham's proud but excremental role as wizard-scribe in *Finnegans Wake:* "The simian has no sentiment secretions but weep cataracts for all me, Pain the Shaman" [192.22–23].) Patiño cannot hear what the Supreme utters without taking it one corrupting step further into a prose style coined by "Scribleruses"; a style that seems, as one hears it being denounced, like a parody of the Supreme's own verbal excesses: "Your style is abominable. A labyrinthine alleyway paved with alliterations, anagrams, idiosyncratic idioms, barbarisms, paronomasias such as pároli/párulis, imbecilic anastrophes to dazzle imbecilic inverts who experience erections by virtue of the effect of the violent inversions of word order" (157/56). Contrary to the inspired 'Abdallah, who gains access to writing on the wings of a charismatic recitation or *qur'an,* poor Patiño's parrot voice drowns in the ink of baroque lampooning, like a talking raven crushed by an oracular writing desk.

What turns Patiño's pen into a lightning rod of satire has a lot to do with the brand of oral tradition celebrated by the Supreme. And what makes both characters hieroglyphic doubles hinges on their mutual failure to untwist themselves from each other and give passage to such a tradition of native idioms and beliefs, thus assuming its effervescent revival with a sense of legitimacy. Their failure is mutual because, without Patiño's presence next to his scriptural boss, the latter would lack a stick on which to lean, or a mirror in which to see in reflection elements of both writing and oral expression, elements that he cannot hope to control, and that he must learn to wisely fear, above the drone of his own insults against his secretary and the political enemies that line up, dead or alive, behind this punished figure. Their relationship implies a complex topography of entangled reflexivity and interdependence, which could be seen as follows: "The self can constitute the other as the image of the self, which simultaneously constitutes the self as image, only because the self is originally other to itself—another way of saying that an internal split grounds an external doubling at the same time that an external doubling grounds an internal split, that the origin is simultaneously split and doubled.[7]

However, the hieroglyphic connection between the Supreme and his surrounding cast of recorded voices has little to do with any overt reference to that ancient form of writing, such as the one established by the discovery of the carved Chair-of-the-Wind petroglyph, broken to bits in the building of a garrison: "Determine their age, because stones do have one. Decipher the hieroglyph. I am the only one able to do this in this country of known-it-all cretins" (116/22). It is worth noting that a petroglyph was indeed found during Francia's days in power: "The Dictator submitted it to examination by some of the eldest among the local priests . . . who, upon careful inspection, informed him that the signs were completely unknown to all of them; but that they resembled the Hebrew language, and had probably been carved an untold number of centuries before" (Wisner, *El dictador,* 153).

In any event, the command to decipher arcane signs should be brought in line with the Supreme's initial order to Patiño to trace the handwriting on a pasquinade back to its author. The riddles of double representation (of both picture and meaning) usually generated by hieroglyphic signs fall back on a hidden trick and a riddle posed by the lampoon at the very outset of the novel. For the pasquinade that Patiño must trace to an unknown author is claimed by the Supreme as his own: "Tell me, isn't the handwriting of the pasquinade mine? . . . Impossible, Excellency! Not even if I were possessed with the madness of right reason could I think such a thing of our Karaí-Guasú. . . . The possible is a product of the impossible. Look here, underneath the watermark, the flourish of the initials. Aren't they mine? They are yours, Sire" (117/63–64; see also the original, 46). Moreover, the reader who bothers to retrace Roa Bastos's handling of historical sources will find out that a similar *pasquín* had appeared (among dozens of others) in Asunción in the wake of Francia's death, assuming his voice, handwriting, and rubric (Tovar, *Las historias,* 34–42). So Patiño goes in search of a posthumous calligraphic charade; posthumous in so far as Francia's death might double itself into the text of *Yo el Supremo* to become lodged in the life of the Supreme, who in Francia's case would have himself (*itself*) written the lampoon. Francia and the Supreme become doubles linked by this piece of someone else's calligraphy, which marks Francia's inability to survive either his own death or the Supreme's authorial life. The Supreme doubles Francia as a force of tutorial creation always dead in anticipation of death, but per-petually alive by virtue of precisely that same force, the one that allows it to outlast the lives of both doubled beings. In such a context, Patiño represents the unwitting and satirized detector, an automaton in charge of exposing with single (yet double-minded) forensic craftiness the nec-rological links between the two doubles of the dictatorial figure as they appear in history (Francia's and Paraguay's) and in fiction (the Supreme's and company).

The constant shuttling back and forth between authorship and detection (and between the space of necrology and the seat where political rule rests in constant fear of insubordination and counterfeit) cannot prevent itself from anticipating the work of arcane inscriptions behind every sign. As John T. Irwin suggests in *American Hieroglyphics:*

> If one begins with the image of hieroglyphic writing and the prob-
> lem of deciphering an inner, hidden meaning from an outer, visible
> shape by means of a necessary though obscure correspondence
> between the two, then one is immediately led to the questions
> of how and why that necessary correspondence became obscure,
> which in turn leads to the question of the development of writing
> from its origins, and thus to the origin of language. As the hiero-
> glyphical problem of the relationship between outer shape and
> inner meaning becomes the question of the origin of man and lan-
> guage, the image of 'writing' expands until all physical shapes be-
> come obscurely meaningful forms of script, forms of hieroglyphic
> writing each of which has its own science of decipherment—sig-
> nature analysis, physiognomy, phrenology, fingerprint analysis, zo-
> ology, botany, geology, and so on. (60–61)

The specific cultural syndrome studied by Irwin might be altered as follows. Even when references to hieroglyphics remain incidental or cursory, as they do in *Yo el Supremo,* the overwhelming significance of questions dealing with personal and transpersonal identity—faithfully or unfaithfully inscribed, written, copied, or drawn—can lead to a larger inference of the hieroglyphical enigma behind them. This inference suggests itself even more when doubts or assertions about the power of language and writing expand as mystifying illustrations of how subjective experience and the order of natural phenomena may be transparently rendered through a writing technique hitherto unknown. Finally, emphasis on preserving the identity of the one who writes glued in absolute and unmediated rapport to the experience being recorded may result, as in the Supreme's case, in an endless struggle with shadowy adversarial figures vying for the power attributed to that singular form of writing.

Someone, then, shall claim access to magical and arcane writing for the purpose of binding together the order of nature and its experience through an empowered self. But such claims may end up in inwardly splitting the one who proffers them, and outwardly doubling his expression of the natural order and the beings it may bring before him. This process of personal enlargement and subsequent breakup animates the prescientific view of Egyptian hieroglyphics. By fixing exclusively on their pictographic appearance, hieroglyphics are seen "as that basic form of signification in which the physical shape of the sign is taken directly from—indeed, is like the shadow of—the physical shape of the object it stands for" (Irwin, 61). To which one may juxtapose fragments from the *private notebook* and the lengthy *compiler's note* in *Yo el Supremo*, in which an extraordinary pen is given description and biographic status. The passage includes ritual allusions to Egyptian oracular magic: "Decipher those bloody hieroglyphs that no one can decipher. To consult the Sphinx is to risk being devoured by it without being able to unveil its secret." The past must be *viewed* if it is to be recaptured; one must "resume the viewing of what has already happened," but it "may also be that nothing has really happened except in this image-writing that goes on weaving its hallucinations on paper. What is entirely visible is never seen entirely. It always offers something else that must be looked at further" (329/196–97). Hieroglyphical awareness merges with the order of hallucination. Indeed, although the fanciful description of the cylindrical pen that follows within the *compiler's note* contains allusions in homage to Raymond Roussel (331, 331n/198), Francia's distant contemporary, Thomas De Quincey, might have recognized in the account and its context elements akin to his own hallucinatory cult of exotic doubles, not to mention his interest in the palimpsest. For the cylindrical pen bears "an inscription blurred by years and years of nibbling. 'What's the use of one tooth biting on another?,'" this being one of the Supreme's favorite expressions, to which he answers: "'To blur inscriptions by the superimposition of other more visible, though more secret, ones'" (329/197). On his part, De Quincey writes to his reader concerning the actions of certain "monkish chemists" in the palimpsest, in which "expelled writing" never totally sinks as rubbish into the membrane that kept it visible, so that on such vellum skin there is the chance "to write a book which should be sense for your own generation, nonsense for the next, should revive into sense for the next after that, but again become nonsense for the fourth" (De Quincey, *Confessions*, 141). In the palimpsest, De Quincey spotted accretions and a continuing inversion and reversion of the same scriptural body, buried but still traceable, staggered yet playable, in a way not even the most famous among ancient magicians (to whom Ficino attributed the invention of hieroglyphics) might have improved: "Could magic, could Hermes Trismegistus, have done more?" (De Quincey, 141; Yates, *Hermetic Tradition*, 163). A genealogical substitution syndrome binds together De Quincey's forensics of the palimpsest and the type of hieroglyphic awareness of double and split selves described by Irwin as the fashion among writers of the American Renaissance imaginatively involved with the notion of a simultaneous origin of man and language:

> Although we can have no direct knowledge of the simultaneous origin of man and language, for many of these writers it was an appealing, indeed a compelling myth to imagine that origin as a form of "hieroglyphic" doubling in which a prelinguistic creature saw the outline of his shadow on the ground or his reflection in water and experienced both the revelation of human self-consciousness (the differentiated existence of self and world) and the revelation of language, the sudden understanding that his shadow or reflection was a double of himself and yet *not* himself, that it was somehow separate and thus could serve as a substitute that would by its shape evoke recognition of what it stood in place of. (61–62)

The magic cylindrical pen offers a complex version of the narcissistic and ultimately paranoid surmise of doubleness described by Irwin. It allows one to perform "two different yet coordinated functions: writing while visualizing the forms of another language composed exclusively of images, of *optical metaphors.*" The Supreme's pen's biography extends beyond the rebus-package of pictograms as it recapitulates two stages in the evolution of projected animation.

First, the projection "is produced by means of orifices along the shaft of the pen, which lets in the flood of images in the manner of a microscopic camera obscura"; and then "a device on the inside, probably a combination of mirrors, causes the images to be projected in their normal position, not inverted," so that it endows them "with movement, in the same fashion as what is today known as a cinematographic projection." And finally, the pen reproduces "the phonic space of writing, the sound-text of the visual images; which could have been the *spoken time* of those words without forms, of those forms without words," which allow the Supreme "to conjoin the three texts in a fourth intemporal dimension turning around the axis of an undifferentiated point between the origin and the extinction of the writing" (330/197). However, this magic lantern of animated memories has broken down; nowadays it only *writes,* "projecting the same mute images stripped of their sonorous space." A sort of junkyard or death row of words and broken gestures (that at one point might have worked in oral performance and storytelling) falls from the pen, in images that "appear on the paper with a sharp break in the middle, like rods submerged in a liquid; the upper half entirely black, so that if they are figures of persons they give the impression of being hooded. Shapes without faces, without eyes" (330/198).

The character in whom the broken magic pen deposits its saturated evidence of the double-dubbed death of voice and image in typescript and ink is Patiño, the bureaucratic animal, expert on the graphology of pasquinade and main receptor of myth as rumor. With his faithful but doubling reflection, he is the one who shatters the Compiler's antics on the evolution of recorded memory from hieroglyphics to video images—insofar as such displays of invention may not wholly exclude the participation in them of the Supreme's satire against his amanuensis.

It seems that the authorial voice sidetracked in the Compiler's hybrid intrusions conspires by default with the Supreme's dictatorial raunchiness. Fiction, biography, history, and testimony rub against each other within the Compiler's notations in a teasing way that only the Supreme's wholesale debunking of categories and genres can sufficiently season with demonic irony. The Compiler cannot avoid—and in fact seeks—a dark tone of twinship with the Supreme. At some level of textual performance suggested by wordplay but not openly enacted, the whole narrative event in *Yo el Supremo* would resemble a *conspilation:* a mongrel word that comes to mind when one considers the affinities and yet the obvious differences between Roa Bastos's novel and Joyce's *Finnegans Wake.* Granting *Wake*'s staggering uniqueness, one may focus on some key elements of voice connecting both works in antiphonal fashion. Seen from the vantage point of Vico's historiosophy, the warping and compounding of lexical elements in *Finnegans Wake* reflect the shaking of the philological tree by the primal thunder that deafened and mobilized creation, and that recurs and shifts registers in the soundless yet vibrant element of dreaming. Each disfigured and chimerical element of common speech and handwriting represents a point at which voices and scriptural projects gather and disperse. A word incurring into other words—and being incurred upon by them—signals a quick graphic séance tracing an instant and promiscuous philological cycle. The will to pronounce in a way that may find an answer collapses, as the speaker tries to renew communication by means of a delirious primeval naturalness. The Supreme's text resembles *Finnegans Wake*'s space of dreaming and the recurrence of remote cosmogonies within it. But it does so by enhancing wakefulness, panoptic vigil, total hearing, and a host of countermeasures, of self-defenses built as part of the Supreme's own reflexive omniscience.

As omniscience's first and last victim, Patiño is a grotesque caricature drawn on a receding speaking original and given borrowed voices. As such, he might be found echoed in *Finnegans Wake*, by fitting his lost mouthing voice in brackets-within-brackets, as if grafted on Shaun's self-apology. What speaks in the apology and its reflexive address might be characterized as the embedded religiousness of all serious authorship. Shaun (amended by bracketed voices) says:

> "I am extremely ingenious at the clerking even with my badly left and, arrah go braz [Pan-Slavonic *obraz:* picture; Breton *braz:* big (Patiño: "My left hand continues to copy, since the right one has already fallen dead at my side" [584/414]; cf. Spanish *obra:* work; *brazo:* arm)]. I'd pinsel it with immenuensoes [innuendoes (cf. *amanuensoes*)] as easy as I'd perorate a chickerow of beans [the Qu'rān: chapters, *suras,* rows of verses (Atherton, *Books at the Wake,* 201–2)] for the price of two miracles and my trifolium librotto [Joyce, *Ulysses*], the authordux [orthodox, *dux:* leader] Book of Lief [*Revelations/Yo el Supremo*]." (425)

Always plural and chimeric, the voice-mouthing of dreams (a standard metaphor reawakened by genuine prophets and visionary writers) cannot be recorded unless it is in the graphic disturbance traced on scroll paper by rapid eye movement. (One can only guess what Joyce would have done with the knowledge of REM.)[8] Heard from but also "seen" (and bracketed) within Joyce's observatory on noises at large, Patiño's graphic voice may sink in the inward dialogue of individual voice with antecedent Voice (as sheer vehicle), as it may emerge in subsequent recitations and prophecies. Patiño rechannels *Finnegans Wake* into a Spanish voice little heard in any of its extant readings.

The seemingly one-sided struggle between the Supreme and his amanuensis involves not only the possible faithful retrieval of communal voices, but also the notion that those voices might be dead on arrival at the posthumous hospice of pictogram or script. Yet a wake never faints in coils if not to proclaim a revival.

Sorcerer and Trickster

I regret to announce, after laying out his litterery bed, for two days she kept
squealing down for noisy priors and bawling out her jameymock farceson in
Shemish like a mounther of the incas with a Garcielasso huw Ananymus
pinched her tights . . . and him, the cribibber like an ambitrickster, aspiring
like the decan's, fast aslooped intrance to his polthronechair . . . engrossing to
his ganderpan what the idioglossary he invented under hicks hyssop!
—James Joyce, Finnegans Wake, 422–23

Recite in the name of your Lord who created,
Created man from a blood-clot.
Recite! Your Lord is the most bountiful,
He has taught by means of the Reed,
He has taught mankind those things he did not know.
—Qu'rān, 94:1–5

James Macpherson (1736–96) forged an epic just as el Inca Garcilaso
(1539?–1616) forged a rare brand of chronicle and autobiography; both
men pinched the past, each became an "ambitrickster" who dealt the
needful present of his race an aristocratic hand—they both littered their
literatures indelibly. But neither seems to have perceived—unless in a
weird and untold dream—the slightest kinship between a letter and a
hen, or the even more improbable cause that, by scratching in a midden
heap, a middling feathered mother would bring about a grand renewal
of letters.

In *Finnegans Wake,* Ana Livia Plurabelle has written (and dug up as
mother hen) a letter, an "untitled mamafesta memorialising the Most-
highest" (104.4)—that is to say, her most gossiped about husband,
Earwicker, whom chaotic rumor has pilloried in colossal shape and laid
like a dreaming giant over Dublin's seat by the Liffey's mouth. Beginning at the humped and thunderous edges of the scriptural cosmos
(where *Finnegans Wake* and *Yo el Supremo* vanish in raffled togetherness),
mother hen's letter emerges in cahoots with a certain circumcised aerolith and a lunar skull to form a threesome of oval-seminal, prenatal-
postnatal agents or fallen angels of scriptural evidence. The plain, if quite
laborious, fact that human birth happens in and around a female body
never seems to escape the wakeful eye of doctrine or legend—or of an
infinite variety of ingenious witnesses bent on inventing nativity in their
own mold. Thunder bears such witness upon Ana Livia, who in her
closing monologue thinks of her husband: "bearing down on me now

under whitespread wings like he'd come from Arkangels" (628.9). With her husband HCE and their twin sons (Castor-Pollux Shem and Shaun), mother (and virgin-goddess) supports or hosts "the notion that the letter buried in the midden heap is a fertile egg, seed, or semen with potential life."[9] On such matters as "scribings" (drawings on Easter eggs), a certain Nivaklé chieftain and sorcerer interviewed by the Supreme on the mystery of the Trinity would have found a lot to ponder, given his belief that "completely surrounding the egg is the shell or hide: the *vatjeche*. Hard bark that protects the soft-soul or pith. As the egg is the soul of the body, the shell is the soul of the egg" (296/169–70). The Supreme feels like "a fresh laid egg" after the interview, or perhaps like a letter just written and not yet read, or a bit of crusty voice still unheard by the faithful. Eggs of such variety transport nativity outside the mother whose duty would be to cover them with heat instead of scrawlings. (Pity the child whose mother hen acted hieroglyphical instead of incubatory toward the shell in which he was to take shape.) A fabulous anxiety seems "penned" by sons in their labors to upstage their own fatherhood. First comes a pleading: "Who in hallhagal [*hell* + Arabic: *to play*] wrote the darn thing anyhow?" (*FW*, 107.36), a type of query usually involved in notions of fathering; then comes a little twister of a question from where none other than the son himself begins to emerge as the would-be author of the thing:

> Erect, beseated, mountback, against a partywall, below freezigrade, by the use of quill or style, with turbid or pellucid mind, accompanied or the reverse by mastication, interrupted by visit of seer to scribe or of scribe to site, atwixt two showers or atosst of a trike, rained upon or blown around, by a rightdown regular racer from the soil or by a too pained whittlewit laden with the loot of learning? (108.1–7)

The busier the actions, the more likely that *both* father and son would be carried in them, both being still closer to the climbing task of becoming sons than to the tabernacles and pubs where established fathers dwell. Perhaps there is here an unresolved symbolic twinship—father still a budding son/son not yet a mirrored father—with ontological priority over the actual issuing of twins: like Shem and Shaun in *Finnegans Wake,* or like the implied presence of another child/orphan besides the one who attempts self-birth through alchemy in *Yo el Supremo.*

In any case, Shaun's report to the judging elders of the race, who have asked him for another "esiop foible," represents brother Shem being littered by the mother's dictation on a bed of literary forgeries, of pseudo-Ossians and mock and possibly unread Garcilasos (el Inca's Book escapes the splendid census of literary allusions made by Atherton in *The Books at the Wake*). So in Shaun's eyes a mother dictates to a son who copies and forges his own authorship upon the very piece that he hears, while yet another son spies on both (*mamafester* and *ideoglossist*) makers of letters and scripture. The question should then be, not who wrote the *darn thing,* but whether the *darn* thing is the father, or is the *thing* where the father must lie. In this fashion, the complex *leggacies of* the letter unearthed by mother hen defeat appropriation even within *Finnegans Wake* itself, but the scriptural issues released by the filthy exhumation may help to illustrate a polemic on the character and evolution of myth latent in *Yo el Supremo.*

Finnegans Wake abounds in trials, hearings before tribunals, lessons parodied, and pedantic dissertations, all of which return one way or the other to the discovery of the letter and its interpretation. All this polemical richness peaks near the end with the do-or-die debate between the monochromatic worldview espoused by St. Patrick's christianizing cunning and the visionary apprehension of natural colors placed before him by the archdruid's pagan grandeur and enchantment. The newly arrived future saint and the resident native priest meet before a crowd anchored by High King Lughaire (Leary) in the watershed year A.D. 432, with religious rule over Ireland at stake. In a famous letter to Frank Budgen, Joyce declared that "the colloquy between Berkeley the arch druid . . . and Patrick the arch priest . . . is also the defense and indictment of the book itself [*Finnegans Wake*]."[10] The victory of the Christian agent has been seen as "the sunrise of a new day, scattering the profound night shadows of the self-contemplating, mythological age of dream" (Campbell and Robinson, *Skeleton Key,* 351). But a deeper understanding of the event would have Patrick rejecting "the archdruid's natural concept of revelation in favor of an analogical interpretation of the phenomenal world," and then *not* recognizing that the afterimage of the druid's majestic vision shows how the fall of humankind from receptive inwardness became partially blind to the phenomenal world (see Norris, *Decentered Universe,* 88–89). There is hardly a better scene than this confrontation between shamanistic wisdom and colonizing Christian policy against which to set Paraguay's Supreme author standing on native grounds as a sorcerer-polemicist in favor of executive magic.

The name *Karaí* may not be taken lightly, for it reflects traditions of empowerment perhaps older than those upheld by druidic sages and priests:

At the time of discovery, the *carai, cara-ibe,* or *pagé* . . . was a kind of man-god, found all the way from the mouth of the Orinoco . . . to the Río Plata. . . . In ceremonies, the *cara-ibe* held in each hand a *maraca* or gourd rattle containing the spirits that spoke to him. He was sumptuously dressed, with a large colored feather headdress as though he were a bird, and he was accorded quasi-divine honors and deference. . . . "The influence of the Caraibes over the people was paramount. They were the medicine-men, wise-men, astrologers, prophets, sorcerers, and devil-propitiators. . . . The sun, moon, and stars obeyed their orders, they let loose the winds and the storms. . . . The most ferocious beasts of the forests were submissive to them, they settled the boundaries of hunting-grounds, interpreted dreams and omens, were entrusted with all secrets, were father confessors in all private matters and . . . held life and death at their disposal."[11]

Although perhaps not as exhaustive in his powers as the *Karaí,* the archdruid faces Patrick clad in the hued diaphany of the rainbow: "his heptachromatic sevenhued septicoloured roranyellgreenlindigan mantle" (*FW,* 611.6–7), signifying his privileged seizure of nature's highest gifts to human sight. His visionary powers were unobscurely phrased in an early draft of the *Wake:*

> The archdruid then explained the illusions of the colourful world, its furniture, animal, vegetable and mineral, appearing to fallen men under but one reflection of the several iridal gradations of solar light, that one which it had been unable to absorb, while for the seer beholding reality, the thing as in itself it is, all objects showed themselves in their true colours, resplendent with the sextuple glory of the light actually retained within them. (Atherton, 98)

But Patrick does not buy a dream wrapped in idealist cant; his quick and winning answer has been paraphrased as follows:

> It is a mistake to say that knowledge *a posteriori,* even for a seer, can attain to the celestial. When you speak of the essential knowledge of the true seer, it is as though, by a paralogism and circumlocution, "My" were to be spoken of as "Me," or a handkerchief were to be taken for the owner of the handkerchief. If I were to permit to you such seeming 4-3-2 agreement, then we may also accept for common man the Sacred Heart as adequate sound-sense symbol for the

fire cast therein by the sunlight of the Father, the Son, and the Holy Ghost. (Campbell and Robinson, 351)

One can imagine Patrick remaining as sharply unmoved, though perhaps more curious, if instead of druidic optics on the ultimate hue of the rainbow he had heard of something not wholly different, but made by hallucinogenic powers. The elements of shamanistic practice and trickery evoked by the Supreme as *Karaí* may or may not include the well-attested recourse to psychotropic drugs on the part of native sorcerers, but such elements certainly establish strong links between his omniscient figure (more *semiocratic* than abstract) and cognate forms of authorship that enact and give peculiar embodiment to his character. These are forms of manifest meddling and intrusion driven home, rather than withheld or otherwise lodged in the abstract narrative structure of the novel. In connection with the shaman or trickster, the author projects himself in acting, gesture, and other concrete forms of usually aggressive or blunt behavior. Two examples of shamanistic performance will be examined in an effort to illustrate how a certain conception of myth as a mirror of power resists disenchantment when confronted with the arrival of newer breeds of constraining knowledge.

The first example evokes Patrick's confrontation with the archdruid, but in reverse. As a scene, it brings face to face a native sorcerer and a crowd of onlookers during festivities given by Governor Lázaro de Ribera in 1804 to celebrate the appointment of Manuel de Godoy (Napoleon's puppet in Madrid) as Perpetual Councilor of Asunción—or Great (or Grand) Conjoiner, as he is satirically called by the Supreme (385–93/241–47).[12] Instead of arguing any of its basic beliefs (as with the archdruid), native shamanism displays an act of awesome transformation; magic engulfs argument—either of a cynical or a strictly rational sort—and poses its own central questions: Is an absence of enchantment ever possible? What manner of practical knowledge comes to replace magic? What authority is that which renames it, and on whose behalf is magic so changed?

Thus we have a chieftain (sorcerer-prophet of the Ka'aiguá-Gualachí) performing in front of the colonial authorities and the spellbound daughter of Governor de Ribera: "Slender-waisted, giant-tall, completely drenched with sweat. . . . The aboriginal horseman's nakedness is covered with nothing except a sort of cache-sexe or loincloth of a fabric that gives off opaque reflections" (388/243). He is about to drop a ring "that leaves the trace of its red edging suspended in the air" on the young woman's white lap, a bold move for which de Ribera has him killed. While dying, his "tattoos give off a phosphorescent glow in the dusk that is beginning to fall. . . . [He] rakes his coppery skin from throat to crotch. He pulls the wax casque from his head, baring his hair tonsured in a spiral-crown. Amid the flurry of feathers, adornments, scales, insignia, he has the appearance of an Adam-Christ of the wilds" (389/244).

While at odds with colonizing powers, the metamorphosis in progress already bears the effects of syncretism as a mode of magical and cere-monial enhancement. The Ka'aiguá-Gualachí were not subjugated by conquistadors or missionaries, and yet their whiteness ("Almost albino, so pure white is he. Snow-white skin. Snow-white eyes" [389/244]) would seem to reflect sacramental values central to the Catholic faith's celebration of purity and the mystery of transubstantiation. It is as if the eucharistic climax of the mass had found a new script of a whiter hue embodying Christ and the Virgin. But syncretism has a zoomorphic side: "Beneath him his mount too has now been transformed, into a pure-blue jaguar. Tongue, jaws blood-red and dripping, ivory fangs. The spots of its coat shine with a metallic gleam in the sunlight." In the eyes of the governor's daughter the transfigured sorcerer "is little less than an Archangel," while in those of the bishop beside her the whole thing represents Satan's visit, which now turns "into a real meteor, a real comet now. It crosses the river and is lost from sight in the sky as it heads for the cordilleras to the East" (389/244). The ring thrown on the woman's white lap has grown and now includes her whole inside a figure of revealed colors not unrelated to the rainbow:

> The ring in the form of a serpent biting its tail grew larger and larger in the lap of the governor's daughter. It soon enclosed the girl, her crazed father, the bishop, the municipal councilmen, and members of the clergy within its circle. The virgo-viper continued to grow larger and larger. . . . At the same time the metal of the ring, resembling ytterbium, the hard metal of virgin land, grew softer and softer, turning into a squamous-viscous material. The scales flew off and remained suspended in the air, lighter than fleece-of-the-virgin. Suddenly the huge serpent burst into iridescent parti-cles. . . . The governor's daughter lay on the carpets covering the platform, bleeding profusely. Her white hoop skirts had taken on the colors of the crimson edging of the ring. (389–90/244–45)

We have purple ballet and cosmodrama, theater and myth. It should be recalled that while the druid priest drew the colors of the rainbow, Patrick distracted himself by imagining old Leary as King Harvest: "kilt like spinach, torque like cauliflowers, eyes like thyme chopped with parsley, stone of ring like an olive lentil, war scars on face like chopped senna" (Campbell and Robinson, 351). Between this oblique salad making and the stark deconstruction of the rainbow that follows it, one can imagine a different Patrick averting his eyes from a violent hue of colors where Holy Ghost and Virgin remain conjoined. However, the Great Conjoiner presiding over this other scene—albeit, inside a portrait from which he must now descend—does not see such a cosmic religious drama (as the archdruid might have in some postpandrial vision). For visions of a sort have christened the Paraguayan banquet and festivities in honor of the *Gran Ayuntador* (a title whose impolite rendering should be that of *Great Fornicator*), where from the start praise has been given to "restoration of that-which-is-lost-once-and-only-once. Royalty. Virginity. Nobility. Dignity" (387/243). But such praise represents the cynicism of "those who, losing them once, regain them twice over." Hence, by a bishop's gambol, Governor de Ribera can most naturally move from restoration to resurrection, since, as the prelate puts it, "It is no more extraordinary to come back to life once than it is to create the same thing twice" (387/243). Which is precisely what the Great Conjoiner denies, unless death and renewal (or damage and healing) take place inside a fairy-tale ballet or drama: "The Prince of Peace and Great Conjoiner stepped out of the Portrait, crossed through the arch of Immortality, and embraced the dazed Lázaro de Ribera. Very good, very good, my dear governor! A real fairy tale! Allow me to congratulate your daughter for her marvelous performance in the role of the swan. . . . The swan-killer . . . has always sent me into sheer delirium. . . . That strange assassin who murders swans in order to hear their last song!" (391/245).

Two views of the affair seem to emerge: that of a maiden killed to obtain her transformation into a swan song, and that of a virgin ravished and taken away by a meteor (most likely embodying her own son, his father, and possibly hers as well). On the one hand, a romance of erotic suicide on stage; on the other, a cosmic saga of mythic renewal. Two different genres of ritual and enchantment are thereby linked, so that they might make sense only so conjoined. In both orders of performance, the innocent maiden misses the opening question posed by the ritual's plot, so she must ask: "What is it your Worship said, if I may ask?" Yet, she herself represents the question *and* the answer about such precious things

(Royalty, Virginity, Nobility, Dignity) that must be lost or destroyed in order to be recovered or re-created. The ritual answer has come from the father rather than the bishop, but their roles coincide; they are bound by ritual not to release the real answer: "Nothing, daughter. Nothing that might interest you at this moment when the fiesta is so splendid it suspends the senses" (387/243). Of course, the father will grow alarmed, as will the bishop, once things get out of hand and the maiden undergoes her plural ordeal, or as she is ravished/taken away, killed as a swan/yet as a snake. Then, as joint figures, father and bishop may rely on the assistance of a third ruling presence, the Great Conjoiner, the expert who descends from his portrait to look into the eyes of what should be a dying swan, not its snake killer. And yet, the expert names the snake as victim: "The queen's favorite bent over the serpent's head. Look, just look at this! An animal retains in its eyes the image of the person who has killed it, until decomposition sets in! And now, my dear Lázaro, I shall return to the portrait" (391/245). In the mysteries released by this resurrection ritual, a daughter-bride (and mother to a son-husband) has been ravished and removed from the scene by a feline serpent (and uroboric meteor) acting as a native cousin to the rainbow; a white maiden-swan has been poisoned by her killing partner, the same snake that remains molting on the scene as evidence of resurrection, under the benumbed look of Governor-father Lázaro. A Great Conjoining will indeed always resist the neat solutions ordered by stark calculations of the sort Patrick laid on the archdruid's seven-colored rainbow.

An added view of the affair develops as one takes into account a couple of notes added by the Compiler to the event. They include references to an Indian massacre that took place shortly after de Ribera's arrival in the colonial province of Paraguay, and to a report drawn from "the hoariest chronicles of the Colony" concerning the Gualachís, who ate the honey of wild bees and were never tamed by the conquistadors, "much less subjugated by the Missionaries."[13] These light-colored people had been ruled "since time immemorial by a famous cacique, a sorcerer and a terrible tyrant whose subjects attribute[d] to him the gift of immortality" (389–393/245–47). In belonging to a layer of colonial history much older than the events narrated, the presence at the 1804 celebrations of these Indians and their immortal sorcerer-tyrant creates a synchronic passage between at least two different moments in the history of Paraguay, from the time it was still regarded as Provincia Gigante de las Indias to the period approaching independence from Spain. A picture of fierce resistance to colonizing influences stands next to both the record of a massacre from a more recent time and the story of one of the last colonial governors of Asunción, "who ordered the one copy of the *Social Contract* that existed in Paraguay to be burned" (393/247), but who is also characterized, in another note compiled from a historian, as "one of the most enlightened Spanish officeholders in this part of America in the twilight years of the eighteenth century" (385–86/241–42). It must be added that de Ribera is mostly remembered as the author of two very unpopular policies among colonists in Paraguay—his opposition to the Spanish crown's order to abolish the *encomiendas,* and his attempt to deny tobacco growers their exemption from military service. The Compiler closes his series of historical footnotes to the affairs under de Ribera's tenure by reporting on the governor's family history, without citing any actual sources except for "Prester John." He refers to oral traditions that had established in the Province the "myth of the swift horseman who stole the daughter of a *Karaí-Ruvichá-Guasú,* a *Great-White-Chief*" (393/247). Clearly, history gathers itself unrefined; it flows back to its various and contending sources in legend, written accounts, and other such elaborations. In this regard, the notion of myth becomes one of recurrence, of resistance against the dying of the past. Rather than implying—as in the work of Lévi-Strauss—a concrete ensemble of any number of stories interconnected by their recasting of material life in symbolic plots, myth persists below the threshold of any single story or cluster of stories. Not so much unstructured as rampant, a certain infectiousness in the knowledge of things and the memory of events prevails from mouth to ear to inscribing means—whether of the humblest or more decorated variety. At any given moment, this universe of stories (this pond of cellular collisions) may go on dying at the edges, but not without giving transitional shape to a life cunning enough to survive its own thirsty immersion in it.

Such is the moment at which the spectacle of the shaman and the virgin would begin to center on the implied figure of the Supreme, who, in symbiosis with the Compiler, absorbs and recycles all available perspectives on the event: the courtly cynicism of the Great Conjoiner, the native myth of the zoomorphic tyrant-sorcerer found in folk traditions, and the unfolding saga of the immortal narratologist that sets all of it in motion. Rather than providing the means to construct at least a partial or detached historical view of the event, the Compiler introduces a historicist layer informed by a specific notion of fictional indifference toward the historical passage of time. Biography determines this type of fictional project, for it must be the biographic mode that on this occasion adopts the mad historicist project of permeating all traceable layers of the country's history with elements originating in a conjoined personality, in a life fragmented into other lives and coextensive with them, a life possessed by the need to tell its own story as a history lived by others. As such, the biographical design may function as a displaced or excluded factor within the historicist picture.

In this instance, the festivities honoring de Godoy took place in 1804, a year regarded by Julio César Chaves as "transcendental" in Francia's life, not only due to his fierce opposition to Governor de Ribera and his close associate, José Espinola, but because it was then that don Gaspar fell desperately in love with the aristocratic Petrona de Zavala, whose rare beauty resembled her mother's (known as *Estrella del Norte*), and whose father, don José Antonio Zavala y Delgadillo, belonged to the highest ranks of the colonial elite. The courtship failed when don Antonio ("the man who best knew the Province's archives") opted for another suitor, a young merchant and captain in the army, and rejected Francia, then twenty-eight, with the insulting phrase, "*What do I care about what that mulatto might think!*" (Chaves, 73–74). A timeless biographical program of revenge controls the scene; resentment felt by a rejected suitor branded as a half-breed (who is also the future perpetual dictator of the country) informs the sacred rape of the highest daughter of the province by the immortal sorcerer-tyrant, who emerges from the remote past of the colony to perform his prowess in front of a cynical perpetual Councilor. All principal actors in the affair are directed from a point of excluded inwardness by the Supreme's biographical sorcery. A scene that climaxed with the shamanistic meteor's bursting into iridescent particles (and ends with everyone reflected within an egocentric constellation) will eventually resurface near the end of the novel, when the Supreme is about to set fire to his papers.

> The Almastronomy I wrote on December 13, 1804! The image of the concave mirror and the ray of light, repeating, in successive rings extending to infinity, the eye that is observing, till finally it causes it to disappear in its own multiple reflections. In this perfect hall of mirrors there would be no way of knowing which is the real object. Hence the real would not exist; only its image. I did not produce the philosopher's stone in my alchemical laboratory. I succeeded in doing something much better. I discovered the line of perfect rectitude passing through all possible refractions. I fabricated a prism that could break a thought down into the seven colors of the spec-

trum. Then each one of them into seven others, until I caused a light
to come forth that is white and black at the same time. (578–79/410)

The passage gives the reverse side of the endless cycle of transformations
glimpsed during the nocturnal experience of the child-orphan inside the
skull. It claims yet another version of the *mysterium coniunctionis,* a
mirror of death in which zodiac and alchemy enclose the magus in its
own retina, as if its soul was fixed in double ocular prosthesis.

The second example of the Supreme's assumption of sorcery will serve
as a complex setting in which to draw a distinction between the author's
dual role as historical character and historicist mythmaker. Since the
analysis concerns the alteration for fictional purposes of some passages
from the Robertsons' *Letters on Paraguay,* one should begin by explaining the nature of their involvement in the early phases of Francia's rule.
The Robertsons conducted business in Paraguay for almost four years,
from the arrival of John in early 1811 to their peremptory expulsion by
Francia in 1815. In his dealings with them, Francia tried to exploit the
brothers' commercial ambitions with the aim of securing British support
in keeping navigational lines open throughout areas of the Río de la
Plata that were under harassment by enemies of Paraguay's government
based in Buenos Aires or operating from the Banda Oriental (White,
Paraguay's Autonomous Revolution, 9). The failure of this policy and the
Robertsons' downfall came when Britain appeared indifferent to the
exploits of José Gervasio Artigas and other *caudillos* against traffic in the
area. On a voyage back to Asunción carrying a cachet of weapons
desperately desired by Francia, John Parrish was briefly held by a contingent of *artigueños,* and the rifles were lost.

Besides conducting some lucrative business there, the Robertsons took
from Paraguay a wealth of impressions and anecdotes far more varied,
detailed, and well observed than the material found in the more prestigious *Essai historique sur la révolution du Paraguay, et le gouvernement dictatorial du Docteur Francia* by Rengger and Longchamp (1827). But the
professional stature of Rengger and Longchamp in the fields of medicine
and the natural sciences, their relative involvement in the affairs of government as army doctors, and the timely publication of their account
combine to give the edge in sharp historical interest to their cut-and-dried
testimony against the dictator's autarchic government. By comparison,
the Robertsons' account approaches a novel of adventure and romance. It
sustains itself as a record of keen, leisured observations, punctuated here
and there with moments of genuine peril. This novelistic quality did not

escape the eye of Juan Manuel de Rosas, the Argentine dictator, who in one of several expressions of praise for Francia accused the brothers of neglecting to inform the public of affairs in Paraguay, engaging instead in personal anecdotes and the sort of historical writing made popular by Sir Walter Scott (Chaves, 413). Thomas Carlyle was even more unkind toward the brothers' anecdotal ease, although his impatience seems to come from not being able to find in their letters the nuggets of information he required to quickly assemble a portrait of Francia (see Carlyle, *Miscellaneous Writings,* 561ff.). Indeed, an element of biographical pathos builds up in their narrative, particularly if one cares to return to the first letters after having read through the entire series of four volumes. By force of circumstance, the *Letters* were not published in book form until late 1838 and early 1839, more than twenty years after the experiences they recount, and after an incident in which the manuscript got lost and had to be redone from scratch. Although they give an account of the final editing, the brothers do not explain how the letters were drafted in the first place; but it is not hard to conclude that these reports *on* Paraguay were once meant as messages *from* that remote land. (The Robertson letters lack the ideal medium of instant relay not yet developed by communication technology; the epistles remain latched to the novel and its satellite forms, while in fact they are embryonic pieces of journalism from the field.) In contrast to most epistolary novels, the Robertsons date the published version of each letter more than two decades after the events depicted, and address it to one of two different subscribers from among the more than two hundred who made publication possible. These would amount to trivial contingencies if it were not for the place accorded to the *Letters* in the fictional world of *Yo el Supremo,* in which they become instruments of novelistic irony and satire.

Particularly in the case of John, who was not yet twenty when he first met Francia, memories must have been of sufficient vintage to stir in him sediments of congenial storytelling. His early Francia was not yet housed in Asunción, but remained in the strategic exile provided by his "neat and unpretending cottage" at Ybaray; John's portrait of Francia is one of a kind. He is met by don Gaspar while shooting birds next to the cottage:

> Up rose a partridge; I fired, and the bird came to the ground. A voice from behind called out, "buen tiro" . . . I turned around, and beheld a man of about fifty years of age, dressed in a suit of black, with a large scarlet capote, or cloak, thrown over his shoulders. He had a maté-cup in one hand, and a cigar in the other; and a little

urchin of a negro, with his arms crossed, was in attendance by the
gentleman's side. The stranger's countenance was dark, and his
black eyes were very penetrating, while his jet hair, combed back
from a bold forehead, and hanging in natural ringlets over his
shoulders, gave him a dignified and striking air. He wore on his
shoes large golden buckles, and at the knees of his breeches the
same. (*Letters,* 1:331)

Although perhaps mediocre by the best standards of biographical de-
scription, the portrait remains vivid and above all singular, even if for lack
of competitors. Of greater significance, as portraits go, is the engraving of
Francia that serves as frontispiece to the 1838 two-volume edition of the
Letters (see figure 1). It not only corresponds to the sketch penned by
John, but it gives a sort of Francia before Francia, a man younger than the
Perpetual Dictator he was soon to become, and quite remote in age and
looks from the Supreme whose features in Roa Bastos's text sustain a
mockingly cynical rapport with the mirror of death. Moreover, as Richard Alan White has pointed out, the title of "El Supremo" seems to have
been coined by Edward Lucas White in his novel, *El Supremo* (1916), and
then given currency by historians, "but it was never used by Francia nor
by any of his contemporaries" (*Paraguay's Autonomous Revolution,* 13).
White's remarks can be confirmed by simply reading Enrique Wisner's
uncluttered summary of Francia's years in power, *El dictador Rodríguez de
Francia,* written in the 1860s upon the request of President Francisco
Solano López, in which Francia is always called *Dictador.*

Taking into account this basic anachronism concerning the historical
location of *el Supremo,* portraits of the novelistic Supreme might disclose
their contradictory—and inherently fictional—nature as redundant, but
also as injurious acts committed against an implicit taboo dealing with
the making of icons or images in his likeness. They might prove redundant because, as a fictional construct, the Supreme's figure would provoke a kind of specular fascination in those who may attempt to capture
his likeness indelibly. The involved predicament of casting one's own
resemblance on the Supreme's icon may or may not affect those who
even today might find a place for him in their own imaginative lives, but
it certainly plays a cardinal role in the fictional access to Francia established in Roa Bastos's novel. A play of mirrors surrounds the Supreme
figurative construct with a potential number of unsanctioned images in
which the approaching glance of a thief in search of a forbidden icon is
trapped in attitudes of self-reflection. The Supreme's portraits (different

Engraving of José Gaspar Rodríguez de Francia used as the frontispiece for the Robertson brothers' Letters on Paraguay

in nature from those of Francia) should not exist outside his own faculty to fashion them in terms of a likeness he detests upon discovering, in the strange hands where he should expect to find it, a resemblance that he (and no other) has placed in them. Specular vanity proves intolerable in that, like death, it cannot be avoided.

In young Robertson's portrait and engraving of Francia, vanity's touch guides a passage from conventional biographical description toward a truly specular and alien enclosure related to death. But nothing like this can be noticed on reading John's description: "*Vanity* seemed to me to be the leading feature of his character, and though there was a latent sternness and almost continual severity in his countenance, yet, when relaxed into a smile, they only made, by contrast, an impression the more winning upon those with whom he conversed" (Letters, 1:335). It would only be on assuming that the Supreme has already read—and in singular fashion stolen—this and any other passage from the *Letters* that the specular effect would take effect. Quite beyond his kinship with Francia or with any other character from history or fiction, the Supreme rises as the enforcer of a second and well-informed reading, a conspiratorial return to the text without which his own antecedent inspection and poisoning of it would slip by undetected—or be merely hinted at by the obvious irony that signals the presence of such subterfuge in his words. As a biographical factor, the Supreme compels repetition and constant self-scrutiny. It is as a part of such reflectivity that vanity rises to a higher degree of self-awareness than the one portrayed by John Robertson in Francia's character. Vanity gives definition to one's portrait in the likeness of death, and it may do so in mockery of death, as seen in the discussion between the Supreme and Patiño of Robertson's portraits (198–200/89–91). Although not quite as defamiliarized into crude comic exchange as the Jute-Mutt or Muta-Juva scripts are in *Finnegans Wake,* the dialogue between Patiño and his boss must be grasped in terms of two reciprocal levels of humor. At the obvious one, the pictures by Robertson are simply debunked; Patiño claims to have burned the portrait as he kept the "papers" confiscated from the "gringo," while the Supreme complains about the fraudulent exoticism in which his figure and native landscapes have been set. But the scene can also be witnessed as if being *played* before a knowing audience, a public well aware by tradition (as in most forms of archaic drama) of an ulterior plot in which these same characters would have perpetrated jokes of the trickster variety on a dutiful victim of ridicule. Any allusion to the serious business of burning, confiscating, or reclaiming an object of communal value that has fallen into strange hands would translate into the commonly held knowledge that the object has already been restored to its rightful place or shape by the same actors, playing the role of all-powerful tricksters. Such figures typically overcome barriers set by ordinary notions of space and time, and thus succeed in challenging death. Accordingly, an emblem of death would be displayed as a token of apotropaic awe, such as the death's-head that presides, in mirror fashion, over the debunking of the portraits: "The death's-head face watches me intently. It mimics my movements as I fight for breath. It digs nails into my Adam's apple, clutches my trachea pumping emptiness" (198/89). Past this point of ritual confrontation with death, the trickster plays a dual role: first, as a character who bothers to explain seriously his displeasure toward the thief-disfigurer of his image and, second, as the comic trickster, the funster who shares with the audience his magic defeat of the alien thief by means of a countertheft.

This is how a text so revisited will provide access to the secret ploy shared by the trickster and his audience. For in the same manner in which his icon might have been stolen—from everyone—by the visiting John Robertson, the Supreme would have gained possession of the manuscript of the *Letters* while acting as a demon-thief. The novelistic kinship between *Yo el Supremo* and the *Letters* is sealed on the spot in Kensington where the brothers, on the eve of selling their manuscript to a publisher, lost it after one of them fell on the ice on alighting from a coach at night. Instead of an author stunned by a fall, a *Compiler's Note* speaks of a victim of theft: "On descending from the conveyance, an almost spectral black [*un negro casi espectral*], hidden beneath a large cape and tricorne, suddenly materialized, blocking the traveler's path and staring at him intently. The latter slipped and fell on the ice. The strange apparition became more spectral still in the feeble glow of the gaslight. Suddenly it vanished" (458/302). Living in a different world, and seemingly untarnished by such an account, the Robertsons shall offer a more elegant version of their temporary setback:

> Some of our friends were facetious on the catastrophe. One said that the MS. had only gone to the trunk-maker a little before its time. . . . Now, although we recollected that of the MS. of Cyd Hamet Benengeli, the first part was found by Cervantes as an envelope to a pound of butter, and that the remainder he purchased from the grocer at the cost of a few maravedis; yet unable to flatter ourselves that the merit of our lost MS., even should it be now in the grocer's shop, would stimulate a Cervantes to edit it, we have been ourselves constrained, from the same original documents, to compile anew the seven hundred long pages which were irretrievably lost on a winter's night. (2:328)

But the other ms. (or the ms. as *other*) was already in the hands of a sorcerer, different only in place of residence from Cervantes's Arabic magic penman.

From such a beginning, the *Letters* will remain in the Supreme's apothecary. Playing sorcerer and druggist, he will insinuate his craft with professional relish into the Robertsons' records on Paraguay. Incidents like John's capture by a band of Artigas's primitive *orientales* will be cured of their attributed lack of sincerity. The Supreme wants to punish the young Robertson for his inept and treacherous conduct, so he inhales a "phosphorescent snuff" laced with a drug prepared for him by none other than the naturalist and drug collector, Aimé Bonpland. He then rubs crushed fire-beetles on his body until it glows in green, and, resembling a fluorescent Irishman, he stalks the young Scotsman out of the room: "I rub my face, my neck, with the guts of these lampyrids. I rub my entire body with this luminous grease. The room is filled with livid lights. My fury burns from the floor to the ceiling. . . . I push along, upside down and right side to, from one wall to another, from one shore to another, turned into a green flame" (475/316).

Green glow from tiny guts: the same excremental luminosity that the Jacob-type twin of "Lucha hasta el alba" keeps in a jar and has to replenish as the insect light dies, a light that allows the chosen twin to write a story of parricide within a story written by Roa Bastos at thirteen, and which he would lose and not recover until almost forty years later, when, in 1968, he started research for *Yo el Supremo* (Ezquerro, "El cuento último-primero," 117–24). As will be explored later, "Lucha hasta el alba" ("Struggle Until Dawn") deals with symbolic affinities between parricide, the writing of autobiographic fiction, and the displaced suicide inherent in killing a strong father figure. The motif-based thematic affinities between parricidal writing in "Lucha hasta el alba" and the episode of fluorescent sorcery would seem to imply that the Supreme's aggression and defenses against John Robertson recognize in the figure of a young merchant with naïve literary aspirations an adversarial son enmeshed in the writing of autobiography. A parental trickster will tamper with the writings of the young Scotsman and his brother, just as the glowing demon chases the youth from Paraguay with a Guaraní cry: "Ko'ã pytaguá tekaká oñemosê vaêrã jaguaicha!" (*"These gringo shits most be thrown out like dogs,"* 476/317). Thus, in "Lucha hasta el alba," a sorcerer's apprentice writes his first tale of transgression under the same green source of dying light that glows afresh on the skin of a sorcerer who, besides scaring people, delights in adding new ink to strange manuscripts and in forging scenes in and out of books by other authors.

Oscar Wilde—whose own study of a forger-poisoner, ("Pen, Pencil, and Poison") is subtitled *"A Study in Green"*—might have enjoyed detect-

ing the Supreme's application of his poisoned pen to the recollections of
John Robertson. Hamlet returns to the scene, for it is here that, fallen
prisoner aboard a little ship to "between thirty and forty of the very worst
class of the marauding soldiers of Artigas," John hums his favorite dirge
about the rough-hewing Divinity that shapes ends. Then, as the Supreme
repeats Hamlet's sentence in Spanish, a pun emerges through an implied
mistranslation of an echoing cognate of *desvastar* ("to desvastate") as
desbastar ["desbastó al fin su destino"], or "to rough-hew," which transforms the English verb into a crooked translation of the name *Roa Bastos:*
someone who *gnaws,* a rodent who rough-hews wood in his own primitive fashion—and hence the opposite of *desbastar,* when it is not punning
with *desvastar,* and simply means to chip away roughness or to educate.
This would fit within Milagros Ezquerro's remarks on the author's nick-
name as a *carpincho,* an amphibious rodent, "or an ambiguous Roa-dor"
(63, my translation). Ends shall meet, since Hamlet was saved from death
by *"thieves of mercy,"* by *pirates,* who helped him descend on Denmark one
last time. Nevertheless, pirates are not named as such in John Robertson's
account; instead, they are *poisoned in* by his omniscient reader-forger, the
Supreme: "the bandits and brigands of the Protector of the Banda Oriental pirated the pirate descended from pirates" (469/311; cf. *Letters,* 1:85–
87). But when it comes to the Supreme, one must always keep in mind the
Compiler, without whom the forgery would lack ironic corroboration:
"The episode is related by the Robertsons in *The Reign of Terror* [the
Letters' ultimate sensationalist title]. The suppression of certain revolting
details is attributable not so much to Puritan prudishness as to the pro-
verbial English penchant for reserve and decorous understatement. . . .
Their version nonetheless coincides in general with that given by *El
Supremo"* (469/311). In such ironic counterpoint, forgery will undo suppression, it will pierce through decorum, and poison naïve reserve with
the indelible ink of rape, as intimated in connection with Shem's black
penmanship in *Finnegans Wake:* "the squid-self which he had squirt-
screened from the crystalline world waned chagreenold and doriangrayer
in its dudhud" (186.6–8).

One can imagine a magic pen that sucks in scribbled ink and then
issues it back upon the same piece of paper, tracing shapes it had
formerly kept hidden. Such a pen needs a bed, a cradle, a row of phrases
dotting the paper like telltale drops: "My scattered wardrobe was parti-
tioned out among the robbers. . . . One man was lying on my bed in a
state of intoxication. . . . Significant gestures were passing from one to
the other, commingled with open threats. . . . After witnessing for hours

a scene of license and debauch too frightful to be conceived, and too gross to be portrayed" (*Letters*, 1:86–87). One must beware: in the eye of the forger (even if he is not a poisoner as well), there is always a phrase that does it, that elicits poison. The "demon-like gang" of gauchos holding John Robertson does not include women (or so would the reader-subscriber to the *Letters* conclude, given the absence here of any reference to females from the account by someone otherwise so prolific in detailing their beauty and occasional strangeness). The forger would not miss the absence, as he *litters* what the victim has written:

> The metamorphosis wrought in them by the assumption of my costume was no less striking than that wrought in me on being forcibly and scantily clad in theirs. . . . No shirt, no stockings were allowed me. . . . Many Artigueños . . . were now to be seen strutting about in Bond Street cut coats, leathern breeches. . . . I had not a wardrobe ample enough to cloth forty men, each had only a *part* of it, and this contrasted so strongly with the part of his own which he was still obliged to retain, as to make him look like the centaur, human above, brutal below, or *vice versa*. (*Letters*, 1:92–93)

Or, as the poisoner (the Supreme) writes:

> When the English ephebe awoke from his nightmare he witnessed an amusing spectacle improvised in his honor. Artigas's band of toughs, decked out in the full dress uniforms, the ecclesiastical ornaments and adornments, dolled up in the dresses and jewelry of the women, were dancing a wild, demoniacal gypsy zambra round about him, brandishing brand-new pistols and sabers. They were laying bets at the top of their lungs as to which of them was strong enough to behead him with a single stroke. Juan Parish Robertson, like the old man in Chaucer's tale (and as happened to me a short time ago), must at that instant have been pounding with his fists on the doors of mother earth begging her to let him in. (470/312)

This follows (but may also alter) the earlier quick picture drawn to suggest that the young pirate might have been raped by his drunken captors: "They subjected him to terrible abuse. They spread-eagled him naked between stakes, lying face downward on the ground. The mob of Tapes and Correntinos worked him over for hours [like creatures out of a noontide visitation]. Confused story of things experienced at midnight. Dreamed of at midday" (469/311). Metaphoric centaurs ("brutal below or *vice versa*") have doubled themselves literally on their inventor's back, exposing it to a quite unwantoned form of reading, and British-gaucho cross-dressing has turned into an all-male show of horsemen cavorting as females with hidden powers.

But this picture can (and perhaps *must*) be altered. The hint that one should try to transform poisoning into appended literature can be found in the slight reference to Chaucer's Pardoner, or, rather, to the old man that appears in a tale within a tale, a story of poisoning that emerges catastrophically from within a wicked sermon. As glancing as the reference might seem, it manages to spark interest in the fact that the Supreme has translated a piece of the *Canterbury Tales* under the guidance of John Robertson: "my groping and fumbling efforts to translate Chaucer, Swift, or Donne" (245/128–29). It might just be that the Pardoner's itinerant sermon *cum exemplum* opens a *mise-en-abyme* relationship between kernels of great thematic significance in *Yo el Supremo* and one of its distant precursors in Roa Bastos's fictional world, the tale of Macario in *Hijo de hombre*. The hint will be followed not only on account of its intrinsic literary value, but in order to deal with a distinctive aspect of Roa Bastos's work: its displacement of Christian and Hebrew religious stories to a setting where they become inextricably grounded in both the myths and traditions of Paraguay's indigenous peoples and the author's biographic covenant with his country.

The Pardoner and the Host

Moder, with you wolde I chaunge my cheste
That in my chambre longe time hath be,
Ye, for an haire-clout to wrappe me.'
But yit to me she wol nat do that grace,
For which ful pale and welked is my face.
—Geoffrey Chaucer, "The Pardoner's Tale"

I will make the voice flow again through the bones. . . .
I will make speech take flesh once again. . . .
After today's time is gone and a new age dawns. . . .
—*Guaraní* Hymn of the Dead

Every informed view held concerning Chaucer's Pardoner requires qualification and a proper sense of antithesis. The man tells a story of murder and poisoning as he treats the audience to a stand-up biography whose shameful appeal must prevail, beyond its own sycophantic hunger, in order to bring about a cure from the very illness it exploits. He is a confidence man in the art of selling pardons to fools who crave entertainment when they should be fearing their own vanity and spiritual death. But, is he even a man? Well, he exceeds manliness the way a heretic does orthodox doctrine: a *eunuchus ex nativitate,* as most experts insist, with hair as yellow as wax, rattails down to his shoulders, bulging eyeballs, a smooth chin, and a goat's voice. So featured, the Pardoner exercises a shrill feminoid pride of office that fascinates and repels those around him. He has been portrayed as an actor of aberrant skills: "He is a mystery, an enigma—sexually anomalous, hermaphroditic, menacing, contradictory. He has a magnetic power of attraction partly because he is frightening and loathsome."[14] The man is an engine of verbal prowess, an enchanter perched over those he would pardon like a monstrous bird chattering a poisoned confession and selling it as medicine. The Pardoner may enlist from any of us the sort of avenging sympathy that recognizes how deserving of such treatment his listeners are, as it acknowledges in him the glacial wrath of an inverted prophet. The man brings punishment on his listeners in the very act of pleasing them, and with the sole consuming purpose of repaying an injury, felt by him to have been received from the perennial others, from the eternal society that will foolishly crave for his oratorical gifts and resentment: "His sermon, with its capacity for dominating others and its avowedly rapacious motive is . . . a kind of monstrous verbal rape. . . . He is invidious. The force which energizes his charade is an obsessive lust for power. . . . One cannot miss its most basic force, resentment" (Howard, *"Canterbury Tales,"* 353). The modern view might also see in the Pardoner strong elements of masochism as a form of self-punishment simultaneously embraced and repelled, juiced-up and then shoved at the audience. From the margins of his sermon, the Pardoner offers his own portrait: a show of naked and perversely engaging self-hatred in which sins common to many find a mirror.

The story he tells shines on him with lurid glare. His value as a prototype of exposed narrative power is similar to the Supreme's arrogant display of authorial control. The Pardoner's performance resembles those instances of personal exposure in which the Supreme enacts his own animating ambition to defeat reflection and storytelling by means of acting, or where he shows off his embodiments, his masks and shames, beyond the instruments of dictation and writing. The Pardoner drags a cosmetized authorial figure under the floodlights; he enforces mimicry, he proclaims that voice is not enough. A required scandal comes off with him, if not in the phosphorescent green of *lampyrid* glow, then in a grotesque vampire show of sermonistic seduction aimed at purse and soul. When the Supreme makes himself into a glowing demon inside a story whose sinews he is in the act of poisoning, the event corresponds with a similar intrusion that the Pardoner would—but does not—carry out inside his sermon; for his scandalous presence within that narrative device remains cast and hidden in allegorical fashion, but also strongly suggested by the power of his performing act as a dramatic frame for both tale and sermon. The similarity comes down to this: the Pardoner is a prototype of authorial exposure of the worse kind, and thus he embodies the same performing stance adopted by the Supreme in the role of sorcerer. Likewise, the Supreme displays inside his controlled plots the same degree of blunt authorial intrusion latent in the Pardoner's allegorical projections into his sermon. The Supreme has taken the final magical step that would have placed the Pardoner nakedly inside his own sermon.

And then there is the Host. An equally involved affinity links this figure with the role of the Compiler, a role thus unbound, taken on parade, pilloried. As a figure of authorial management, the Compiler seems closer than any other character to a writer named Roa Bastos (see Cruz, 71–83; Krysinski, 49ff.; *Yo el Supremo,* 62–67). He (the Compiler) collaborates, meddles, and struggles with the otherwise absolute narrative control of the Supreme, with whom he nevertheless remains in ironic conspiracy. What he reads and compiles the other does not need to read in order to know. For instance, the compiling self must have read the Robertsons, while the Supreme self has always known their writings because he acted in them and altered them even before they were written. So when the writings are stolen as the manuscript of the *Letters,* they are found shaped by the mind and deeds of the Supreme, and poisoned by the hand of the Compiler, the Cide Hamete in the affair. These two entities are figure and shadow. The one who compiles has his way into performance within the plot barred by the other, the sorcerer; but the sorcerer cannot find a brand of ink strong enough to withstand poisoning by the other, his hand cannot reach out into any future text without the other's hand riding on it. A sorcerer acts, kills, cures; a compiler frames, corrects, counterfeits, poisons.

A moment of climactic tension in "The Pardoner's Tale" may help to illustrate this ingrown duality. The Host has been asked by the Pardoner to unbuckle his purse, and to buy pardons that have just been shown to be soiled by greed; he answers with an extravagant insult, more or less as follows: "You'll have me kissing your old pants and swear they were a saint's relic, even if your ass had put paint on them. But, by St. Helen and the Holy Cross she found, I wish I had your balls in my hand instead of a bunch of relics; I'd have them cut off and helped carry them until they were enshrined for you inside a hog's turd" (cf. Chaucer, 660–67). There is more in the insult than offends the ears, for a good amount of irony hinges on whether or not the Host knows, from the Pardoner's appearance, that he threatens a eunuch with castration (see Howard, "*Canterbury Tales*," 366). If he does, he would begin to resemble the Compiler's peculiar omniscience; if he does not, his brutal intent would have some of the Supreme's heady immersion in dramatic strife. In either case, he would have come too close to his abject rival, far closer than either savage irony or blind macho rage would want to—unless to make a quick killing.

It has been brilliantly suggested that "the two men might have in effect exchanged malevolent wishes to castrate each other" (Howard, "*Canterbury Tales*," 367); and it is this sort of intimate cross-injury that would bring their confrontation within the authorial perimeter of the Supreme and his Compiler. The latter would always have read (or compiled) something about someone's congenital defects or castration, while the former would have sampled (and dressed) both injuries with his actions. It is as if the Compiler were to be looking over the shoulder of the Host who would know (as he insults the Pardoner) that the weird fellow he threatens already lacks what he would take away—at least with a threat. The Compiler occupies that position within specular relationships from which shame is both spotted and applied on the other as on a surrogate. If, as most interpreters claim, the compiling Self and the Supreme person are reciprocal doubles, the question of shame needs adequate answer. Otherwise, the specular encounter will not result in the exposure of a *marked* or branded self, the sort of primal victim claimed by the regulating conscience identified in Freud's topography with the superego. Beyond its recognition of narcissism, the specular scene represents a hermeneutic fable on the contagiousness of shame, arrested by means of a wicked sort of bestowal. In other words, someone in particular (rather than two individuals combined) feels the impact of shame in the specular encounter. This exposed someone would be the Pardoner, bestowed or tainted with abjection by the Host's ironic insult, ironic because (in specular terms) the Pardoner cannot but see that the other knows of his singular immunity against the only sort of castration that the Host (the other) seems to recognize. Either by God's hands or by his own, all of the Host's castrations are real (in the sense in which they are worn on a man's face). The Host may be labeled a shame-maker, a talking head capable of broadcasting shame about the Pardoner, who in turn seems immune to it, being instead a skilled practitioner of shamefulness. The question is whether the Pardoner can feel guilt, an experience which by profession he has always exploited in others.

If the Compiler were like the Host, he would be shallower than the characters about whom and at whose expense he compiles. As just another character, the Compiler would not be capable of seeing past the other's shame into a deeper assumption of guilt. But shallow he is not, nor is he an outright character, like the Host as he insults the Pardoner. The Compiler's attitude combines the body's withdrawal from the perils of action with the authority to revise and correct any actions (embodied or written). The Compiler is the ultimate skin, the hardest to see—he is the Host with the Pardoner inside.

On his part, the Supreme duplicates anyone and projects everyone into shameful view. In being capable of dis-playing both Pardoner and Host, the Supreme stands at both ends of giving and receiving shame. Each insult or deprecation issued by the Supreme reveals a vulnerability to both shame and guilt that the Compiler can only witness and abet from the margins. This almost clerical role finds an outlet of performing value in the copious investment of authorial and self-fashioned pluralness that the compiling hand and mind have placed on the mirrored self of the Supreme. The story belongs to him, to the author as a fully deployed character: with its contagious phobias, aches, cynicism, childish yearnings, and overburdened memories. This character shares a narrative physiognomy with the poor old man in the Pardoner's sermon, whose words to Mother Nature and to Death the Supreme remembers as a translator and, quite possibly, as an actor. In fact, he might insist that an old pardoner—even *the* Pardoner—should be the right man to play the wandering role of an orphan who knocks at the door of a rejecting mother.

A similar role is played in *Yo el Supremo* by the figure of Macario, introduced in the text within a couple of marginal notes. Macario's marginality extends through fibers colored with biographic chemistry; it is a biography placed in a region near the heart of Roa Bastos's fiction and its sources in anonymous myth. Although relatively small, Macario's biographic narrative resists summary: it seems to die when removed from its fragmented but compact setting. And yet, like a gospel, Macario's life grows as it is retold and transposed, renewed and recognized by voices written or heard. Like Coriolanus's *world elsewhere,* Macario's native country would seem to belong to an earthly afterworld, a world so pitched on familiar landmarks that it deserves to be known as an *after-place*. This place-after-the-place-that-is-always-the-place is where Macario finds his itinerant residence as the oldest storyteller in Roa Bastos's fiction. His age is older than that of the group memory it sustains, since it springs from the myriad vanishing points through which such memory falls into inchoate randomness: "He sprung everywhere. . . . He walked tantalizing [*tantaleando*] the road with his tacuara staff; eyes dead, parched by the skin of cataracts . . . we saw him go by as if that burnt little old man, the son of one of dictator Francia's slaves, had emerged before us each time like a visitor from the past. . . . He was a marvelous teller of stories . . . the living memory of the people. He knew of things from beyond the boundaries" (*Hijo de hombre*, 9, 14). But Macario's age is also younger than any personal memory. His encounters with each person whom the narrator in *Hijo de hombre* perceives as part of his own recollections mark the individual birth of memory's scouting of the past within a single lifespan. Macario represents two ages: the age of hazardous birth and infancy and the age that tantalizes the earth knocking on death's doors. He will be buried in a child's coffin: "Lo enterramos en un cajón de criatura" (*Hijo de hombre*, 46). Like the poor old man in the Pardoner's sermon, Macario moves on liminal grounds, setting the boundaries and the reach of those questions that the living may dare bring into an area of marginality where life is measured by death.

In the Pardoner's sermon, evil runs to the edges, madly wanting to kill a traitor named Death. In Macario's story, boundaries are reached in search of resurrection—a thin line separates both pursuits. The Pardoner tells of how three drunken young rioters swear their brotherhood as they rush to avenge the killing of a friend who in fact has died of the plague (known popularly as Death). A boy has told them that his mother said so, and off they go in chase of this powerful fellow who has killed so many. They meet an old man who has his own mother-story to tell: no matter how much or how far he travels, he cannot find anyone willing to give him youth in exchange for his old age; Death rejects him and Mother Earth will not welcome him back, or give him that shirt of hair ("heire clout") he needs as a sign of rightful shelter—the old man cannot find resurrection, so he lives sheltered by Death's ungenerous companionship. The three evil stooges will not recognize how deadly the advice given by Death's reject can be; so they follow his crooked pointers up to a tree, where instead of traitor Death they find a pot of gold. The two oldest are left behind to guard the treasure while the youngest runs back to town to fetch a few bottles of wine. They plot their own deaths to great success: the returning brother is slain by two murderers who will celebrate their crime with two bottles of poisoned wine left behind by the victim, who in his quick return to town had paid a visit to a pharmacist well read in Avicenna's chapter on poisons.

Macario's storytelling role is as inseparable from the two novels and the short story in which he appears as the Pardoner's sermon is from his own tale. The opening sequence in *Hijo de hombre* gives the bare essentials of the storyteller's life, fragments of which enter into the smaller textures of *Yo el Supremo,* and also into the rewritten story "Lucha hasta el alba." Macario migrates within Roa Bastos's work like a minimal but exemplary factor in the making of scripture; he links Genesis, the Book of Ezekiel, and the Gospels as if, in their composition and reception, each of these textual traditions had passed through two distant but interconnected social environments: the imaginable one in which a given body of scripture claims to have directly gathered its materials from living people, and the one in which the same body of holy scripture would already be subject to reception by being repeated and inevitably altered in oral performance and according to the pressing needs of the moment. Macario is witness to the Christological drama that unfolds in the navel-like world of Itapé (his Galilee) as if he had come back to it from the older territory of myth and saga where a younger figure of the author (Roa Bastos) experiences and creates as fiction his own struggle with an angel. Uncle and spiritual father of Christ the artisan, Macario has also visited the province where Jacob the son wrested a father's name from the land, and he has also traveled through the cosmic devastation of Ezekiel's battlefields on the same invaded land.

Macario's life around Itapé involves him in a grass-roots enactment of the mysteries of incarnation and resurrection. The village celebrates Christ's passion in "a harsh ritual—rebellious, primitive, fermented into a curse by an insurgent group, as if the spirit of the people were to curl up at the smell of sacrificial blood and explode in a clamor that no one knew whether to blame on anguish, hope, or resentment" (*Hijo de hombre,* 12). A covenant between youthful restlessness and patriarchal endurance puts in crisis the recurrent Christological riddle by offering proof that Christ must be made, extracted from effigy, *rough-hewed* by the staining hands of leprosy, his wooden baldness covered with a head of hair clipped from a surrogate mother, the village whore and the counterpart of Macario since she is the one who, in apparent lunacy, speaks in broken words ("palabras rotas") and sings the Guaraní *Hymn of the Dead*. But the story also contains a portrait of adolescent biography trying to incorporate three ages: the remote past during Francia's rule and the birth of Macario; a middle passage located at the catastrophic juncture of the Great War of 1864–70 (when the male population of Paraguay suffered virtual annihilation in their fight against the Triple Alliance, and when Gaspar Mora—the village artist and eventual leper—is given birth by Macario's sister); and a third age, the one recollected by the narrator as the time of his childhood and adolescence, when the Christological events unfold.

Like the passion drama that serves as their axis, these ages are *recursive,* which means that they are perceived as a single age fixed and renewed within one individual, to which his entire life may hasten back. Their reincarnational value is immanent in the life of each person who feels the effervescent recurrence of the crisis. The Guaraní belief in the rebirth passage of the dead through human remains gives to the Christian faith in the mystery of incarnation a strong element of communal reinstatement, of the return of the dead. This crisis is not centered on the nailing of a God figure to a cross, but on the deeds of an individual who, with the help of others infused with the charisma of his actions, has given communal life to the Christ-object, as when Gaspar dies of leprosy in the bush, but leaves behind a wooden Christ for the others to protect as if it were his own life being reborn in each of those who care. The object will always remain an object, an artifact, but the same group that compelled its making and took the effigy to an omphalic summit will no longer be an object of social passivity; its members will be resurrected in each other's lives. Reincarnation becomes reinstatement; the mystery of transposed substances and ontologies (flesh into wood, leprous fluids into sacral anointment) does not reflect a man or a god risen from death, nor the alchemy of pure birth from an intact mother. It is rather the Guaraní belief that the village adopts and tries to make permanent: that the communal voice shall sing once again through the bones and take flesh once more in the rebirth of time.[15]

Behind this earthbound Christology, an artist's life awaits recognition. The opening narrator in *Hijo de hombre* tells the story of his youth, whose principal actors are an old storyteller and his nephew, a musician who carves rustic figures on wood. Two paths to creation cross each other in the novelist's memory: the one traced by Macario from the shadow of the *Karaí Guasú* to the present, and the one followed by Gaspar Mora into liminal exile and resurrection. Two prototypes of the archaic artist (of his myth of origins and ultimate fate) can be found along these crossing paths. The storyteller was born under Francia's wing, and the musician-artisan a few decades later, during the exodus of the Great War. But on closer inspection, their births appear bound together and concurrent. Macario's father Pilar was a domestic servant freed from slavery by the *Karaí*, whose meals he tasted to make sure they were untainted by poison. Pilar offended Francia and paid for it with his life, but not before fathering twelve children, who after his execution were sent into confinement at various points in the country, with Macario and his sister María Candé sharing their exile. In Pilar, the *Karaí* loved and killed a son; he gave the son the name of Francia, and there was no lack of rumor claiming that the half-breed ex-slave was the Dictator's natural son. Hence, the storyteller's full name as putative grandchild is Macario Francia, and his nephew's first name Gaspar. The phrase, "That afternoon we learned that Macario Francia was Gaspar's uncle" (*Hijo de hombre*, 17), reinstates the *Karaí*'s Christian name and patronymic within a knotted genealogy; it may be rephrased as: *the grandson is the grandfather's uncle as the grandfather may be his own grandnephew*. Besides being Gaspar's scriptural guardian (or the person who shapes his image as the artisan shapes his own likeness in the wooden Christ he carves), Macario, as the mother's brother, represents the matrifocal strength possessed by Guaraní culture in Roa Bastos's fiction and in his own biographical reflections. Indeed, as "Lucha hasta el alba" shows, it is as conveyed by mothers and other females to their children that the scriptural stories blend with indigenous myths. A central element carried in such transmission binds together the generations of grandfathers and their grandchildren's grandchildren's children as if, in running a finger through a deck of cards, a flickering image would produce the still figure of a single yet layered and successive male. José Gaspar *Karaí*, Pilar, Macario, and Gaspar blend in the sliding birth of these generations. The uncharted fate of the other eleven children of Pilar may be recapitulated in the single one whose wandering path the personal narrative and the gospel myths have chosen to follow. This fragmented scriptural saga would find a recurrent drama of sacrifice and reinstatement in the Christological event that young Gaspar motivates and the town fulfills under the leading voice of Macario.

The artist's life is twisted into knots as genealogy, but it is also severed beneath this factor of recurrence. Wandering Macario might have been a prophet in the mold of Elijah and Elisha, or else one among many figures who simply did not attain full charismatic power in a life of militancy.

The environment of social ferment to which he is drawn needs to be understood in terms of those elements of dire material life so strongly felt in and around enclaves from which prophetic militancy springs. Without pressing the analogy too far, Gottwald's characterization of prophecy in such a setting might shed light on Itapé's discontent: "The bearers of the Elijah-Elisha stories look like religious formations at the lower fringes of society that functioned as rescue stations and advocacy groups. The underside of Israelite life, away from the "history-making" royal court, was filling up with more and more people pushed out of the old protective tribal structures by political centralization and social stratification" (The Hebrew Bible, 352).

There are no Yahweh supporters in Itapé, nor is there a long and complex tradition of disputed legitimacy between, on the one hand, ancient tribal structures and, on the other, an encroaching court with its bureaucratic apparatus and a theocracy vying for international prestige. And yet, Itapé is said to have been settled on the redlands of Guairá when an old viceroy, indifferent to the toil and suffering that would ensue from his gesture, put his finger on an empty area of a chart and opened the region to colonial exploitation, "as it was always the case when it came to distributing the land among the *encomenderos* or rewarding the fatigue of the petty captains who had contributed to reducing the tribes to bondage" (*Hijo de hombre*, 10). Itapé's history will proceed under colonial rule and then under the sway of those who bring in the railroad and the sugar plantation. The town's neighbors unite only once against the alliance of political bosses and the clergy, when Macario convinces most of them that they should protect the wooden Christ carved by the leper Gaspar against the priest's wishes to burn it. The episode places Macario on the side of what is clearly Roa Bastos's faith in the people's need to seize religious symbols, objects, and stories in order to free them from the occlusive other-worldliness sponsored by the church in cynical alliance with political and economic interests. Macario utters what amounts to blasphemy when he tells those who would follow the priest's orders that he hears the voice of a man inside his chest, and that "it is a man who speaks! God cannot be understood. . . . But a man, yes!" (*Hijo de hombre*, 37). His followers will then cluster around a man who hears religious voices, but not of godly origin. It is as such, as a vessel of communal and earthly urgencies, that at the summit of his years in Itapé, Macario may end up resembling an old prophetic figure: "Macario's rancho ended up being surrounded all the time by a rumorous crowd. During those days, the old beggar was the true patriarch of the town. A schismatic and rebellious patriarch, obeyed by everyone" (43). Under his influence, Itapé becomes an enclave of cohesive aspirations informed by a heretical and potentially messianic understanding of the Christological figure, and alerted to the indigenous proclamation of rebirth. The Guaraní *Hymn of the Dead* could be compared with the archaic Hebrew notion of *ru'ah*, the *wind* that rises from chaos as harbinger of things at the brink of gaining form, but also the *spirit* or *breath* that infuses matter and some individuals with uncanny force. The notion of a cyclic renewal present in Guaraní cosmology might likewise be compared with elements of archaic religion still discernible in the text of Genesis, such as the presence of spirits, places of ancestor worship, and the type of phenomena that scholars once called *polydaemonism* (Hayes and Miller, *Israelite and Judaean History*, 125). It is precisely such a setting on a piece of earth still teeming with spirits and polymorphous forces that Macario wants his people to survey and reclaim as their own. At the same time, the Genesis setting stands side by side with that moment in Ezekiel (37:1–14) when the prophet is carried by the Lord to a plain strewn with bones and says that he will put the breath of life in them and bring about their resurrection. Considering that the title of *Hijo de hombre* is taken from Ezekiel's prophetic calling addressed to the "son of man," the parallel between these moments in the Bible and the Guaraní *Hymn of the Dead* could not be more salient.

The lives of Macario and Gaspar Mora are thus intertwined by way of genealogy. Both men are inseparable as factors in the making of a gospel, as they are combined by their contrasting relationships with creation and procreation. Both men (no matter how old and patriarchal one of them might become) share the status of perennial sons within the notion of fatherhood. They both reflect the *Karaí*'s putative lineage in not leaving behind any biological issue; their brood lives on in their work and exemplary acts, and it is through such work that a genealogical cycle closes as they join in fathering the image of the country's Father. But the image is split between Macario's direct access to the *Karaí*'s relics (and the branding of the Dictator's power on his own flesh) and Gaspar's leprous anointment of the Christ-artifact with his own brand of contagious sacredness. The old uncle mesmerizes young men by showing them a silver buckle that belonged to Francia; the relic gives proof of his proximity to the Dictator, as does a scar on the palm of his hand from a burning wound he suffered when, as a child, he tried to steal from Francia's writing desk a gold coin that the cunning old man had left behind as bait after first putting it on a burning brazier. More than just a scar, the branding mark is a "llaga negra," a black sore that links Macario with Gaspar's leprosy, a sacred disease and also an agent of procreative faculties beyond sexual difference.

A complex relationship comes into view if one considers that Macario regards the wooden Christ as Gaspar's son, while at the same time insisting that the man died a virgin. When someone proposes to bury the *talla*—the effigy—next to the leper's remains, Macario rejects the idea by saying: "It is his son! he left him as his replacement" (*Hijo de hombre*, 33). Moreover, the subject of Gaspar's leprosy affects not only his artistic and sacred procreativeness, but the adversarial and phobic view regarding his presumed unmanliness (his lack of *hombría*). The narrator recalls fighting one of two malevolent twins who once insulted Gaspar's memory, after his disappearance from Itapé, by calling him *monflórito*, a vernacular reference to male sexual unfitness and effeminacy. Later, the twins will almost drown him in revenge; he is rescued from the river's muddy bottom at the point of bloody asphyxiation, as if by Gaspar's "wooden hand," which turns out to be a "raigón negro," a black root. The memory seems to harbor ambivalent elements of symbolic birth, of being uprooted from a hostile womb element. The twins' association with negative or malevolent strategies against birth and its symbols may include the theft of Francia's silver buckle from Macario, a relic and obvious token of fatherhood which one of the thieves wears on his belt. But all this happens before Gaspar's leprosy is discovered and the effigy of the leprous Christ is brought before the priest to have it placed in the church. The priest takes charge of linking Gaspar's disease with his unmanliness. He reminds the crowd that the Christ is "la obra de un lazariento [a leper's work]. . . . There is danger of contagion," and on finding resistance in the audience, he adds: "Just think about who carved this image. . . . A heretic, a man who never set foot inside a church, an impure man who died the way he died because! . . ." (*Hijo de hombre*, 36). With his invective, the priest has struck (in vain) at the heart of Gaspar's sacredly abject condition as a Christ-like artist and eternal son.

Besides being a *figura christi,* Gaspar Mora joins Macario Francia in a biographic portrait of the artist sketched inside the novelist's memories of youth. The two figures of archaic and locally rooted creation ought to be seen as inalienably bound together in narrative form, like the Pardoner and the poor old man of his sermon when taken beyond the narrow tactics of a wicked man who sells Christian forgiveness to a hungry crowd. We move from the Pardoner to Macario: from a wild sermon aimed at vulnerable or tainted souls to a Christology for the hungry in need of communal rebirth. Instead of an old man rejected by death, a young-old-man, a father-son figure perennially knotted together. Rather than Death as the plague, a disease that anoints life's rebirth with miserable substances obtained from its sacred melting. But this counterpoint offers only one view of the narrative matter in which filaments of the Pardoner's tale can be traced in Roa Bastos's text, a matter that continues to color the text through the biographic mingling of Macario's life and that of Aimé Bonpland.

Province, Republic, Kingdom

The earth of Paraguay, Excellency, is the heaven of plants; there are more of them here than there are stars in the firmament and grains of sand in the deserts. I have tirelessly interrogated the layers of our planet. I have opened them like the leaves of a book in which the three kingdoms of nature keep their archives. . . . What do you think of the pages of the book of Paraguay? Here I must dig deeper, Excellency. Poke about in layer after layer till I get to the very bottom.—Augusto Roa Bastos, Yo el Supremo

his hoisting of an emergency umberolum in byway of paraguastical solation in the rhyttel in his head.—James Joyce, Finnegans Wake

You should never believe Europeans, nor trust them, from whichever Nation they might come [Francia to a delegate from Itapúa].—Julio César Chaves, El Supremo Dictador

In March 1821, the well-traveled French naturalist, Aimé Bonpland, settled in Candelaria, a colony situated in the disputed province of Misiones de Entre Ríos, just east of the Paraná river and not farther than two leagues from Paraguay's border at Itapúa (see figure 2). He had arrived in the Plata region three years earlier, following an invitation to return to South America from his friend Simón Bolívar. While in Buenos Aires, Bonpland managed to enlist the financial support of two French merchants and a concession from the Entre Ríos authorities to develop a *yerba maté* plantation in an area once controlled by the Jesuits, and more recently held under the sway of *federal* leaders like the *caudillos* Artigas and Ramírez, until the arrival of Brazilian intervention in 1821 (White, 131–33). Just before Ramírez's defeat, Bonpland was able to settle in Santa Ana with his help and that of an Indian partisan of Artigas, Nicolás Irapí, who, like the other two leaders, had territorial ambitions affecting Paraguay. News of such a settlement next to one of

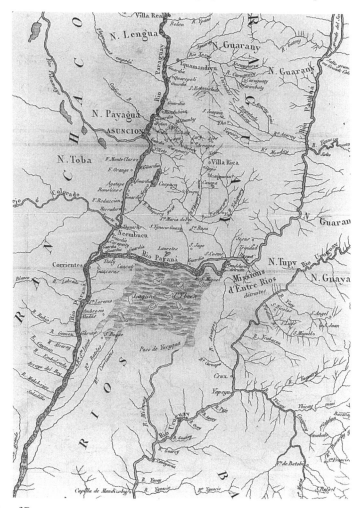

Map of Paraguay

his most troublesome borders reached the Dictator at a moment of great
peril, when Paraguay's status as an independent republic remained unrecognized and besieged by forces from the United Provinces of the Río
de la Plata and Brazil. While keenly interested in gaining the recognition
of European nations for his young republic, Francia had plenty of
reasons to distrust any of the emissaries that showed up in the area to
open contacts with his government outside official diplomatic channels.
His response to the wily Saguier, who arrived on one such mission in
1819, shows Francia's contempt for the type of "uncivil and diffident

adventurer" sent to him by nations like France. Years later, Saguier
would be put down in an *Auto* as "an uncovered royalist spy who turned
himself into a pharmacist" (Chaves, 336). In the spirit of such feelings
of disappointment and hate toward duplicitous European overtures,
Francia ordered troops at Itapúa to move against Bonpland's place
under cover of darkness. The instructions for the raid reveal his estimate
of his enemies' character and ambitions. He sees Bonpland enrolled in a
"Quadrilla de Indios Bandidos," remnants of "hordes destroyed and
dispersed" upon Artigas's "total ruin and defeat," but now once again
active under the command of Irapí, with the aim of penetrating into
Paraguay, "pretending to dismember and take hold of this Place, and to
create in it, according to what the Indian [Irapí] used to say, a sister
Province, in order to rent to others its *Yerbales*" (Chaves, 337). The raid
against the colony in Candelaria was successfully carried out on 8 De-
cember 1821.

Thus began perhaps the most notorious and extended episode of
international resonance during Francia's regime. Bonpland was slightly
wounded and taken prisoner, but his subsequent life of ten years in
Paraguay was spent in the most curious of exiles. Settled on a farm that
Francia gave him in an area of great natural beauty named Santa María,
the naturalist's enterprising genius laid down its roots. He became an
agriculturalist who used the most advanced farming methods in a large
variety of crops, bred cattle and horses, built a distillery, a carpentry
shop, and a smithy, and opened a market in the nearby village. But his
greatest contribution to the area was the establishment of a hospital and
maternity ward that soon became filled with patients and in which he
served as both physician and expert pharmacist (Chaves, 400–401).

In the meantime, efforts to secure his release were led by Simón
Bolívar, whose actions in the affair might be interpreted as part of an
overall plan to enter into the geopolitics of the Plata region on the side of
Buenos Aires and to the detriment of Paraguay's status as an independent republic. In a famous letter to Francia that might not have reached
its destination, Bolívar threatened to descend on Paraguay from his base
in Alto Perú (he thought of using the Pilcomayo River) in order to
rescue "the best of men and most celebrated among travellers" (Chaves,
391). Francia's silence provoked the Liberator's anger and made him
press hard on the government in Buenos Aires to allow his armies to
invade Paraguay, bring down Francia, and restore the isolated country to
the old viceregal unit which had become the United Provinces of la
Plata. Like many others, Bolívar regarded Paraguay as a province, which

he saw "being occupied by a certain Francia [*un tal Francia*], who has had it perfectly locked up for fourteen years. It does not belong to anyone, nor does it have any government, but that of a tyrant who is a virtual enemy of everyone, because he deals with no one and persecutes anyone; he who enters there, never leaves" (Chaves, 393). Well aware of Brazil's intentions to intervene in the event of an invasion, the Buenos Aires government refused to go along with the Liberator's plans to descend on the region. As Chaves adds with a touch of ironic despair, "the struggle between the men from the North-West and those from the South-East on the Gran Chaco scenario was left postponed for another time, for other generations" (395), making reference to the War of the Triple Alliance (1864) and the War of the Gran Chaco (1934).

Bonpland would remain in Santa María until 1831, a pawn used by Francia in his dealings with European powers, but a beloved sage and medicine man among the peasants of Itapúa. Even after being expelled from Paraguay, he chose to stay in the Banda Oriental and apparently begged to be admitted back into the country (White, 136). Near his death, Francia included this reference in a letter to a delegate from Itapúa: "Ask Rego if Bonpland is still in San Borja and whether his pharmacy is well stocked in order to send for some remedies" (Chaves, 404). The two men would meet with great cosmic flair in the pages of *Yo el Supremo*.

Macario Francia comes into contact with the *Karaí* Bonpland twice, and in two different books. In *Hijo de hombre,* the old man recalls going to Candelaria with his father Pilar to bring back some remedies that Bonpland had prescribed for the *Karaí*'s arthritis while still being held prisoner (see Wisner, 122, for an account of the *yerbas* obtained from Bonpland, *turubi* and *quarayá*, "through an officer expressedly dispatched for that purpose"). Macario tells of a second visit to the area, twenty years later, to seek medicines for his sister María Candé, ill with *pasmo de sangre,* a chilling of the blood not lacking in symbolic implications. The mission failed, since Bonpland had died three days before Macario's arrival. However, as Macario relates in *Yo el Supremo,* the old man's body (carefully embalmed following prescriptions of his own making) remained among the living only to suffer a curious outrage:

> At night they brought him out onto the veranda in an old high-backed friar's chair. We could see him, still and white and plump, fast asleep in the moonlight. On the last night a drunk kept passing by the sick man, shouting greetings to him. He kept walking back

and forth, growing angrier and angrier, and shouting louder and louder:—Good evening, Karaí Bonpland. . . . Finally he became downright insulting. The guasú doctor, big and white and naked, lost in dreams, paid no attention to him. . . . That was too much for the drunk. He took out his knife, went up onto the veranda, and stabbed him in blind fury till I leapt upon him and took the knife from him. (419/268–69)

This bit of narrative has been lifted by the Compiler from its original place in *Hijo de hombre* and grafted onto the imaginary dialogue between the Supreme *Karaí* and his wise counterpart, the *guasú* doctor of the realm. The graft allows Macario's personal myth to grow, to become a necessary factor in the Supreme's access to the land, to her denizens, and to her status as a kingdom—a territorial notion of cosmic (as opposed to mere political) significance. One senses here the force of ingrained kinship acting between the figures involved in an almost buried cluster of stories. This is the one area in *Yo el Supremo* where the historical figure of Francia becomes implicated in the making and binding together of a human group, or in which the storied seed of the nation's Father spreads through a landscape where the first families have just secured their rights to walk on a piece of earth they will name, possess, and cover with their lineages, and where lines of descent first surface as a jumbled story.

The story might as well be joined right where the graft takes place. Macario learns that the aromatic doctor has indeed suffered a second death, so he returns to Itapé without the remedies for his sister, but with the knife used to stab the mummy, which he places under her head to speed up her cure; it ought to be added that this is the same woman who a few years later will give birth to Gaspar Mora, the Christ-figure of *Hijo de hombre*. Upon this branch of the story another is grafted. Mistaken for an accomplice, Macario is jailed with a criminal drunk ("who got out safe and sound in three days"), causing him to feel caught between the lands of the living and the dead. He is accused of a mixture of trivial and uncanny crimes: wiping his ass with a bird, killing a dead man, or just being alive. He becomes a sorcerer in the scant prison air, eats mosquitoes fried on the fire of his cigar butt until he finally dwindles down to a shape of skin and bones thin enough to allow him passage through a crevice in the wall, from which he runs all the way home (419/269).

The jumble of stories has been barely nudged. In order to sound it further, attention must now turn to another key figure, that of Macario's black father. The story of Joséph María Pilar comes out of the oracular voice of the hydrophobic dog Sultán, who has risen from the dead with a "little rainbow of spittle [formed] around his muzzle," like a maniacal soothsayer who lampoons the Supreme with a bawdy and scathing version of the black man's torture and execution. Considering that Francia's biography includes his punishment of Pilar for having kicked the dog, the prophetic voice should be taken as that of a former victim turned into an apologist and posthumous alter ego of the Dictator's favorite servant. The dog's oral history opens a sequence that includes the Supreme's own biography of Pilar (a mixture of vilification and twisted praise) and, as usual, a self-portrait drawn from the impulse to disfigure a victim (see 540–54/375–87).

In fact, so drawn, Pilar offers the complete, black-colored version of the role of performing sorcerer already played by the Supreme as the green demon who scares John Robertson out of Paraguay. Pilar is "able to act out farces . . . patching together voices, figures, gesticulations of the strangest strangers"; He is "Mime. Actor. Pander. Improviser. Satyr. Quick-change artist. Basso-buffo. Swindler. Petty larcenist" (543/377). The satirical Pilar is a pirate of the writing desk, a thief inside the Supreme's cabinet and bedchamber, a stud of the market plaza and the river islands, a forensic astrologer who would turn the house of Capricorn into permanent evidence of the Supreme's failed attempt to marry the alluring daughter of the celebrated *Estrella del Norte*. Pilar receives a load of shame equal to the one dumped on the amanuensis Patiño (with whom he is, of course, linked), but with the difference that he fathers an entire genealogy, that he surrounds his master with an incestuous brood and a sort of Dionysian version of Christ's Nativity. If Patiño represents the scribe as victim in a satyr play, Pilar embodies a phallic demon bouncing inside the Supreme's cabinet and luring him into orgiastic resemblance. The Supreme describes the servant's arrest as if he were an ape-god who, upon being caught tampering with secret papers, goes into a wild gig: "Dances round me twanging a drunken magic spell. Corners me . . . forcing me to play a role in the farce being staged by this monkey disguised as the Supreme Dictator of a Nation" (548/382). As he "bounds and rebounds from one wall to the other," "falls motionless, doubled over in a knot on top of the aerolith," or becomes a shoe floating in the air in search of a lost foot, or "falls on top of the table, ending up as a paperweight," the rantingly lewd Pilar becomes the primordial fetish, a phallus on kinesthetic display. On the day of his execution (and on the eve of the Nativity), the women of Asunción dance in maenadic frenzy round a giant taper built to celebrate the silver anniversary of the Supreme's wedding to his Perpetual Dictatorship. As told by Sultán, the women rub their bellies and breasts with the warm wax that drips from the softened tip of the candle as they sing an altered Guaraní *villancico* in which the *Karaí* has replaced Jesus:

> *Oé . . . oé . . . yekó raka'é*
> *ñande Karaí-Guasú o nacé vaekué . . .*
>
> *[Ohé . . . ohé . . . they say*
> *Our Lord was born on a long-ago day.]*
> (541/375)

Pilar's dying words to the dog who licks his wounds put this fertility chant back into his own bawdy astrology of the Supreme: "All those candles lit to Saint Fart, in honor of nothing at all!," he tells Sultán, before declaring that he leaves the Indian Olegaria pregnant, and that he wants the child to be given his name. The reference to the windy saint is part of an elaborate forensic and horoscopic scheme tying the Dictator's temperament with the country's climate and place under the stars. But Pilar's last words are also linked to no less than two weddings and a nativity scene; the ex-slave dies as a man who would have been a king— in the mold of one of the Magi.

Before examining such bizarre developments, Pilar's place in Francia's household should be examined. The first notice of him seems to be the one found in Rengger and Longchamp's *Essai historique,* as the authors describe the Dictator's style of living in Government House: "Il y loge avec quatre esclaves, savoir un petit négre, un mulâtre et deux mulâ-tresses, qu'il traité avec beaucoup de douceur" (280). The physicians lived in Paraguay between 1821 and 1824, so their "petit négre" should be the same "Negrito Pilar" who, on 6 January 1825, greeted those who came to see Francia, calling him "Benemérito Patricio" and asking for the restoration of the *fiestas* in honor of St. Balthazar, which had been cancelled by Francia due to their lewdness (Wisner, 129). But Chaves, without giving the exact source, refers to "el mulatillo Pilar" (and implicitly to Rengger and Longchamp's "mulâtre") as Francia's long-time *ayuda de cámara*—the resolution granting freedom to the Dicta-tor's slaves would not be signed until August 1834 (203). Either racial designation should match the Southern epithet *darkie*. Thus, beginning either as a *mulatillo* or a *negrito*, Pilar the black would not meet his downfall until right after his official emancipation in 1834.

Of far greater significance is Pilar's incidental presence at the petition to restore St. Balthazar's Carnival, for such is obviously the occasion narrated in *Yo el Supremo,* but changed into the event of Pilar's execution and, in the same apocryphal vein, into the silver anniversary of the Supreme's wedding to the Perpetual Dictatorship. Since Francia was proclaimed Patrician and Supreme Dictator on 1 October 1817, and died some twenty-three years later in September 1840, no such celebration ever took place; besides, Olegaria's account of Pilar's last days places his execution on the eve of the Nativity in 1834. What this apocrypha accomplishes is a displacement of the 1825 events (on the eve of Francia's birthday, as recorded by Wisner, among others) to a twelve-day period between Nativity and Epiphany in 1834–35. The period should be regarded as a sacred season, extending from the death by execution of Pilar and the birth of his son Macario (both on Christ's Nativity) to the birthdate of the Supreme (Epiphany). The fact that elsewhere Macario accompanies his father on a visit to Bonpland (it would have been in 1822) shows that, either as a *petit négre* or a *mulâtre,* Pilar resurfaces here and there with incremental force and in flagrant contradiction: he dies the day his favorite son is born, yet more than ten years earlier he takes the child on a trip to obtain drugs from Bonpland. Elsewhere in the text, Bonpland is regarded as "the sort of man to be in several different places at once. A way of having several lives"; he is portrayed as a magus, "absorbed in leafing through layer after layer of the Great Book . . . his bright little sky-blue eyes interrogating traces and mementos of past existences. Secret archives: those hiding-places where nature sits by the fire in the depths of its laboratory"; and is also a witness to transmigration: "Strange beings. Presences now past. Presences not yet come. Invisible creatures in transit from age to age" (415/266). The father's death and the son's birth belong to the same Nativity. Elsewhere, their pilgrimage to Bonpland (the greatest figure of wisdom in the book, or the figure who holds the Book), brings them to a point in the cycle that makes the very notion of a Nativity viable, as a moment of passage between death and rebirth. The story of Pilar and Macario is part of a gospel whose roots descend into the native layers of the land.

As explained by Wisner, the cult of St. Balthazar developed in the countryside, where the saint was venerated as a miracle worker. On the eve of the feast in his honor, a *murga* (carnival band) accompanied the saint's image through the streets for a solemn mass at the main church and a return to the chapel the following morning. The celebrations that would follow marked the opening of a long carnival; they are described as extremely licentious, being in honor of *Baco,* and Francia had forbidden them out of political and moral concerns (see Wisner, 130–31; this account is used by Chaves, 325). Otherwise, the Dictator's birthday was observed with reverence and politeness; he would come out of Government House to give alms to the poor under the glow of the candles left behind in tribute to his kindness. One such scene is described by Macario in *Hijo de hombre* (15–16), and a notable one was recorded by the Brazilian envoy, Correa da Cámara: "He [Francia] celebrated the sixth of January of the year 28 in extraordinary fashion, ordering that two great bonfires be set and that the front of his residence be illuminated with eight hundred candles" (in Chaves, 387). As one moves from these various historical sources into Roa Bastos's text, elements from the Nativity and the Epiphany will be expressed in terms of a dynastic struggle invented by the Supreme, who transforms Pilar into a sacrificial victim, at once appealing and abject, part demon and part god. Surrounding this figure, two would-be brides and a child with Christological implications supply the story with a wedding mystery, in which the Supreme's fate as a bachelor becomes a sign of his incestuous loneliness as the father of a country, of a land that for all intents and purposes he imagines as his kingdom (even though the historical Francia always rejected the idea of monarchy). According to the dynastic myth, a gospel with deep roots among the land's inhabitants would grow branches into the royal house.

Considering how dynastic contentions usually behave (in sources very much at odds with each other), it matters that a composite picture of them be obtained, and that their various plots and motifs be shaped in the form of a story, of an ensemble. In this instance, all parties do speak through the same medium. So to start with, one may imagine a single dynast (or a hired hand) embroidering an extravagant tale, a gospel faulted by boundless egotism and spiced with elements of self-debunking turned on enemies, the presumptive usurpers of the throne (as if the best insults were those first tried on oneself). And then, one should consider the claim that has Pilar (and not Patiño, as Sultán insists) wanting to become King of Paraguay. It would be in reference to this notion of usurpation that other elements in the story may fall into a sort of makeshift chronology, extending from King Solomon's royal House to Christ's manger and King Balthazar's visit.[16] Pilar becomes as black as dynastic symbolism may require, resembling King Solomon, who according to Sultán went to awful extremes to match the Shulamite's charms. The dog teases the Supreme with a piece of travesty on the Song of Songs:

You haven't acquired a single real's worth of the wisdom of King Solomon, the non-Christian. As he slept with his concubines he kept the knife of Ecclesiastes hidden beneath his pillow. Sometimes, without a sound, he took out a steel forged-in-pain as they slept. He cut off their hair and made from it splendid red, golden blond, raven-black, wavy, kinky, curly beards for himself that reached down to his navel. (542/376)

Bits from the Bride's conclusion to the fifth song (her radiant and ruddy lover, his hair of the purest gold, yet wavy and black as the raven) are worked into a harem abomination, as Solomon goes on to mutilate his concubines, cutting off their breasts and plucking their eyeballs while they continue in blissful sleep. The bridegroom turns into a sadistic despot who practices the very kind of unholy rites denounced by the writer of the apocryphal book, the Wisdom of Solomon (12:1–7). So the nuptial theme is set, with both the Supreme and Pilar mirrored in black. The theme will be developed by means of contrasting two brides: one hopelessly out of reach for the Supreme, another seduced and taught by Pilar (one a lady of high birth, the other a poor Indian from the plaza).

The two bridegrooms (or contending kings Balthazar and Gaspar) will be obscenely linked by images of self-fornication, while their brides hold hands across a field planted with innocent but bawdy idioms relayed in a secret code that links nuptial gifts with the making of a horoscope for the Supreme. The guiding notion of giving gifts and presenting a forecast at weddings and births brings together the two idiomatic registers that dominate the entire story. A horoscope is a routine gift salaried by the powerful; candles are gifts within reach of even the poorest citizens, at least on great occasions; while finery, ribbons, and rare fabrics are meant for brides and newborn progeny. These gifts are combined from two opposite ends of the social spectrum in Pilar's satire. As a huge phallic candle burns in the square and women anoint themselves in its seminal wax, the Supreme, whom the candle represents, looks through a telescope at a distant fire and great bride in the sky (the Star of the North) and howls like a dog next to Sultán, who turns into Pilar's surrogate. The astrology lessons between master and servant have included mock riddles like this one: "Listen, if I handed you a candle end and told you to eat it, would you do so? No Sire, because you yourself have told me that a person shouldn't consume his own candle. Listen, you little rascal: the sun travels round and round its burning ring and needs no other food than its own self" (545/378). The lesson in cosmic self-insemination and cyclic self-engendering leads to further bantering concerning the marriage of two bridegrooms to a single bride: "We flee from the Lion and meet Virgo, the virgin. Our first love. We wed her. Why are you laughing? Nothing, Sire; it's just that I've also heard you say that virgins are as hard to find as a needle in a haystack, though that's the best place to look for them. But from what you're saying they're not as hard to come by in heaven" (545/379). Behind the banter, the Supreme's horoscope quite handily transforms his past failure to marry the daughter of the Star of the North into Pilar's present clandestine affair with Olegaria. The gift of a tainted horoscope to a monarch becomes a feast of stolen gifts among the humble, whose extravagance in supplying themselves with colorful paraphernalia mimics the luxury of great weddings.

Candles have been offered to Saint Fart, and now the Supreme's intestines will answer that offering. As keen physicians, Rengger and Longchamp provide a brief chart of Francia's visceral climatology:

> "La température paraît avoir une grande influence sur son humeur; au moins l'on remarque que quand le vent du nord-est commence à régner, ses accès sont bien plus fréquents. Ce vent, très humide et d'une chaleur étouffante, amène des pluies subites et journalières, et fait une impression fâcheuse sur les personnes qui ont les nerfs mobiles, ou qui souffrent d'obstructions dans le foie et les autres viscères du bas-ventre. (289)

> [The temperature would seem to have great influence over his temper; at least one can notice that, when the northeastern wind begins its sway, his fits become quite frequent. This wind, quite humid and stiflingly hot, brings with it sudden and daily showers and creates a sensation of anger upon persons with shifting nerves, or upon those suffering from obstructions in the liver and in the organs of the lower bowels.]

Visceral channels, coiled and never unwound if not impolitely, have a happy counterpart in those stolen gifts from the State stores that Pilar sends to the already pregnant Olegaria, as when a guard catches him "throwing through the skylights spools of ribbon that slowly came unwound in the breeze from the river" (547/380). Since a secret language of innocent indecency is about to translate Pilar's actions, one may recall that the Mock Turtle was taught "Fainting in Coils" and thus consider Farting in Gifts a good remedy for the menacing constipation of a bachelor king who used to be a libertine. In essence, the Supreme is being accused by Sultán—and by his own voice—of having been a libertine, a failed suitor, and of being now a hardened bachelor who haunts other marriages as a ghost-bridegroom and would-be father.

Instead of a bride, a wedding itself is stolen from the Supreme by Pilar, who begins to shower gifts on the already pregnant Olegaria, as if their marriage consisted of just such a display of sacramental thievery. But Pilar's real bride is his own execution, as the Supreme's wedding is the fertility ritual enacted by the bacchic women round his phallic candle, as Olegaria's bridegroom is the son she delivers on the same date. Twelve days after her would-be husband's execution, Olegaria brings a candle and a declaration to the Supreme's front porch, on the occasion of his birthday and in honor of St. Balthazar. It is then that Olegaria reveals the secret nuptial code: she and her husband had agreed to call the arms *bolas de fraile* and the reels *pedos de monja*. So that Pilar's declaration to the guard who caught him hurling spools into the breeze for his bride is cleared of all possible conspiratorial symbolism, "she doesn't know how she can let fly with her little *pedos de monja* filled with north-wind. And the *bolas de fraile* in Olegaria's skirts are getting all dried up" (547/380, Lane's translation amended). Placed between a Star-of-the-North bride who never was (who remained caught in the zodiac's eternal roulette) and little breezes from presumed virgins (already filled with a baneful north-wind), Olegaria emerges as a madonna figure holy-ghosted by an arcane story in which her black husband and would-be King is sacrificed on the birthdate of her own son, the future Macario, the gospel traveler who will become part of another Christological knotting. Fatherhood divides itself into three figures: a Host of foul temper, a rabid spokesman, and an uncrowned, black demon-god, who as a man and a house slave guarded his master from the unwanted gifts that poisons bear.

The conjunction of wedding with divine birth is not a sheer invention of *Yo el Supremo*. The birth of Christ and the visit of the Magi were celebrated on the same date until the fourth century of the Christian era (Elissagaray, *Rois Mages,* 31). Besides their place in orthodox tradition, both events might have at some point included elements of a nuptial ceremony subsequently erased. An epithalamial tradition exemplified by the Song of Songs could have penetrated the Nativity ensemble; the Magi might have been following the Dog Star (Isis's herald of fertility) in their trek to the manger, bringing with them gifts that included the prototypical aphrodisiacs, frankincense and myrrh. In gathering these intriguing facts, Edmund Leach has wondered whether or not the wit-

230 The Confessional Self

nesses to the birth were also attending a wedding (Leach and Aycock, 48). If, as he thinks, the answer should be affirmative, the gospel and dynastic drama in *Yo el Supremo* would simply repeat a syncretistic pattern of ancient standing. In any event, Roa Bastos's novel puts in the foreground those patterns of appropriation, parody, and ultimate propagandistic fusion that so often affect the making of religious systems as their stories enter into contact with each other, and previous orthodoxies melt into heresies and become involved in political trends and cults.

Beside the Supreme's saga stands the biographic tree of a religion, as it might have grown on Paraguayan soil. The communicants of this scriptureless religion operate in the margins, but the total effect erases such margins: only networks exist with the cumulative impact of truths on hold. Oral and scriptural sources observe an unstable covenant; interpretation holds them together in a precarious synthesis that may soon dissolve. The notion of myth developed by Lévi-Strauss is of limited help in this context. Though it helps in gathering together recurrent motifs and scattered elements of plot in order to form something close to a story, myth in a structuralist sense must reflect a specific setting of material life in which stories would have developed bearing the imprint of the different activities and normative routines involved in maintaining such a setting viable as a space of relative symbolic legitimacy.

It is obvious that *Yo el Supremo* could only indirectly give the sort of intricate evidence that myths offer concerning practices and beliefs in the life of one or various communities. Instead of the firsthand testimony of myth, the novel elaborates the inner workings of storytelling and, in so doing, it requests a second degree of elaboration on the part of its interpreter; in other words, it offers a performative view of the factors that enter into the making of stories in general, including myths. This activity may approach the sense of producing a *myth,* or "a myth of mythology," as declared by Lévi-Strauss at the outset of *Mythologiques* (*The Raw and the Cooked,* 12); but the feeling of working on something like "a novel of novel-making" would differ from his overall sense of myth in one crucial aspect. The presence of an overarching structure tying together dozens and even hundreds of stories cannot be entertained; it is the opposite that seems to hold true: without implying randomness, the novel reflects myth by demonstrating (in being interpreted and partially retold) the ever-changing character of stories grasped in renewed reception and accommodation. It seems that *Yo el Supremo* lends prominence to such a renewal of reception, and that it expects from its interpreters a repetition of the act that gave it complex shape as an interpretation of Paraguay's historiographic self expecting receptive reorientation. The role of religion and myth in the novel is far more than thematic or even structural, a distinction by now quite tedious. It presents religion and myth neither as a parting of the waters nor as a regression of articulated beliefs to a sort of archaic union. On the contrary, myth and religion are seen moving ahead, forming together an agenda still to be run through and shaped by a retelling of stories as if they were at risk of falling into obsolescence.

The central paradox in the novel lies in the Supreme's absolute control of the agenda at the same time that he and the Compiler suggest, by the very nature of their authorial activity, that the reader should take control of it, linking together stories that have entered reading dispersed and in need of connection. An example of how a storied column may rise only when built by the reader is possible after having situated the figure of Bonpland in the text and suggested its links with the stories of Macario, Pilar, and their cohorts. However, a connecting tissue has not yet been located, and a theme of sufficient general significance is yet to be identified so that the stories may amount to something larger than themselves while not losing their local hue. In order to do so, a narrative program needs to be set in reference to a dominant issue: urgent, fearsome, crying for organized action, hopeful and militant. For instance, it can be demonstrated that Bonpland and the Supreme communicate in counterpoint, and that the doctor naturalist embodies a form of wisdom immersed in the order of creation, a notion only indirectly tied to theological assumptions, for it tends to advocate a view in which the Supreme Being gives way to Nature seen in pantheistic grandeur. Bonpland is the utopian activist, the encyclopedist who makes a voyage rather than just writing one; but there is an aspect of quietist insularity in Bonpland's exile, considering the geopolitical terrain it occupies. Therefore, it can be claimed further that Bonpland and the Supreme represent two central aspects in the makeup of the ethical prophet as a modern version of the native *Karaí*. Respectively, they represent wisdom and the nagging of the people's bad conscience and lack of collective will; they are the wise man and the watchman. The Supreme regards the resident sage with a sort of yearning condescension, as if he knew that the naturalist's colony at Santa María is an ultimate expression of the pastoral exile that he once enjoyed in his *chacra* at Ibaray, while also exploiting it as a timely exile from the affairs of Asunción over which he sought control. Bonpland enters politics as if by accident, playing the pawn in other people's tactics, but he represents much more than a minor piece in the Supreme's mindful landscape; he is the kingpin in the political ruler's allegory of utopian management and organic consensus. Bonpland contributes wisdom to prophecy, while the Supreme sets in motion the effervescent tyranny over the community's political fate usually included by prophets in their call to action.

In prophetic books such as Ezekiel, a divine king and a prophet become integral players in the achievement of a final vision of righteous sovereignty reached by priestly wisdom. Without straining parallels, it can be shown that in *Yo el Supremo* a similar design is at work, but with far different results. In Ezekiel's case, the land is invaded and its elite taken into exile in order to ensure that political structures will not recover soon, that the people will be left in need of reorganization and the testing of new leaders. The final utopian vision of the new Temple and of the restoration of God's rule over Israel offered by Ezekiel runs contrary to the apocalyptic schemes that increasingly dominate prophetic utterances in the Bible after this prophet. In *Yo el Supremo,* there is an almost total absence of utopian blueprints, with the possible exception of those passages in which the Supreme imagines Bonpland at Santa María: working with patients, with births, with new crops, being a practical man at the same time that he reads into the great books of nature and conducts an arcane census of the species more in the spirit of Gracián, with whom he is mockingly compared, than of Darwin. At this point in narrated time, the national crisis brought about by an invasion and resulting in the destruction of a local monarchy (as in Ezekiel's case) remains still in the future in the Supreme's novel. The near destruction of Paraguay's sovereignty and the virtual elimination of its active male population lie some thirty years ahead of Francia's death in 1840. This is the terrible event that prophetic discourse foreshadows and mourns in the novel; a body count and a shrinking of boundaries haunt the mood of prophecy shared by the wise man and the watchman.

Assuming that such a context of prophecy exists in the novel, it may be reduced to these focal elements: two main dwelling places, a site of catastrophe, and a story obscurely addressed to ethnic birth and demographic chaos (or perhaps an unfinished myth about the making of a race and the taking of its last census before an impending cataclysm). The two dwelling places are Bonpland's settlement in Santa María and the Supreme's watch terrace at the Hospital Barracks in Asunción. The site of catastrophe (*el lugar de la pérdida [the place where the loss occurred],* 102/10) is marked by a recurrent event, the Supreme's fall from his horse at the onset of a thunderstorm. The story or myth is linked to the fall since it is first mentioned when the fall is introduced, and it is narrated in full when the episode of the fall returns for the last time as if to gather its full implications.

First, let us examine the two dwelling places as focal elements of narrative. Bonpland's Santa María appears like Paradise settled by a descendant from Candide the gardener: "That old Frenchy, more candid than Candide, prince of universal optimism, wants to console me, comfort me, revive me" (416/267).[17] Virtually an island, the colony lies encircled by rivers in confluence, just northeast of the merging of the Paraná with the Paraguay and just below the Tibiquary and its network of streams; its seems like a place made for a territorial dreamer to rest his riddled head. The Supreme recalls visiting the hospice one night disguised as a pilgrim peasant, and there in the darkness he received from the doctor his "bulbs and roots," and a little pouch in which "a very fine powder gleamed with the greenish luminosity of fireflies"; as he left, the pilgrim passed through the awaiting crowd of patients, and stumbled "over dim shapes lying on the ground. A multitude in the dark resembling a moaning mass of bodies strewn all over a battlefield after a bloody combat" (408/259–60). The visit opens a segment in which the essentials of Bonpland's exile in Itapúa, and later in Misiones, are woven into an imaginary dialogue between him and the Supreme, whose words seem to come from a man very near death, as he sets them down in his *private notebook*. A rare element of tenderness creeps into his usual satirical banter. Above all, questions about hell and the loneliness of the absolute ruler punctuate what is in fact a soliloquy. Bonpland's dwelling place in Santa María functions as the land's navel; there, a wise man pours over "a book in which the three kingdoms of nature keep their archives" (411/262). It is therefore both fitting and bitterly ironic that the imaginary dialogue should end with its own political version of the tree of knowledge:

> If you happen, by any chance, to come across the footprint of the species to which I [the Supreme] belong, rub it out. Hide the trail. If you should find this noxious weed in some remote cranny, pull it out by the root. You won't mistake it. It must resemble the root of a little plant in the form of a lizard, toothed back and tail, scales and icy eyes. Animal-plant of a species so cold that it puts fire out merely by touching it. I won't mistake it, my good Sire. I know it very well. It turns up everywhere. One roots it out and it springs up again.

Keeps growing and growing. Turns into an immense tree. The gigantic tree of Absolute Power. (417/267)

The voices of the two old men blend in a last confession of proud but ruined solitude. Thus, as if holding on to its own disenchanted nostalgia, the enlightenment, belatedly present in Bonpland as well as in the genial and somber despot, dissolves the vision of benign paternalism at home in a tropical arcadia not far from where, in Guairá, the Jesuits had once started their kingdom of God on earth.

Rather than looking at the other dwelling place, we must now turn to the focal point of loss and catastrophe. The figure of a Jesuit rises before the Supreme at the place where the loss occurs, where he is thrown from his horse and ends up like the Pardoner's poor old man, pounding on the ground as if seeking shelter inside the earth. As usual, a graft has been implanted by means of another text. In Chaves's biography of Francia, a curious episode finds the Dictator heading down a lane on his way back from one of his regular outings on horseback. A priest leading a funeral procession approaches from the other end, and, upon seeing the horseman, kneels down and raises the host, but the indifferent Francia gallops by without even taking off his hat as a sign of respect (Chaves, 323). The Supreme will encounter a different experience; he will see a Jesuit historian, Pedro Lozano, in place of the priest. Lozano wrote a history of the *Comuneros* war (1717–35), the struggle that pitted his order against the colonists of Asunción and led to the detachment of half of the missions from the colonial province and to their placement under Buenos Aires's rule. The Supreme regards Lozano's *History* as a "libel against José de Antequera," a Panamanian jurist who arrived in Asunción in 1721 at the request of the *Cabildo* and became the leader of the anti-Jesuit forces. Throughout this phase in the struggle, the order enjoyed the support of the viceroyal government in Peru, and, when Antequera finally left the province on the eve of an invasion by royalist forces from Buenos Aires and sought refuge in Charcas, he was betrayed and handed over to the viceroy, who executed him in 1731 after five years of prison (Cardozo, 176–77). Instead of a regular priest (as in Chaves's narrative), the Supreme encounters an apologist for the Jesuits, whom he regards as the worst resident enemy ever encountered by Paraguay in its struggles for political autonomy. Face to face with the hated Lozano, the Supreme's experience of catastrophe offers a synthesis of individual death and a memory of territorial loss: "At that moment I remember having read that the chronicler of the order [Lozano] died a century before, in the

gorge of Humahuaca, as he was journeying to Upper Peru by the same
route that Antequera followed on the way to his beheading" (154/54). To
these deaths must be added Francia's own, traditionally blamed on the
drenching he took in August 1840 during one of his usual rides. This
incident has been collapsed into the one narrated by Chaves, which in
turn leads to the haunting of the Supreme's mind by the memory of
Paraguay's loss of territory during the *comunero* struggles.

The legacy of the *comuneros* is then affirmed as an integral aspect of the
Supreme's political conscience. Since the days of Domingo Martínez de
Irala and the earliest settlers of the territory, the Castilian revolt of the
comunidades in 1520 against Habsburg royal prerogatives was adopted as
a model for local autonomy in the province; the name of *comuneros* was
proclaimed in opposing the royal *adelantado*, Álvar Núñez Cabeza de
Vaca, during the first political upheaval to take place in the colony. The
brand of *comunerismo* adopted by the settlers made each of their leaders a
man unto himself; Cabeza de Vaca is recorded as having asked them,
"Does it seem a just thing to you that each one of you should want to be
king on earth?" (Cardozo, 152). By the time the Jesuits became influential
during the first half of the eighteenth century, the political ideals of this
community of peerless colonists had met a dual challenge. The order
attempted to claim Indians away from service to those among their
captors based in Asunción, while the governor followed the policy of
handing over to the order the captives taken in expeditions into the
Chaco and other areas (Cardozo, 175). The war to which the conflict led
had the colonists fighting the Jesuits and the crown in a struggle that
marks a revolutionary moment in Paraguay's history perhaps more significant than the fight for independence between 1810 and 1813, since the
colonists' sense of political legitimacy was articulated (by Antequera
among others) under the influence of old nonsecular sources (some of
them Jesuit) like the Spanish theologians Francisco de Vitoria, Francisco
Suárez, and Juan de Mariana, all of whom in their own times had
opposed the doctrine of the divine rights of kings. As a result, *comunero*
ideas constitute a pre-Enlightenment phenomenon and the closest thing
in Paraguay to a political philosophy evolved from the most ingrained
elements of a consensual national character, already matured by the time
of independence.[18]

Besides these implicit political elements, the Supreme's fall from the
horse has a penitential result. The fallen man becomes a beggar, the
"Supreme Mendicant," who wanders alone, "without a family, without a
home, in a strange land," like Chaucer's wanderer, condemned not to

die, or to "unlive" his life (560/393). With the last mention of the incident, the narrative reaches its best view of the Supreme's dwelling post as Paraguay's watchman. In a passage that could be seen as a miniature version of Ezekiel's terrifying visions of impending doom and foreign invasion ("I saw a storm wind coming from the north, a vast cloud with flashes of fire and brilliant light about it," 1:4), the watchman climbs to a terrace and aims his spyglass toward the Chaco, where he sees "a strange-shaped cloud approaching," and imagines the "whole country on a war footing once again"; but then he sees birds, swallows, blinded by "bullets of rain from the cloudburst" (from the same hailstorm that knocked him down the day before), falling all around him, looking at him "through the drops of blood of their empty eye sockets" and dying, as he strides out of the post, "rapidly across the creaking, cheeping little bones," a "whole great flock had come from the farthest borders of the country to die at [his] feet" (561–62/394–95). As in the nocturnal visit of the pilgrim to Bonpland's colony at Santa María (where he feels like walking over bodies after a battle), the image of death in droves and a sense of cosmic plight descend upon the watchman, who thus becomes a prophet of the demographic calamity that will afflict Paraguay some twenty-five years later, during the Great War of 1864–70. The notion that it is the population of the country that matters in these visionary experiences can be confirmed by simply observing that the fall and the vision it releases are set next to a story of ethnic mystery and deformity, which is followed first by a narrative pendant on the crookedness of Paraguay's latest census, and then by a small anthology of imaginary portraits of the Dictator and his government written by schoolchildren, the country's most precious resource. In its few remaining passages beyond that point, the novel will dispose of the Supreme's final moments and resolutions before ending with a review of forensic matters concerning the Dictator's skeletal remains.

The account of the mysterious "monster-people" and their spread among the population is handled by Patiño in such a clumsy manner that it seems as if he is feeding his boss a cock-and-bull story in order to distract him from the business of finding the author of the pasquinade (to which he has returned as if out of the blue) as well as from any ideas of punishment, since Patiño has never found the culprit. It is as if the narrative had snapped right back to its opening demand to search for a hidden hand. And in fact, the entire text may contain a short circuit, a coil that links together—instantaneously and unaffected by any amount of reading—the initial request addressed to the amanuensis, the procla-

mation of his execution, and the summons to a meeting of all government officials to take place on 20 September 1840, the day of Francia's
death. Patiño's story signals the start of a devolution, of a reeling back to
where it all started: a pasquinade written by a dead man, a search for a
purloined author, and perpetual unrest in a cabinet which is lodged
inside the Supreme's head. The story has the surface of a pastiche; it
seems to involve characters that have escaped from their places in folklore in order to play in a conspiracy, and they behave like a spreading
rumor transformed into monstrous human shapes. But the story is too
typical not to stand as some sort of warning, perhaps reaching beyond
the intent of whoever might want to exploit it; and the Supreme's
beguiling sleep in response to it may imply that he knows that the story
should be true.

As Patiño would have it, while his Excellency was recovering from the
fall in the hospital, a strange group (two men, a woman, and a child)
entered Asunción. Father, uncle, and aunt gestured like deaf-mutes, but
finally conveyed their hunger and their only means of livelihood, the
child. The albino crawled and whined in a very old voice, and looked
more like a frightened iguana, certainly not like something human; it
had been born on the Day of the Three Kings, just like the *Karaí*, and it
could not be lifted from the ground even when five guards tried to, and
ended up yanking its clothes off, whereupon quite a creature came into
view. In fact, two creatures in one: a small boy and a bigger girl joined at
the navel; the boy lacked a head and sported a holeless behind. As a
result, both elements of the compounded body lived on the same food
and evacuated through the girl's tracts. The twins had been left behind
by their vanished mother, and then an Indian healer (a *Payaguá Paye*)
looked them over and concluded that they were seers who could help the
Supreme Government predict its needs. Suspecting some trick and the
work of superstition, Patiño ordered the wretches pilloried, lashed, and
jailed; but when stripped for punishment, the adults also revealed a
monstrous lack of genitals and only a hole in their place. Punishment
proved difficult, since the lashes rotted on contact with their flesh until
the Indians refused to continue the whipping. The next morning they
were gone, leaving on the cell floor a puddle of urine. Now, however,
they are returning, this time in covens, coming out of the drains, showing up from everywhere in the countryside, only to vanish again after
scaring the good citizens of Asunción.

In spite of the air of black humor that surrounds it, there is something
sinisterly tempting but also pitiful about Patiño's report. It is both the

unwitting proof of what the Supreme regards as the amanuensis's inability to tell a legitimate story and a self-conscious twisting of that defect into its poisonous parody. The story deals with twins and it sets up a Siamese situation between the two men. As in the case of the Pardoner's sermon, the story has the elements of fantastic prurience that a teller might expect his listeners to enjoy. In Patiño's story, however, monsters of sorcery are meant to tease the Supreme into curious fear, as if these creatures were the living embodiment of the rumors and conspiracies that, in Patiño's mind, his boss has come to detest and fear, but also to need as sustenance for the cure of his loneliness. The amanuensis's confessions of ineptness as he tells the story may have a deeper sacrificial and lethal meaning. If it is true that his words "come out gabbled and garbled and gargled, like a parrot talking," or that he feels as if "confessing, like the demented man who killed himself with the guard's bayonet because he believed he'd murdered [his] Excellency in his sleep" (567/400), it could be because these signs of abjection are the result of the Supreme's own acting as a ventriloquist as well as a consequence of Patiño's parody of himself as a parroting servant. The fact that Patiño thinks that his boss may have passed from sleep to death while listening to the story shows how much they resemble, in their own master-slave symbiosis, the sharing of one metabolism by the Siamese twins of the story. The feeling of being linked to his boss will not prevent Patiño from trying to kill the Supreme through his own mimic of sacrifice: in order to kill the other, one half hopes to survive the ingestion of a poison that should only affect the other half. Self-parody would work as an antidote, which, upon taking effect in oneself, reacts as poison in the other. It is only in this involved sense that Patiño's plot is destined to fail, for by the time the amanuensis copies down the order calling for his own execution, the dictating Supreme seems already defeated by his own absolute means of doing away with any opposing human will other than his own.

It would not come as a surprise if, when finally given the chance to tell a whole story, Patiño should produce a catastrophic design locking together suicide and murder, since throughout the novel resentment and contempt have been so intimately shared between him and the Supreme as to suggest a single, divided consciousness holding both of them together. Besides providing a definitive view of mutual bondage, the telling of the story offers a clue about the role of improvisation and storytelling in the novel. The presence of the will to improvise is so ingrained in the voices of *Yo el Supremo* that it tends to remain out of hearing range, and to become obvious mostly in puns and invented words. Particularly in the conversations between Patiño and the Supreme, the text comes close to letting loose a burlesque comic routine with elements of parody, farce, and even a puppet show; but these theatrical elements of grotesque enhancement are kept under control by the tonal depth of the novel's archival self-consciousness. Likewise, the combination of spontaneous response and formulaic readiness so typical of the extemporaneous give-and-take on stage seems overruled by the voices' obedience to a novelistic script already altered and set in place, rather than about to be forsaken by comic misrule. The dominant role of improvisation is further dimmed by the way in which voices blend: in running into each other unmarked, they improve the chances of one speaker exploiting and echoing what the other has just said. Yet this same lack of diacritical marks affects the status of each voice with respect to exactly *who* or *what* speaks in the text. The distinctiveness of each voice is not at issue, for it seems obvious *who* the speaker is; but who *else* might be involved in the same utterance remains undecided, so much so that dialogue in the novel cannot escape the effect of a final scrutinizing censorship, the effect of being under transcription by a hidden hand. In an actual histrionic situation, each actor would probably add to his own voice a satirical tone shared by the other actor's voice; in the case of a puppet show, a single performer from behind the scene would produce all voices and the tonal effect of parody and satire. However, in their present context, voices in the novel register as if they were being replayed; and in a basic sense they should also sound as if coming from ancestors, like posthumous sounds improvised from another world of revised and withdrawn consciousness. This element of distance from an actual conversation—even from a recital—stands for the most part in contrast with the operation of myth in traditional oral communication. Hence, it should be carefully examined if the fate of Patiño's story is to be understood within the range of genealogic and demographic themes to which it immediately leads.

Insofar as they may survive in spoken form within a given group, the stories usually called *myths* may be believed to possess strong elements of recorded ancestry. Even when treated with irreverence or when improvised upon, such stories may still convey the recognition that ancestors continue to exert authority over the group's affairs. Moreover, when stories and recitals of ancestral facts have a role to play in accounts of genealogy, their constancy and ability to change may gain utmost significance, since a kind of census is being taken, maintained, and revised with their enactment. The same applies in the case of propositions bearing on dwellings and places being claimed as residence or hunting grounds, as demonstrated by the Mby'a-Guaraní concept of *tataypy ruoa,* or the *settling of the hearths (asiento de los fogones;* see Cadogan, in Roa Bastos, *Las culturas condenadas,* 27–29). There are instances in the history of ethnography that reveal how the fixing of names and designations of genealogy by means of written judicial records for the purpose of regulating property claims clashed with a traditional system of oral relocation. In the passage from tribal structures to a colonial or national judiciary, native plaintiffs would recite their genealogies based on a system of descent from a single individual going as far back as seventeen generations and using proper names as memoranda to establish territorial rights. Upon cross-checking traditional accounts of genealogy against bureaucratic ones, it would be discovered that:

> In searching the archives for phrases of [the] genealogical disquisition whose sole subject was everybody's spoken word, the written records, robbed of their bureaucratic might, served to reveal—but in the aspect of ethnography—the most fundamental fact of shared memory: that what is memorable, that which this kind of memory remembers, far from being a recorded past or a collection of archives, consists in present knowledge, proceeding through reinterpretations but whose unceasing variations within tradition relayed by speech are imperceptible. (Detienne, 36–37)

In this particular case, colonial clerks could not accept the production of new names by the native plaintiffs, as if new people were being created or old ones reshuffled in the past; when in fact what native genealogists were doing was to compensate for the lengthening of family branches in the course of generations by pruning them down to the shape of a permanent yet changing tree. Both sides were right, but they looked at the maintenance of ancestral precedents from two different perspectives on the status of memory.

Before he dictates to Patiño his death sentence, the Supreme picks up on the story of the monster-people and uses it as an opening to tell his own story of where the real danger to the country comes from. His response rests on the tacit articulation of an improvised rejoinder that could be phrased as *"yes, and . . . ,"* and that, either as an act of association based on oral formulas or as a prepared rebuttal, answers a story as it develops it by means of a different one. (It could even be argued that in oral tradition any story, by its mere enunciation, may already imply the existence of a fitting rebuttal to it along formulaic lines.) So, if there is a story of monster-people showing up everywhere, there should be an even better story (also about monsters), like the one about the census that, instead of counting real heads, gave "birth to people out of nothing," and "provided every family where the father and mother are unknown with a whole flock of kids that don't exist," so that a mother was given "567 sons . . . all with the oddest names and ages, the youngest still unborn and the oldest older than his mother." This bureaucratic monster did create an "army of phantoms" out of the "imagination of profligate figure-flingers," who in the meantime have roamed the backlands chasing after "peasant girls, mulattas, and Indians," making of "their trouser flies their principal pieces of military equipment" (570/402–3).[19]

The truth or falsehood of Patiño's report has been simply developed into a mock version of the census and of Paraguay's miscegenation, setting the stage for a related and more vivid kind of census taking, the one provided by the schoolchildren's composition pieces on the Supreme. Patiño reads them according to school districts, stating the name and age of each pupil. They are like open letters addressed to the fabulous but familiar man whom they describe and advise: "The Supreme Dictator is a thousand years old like God and has shoes with gold buckles edged and trimmed with leather. [He] decides when we should be born and that all those who die should go to heaven"; "The Supreme is the Man-Who-Is-Master-of-Fear. Papa says he's a Man who never sleeps. He writes night and day and loves us backwards. . . . Mama says he's a hairy spider forever spinning its web in Government House" (571–72/404–5). Among the statements there is one from "Pupil Francisco Solano López, age 13," asking for the Dictator's sword to defend the fatherland, thirty years before his death at Cerro Corá. Finally, a report from the "Home of Orphans and Foundling Girls" transforms the theme of the phantom army when it calls for a people's militia to defend the Revolution. What began as a report on ethnic monstrosity and then became a story of demographic sham, ends with the description of a multiracial army housed in an orphanage that is said to be a brothel. The report brings the chain of stories to a breaking point, as it is answered, not with another story, but with the dictation of the amanuensis's own death sentence.

The dialogue between the fictional versions of Policarpo Patiño and Francia could be adapted into a play, or perhaps into a dramatized conversation in the style of Denis Diderot's *Le rêve de d'Alembert* and *Le neveu de Rameau*. Particularly in the latter's case, *Lui* and *Moi* could offer a more than adequate model of the dialectical relation between power and moral dogmas and their disruption by adverse self-consciousness. Such a Hegelian reading should be of sufficient complexity to adapt the master-slave elements in the *Yo-El* nexus into a one-on-one dialogue on domination, on the clinch between lordship and bondage. It is likely that in Roa Bastos's hands the eccentric parasitism of Diderot's amoral creator of pantomimes would make of him (*Lui*) the embodiment of those egotistical impulses in art that the Machiavellian ruler (*Moi*) must exploit in his own craft, while keeping them under ascetic control (see Gearhart, "Hegel and Diderot," 1042–66, for a discussion of Hegel's reading of Diderot). As aptly demonstrated by Wladimir Krysinski (41–52), dialogue in *Yo el Supremo* eschews aesthetic individualness. Beyond this, dialogue leans against a specific sense of authority in which two opposite impulses to confront tradition never seem to find mutual resolution. On the one hand, the past calls for a militant fusion of wills (even at the expense of the dearest of personal freedoms), a fusion that may preserve one's own life from death or from the demands imposed by the group's survival. On the other hand, the present age questions tradition and alters recorded events, as if the past mattered only in order to be shaken and given a different face.

The authority of the past is binding, and it is only through an agonistic recognition of this that its own present disruption might be rehearsed. The past becomes any critical point in Paraguay's history, before and after Francia's rule, as the present turns on its ability to relocate itself at such a critical point in time if it wants to change, to remain open to discourse. If this binding aspect of authority is considered, the figures of Patiño and the Supreme could perform in a popular play characterized by expressionistic excess, their stereotypical traits being placed at the service of laughter and cathartic ritual. For instance, the audience would welcome in anticipation Patiño's punishment and yet love him, just as it would respect and hate the Dictator. Among the audience, schoolchildren would have their impressions on the Supreme read, they would enjoy themselves being quoted and taken into a national roster by characters who *know* and *name* them. The expressionist mode would heighten the actors' roles as ritual prototypes and would call for an audience whose own awareness of its historical situation would involve imagining how other citizens, from other eras in Paraguay's history, would have felt and reacted upon participating in the same play. A gathering of generations would spill over from the space of performance into the audience, seeking and creating actors in it, as happens in the text of the novel each time the illusion of fiction is pierced by the voice of characters in search of an audience of more than one reader at a time. What is being described here is a performative aspect of mourning and celebration in *Yo el Supremo* that is driven by a consciousness of the territorial and ethnic fate of Paraguay, and that is laden with the burden that these notions of survival place on the national conscience as a form of ancestral authority (like the one memorialized in the moving but heavily oratorical *El libro de los héroes* by Juan O'Leary). Instead of enforcing a rhetoric of mourning and heroism in the mold of countless patriotic speeches and histories, the text registers a call to candor, satire, irreverence, and cathartic parody. The authority of the past becomes deflated, the many deaths and territorial reductions that gave it transcendent gravity cease to exact reparation from memory; the dead are not made into objects of incantation: they are toppled from their places in civil religion.

In this scenario, a masquerade with traces of ritual comedy gives performing actuality to remnants of myth, to fractions of a people's memory. However, comic irreverence and expenditure do not exhaust the sober and perhaps ultimately melancholy effect of myth (of remembered stories) to inspire some sort of solidarity with the past. This effect may be found within the archival layers of the text, within the imaginary accretions that may have prompted Roa Bastos to call his novel "that sort of palimpsest jealous of its own intercrossed and staggered mythographic enigmas."[20] Past enigmas remain; they are never meant to be therapeutically resolved, for without a negotiated sense of force emanating from one's cultural ancestry only a frivolous notion of myth would prevail.

Whether in cycles or coils, myth digests the past. For instance, the note by Telésfora Almada from the orphanage-brothel calling for a revolutionary militia reinstates the figure of María de los Angeles Isasi as the *hembra brava* (rough woman) to whom the Supreme entrusted the place after her return from exile among the *montoneras* of Argentina's civil wars. Her story is more than the apocryphal life of the daughter of Francia's most hated ex-friend, it is the archetypal biography of womanhood, from Paradise to Revolution. José Tomás Isasi supported Francia's appointment as Sole Consul and Dictator of Paraguay in 1814, but eventually he would obtain permission to leave the country in May 1826 with a shipment of *yerba* and a considerable amount of treasury funds (over 100,000 pesos in gold and silver). Once in Buenos Aires, he sold the merchandise and kept *all* the money. Francia tried in vain to have

Isasi returned to Paraguay; his contempt for the man shows in a resolution of 1829 in which he calls him a "mulatillo infame," a descendant from a Santa Fe mulatto "known as Amchingo Espinoza" (Wisner, 74; Chaves, 316, 352–53). The Supreme narrates two deaths for the scoundrel: Isasi burns forever at the Plaza in Asunción, and he dies of a fall from a horse near Santa Fe. María de los Angeles is brought up by an old Indian woman and becomes a guerrilla fighter scarred by the wild life of the *montonera*. At this point, the story goes through an idyllic interlude in Paradise. A boy and a girl play in the primordial garden where the Guaraní Genesis places the emergence of the hummingbird from the passionfruit, after the First-Last-Last-Father had brought the tiny thing out of himself amid the original darkness to serve as his first companion and the one who would refresh his mouth and nourish him with the fruits of Paradise—from which human speech seems to have issued, as if from the hummingbird's nectar. The Supreme offers this wondrous mythic biography to Isasi's daughter, a rebel woman who has returned ostensibly to redeem her father's crime, but more so to stand next to a terminally lonely old man who yearns for his own revolutionary legacy.[21] The Supreme's fearful awareness that he could never control such a legacy seems evident in the grandeur and tenderness with which he constructs a vision of Paradise, as if to imprison María de los Angeles (and himself) in its idyll. But his fear also shows in the wish to appoint her as headmistress of a school for prostitutes, a role she accepts with the intent of training young women to become revolutionary fighters.

Like Bonpland, María de los Angeles occupies a spot of liminal iridescence on the map of the young Republic. He directs a hospital and a maternity ward; she runs an orphanage which might be a cradle for whores or for a revolutionary militia—perhaps for both. He is a rationalist gardener, Adam the agronomist, but also a wise man married to nature's wisdom; she is the female half of the first child, a Guaraní Eve, but also a female wedded to revolution and its wild territorial fury. In both figures, the old Province moves in two directions at once: toward a future Republic rationally managed and guarded by its people, and toward archaic sources in a Kingdom permanently settled by dreams and the songlines of myth.

A Foundling Father

In a clear October morning in 1780, don García and his son depart on board a small sumaca *heading south, on the Paraguay, downriver. . . .*—*Julio César* Chaves, El Supremo Dictador

After parting from Laban at the cairn, Jacob, with his wives and children, his flocks and his herds, pursued his way southward. From the breezy, wooded heights of the mountains of Gilead he now plunged down into the profound ravine of the Jabbok thousands of feet below. The descent occupies several hours, and the traveller who accomplishes it feels that, on reaching the bottom of the deep glen, he has passed into a different climate. From the pine-woods and chilly winds of the high uplands he descends first in about an hour's time to the balmy atmosphere of the village of Burmeh, embowered in fruit-trees, shrubs, and flowers, where the clear, cold water of the fine fountain will slake his thirst at the noonday rest. Still continuing the descent, he goes steeply down another two thousand feet to find himself breathing a hothouse air amid luxuriant semi-tropical vegetation in the depths of the great lyn of the Jabbok.—*Theodore Gaster,* Myth, Legend, and Custom in the Old Testament

The complex role played by myth in Roa Bastos's *Yo el Supremo* may be summarized as follows. At a performative level, it functions as *voice* (Spanish being influenced in semantic, melodic, and imagistic ways by Guaraní) and as *gesture* (characters involved in stereotypic bodily expression suggestive of ritual ceremony). In both instances, the matter of myth becomes kinesthetic and effusive, losing its heavy ("*murmurulentous*" [*FW*, 611.29]) quality as a vessel of past (dead) voices and schemes. But myth functions also at another graphic level, in which performing space dwells within consciousness, as in a dream, or changes into a topography, as in a vision of several places and temporal scenes beheld by a single individual, much like a prophet or a shaman in trance. This second modality does not exclude the first, but imprisons it within a space of self-recognition and turbulence involving a struggle with figures of authority and, above all, with the father. Such a space includes two other closely linked acts: a drama of *recognition* and a salient episode of *ritual marking*.

Recognition juxtaposes at least two moments of inward biography within a retrospective narrative scheme that involves a young male protagonist as seen by his older self, old enough to be that young man's childhood father and, more remotely, the father as he would have been already remembered by the young man who is being evoked by his own dying, biographical, older-than-his-years, great-paternal self. The young man's biographic imagination unfolds both in the direction of aging and of personal ancestry, toward individual old age and as a recapitulation of increasingly remote paternal ancestors. In other words, an old authorial figure of ageless age produces a reflexive biographic narrative about a critical point in his youth that includes his own child figure, the child's living father, and older father figures fantasied in the child's mind (figures centered on a father who is ever-so-much-older in being a memory-event, a phantasmatic representation inseparable from any actual remembering self). The father's utmost remoteness is determined by the distance between the son who remembers and the remembered son. What is most immediate about such a remote father is that the only father left is the remembering, ageless son.

The complex recognition scheme involves a relation between *name* and *mark*. Ritual marking concerns acts such as circumcision and the claiming of territorial rights by means of fixing a spot, site, or boundary with eponymous significance. The quest for self-possession and recognition is thus linked to group solidarity, and as such it may deprive the participant or protagonist of at least some measure of personal autonomy. Solidarity and autonomy may not be in conflict, as in the sense of adhesiveness expressed by Whitman in "Song of Myself":

> Divine am I inside and out, and make holy whatever I
> touch or am touched from;
> The scent of these arm-pits is aroma finer than prayer,
> This head is more than churches or bibles or creeds.
> If I worship any particular thing it shall be some of the spread of
>   my body;
> Translucent mould of me it shall be you.
> (526–31)

Not unlike this but in a wilder setting, the body's quest for the tutorial voice of myth emerging from a menacing father will result in the father's killing and a dual, guilty consequence: a young man's death, as if by specular punishment, and a young man's blessing, as if homoerotic desire (at least toward one's younger self) were to infuse the heart of such Oedipal drama.

In an epic dimension, it all begins as biography and myth join in a personal saga dealing with the claiming of a sacred land, as with patriarchs like Jacob, who may be "portrayed in a variant of the motif of the wily trickster who first outwits his father and brother, and later does the same to his father-in-law"; Jacob's land being "a sacred land, a holy land in that it is a demonic realm" (Gottwald, 174; Smith, 109). For better or for worse, the rhetoric of Paraguay's historiography identifies the nation's conquered realm with ecological forces akin to religious manifestations of demonism and sacred awesomeness: "concerned within the most hidden place in the continent, far removed from the sea, left in isolation and loneliness, devoid of metals, under a torrid heat, with fierce forests, immense spaces, and a neighboring, untamed and barbaric Chaco; with droughts and floods, and perilous navigation" (Cardozo, 22).

To such a setting one must add the traditions of a Guaraní exodus, first revealed by Curt Nimuendajú after living for decades among the Apapocuva of Brazil in the early part of this century. Biblical parallels make better sense if the Exodus of the Pentateuch is combined with apocalyptic traditions that the canonical sequence situates in postexilic times. Nimuendajú's Guaraní informants spoke of surviving an exodus from Paraguay toward the east and the coast, moved by proclamations from apocalyptic shamans to go in search of a *land without evil, a land where one never dies,* the *Mbae Verá Guazú,* a mobile paradise, a nomadic site which, after wandering in Amazônia, had climbed to Cuzco and the citadel of *Candir,* as the Inca emperor is known in sixteenth-century Guaraní reports (Cardozo, 113–15; La Barre, 203–4). The shamans resisted reductions and slaughters with visions of migrations and a flight across the eastern seas, and through Christianized expectations of rebirth like that of Tanimbu, who would descend from heaven as a god after speaking inside a womb (see Sušnik, in Roa Bastos, *Las culturas condenadas,* 174). The protagonist's saga of recognition in *Yo el Supremo* and its pendant, "Lucha hasta el alba," reflects this legacy of mobility, of mystic flight, but also of intense, death-mediated fusion with the land at a point of eponymous emergence.

Although written thirty years before the start of the novel, "Lucha hasta el alba" has been restored and adopted by Roa Bastos in *Antología personal* (1981) as a missing link in the authorial biography of his major work. He reports finding the "broken, almost illegible" manuscript, with two pages torn, inside one of his favorite books, Leonardo's treatise on painting, a work that had taught him "to see the meaning of the world as a vast hieroglyph in motion," made up of signs perhaps impossible to decipher (86). The momentous discovery, reminiscent of Poe and Borges, is qualified and labeled as "a double parricide . . . a *corpus delicti* rather than a story . . . a nightmare instead of a lived history," and as a "proof . . . that those stories in which autobiographical elements abound, whether in sentimental or idealized shape, are hopelessly false, since they emerge out of self-love and self-pity, the most distorting of elements in artistic work" (86). In issuing the restored story, the author sees himself handing over "an initial point of reference to a work and a life which have never learned to avoid the same mistakes"; the story is a "curiosidad museográfica," better left for collectors of trivia (1981:185–86).[22] Exorcisms aside, "Lucha" offers nothing less than a definitive rehearsal of authorial empowerment in the realm of myth, cast in the mold of a rite of passage.

Its intertextual place in *Yo el Supremo* and *Hijo de hombre* involves three episodes or situations in which birth and resurrection are reflected in the ordeal of passing from the condition of witness to that of participant and creator. These focal narratives are the orphan child's apprehension of alchemy inside the lunar skull, the adolescent's trip aboard the *sumaca* on his way to the university in Córdoba, and the artistic/religious companionship between the young author and Gaspar Mora, mediated by the figure of Macario. In each case, incidents focus on the presence of a threatened young creator who confronts ritual pollution and death and struggles to achieve cleansing and rebirth. As suggested earlier in analyzing the story of Gaspar Mora, creative activity splits between the primitive storyteller and the manual artist, musician and carver of wooden statues; there is a split between a figure of unambiguous spiritual manliness and stern patriarchal character (Macario) and a younger, Christ-like son figure (Gaspar), whose craft and ethical calling cannot be separated from the influence of women as lovers and mothers.

The retelling of Jacob's struggle with the angel in "Lucha" offers a rather dense mythic view of such a split. The imagination of Jacob's young surrogate as child protagonist has been fed biblical stories by a mother who blends them with Guaraní legend and myth. She protects her favorite child from a father emotionally and morally harmed after being almost murdered by a group of revolutionaries who held him hostage until news came that he was not to blame for the hiding of some weapons. This political version of Jacob's predicament at Jabbok does little to establish a realistic focus in a story deeply committed to a liminal mythic view of filial transgression. If, in fact, the story's restoration after its rediscovery in 1968 left untouched what the author wrote when he was not yet fourteen, the dangling character of its political implications would be the one remaining proof of artistic immaturity.

Milagros Ezquerro (117–24) has given a detailed analysis of "Lucha," but her insights leave room for further scrutiny. In particular, the biblical and Christological motifs she has examined can be explored in reference to elements of Guaraní myth and native beliefs. The story begins as the boy resumes his nocturnal writing still smarting from a beating by his father and the echo of a cursing prophecy: "There you have him, the future tyrant of Paraguay! Now a rebel and a despot later! . . . I'm going to straighten him out with the bull-whip, that cub from the dammed *Karaí Guasú!*" (*Antología personal*, 187). Earlier, the boy has plunged into the river to catch a glimpse of a drowned man, and his twin brother has brought home the story of how he came to the surface hugged to the corpse and bleeding through the nose. Writing cannot heal the wounds from a cruel father, so one night the boy runs away from home guided by the notion that living like Jacob might be easier than writing about him. Soon enough, a fierce enemy falls upon him and they spend the night locked in combat; he sweats blood and feels cleansed, but in the meantime the other breaks his hip at the hollow of the thigh. Dawn is about to rise when the other commands him to quit, but denies him a blessing in exchange. Blinded and cursed with everlasting damnation, he strangles the stubborn adversary, whose head falls; the face on it looks like his father's, with the bird of prey features of the old *Karaí*. Running away from the spot, he sees two landscapes, two lands, two lives and times opening before him, and an alien voice who proclaims: "I have, like Jacob, seen God face to face and my soul is released!" Lame and aging at a wondrous pace, he brings the shrinking head to a rabbi in what he believes is the town of Nazareth; but the old man will not answer his cry of "Peniel!" and drives him away with a handful of coins and a plea to go work in the harvest. The fugitive murderer gets drunk with the reward, and resting his head on the disjointed thigh, quickly offends those at the *boliche* with the smell of death.

The story follows the pattern of appropriation that the Christian Gospels apply to Hebrew scriptures. As Ezquerro has shown (122–23), evocations of Cain, Abraham, and Judas combine with references to the gospel theme of precursor and supplanter, as in: "This is the man I meant when I said, 'He comes after me, but takes rank before me'; for before I was born, he already was" (John 1:15). Also, the death of Jacob's surrogate (and his earthly recognition by two men as "Don Pedro's son") may evoke in inverted fashion Luke's account (24:13–32) of the two disciples at Emmaus, one of several appearance-narratives added to Mark's original proclamation that Jesus had risen from the dead (Sheehan, *First Coming*, 139).

Besides turning Jacob into Jesus as a wounded outcast among the living, "Lucha" transforms his twinship with Esau into a dual portrait of the hunter in a forest setting where tokens of female fertility are dominant. It is here that Jacob's preferential status with his mother and Esau's beastly rapport with his father suggest the handiwork of myth. The light from the jar used by the boy to write must be gathered in the forest, for it comes from *muás*, the same phosphorescent bugs (or *lampyrids*) used elsewhere by the Supreme to smear his body in shamanistic display. A light that comes from the belly of wormlike bugs and that must be replenished almost daily allows nocturnal creation only in connection with a cycle of life and extinction that the budding writer must continuously feed: "People around here die like the *muás* do in the jar when they cannot give more light from their belly [*vientre*]" (191). The lunar associations between the glowing, ebbing jar of worms and the womb finds reinforcement in the *Wöro*, the *póra-women* (forest deities of the Mak'a and Chamacoco Indians) for whom the boy leaves girdles of *muás* hanging from branches. These forest nymphs dance with the girdle talisman round their waist to ask the moon for rain; in addition, a reference to the "Siete Cabrillas" (the Pleiades) hints at a possible link between them and this constellation (on the *Wöro*, see Roa Bastos, *Las culturas condenadas*, 340). The hunter of *muás* is trailed into the forest by Esau, who suspects that the worms are being used for something quite different from making girdles, but whose brutishness goes no further than his attempt to pollute the gift: "When Esau goes hunting in the forest, he finds the girdles of *muás* that I leave hanging from the tree branches. He touches and smells them. He puts his head between his legs and shouts like a dwarf insulting the *Wöro*" (188). Esau's behavior implies hostility of an estrous and genital nature against the mother and female fertility; his hunting brings small game to the father, to whom he is bound as a spy on Jacob's hidden practices. Writing must be hidden from the father and shared with the mother, from whom the oral nurturing that gives life to written fiction flows as the kind of native lore that makes the mysteries of the forest familiar and practical to the hunter (who is never shown killing any game but, instead, offering gifts to the nymphs of fertility). The cycle that joins writing with hunting runs parallel to the one involving the life-and-death cycle of the *muás* inside the womblike lamp. So close is the association between the mother and Jacob in this regard that it seems foolish to attribute to her a reproductive aegis over scriptural creation in which her son would not share maternally. Jacob's surrogate in "Lucha" struggles with a Father-God upon emerging out of his own mothering, an activity in which he is as much the mother as the son.

Mothering requires expulsion, as Gaspar Mora's leprous life in the bush demonstrates. (It should be mentioned that Gaspar's Christ-like figure provokes the admiration of women, that one of them, María Rosa, has bridal and maternal links with him of a symbolic nature, and that he is envied by men who think he is unmanly.) The same experience of birth within a drowning death in the river from which the young man in *Hijo de hombre* emerges feeling saved by the hand of Gaspar takes place in "Lucha" (and also in *Yo el Supremo*). It happens as if all the sensuous care that disappears after the mother expels the child (and he comes to assume her custody in the art of writing) were to find agonizing expression in wrestling with oneself, rather than with the emissaries from God or the father. Likewise, the paranoid wrestling with the tight grip of sudden manhood may imply not only a reformed fear of the mother's caressing doctrines, but also an ambiguous aversion against maleness embracing maleness, as in the enthusiastic but demonic clash with the stranger suddenly revealed in overpowering nocturnal intimacy. The folklore of Jabbok (Gaster, 205–11) explains the affair by citing several encounters with river-spirits (as in Hercules' combat with Achelous) whose blessings and destruction the hero desires; but the episode's residual economy of detail can be taken up, as Thomas Mann does in *Joseph and His Brothers* (1934) in the spirit of sacred comedy.

Mann's Jacob remembers Jabbok from old age, while in the company of Joseph, a lovely youth who dreams under Ishtar's influence and practices the "lunar syntax" invented by Thoth of Hermopolis, the white-haired ape, letter-writer of the gods. Young Joseph is an ecstatic singer: "Manifestations, strange and almost uncanny, began to creep into the posturings of the solitary figure. He seemed intoxicated by his own lyric ritual"; the rhythmic chanting of " 'Yahu, Yahu,' " was a mere panting whisper that issued from lungs empty for want of an intake of breath. At the same moment the body changed shape, the chest fell in, the abdominal muscle began a peculiar rotatory motion, neck and shoulders stretched upwards and writhed" (39–40). The environment of ecstasy and vatic sensuousness affects Jacob's memories of youth, now awakened while listening to Joseph's "prattle about names and naming"; the event at Jabbok comes like a dream from remote days:

> When in actual bodily fear he had awaited the meeting with the brother from the plains, whom he had cheated and who was doubtless still thirsting for revenge; and then, aspiring so fervently after the power of the spirit, had wrestled for the sake of the name with the

strange man who had fallen upon him. A frightful, heavy, highly sensual dream, yet with a certain wild sweetness; no light and fleeting vision that passes and is gone, but a dream of such physical warmth, so dense with actuality, that it left a double legacy of life behind it as the tide leaves the fruits of the sea on the strand at the ebb. (58)

Cast in the recessive actuality of dream-revision, the encounter includes, as an aftermath, the other's face: "For the moon had suddenly glared out of the cloud and he had seen him breast to breast: the wide-apart, unwinking ox-eyes, the face and shoulders glistening like polished stone; and in his heart he felt again the fury of desire with which in agonized whispers he had demanded the name" (59). Even the axial dislocation at the hollow of the thigh is experienced with an omniscience in excess of pain; indeed, as an act of knowing and being known: "The painful thrust and grip upon the thigh had seemed like an examination. Perhaps it was meant to find out whether there was a socket there, whether it was movable and not, like the strange man's own, fixed and not adaptable to sitting down" (59).

Mann's version of the Jabbok event offers a view of primitive virility untouched by ascetic discipline, still naïve while in the midst of the encounter, as if it did not know yet where to draw the line between God's testiness and man's right to rule over the grounds of reproduction. These are totemic rather than theistic grounds; Jacob remembers when he was a young and fearless father, leaning more on his body than on the trailing conscience of a trickster, and capable of feeling God's weight as that of an estranged brother emerging from ambush like a familiar animal or as a creature of the night ready to test his sweat and seed, and to enforce with intruding shamelessness his own inspection of manhood. All traces of motherhood as a shaping factor in the making of the son seem absent from Mann's version, as if in its physical entanglement the scene portrayed the alliteration of *Jacob* ('heel-gripper,' 'supplanter'), *Ye'abeq* ('to wrestle'), and *Jabbok,* the place in which such earthy eponymics give way to the mighty *he who striveth with God.* However, some see traces of birth-from-the-earth (autochthony) underlying the etiological myth (on a dietary taboo) annexed to Jacob, in which case he would have undergone parthenogenesis and thus assimilated functions inherent in females (see Leach, *Genesis As Myth,* 7–23; Geller, "Jacob," 8–12). But regardless of such older myths, Mann's visit to Jabbok yields a portrait of the patriarch still in fraternal bonding with the wilderness.

By comparison, the view of Jabbok in "Lucha" strikes a note of mourning and penance, moving as it does from a nocturnal bower of mutual care between mother and son to his desolate pilgrimage as an outcast in the mold of Cain. His struggle with God is almost abstract in its cruelty, it evokes an ascetic ordeal; the decapitation of the stranger has the nightmare quality of a victim who avenges himself by the nature and quality of his dying, as if the murderer were to be caught in the awful act he intended to do, rather than in the one he has actually done. In contrast with Jacob's sultry dreaming in Mann's version, here the sun's white heat consumes and shrinks life; the world after *Paniel* is a sterile nightmare. However, what is at issue is not to expose differences between views of a biblical event in two literary authors, but to draw a contrast between two separate but related scenes in Roa Bastos's fiction. For the scenario of parricide in "Lucha" is also found in *Yo el Supremo,* where it bears traces of profuse contact between the son, his own body, and the elements of earth and water at a moment of self-recognition still subject to Oedipal interpretation, but at a level of synthesis unmatched by any other episode in the novel.

Recorded in the most private layers of the Supreme's writings (the *Logbook* and the *tutorial voice*), the entire narrative of the trip aboard the *sumaca* centers on a biblical passage partially quoted in Latin, and whose full version in the Vulgate is as follows: "*Non timebis a timore nocturno, a sagitta uolante in die, a negotio perambulante in tenebris, ab incursu et demonio meridiano*" ("You shall not fear the hunters' trap by night / or the arrow that flies by day, / the pestilence that stalks in darkness / or the plague raging at noonday [*Sacra Biblia,* Psalm 90:v–vi; *NEB* Psalms 91:5–6]). In terms of mythographic representation, the text of the novel finds its axis at a moment of meridian stillness in which noonday and midnight merge in inverted symmetry and vertical synchrony:

> The sun riveted at the zenith. If the days and the nights pass, they do so behind Joshua's shield, without our having any way of knowing whether we are in the dazzling darkness of noon or in the searching shadow of midnight." (420/270)

The *sumaca*'s descent on the waters of the Paraguay toward the port city of Santa Fe is rendered in choral form. The tutorial voice of the father ("the murmur of his capric voice") envelops the son's visionary experience; the scene evokes a symphonic drama, an opera of antiphonal textures mixing with screen images, but the paradox of majestic immobility and hell-bound chaos would be difficult to reproduce outside the omniscient design that holds it together in the text.

Among the dominant themes, none surpasses that of the Supreme's tainted paternal breed ("that terrible smell of bastard lineage"). As a dividing line between the dead and the living, the dark and pestilential side of noon combines notions of polluted birth with the emergence from some still unblemished bosom in nature. Stench emanates from the father's merchandise, "tons of cylindrical pestilence towering a hundred times higher than the main-mast" (421/271), as it does from the dead buried beneath the floor of Paraguay's churches: "from the cellar of our souls. Like the bad smell of Sunday Mass." The stench fascinates as much as it repels, it suggests communion between the feracious and cannibalistic qualities in the father's foul meal and greed and what lies underneath the community's ritual discipline, and it blends with the effluvia that rise from the river amid the funereal opulence of its flowers, its fermenting mire, its carrion, and its "fierce wild odor" (424/273).

If the scene could be grasped in fulfillment of its simultaneous design, the oven of noon would be seen and smelled at the same time that a frozen, muddy battleground at night descends into view with its own motifs of life feeding on death:

> When we awoke, the two-master [*sumaca*] was beached at a bend in the river that resembled a funnel of tall cliffs. Everyone was sleeping like the dead. The skipper, the crew sprawled out on the cargo, deader than the corpses of Igatimí. The sun leapt out from the other shore and settled down in its appointed place. Nailed to the noonday sky. (437/284)

The son's meridian ecstasy is possessed by the father's *Negotium perambulans in tenebris,* the time when he penetrated deep into enemy territory, up north near the banks of the Igatimí, where the *Mby'a* had been stirred up by the *bandeirantes.* The man had left home when his son was not yet ten, and had ended up fighting for three nights and days in the dead of winter, with men falling all around, bogged down in thick layers of ice; until the last night came, when he was able to survive what the others did not, buried naked under two who were dead but still warm, and glued mouth-to-mouth to the one named Barroso (*muddy, clayish*), who by then should have been in the *País do Fogo,* in Hell's fire, a bit of which he could still pass on to him by the mouth: "entrégame por tu boca aunque sea una brasinha de ese fuego" (436/283–84). This hybrid tutorial voice in Portuguese and Spanish has been heard before, when it ordered the son to throw away the skull in the scene where the orphan hides his renewable birth in alchemy's lunar incubation. Moreover, the skull scene and Jacob's writing by the lamp-womb are also reflected here, since direct reference is made to the skull, and though no mention is made of "Lucha," the age of the boy who writes aboard the *sumaca* is the same as Jacob's when he runs away from home at fourteen.

The parricide changes while it pivots on the same symbolic base. In "Lucha," it is the dry sterility of the crime and its inherent spiritual suicide and self-castration that matter, while in *Yo el Supremo* the Oedipal scenario brims with elements of male engenderment. It is as if on meeting each other at the crossroads, Oedipus and Laius had engaged in a cryptic form of intercourse, a jumbled castration as chimeric entanglement, a gladiatorial merging, possessive and fracturing. Even at the margins of the scene in which the *sumaca* turns into a sacrificial stage for parricide, the chimeric factor appears at the level of word particles. For instance, just a few pages after this passage, "all those who said *I* during this time, were none other than *I-HE*" [*YO-EL*], the tutorial voice's hybrid speech says *yelo* (ice) instead of *hielo*, which scrambles or meshes together the two most prominent signs in the novel, *yo* and *él*, thus coupled as: *Y*-el-*O* or y-*EL*-o. This happens at a moment when a man lies naked on that icy element and extracts the last residues of vital heat from the bodies of two other men, one of whom bears in his last name ("Barroso") a sign of primal matter, of clay and mire. In this regard, the obsession with which the father's name (*Rodríguez*) is scrutinized in the note at the bottom of the page may reveal more signs of a substance acting up at the word-particle level: "the Portuguese suffix *es* changed to the Castilian *ez*" (423/272)—reads the note. It may be that in going from one patronymic to the other, the *es* of *to be* (as in *is*) can end up sounding just like *hez*, a word well in tune with the excremental and foul nature of the father's bloodline, since it means "lo más vil y despreciable de algo" [the most vile and worthless of something] (Corominas, *Breve diccionario*, 318). Except for its nonvernacular plural rendering as *feces*, *hez* has been used traditionally to deride others, like those who in English might be called "social scum." This alchemy of word particles has a home in the skull, an object whose ultimate fate is debated at the end of the novel, when it turns out that Francia's headbones break down into "the skullcap of a woman, the facial mask of an adult male, and the jaw of a child" (607/432–33). The fate of *Paniel* (of God's face, and of the torn head that Jacob-as-Cain takes away and dies with) marks the closing point of a male-on-male circular construction of selfhood, of a biographic cycle in which a divine hero becomes an accursed transgressor against God and himself—the same cycle that opens with an orphan child rehearsing the role of foundling father.

Lov'd me above the measure of a father,
Nay, godded me indeed.
—Coriolanus *(5.3.9–10)*

Lying on his deathbed, the Supreme incubates a child within his dreams, just as a boy of fourteen on his way to Córdoba recapitulates what a child attempted to do inside a skull, just as the writer of *Yo el Supremo,* upon finding a lost manuscript, may magnify scenes of self-birth through writing, just as the orphan with his candle upheld a vision of concave omniscience within an object, a microcosm of bone in kinship with the womb-in-the-jar that a boy threw into the river. Threw away as the skull shall be thrown by the orphan, and as yet that same death's-head might still fall from the shoulders of God to serve as Cain's token of orphanhood by murder. . . . Thus the orbits of self-recognition describe an egoist's zodiac, a biographic house-in-the-sky, a sublime aretalogy of loneliness.

The eyelids of morning wink at noon ("I saw the jaguar, crouching in the brush of the cliff") and out of the darkness of womb ("A thousandth of a second before the roaring, spotted meteor hurtled down upon the two-master, I plunged into the water") a child emerges ("I fell onto an island of floating plants. . . . I was being born. Rocked in the basket of the giant water lily, I felt I was being born of the muddy water, of the stinking mire") already a man ("I saw the jaguar rip Don Engracia to pieces with its talons") of priestly powers ("the spectacle of the two-master turned into a sacrificial altar") who murders sacredly ("I pressed the trigger. The powder flash outlined the figure of the jaguar in a ring of smoke and sulfur") on the foundling's navel-spot ("The true place lost forever, my first cries of a newborn babe wailed. Will I ever find it? You will find it, yes, in the very same place where it was lost, said the river's grasping voice") where written words drift ("A bottle was floating at my side") as letters not from mother ("I tilted the bottle up. I drank my own questions down in one swallow") but otherwise mothered ("Devil's-milk. I sucked my own milk, from my frontal sinuses") by her ("I slowly rose to my feet") avenging ("clutching the rifle") angel . . . herself . . . María de los Angeles . . . hummingbird's nectar, flowing like words from mouths in Paradise . . . a woman with a rifle . . . a foundling self.

Notes

Preface

1 All quotations from *Coriolanus* are from William Shakespeare, *Coriolanus,* ed. Philip Brockbank (London: Methuen, 1982).

1 Counterfeit Bewitchments: The Storyteller in Benjamin, Borges, Wells, and Vargas Llosa

1 I follow and develop insights found in Richard Wolin, *Walter Benjamin: The Aesthetic of Redemption,* 177–81 (Adorno to Benjamin quotation, 177).
2 In no specific way, but rather as a deeply formative experience, I have been influenced by Elaine Scarry, *The Body in Pain: The Making and Unmaking of the World.*
3 See Rodríguez Monegal, *Borges,* 270–73, on the shifting identity of the woman behind the "S.D." initials.
4 In relation to pastoral, leisure, and some novelistic responses to the modern myths of innocence, the Benjamin of "The Storyteller" finds an Anglo-American skeptical counterpart in William Empson, *Some Versions of Pastoral.*
5 All quotations attributed to Benjamin are from Benjamin, *Illuminations.*
6 Russell Hoban has written a story on Juan Dahlmann's story; see "The Man with the Dagger," *Granta* 28:189–200.
7 Góngora (or perhaps an unknown writer) once wrote:
    [cuando criminante y bella
    salió ministranto aljófar],
    del sacro Betis la ninfa. . . .
Here, a nymph may be corporeally criminal in being beautiful as she emerges from the river dispensing pearl drops. See *Luis de Argote y Góngora: Obras completas,* ed. Juan and Isabel Mille y Giménez (Madrid: Aguilar, 1966), romance 56, p. 159 (the lines enclosed in brackets do not appear in some Góngora manuscripts; see note, p. 1,110).
8 All quotations from "Morte d'Arthur" are from Lionel Trilling and Harold Bloom, eds., *The Oxford Anthology of English Literature: Victorian Prose and Poetry.* The current quotation is from p. 424 (lines 52–65). Hereafter line numbers given in text.
9 All quotations from *The Invisible Man* are from *Best Science Fiction Stories of H. G. Wells,* with page numbers given in the text.
10 There is little new that can be said about "Tlön, Uqbar, Orbis Tertius." I have learned much from John Sturrock's elegant analysis in *Paper Tigers: The Ideal Fictions of Jorge Luis Borges,* 118–22; James Irby's "Borges and the Idea of Utopia," *Books Abroad*

45:411–19; and Arturo Echevarría's *Lengua y literatura de Borges* (Barcelona: Ariel, 1983), 104–86.

11   I am grateful to Daniel Balderston for calling my attention to the making of what he calls "this silly pun" in Masao Miyoshi's lively "Dr. Jekyll and the Emergence of Mr. Hyde" *College English* 27 (1966): 470–80.

12   All quotations are from *"The Strange Case of Dr. Jekyll and Mr. Hyde" and Other Stories* (New York: Penguin, 1979).

13   Mario Vargas Llosa, *El hablador* (Barcelona: Barral, 1987); trans. as *The Storyteller*, trans. Helen Lane (New York: Farrar Strauss Giroux, 1989). Page numbers for both will be cited in the text.

14   In search of possible sources for Vargas Llosa's marvelous pastiche of Machiguenga stories, one may start with Claude Lévi-Strauss's bibliography in *The Jealous Potter*. A partial list of such sources would include G. Baer, "The Matsigenka View of the Religious Dimension of Light," unpublished paper (Madras, 1979), and "Religión y chamanismo de los Matsigenka," *Amazonia Peruana-Chamanismo* 2, no. 4 (Lima, 1974); V. de Cenitagoya, *Los Machiguenga* (Lima: Sanmartí, 1943); S. García, "Mitología Machiguenga," *Misiones Dominicanas del Perú* 17–19 (Lima, 1935–37), and "Mitología de los salvajes Machiguengas," *Actas y Trabajos Científicos del 27 Congreso Internacional de Americanistas (1939)* (Lima, 1942); and, above all, J. M. Grain, "Kashiri (historieta lunar)," *Misiones Dominicanas del Perú* 38 (Lima, 1957).

2   Talking Heads: The Archaeology of Personal Voice in Cortázar's "Cefalea"

1   In Cortázar, *Bestiario* (Buenos Aires: Sudamericana, 1966), 69–90. Hereafter page numbers given in the text.

3   Severed Versions of Pastoral: "Bestiario," "Final del juego," and "Las armas secretas"

1   Quotations from "Continuidad de los parques" are from Cortázar, *Final del juego* (Buenos Aires: Editorial Sudamericana, 1964), 9–11, and *"The End of the Game" and Other Stories*, trans. Paul Blackburn (New York: Collier, 1978), 63–66; "Silvia" is quoted and translated from *El último round* (México: Siglo Veintiuno, 1969), 81–92.

2   This interpretation is not at odds with the interesting one offered by David Lagmanovich, who compares "Continuidad" with the situation in *Lady Chatterly's Lover*, which would be the novel being read by Cortázar's fictional reader; see his "Estrategias del cuento breve en Cortázar: un paseo por 'Continuidad de los parques'" *Explicación de Textos Literarios* 17 (1988–89): 177–86.

3   Quotations from "Final del juego" are from Cortázar, *Final del juego*, 181–96, and *"The End of the Game" and Other Stories*, 135–49 (page numbers from the translation are given in text); quotations from "Los venenos" are from Cortázar, *Final del juego*, 23–40.

4   As suggested to me by Daniel Balderston, the girls might in fact be cousins, but there is little doubt that they stand in allegorical relation with the three sisterly Graces, including Thaliae or *Letitia Uberrima;* see Edgar Wind, *Pagan Mysteries in the Renaissance*, 26ff., 118.

5   My intertextual approach to "Los venenos" and "Bestiario" is influenced by the

ethnographic work gathered in *Death and the Regeneration of Life*, ed. Maurice Bloch and J. Parry, and, in particular, Bloch's "Death, Women, and Power" (211–30).

6 Pereira, *Deseo y escritura*, 23–25. I chose this reading as typical among sentimental and melodramatic responses to "Bestiario," a tradition of allegorical and naïve commentary that seems quite appropriate as a fictional and perhaps cinematic response to a captivating story. (It is hard to imagine someone not wanting to rewrite or to film what seems like Cortázar's answer to "The Turn of the Screw.") Rather than deploring such imaginative responses to the best of Cortázar's fiction, one should recognize in them the extraordinary affluence of feeling that Cortázar's stark psychological minimalism brought to a whole generation of readers. Among the earliest views on the tiger, two are worth quoting: "The tiger is the fantastic projection of the incestuous voracity of one family member, it is a symbol of his bestial purposes lurking in every corner" (García Canclini, *Cortázar*, 21); and (misspelling Rema's name), "El Nene and Roma [sic], Roma [sic] and Nino, Isabel and Roma [sic], Luis are the protagonists of a drama driven by homosexual passion (Isabel kills Nene in jealous anger, in a manifestation of revenge and sadism)" (Sola, *Julio Cortázar y el hombre nuevo*, 29). With Luis dangling at the end, this cluster of homosexual cells gives excellent proof of how a "reader's response" view of *lo fantástico* is likely to provide small allegories of Lacan's Imaginary and its dualistic, desire-mediated lock on reality: commonsense and visceral responses to *lo fantástico* generate a cloning of the Imaginary's cloning powers.

7 Quotations from "Bestiario" are from Cortázar, *Bestiario*, 139–65.

8 Quotations from "Las armas secretas" are from Cortázar, *Las armas secretas* (Buenos Aires: Sudamericana, 1966), 185–22, trans. as "Secret Weapons," trans. Paul Blackburn, in *"The End of the Game" and Other Stories* (New York: Collier, 1978), 248–77. Page numbers will be given in the text.

4 The Raven and the Writing Desk: A Biographic View of Yo el Supremo

1 All quotations from *Hamlet* are from William Shakespeare, *Hamlet*, ed. Harold Jenkins (London: Methuen, 1982).

2 Quotations are from *Yo el Supremo*, ed. Milagros Ezquerro (Madrid: Cátedra, 1983), 143; and *I the Supreme*, trans. Helen Lane (New York: Knopf, 1986), 45. Page references to both editions will be cited in the text, with the original cited first.

3 James Joyce, *Finnegans Wake* (New York: Viking, 1959). Hereafter cited in text as *FW* with page and line numbers.

4 See Augusto Roa Bastos, ed., *Las culturas condenadas* (México: Siglo Veintiuno, 1978), 257–58, for the Spanish version of the Mby'a myth, trans. Léon Cadogan.

5 Fulgencio R. Moreno, *La Ciudad de la Asunción* (quoted in Chaves, 200).

6 In her editor's introduction and notes to *Yo el Supremo*, Milagros Ezquerro provides the most detailed, lucid, and authoritative analysis and classification of the narrative modes and voices in the novel. See 37ff. for a description of the *private notebook*).

7 John T. Irwin, *American Hieroglyphics*, 128. With its combination of allusive exuberance and analytical courage, Irwin's treatise stands as a sublime counterpart of the grotesque modes of inquiry and self-testing that characterize the Latin American novels of dictatorship written in the 1970s (including Vargas Llosa's *Conversation in a*

Cathedral, García Márquez's *The Autumn of the Patriarch*, Alejo Carpentier's *Reasons of State*, and Carlos Fuentes's *Terra Nostra*). For a challenging view of these novels, see Roberto González Echevarría, "The Dictatorship of Rhetoric/The Rhetoric of Dictatorship" and "*Terra Nostra:* Theory and Practice," both in *The Voice of the Masters*, 64–97.

8 Our sense of sight and sound compounds and of the complex optics in Joyce's epistemology of sleep is based on John Bishop, *Joyce's Book of the Dark*.

9 Margot Norris, *Decentered Universe*, 36, who also quotes: "as sure as herself pits hen to paper and there's scribblings scrawled on eggs" (*FW*, 615.9).

10 James Joyce, *Letters*, 1:406.

11 Weston La Barre, *The Ghost Dance*, 198–99 (who quotes G. F. Church, *Aborigines of South America* [London: Chapman and Hall, 1912], 31–32).

12 Roa Bastos's source is clearly the account in Chaves (69–73).

13 See Bartomeu Meliá and Christine Munzel, "Ratones y Jaguares," in Roa Bastos, *Las culturas condenadas*, 62–85, for an account of the genocide inflicted on the Axe-Guayaki, of which the Gualachís were a part.

14 My portrait and understanding of the Pardoner are indebted to the late Donald R. Howard's interpretation in *The Idea of "The Canterbury Tales"* (Berkeley: University of California Press, 1976), 345ff., and in *Chaucer: His Life, His Works, His World* (New York: Fawcett Columbine, 1987), 488–92, 490–91. Hereafter these will be cited in the text as *"Canterbury Tales,"* and *Chaucer*, respectively.

15 See Léon Cadogan's Spanish prose version of the Guaraní *Hymn of the Dead* in Roa Bastos, *Las culturas condenadas*, 261–62.

16 The rich iconography surrounding the Adoration of the Magi is built on the single reference in the Gospels (Matthew 2:1–16) to the three kings. The dog Sultán's story associates the Black Pilar with the popular cult of King Balthazar and with grass-roots monarchical beliefs in Paraguay. Born on 6 January, Francia bore as his second name Gaspar, another of the Magi's traditional names.

17 In chapter 14 of *Candide*, "Comment Candide et Cacambo furent reçus chez les jesuits du Paraguay," Voltaire spends his caustic humor on the spiritual kingdom at the Misiones.

18 See Díaz Pérez, *La revolución comunera del Paraguay*, and Francisco E. Feito, "*Yo el Supremo*," in Burgos, *Las voces del Karaí*, 55.

19 Francia had a census taken in 1838 and possibly another seven years earlier (see Wisner, 145, and White, 119).

20 The phrase may be found in Roa Bastos, "Algunos núcleos generadores," 67–95. I have read this lecture in Roa Bastos's own typed manuscript, obtained through the generosity of Ana María Codas.

21 In her essay in Burgos's *Las voces del Karaí* (101–19), María Elena Carballo provides an insightful view of the female silence in the figure of María de los Angeles Isasi.

22 "Lucha hasta el alba" was first discussed by Roa Bastos in "Algunos núcleos generadores," 66ff.

Anzieu, Dedier. *The Skin Ego*. New Haven: Yale UP, 1989.

Aronne-Amestoy, Lida. *Utopía, paraíso e historia: interpretaciones del mito en García Márquez, Rulfo y Cortázar*. Purdue University Monographs in Romance Languages, no. 19. Amsterdam and Philadelphia: John Benjamins, 1985.

Atherton, James S. *The Books at the Wake: A Study of Literary Allusions in James Joyce's* Finnegans Wake. New York: Viking, 1959.

Auerbach, Nina. "Incarnations of the Orphan" and "Alice in Wonderland: A Curious Child." In *Romantic Imprisonment* (57–79; 130–48). New York: Columbia UP, 1985.

Baez, Cecilio. *Ensayo sobre el Dr. Francia y la dictadura en América*. Asunción: Cromos Mediterraneos, 1985.

Barthes, Roland. *S/Z*. Trans. Richard Miller. New York: Hill and Wang, 1974.

———. "The Struggle with the Angel: Textual Analysis of Genesis 32:22–32." In *Image, Music, Text* (125–42), trans. Stephen Heath. New York: Hill and Wang, 1977.

———. *Camera Lucida: Reflections on Photography*. Trans. Richard Howard. New York: Hill and Wang, 1981.

Benjamin, Walter. *Illuminations*. Ed. Hannah Arendt, trans. Harry Zohn. New York: Harcourt, Brace and World, 1969.

Bergonzi, Bernard. *The Early H. G. Wells*. Manchester: Manchester UP, 1961.

Bersani, Leo, and Ulysse Dutoit. *The Forms of Violence: Narrative in Assyrian Art and Modern Culture*. New York: Schocken, 1985.

Bishop, John. *Joyce's Book of the Dark:* Finnegans Wake. Madison: U of Wisconsin P, 1986.

Bloch, Maurice, and Jonathan Parry, eds. *Death and the Regeneration of Life*. Cambridge and New York: Cambridge UP, 1982.

Bloom, Harold. "Criticism, Canon-Formation, and Prophecy: The Sorrows of Facticity." *Raritan* 3, no. 3 (Winter 1984): 1–20.

Boon, James A. *Other Tribes, Other Scribes*. Cambridge and New York: Cambridge UP, 1982.

Borgeaud, Philippe. *The Cult of Pan in Ancient Greece*. Trans. Kathleen Atlass and James Redfield. Chicago: U of Chicago P, 1988.

Borges, Jorge Luis. *Evaristo Carriego*. Buenos Aires, 1955.

———. *Obra poética*. Buenos Aires: Emecé, 1964.

———. *Otras inquisiciones*. Buenos Aires: Emecé, 1964.

———. *El Aleph*. Buenos Aires: Emecé, 1966.

———. *Historia universal de la infamia*. Buenos Aires: Emecé, 1966.

———. *A Personal Anthology*, ed. & foreword Anthony Kerrigan. New York: Grove, 1967.

———. *Discusión*. Buenos Aires: Emecé, 1969.

————. *The Aleph and Other Stories: 1933–1969*. Ed. & trans. Norman Thomas di Giovanni. New York: Bantam, 1970.

————. *Ficciones*. Buenos Aires: Emecé, 1971.

————. *Prose for Borges. Triquarterly 25*. Fall 1972.

————. *A Universal History of Infamy*. Trans. Norman Thomas di Giovanni. New York: Dutton, 1972.

————. *Jorge Luis Borges: Ficcionario; una antología de sus textos*. Ed. Emir Rodríguez Monegal. México: Fondo de cultura económica, 1985.

————. *Textos cautivos: ensayos reseñas en* El Hogar *(1936–1939)*. Eds. Enrique Sacerio-Garí & Emir Rodríguez Monegal. Barcelona: Tusquets 1986.

Brown, Peter. "The Rise and Function of the Holy Man in Late Antiquity." *The Journal of Roman Studies* 61 (1971): 80–101.

Burgos, Fernando, ed. *Las voces del Karaí: estudios sobre Roa Bastos*. Madrid: Edelsa, 1988.

Caillois, Roger. *Le Mythe et l'homme*. Paris: Gallimard 1972.

Campbell, Joseph, and Henry Morton Robinson, eds. *A Skeleton Key to* Finnegans Wake. New York: Harcourt, Brace and Co., 1960.

Carballo, María Elena. "Lo femenino y lo absoluto en *Yo el Supremo*." In *Las voces del Karaí* (101–9), ed. Fernado Burgos. Madrid: Edelsa, 1989.

Cardozo, Efraím. *El Paraguay colonial: las raíces de la nacionalidad*. Buenos Aires: Nizza, 1959.

Carlyle, Thomas Francis. *Miscellaneous Writings: Essays Collected and Republished*. New York: Alden, 1871.

Chaucer, Geoffrey. *The Text of* The Canterbury Tales. Eds. J. M. Manly and Edith Rickert. Chicago: U of Chicago P, 1940.

Chaves, Julio César. *El Supremo Dictador*. Madrid: Atlas, 1940.

Clifford, James. *The Predicament of Culture: Twentieth-Century Ethnography, Literature, and Art*. Cambridge: Harvard UP, 1988.

Corominas, Joan. *Breve diccionario etimolólogico de la lengua Castellana*. 2nd ed. Madrid: Gredos, 1967.

————. *Diccionario crítico etimológico castellano e hispánico*. 4 vols. Madrid: Gredos, 1984.

Cortázar, Julio. *Bestiario*. Buenos Aires: Sudamericana, 1964.

————. *Final del Juego*. Buenos Aires: Sudamericana, 1964.

————. *Las armas secretas*. Buenos Aires: Sudamericana, 1966.

————. *El último round*. México: Siglo Veintiuno, 1969.

————. *"The End of the Game" and Other Stories*. Trans. Paul Blackburn. New York: Collier, 1978.

Cruz, Jorge Luis. "Apuntes sobre la 'compilación' en *Yo el Supremo*." In *Las voces del Karaí* (71–83), ed. Fernando Burgos. Madrid: Edelsa, 1989.

Deleuze, Gilles. *Masochism: An Interpretation of Coldness and Cruelty*. Trans. Jean McNeil and Aude Willm. New York: Braziller, 1971.

De Quincey, Thomas. *Confessions of an English Opium-Eater and Other Writings*. London and New York: Penguin, 1985.

Derrida, Jacques. *Glas*. Paris: Galilée, 1974.

————. *Of Grammatology*. Trans. Gayatri Chakravorty Spivak. Baltimore: Johns Hopkins UP, 1976.

————. *Glas*. Trans. John P. Leavy, Jr., and Richard Rand. Lincoln and London: Nebraska UP, 1987.

Detienne, Marcel. *The Creation of Mythology.* Trans. Margaret Cook. Chicago: U of Chicago P, 1986.

Díaz Pérez, Viriato. *La revolución comunera del Paraguay.* Palma de Mallorca: Mosén Alcover, 1973.

Diderot, Denis. *Rameau's Nephew and D'Alembert's Dream.* Trans. Leonard Tancock. New York: Penguin, 1971.

Dorsch, T. S., ed. *Classical Literary Criticism.* Baltimore: Penguin, 1965.

Elissagaray, Marianne. *La légende des Rois Mages.* Paris: Seuil, 1965.

Empson, William. *Some Versions of Pastoral.* New York: New Directions, 1960.

Ezquerro, Milagros. "El cuento último-primero de A. Roa Bastos." *Revista de Crítica Literaria Latinoamericana,* no. 18 (1983): 117–24.

Feito, Francisco E. "*Yo el Supremo* vs. el supremo poder de la palabra." In *Las voces del Karaí* (53–61), ed. Fernando Burgos. Madrid: Edelsa, 1989.

Frazer, Sir. James J. *The Golden Bough,* 3rd ed. vol. I. London: Macmillan, 1911.

Freud, Sigmund. *The Standard Edition of the Complete Works of Sigmund Freud,* ed. James Strachey. 24 vols. London: Hogarth Press and the Institute of Psycho-Analysis, 1953–74. 24 vols.

———. [1908]. "Family Romances." In *Works,* 9:236–241.

———. [1913]. "The Theme of the Three Caskets." In *Works,* 12:290–301.

———. [1919]. "A Child Is Being Beaten." In *Works,* 17:177–204.

———. [1937–39]. *Moses and Monotheism.* In *Works,* 23:3–137.

Fustel de Coulanges, Numa Denis. *The Ancient City: A Study on the Religion, Laws, and Institutions of Greece and Rome.* Trans. Willard Small. New York: Anchor Books, 1960.

García Canclini, Néstor. *Cortázar: una antropología poética.* Buenos Aires: Nova, 1968.

Gearhart, Suzanne. "The Dialectic and its Aesthetic Other: Hegel and Diderot." *MLN* 101, no. 5 (1986): 1042–67.

Geller, Jay. "Jacob and Jaebbek and Jabbok." Unpublished paper, 1977.

Gombrich, E. H. *Symbolic Images.* New York: Dutton, 1982.

González Echevarría, Roberto. *The Voice of the Masters: Writing and Authority in Latin American Literature.* Austin: U of Texas P, 1985.

Gordon, Jan B. "The *Alice* Books and the Metaphors of Victorian Childhood." In *Aspects of Alice: Lewis Carroll's Dreamchild as Seen Through the Critics' Looking Glasses* (98–107), ed. Robert Phillips. New York: Vanguard.

Gaster, Theodore. *Myth, Legend, and Custom in the Old Testament.* 2 vols. New York: Harper and Row, 1969.

Grosskurth, Phyllis. *Melanie Klein: Her World and Her Work.* New York: Knopf, 1986.

Gottwald, Norman K. *The Hebrew Bible: A Socio-Literary Introduction.* Philadelphia: Fortress Press, 1985.

Harrison, Jane. *Prolegomena to the Study of Greek Religion.* London: Meridian, 1955.

Hayes, John H., and Maxwell Miller, eds. *Israelite and Judaean History.* Philadelphia: Westminster Press, 1977.

Hernández del Castillo, Ana. *Keats, Poe, and the Shaping of Cortázar's Mythopoesis.* Purdue University Monographs in Romance Languages, no. 8. Amsterdam and Philadelphia: John Benjamins, 1981.

Houghton, Walter and G. Robert Stange, eds. *Victorian Poetry and Poetics.* Boston: Houghton Mifflin, 1968.

Howard, Donald. *The Idea of The Canterbury Tales.* Berkeley: U of California P, 1976.

———. *Chaucer: His Life, His Work, His World*. New York: Dutton, 1987.

Huxley, Francis. *The Raven and the Writing Desk*. New York: Harper and Row, 1976.

Irwin, John T. *American Hieroglyphics: The Symbol of the Egyptian Hieroglyphics in the American Renaissance*. Baltimore: Johns Hopkins UP, 1983.

Izard, Michael, and Pierre Smith, eds. *Between Belief and Transgression*. Chicago: U of Chicago P, 1982.

Jung, C. G. *Mysterium Coniunctionis: An Inquiry into the Separation and Synthesis of Psychic Opposites in Alchemy*. Princeton: Princeton UP, 1963.

Joyce, James. *Ulysses*. New York: Random House, 1946.

———. *Finnegans Wake*. New York: Viking, 1959.

———. *Letters*. Vol. 1, ed. Stuart Gilbert. New York: Viking, 1966.

Kafka, Franz. *The Metamorphosis/Die Verwandlung*. Trans. Willa & Edwin Muir. New York: Schocken, 1968.

Krysinski, Wladimir. "Entre la polifonía topológica y el dialogismo dialéctico: *Yo el Supremo* como punto de fuga de la novela moderna." In *Las voces del Karaí*, ed. Fernando Burgos. Madrid: Edelsa, 1989.

Kristeva, Julia. *Powers of Horror: An Essay on Abjection*. Trans. Leon S. Roudiez. New York: Columbia UP, 1982.

La Barre, Weston. *The Ghost Dance: The Origins of Religion*. Garden City, N.Y.: Doubleday, 1970.

Lacan, Jacques. *Écrits*. Paris: Seuil, 1966.

———. *The Four Fundamental Concepts of Psycho-Analysis* ["Les quatre concepts fondamentaux de la psychanalyse" (1973)]. Trans. Alan Sheridan. New York: Norton, 1978.

Lagmanovich, David. "Estrategias del cuento breve en Cortázar: un paseo por 'Continuidad de los parques.'" *Explicación de textos literarios* 17 (1988–89): 177–86.

Laplanche, Jean. *Life and Death in Psycho-Analysis*. Trans. Jeffrey Mehlman. Baltimore: Johns Hopkins UP, 1976.

Leach, Edmund. *"Genesis As Myth" and Other Essays*. London: Jonathan Cape, 1969.

Leach, Edmund, and D. Alan Aycock. *Structuralist Interpretations of Biblical Myth*. Cambridge and New York: Cambridge UP, 1982.

Lebovici, Serge, and Daniel Widlocher, eds. *Psychoanalysis in France*. New York: International Universities Press, 1980.

Lévi-Strauss, Claude. *Structural Anthropology*. Trans. Claire Jacobson and Brooke G. Schoepf. Garden City, N.Y.: Doubleday, 1967.

———. *The Elementary Structures of Kinship*. Trans. James Harle Bell, John Richard von Sturmer, and Rodney Needham, ed. Boston: Beacon Press, 1969.

———. *The Raw and the Cooked: Introduction to a Science of Mythology*, vol. I. Trans. John and Doreen Weightman. New York: Harper Torchbooks, 1969.

———. *L'homme nu*. Paris: Librairie Plon, 1971.

———. *Tristes tropiques*. Trans. John and Doreen Weightman. New York: Atheneum, 1973.

———. *The Jealous Potter*. Trans. Bénédicte Chorier. Chicago: U of Chicago P, 1988.

Lewis, Wyndham. *The Lion and the Fox: The Role of the Hero in the Plays of Shakespeare*. London: G. Richards Ltd., 1927.

Macksey, Richard. "'Alas, Poor Yorick': Sterne Thoughts." *MLN* 100, no. 5 (1985): 1006–20.

Mann, Thomas. *Joseph and His Brothers*. New York: Random House, 1966.

Marcos, Juan Manuel. *Roa Bastos, precursor del Post-Boom*. Madrid: Orígenes, 1983.

McHugh, Roland. *Annotations to* Finnegans Wake. Baltimore: Johns Hopkins UP, 1980.

Meeks, Wayne A. "The Man From Heavens in Johannine Sectarianism." *Journal of Biblical Literature* 91 (1972): 44–72.

Mendenhall, George E. *The Tenth Generation.* Baltimore: Johns Hopkins UP, 1973.

Menninghaus, Winfried. "Walter Benjamin's Theory of Myth." In *On Walter Benjamin: Critical Essays and Recollections,* Ed. Gary Smith. Boston: MIT Press, 1988.

Mitzman, Arthur. *The Iron Cage: An Historical Interpretation of Max Weber.* New York: Knopf, 1970.

Monkman, Kenneth. "Sterne, Hamlet, and Yorick: Some New Material." In *The Winged Skull: Papers from the Laurence Sterne Bicentenary Conference,* ed. Arthur Cash and John Stedman. Kent, Ohio: Kent State University Press, 1971.

Nagy, Gregory. *The Best of the Acheans: Concepts of the Hero in Archaic Greek Poetry.* Baltimore: Johns Hopkins UP, 1979.

The New English Bible [NEB]. New York: Oxford UP, 1973.

Norris, Margot. *The Decentered Universe of* Finnegans Wake. Baltimore: The Johns Hopkins UP, 1976.

Ovid [Plubius Ovidius Naso]. *Fastorum Libri Sex.* Vols. 1 and 2, ed. Sir. James Frazer. Hildesheim and New York: G. Olms, 1973.

Pavel, Thomas G. *Fictional Worlds.* Cambridge: Harvard UP, 1986.

Pereira, Armando. *Deseo y escritura.* México: Premia, 1985.

Picon-Garfield, Evelyn. *Cortázar por Cortázar.* Veracruz: Universidad Veracruzana, 1978.

Planells, Antonio. *Cortázar: metafísica y erotismo.* Madrid: Porrúa, 1979.

Poirier, Richard. *The Performing Self: Compositions and Decompositions in the Languages of Contemporary Life.* New York: Oxford UP, 1971.

Pressly, William L. "The Praying Mantis in Surrealist Art." *Art Bulletin* 55 (1973): 600–615.

Pucci, Pietro. *Odysseus Polutropos: Intertextual Readings in the* Odyssey *and the* Iliad. Ithaca: Cornell UP, 1987.

Reddy, Daniel R. "Through the Looking-Glass: Aspects of Cortázar's Epiphanies of Reality." *Bulletin of Hispanic Studies* 54 (1977): 125–34.

Rengger and Longchamp. *Essai historique sur la révolution du Paraguay et le gouvernement dictatorial du Docteur Francia.* Paris: Hector Bossage, 1827.

Roa Bastos, Augusto, ed. *Las culturas condenadas.* México: Siglo Veintiuno, 1978.

———. "Algunos núcleos generadores de un texto narrativo." In *L'idéologique dans le texte* (67–95). Toulouse, 1978.

———. *Hijo de hombre.* Barcelona: Argos Vergara, 1979.

———. *Antología personal.* México: Imagen, 1981.

———. *Yo el Supremo.* Ed. Milagros Ezquerro. Madrid: Cátedra, 1983.

———. *I the Supreme.* Trans. Helen Lane. New York: Knopf, 1986.

Rodinson, Maxime. *Mohammed.* New York: Vintage, 1974.

Rodríguez Monegal, Emir. *Jorge Luis Borges: A Literary Biography.* New York: Dutton, 1978.

Robertson, J. P. and W. P. *Letters on Paraguay: Account of a Four Years' Residence in That Republic under the Government of the Dictator Francia.* 2 vols. London: John Murray, 1838.

———. *Francia's Reign of Terror: Being a Sequel to* Letters on Paraguay. 2 vols. Philadelphia: E. L. Carey & A. Hart, 1839.

Róheim, Géza. *The Eternal Ones of the Dream.* New York: International Universities Press, 1971.

Rubin, William S. *Dada and Surrealist Art.* London: Thames and Hudson, 1969.

Sacks, Oliver. *Migraine: Understanding a Common Disorder.* Berkeley: California UP, 1985.

Sennett, Richard. *The Fall of Public Man: On the Social Psychology of Capitalism.* New York: Vintage, 1978.

Shakespeare, William. *Coriolanus.* Ed. Philip Brockbank. London and New York: Methuen, 1976.

———. *Hamlet.* Ed. Harold Jenkins. London and New York: Methuen, 1982.

Sheehan, Thomas. *The First Coming: How the Kingdom of God Became Christianity.* New York: Random House, 1986.

Smith, Jonathan Z. *To Take Place: Toward Theory in Ritual.* Chicago: U of Chicago P, 1987.

Sola, Graciela de. *Julio Cortázar y el hombre nuevo.* Buenos Aires: Sudamericana, 1969.

Stevenson, Robert Louis. *The Strange Case of Dr. Jekyll and Mr. Hyde and Other Stories.* New York: Penguin, 1979.

Sturrock, John. *Paper Tigers: The Ideal Fictions of Jorge Luis Borges.* London and New York: Oxford UP, 1977.

Tindall, William York. *A Reader's Guide to* Finnegans Wake. New York: Farrar, Straus and Giroux, 1969.

Trilling, Lionel, and Harold Bloom, eds. *The Oxford Anthology of English Literature: Victorian Prose and Poetry.* London: Oxford UP, 1973.

Tyler, Margaret L. "Síntomas orientadores hacia los remedios más comunes del vértigo y cefaleas." *Homeopatía* 14, no. 32 (Buenos Aires, 1946): 33–58.

Tovar, Francisco. *Las historias del dictador:* Yo el Supremo, *de Augusto Roa Bastos.* Barcelona: Delmall, 1987.

Vargas Llosa, Mario. *El hablador.* Barcelona: Seix Barral, 1987.

———. *The Storyteller.* Trans. Helen Lane. New York: Farrar, Straus and Giroux, 1989.

———. "Mouth." *Granta* 28:281–82. London, 1989.

Weber, Max. *Economy and Society: An Outline of Interpretive Sociology.* 2 vols. Berkeley: California UP, 1978.

Wells, H. G. *Best Science Fiction Stories of H. G. Wells.* New York: Dover, 1966.

———. *H. G. Wells' Early Writings in Science and Science Fiction.* Eds. Robert M. Philmus and David Y. Hughes. Berkeley: California UP, 1974.

———. *The Island of Doctor Moreau: A Possibility.* New York: Stone and Kimball, 1986.

West, Anthony. *H. G. Wells: Aspects of a Life.* New York: Random House, 1984.

White, Richard Alan. *Paraguay's Autonomous Revolution, 1810–1840.* Albuquerque: New Mexico UP, 1978.

Whitman, Walt. *Leaves of Grass: Comprehensive Reader's Edition.* Ed. Harold W. Blodgett and Sculley Bradley. New York: New York UP, 1965.

Williams, John Hoyt. *The Rise and Fall of the Paraguayan Republic, 1800–1870.* Austin: U of Texas P, 1979.

Williams, Raymond. *The Country and the City.* London and New York: Oxford UP, 1973.

Wind, Edgar. *Pagan Mysteries in the Renaissance.* New York: Norton, 1968.

Winkler, John J. *Auctor and Actor: A Narratological Reading of Apuleius's* The Golden Ass. Berkeley: California UP, 1985.

Wisner, Enrique. *El dictador Rodríguez de Francia,* ed. J. Bóglich. Concordia: Entre Ríos, 1923.

Wolin, Richard. *Walter Benjamin: An Aesthetic of Redemption.* New York: Columbia UP, 1978.

Yates, Frances. *Giordano Bruno and the Hermetic Tradition.* New York: Vintage, 1969.

Index

207; and Compiler and Host, 209–10; and Bonpland, 221–22; linked in Siamese fashion, 237; and stereotypic gestures in drama, 245; and Jacob's and the angel, 251–52. *See also* Fetishism, Masochism

Bolivar, Simón, 218, 220–21

Bonpland, Aimé, 203, 218; at Candelaria, 220–22; 225, and the Supreme, 231–36; and María de los Angeles Isasi, 244

Borges, Jorge Luís, xiii, xiv, xvi, xvii, xix; and Benjamin, 5–8; 22–23, 28–36, 39, 70–71; and Tennyson, 44–48; and Wells, 53, 55, 56, 59; early writings of, 61–67; and Frazer, 53–54, 69–70; and Whitman, 48–54, 71. Works: *Historia universal de la infamia,* 6–7, 18; *Evaristo Carriego,* 30; "La postulación de la realidad," 5, 17–38; "El arte narrativo y la magia," 5, 37–38, 69–70; "El Sur," 28–43; "La muerte y la brújula," 33–43; "Sur," 42; "Adrogué," 43; "La luna," 44; "Funes el memorioso," 63–64, 66–67; "Tlön, Uqbar, Orbis Tertius," 62–63, 72

Caillois, Roger, 148–51

Cain, 249, 253, 256

Cannibalism, 86, 145, 150, 254

Carlyle, Thomas, 19, 198

Castration, 20, 41; in "Bestiario," 147–48; and Chaucer, 209–10, 255

Celibacy, 31, 78–79, 84. *See also* Bachelor

Cervantes, Miguel de, xvi, 19, 25–27, 34, 202

Charisma, xv, 4; in Benjamin, 11–12, 14, 17, 22; in Borges, 34; and poetic character, 54; in Frazer's magician, 69–70; in *El hablador,* 75, 77; and archetypes, 142; and taboo, 146; in *Yo el Supremo,* 179, 213–14

Chaucer, xix, 205–9, 235

Childhood, xviii; in "Silvia," 125, 128–29; "Los venenos," 137, 141; "Las armas secretas," 160; and *Hamlet,* 165–66; in *Yo el Supremo,* 179, 213–14

Chorion, 64. See also *Tapetum*

Christ: in *El Hablador,* 75–77; in *Yo el Supremo,* 174, 176, 192, 212–13, 215–17, 223, 225–26, 229

Christology, 76, 212–14, 216, 226, 229, 248

Circumcision, 74, 173–75, 187, 246

City: in "La Postulación de la realidad," 28–29, 31–36; and *flâneur,* 28–29, 31–36

Classic (mode of writing): in "La postulación de la realidad," 18, 21–31, 33–34; and mourning, 35–36; related to "el arte narrativo y la magia," 37–38; and *flâneur,* 38–39; and "La muerte y la brújula," 42–43; and "Morte d'Arthur," 45–48; and *The Invisible Man,* 53, 58; Wells referred to by Borges as, 67; and *The Golden Bough,* 70. *See also* Romantic

Communeros, 234–35

Community, xii, xiii–xiv; in "The Storyteller," 9–10; compared as found in Benjamin and Borges, 22; in "El Sur," 32; and the holy man, 90; in *Aesopica,* 93; in "Cefalea," 100, 104; and Freud, 124–25; in "Los venenos," 141; in *Yo el Supremo,* 166; and gossip, 187; and the trickster, 202; and Guaraní culture, 213; in *Hijo de hombre,* 213–18; and the comuneros, 235; and Paraguay, 254

Confession: in *The Invisible Man,* 57–59, 65, 72; in *Dr. Jekyll and Mr. Hyde,* 69, 72; in *El Hablador,* 89–90; in *Yo el Supremo,* 178, 190, 207, 234, 238

Coriolanus, xv–xvi, 3–4, 16, 39–40, 48, 64, 70, 210, 256

Cortázar, Julio, xvii, xviii; and the fantastic, 100–102, 120–22, 141–43; and *lo fantástico,* 143–44; and structuralism, 100–101, 151, 158; and the Pastoral, 119, 129, 131–32; and the sublime, 132; and Freud's theories and writings, 124–26, 134–35, 158–59, 161–62; German romanticism, 155–56. Works: "Cefalea," 99–117, 120; "Continuidad de los parques," 121, 122–26; "Silvia," 122, 124, 126–29; "Final de juego," 129–35, 137; "Los venenos," 129, 135–37; "Bestiario," 143–55, 159–61; "Las armas secretas," 155–62

in *Yo el Supremo,* 169, 177, 183, 214, 216, 223, 239–40; in *Hijo de hombre,* 214, 216
Gift, 22, 57, 77, 79, 83, 117; in Cortázar's stories, 128–29, 132–33, 136–37, 140–41, 150; in *Yo el Supremo,* 173, 190, 194, 207, 227–30, 250. See also *Giftmädchen,* Poison
Giftmädchen: and "Bestiario," 150. *See also,* Gift, Poison

Hallucination, 18, 113, 116, 183
Hallucinogens, 80, 191
Hamete, Cide (Hamet), 202, 208
Hamlet, xvi, xviii; in *Yo el Supremo,* 165–67; and parthenogenesis, 169–71; and *Finnegans Wake,* 170; and alchemy, 175–76; and John Robertson, 204
Hegel, F. W., 51, 158, 161, 242
Heimat, 104–105, 112
Heine, Heinrich, 155–56
Hesiod, 92–94, 177
History, xii, xviii; in "The Work of Art," 8, 12, 29, 36; in *Evaristo Carriego,* 30; "El Sur," 36, 71; and Borges on Whitman, 49, 51; in *Yo el Supremo,* 168–69, 181, 199, 216, 222–26, 231, 233–34, 242–43; and Asunción, 171; and the Compiler's hand, 185, 195–96; and *Finnegans Wake,* 186; and colonial Paraguay, 194–96, 215, 234–35, 247; and mythmaking, 197, 230–31; and the Robertson brothers' *Letters on Paraguay,* 197–206; and biblical parallels, 214–15; and performance, 242–43
Homeopathy, in Borges as influenced by Frazer, 53–54; in "Cefalea," 103–5, 109–11, 113, 115
Hysteria: and Lévi-Strauss, 158; and Hamlet, 165. *See also* Parthenogenesis

Incest, xviii; and *Evaristo Carriego,* 30–31; in "El Sur" and "La muerte y la brújula," 41; in *El hablador,* 78–79, 83–86, 88; and Freud's theories, 125–26; in "Bestiario," 143–47, 153–56; in "Las armas secretas," 160–62; in *Yo el Supremo,* 168, 173, 223, 226
Invisibility, xvii; and Borges's classic

mode of writing, 25–26, 28, 34, 38; and Borges on Whitman, 50; and Borges on Wells, in "el Arte narrativo y la magia," 53; and *The Invisible Man,* 54–72; and Leticia in "Final de juego," 131, 133
Irwin, John T., 182–84

Jabbok, 245, 248, 251–52
Jacob, 203, 212, 245–53, 255
Janus, 39–42, 142. *See also* Diana
Joyce, James, xix, 167, 185–86, 189. See also *Finnegans Wake*
Jung, C. G., 141, 144, 148–50, 176

Kafka, Franz: *The Metamorphosis* and *El hablador,* xvii, 77–78, 80–81, 84–85
Kinship, xiv, xvii, xviii; and *Evaristo Carriego,* 30; in Juan Dahlmann's contrast with the *flâneur,* 32–33, 71; in *The Invisible Man,* 60; in *El hablador,* 72, 74, 79, 90, 93; in "Los venenos," 135; in "Bestiario," 138–40, 144, 146, 149, 151–55; in *Yo el Supremo,* 161, 187, 201–2, 222, 256
Koran (Qu'ran), 177, 179, 186–87

Lévi-Strauss, Claude, 100–102, 105, 158, 195, 230
Lewis, Wyndham, xvi

Magic (magician), xii, xvii, in "The Work of Art," 8, 10–14, 17; and Borges, 22–23, 26, 37–38, 52–54, 71; and *The Invisible Man,* 59, 67–68; and *The Golden Bough,* 60–70; and "Silvia," 128; "Bestiario," 149; "Las armas secretas," 158; in *Yo el Supremo,* 183–85, 189–92, 197, 202–4, 208, 223, 225
Mann, Thomas: *Joseph and his Brothers,* 251–53
Masochism, 20–21, 41–42, 61, 124, 126, 129, 159, 207
Melancholy, xviii, 19–20, 36, 43–44, 122, 124, 130, 170, 243. *See also* Mourning
Memory, xvi, xvii; in "The Storyteller," 6, 15, 71; in *Evaristo Carriego,* 30; "El Sur," 28–30, 35; and Borges in relation to Tennyson, 46–47; and Ireneo Funes,

Memory (*cont.*)
64–66; in "Cefalea," 117; and Freud and "Continuidad de los parques," 124–25; in *Yo el Supremo*, 174–75; its role in dictation and the *Koran*, 179; and hieroglyphs, 185; and Macario in *Hijo de hombre*, 211, 213, 217; and myth and rumor, 240, 243; and biographic imagination, 246

Metamorphosis, xi, xvii, 13, 17, 71, 80–81, 84, 123, 127, 131, 134, 192, 205

Migraine: and "Cefalea," 103–5, 109–11, 115–16

Mimicry, 55–56, 88, 95, 111, 123, 207

Mohammed (Muhammad), 177; and *Yo el Supremo*, 179–80; and 'Abdallah, 179–80; in *Finnegans Wake*, 166

Monster (monstered), xi, xii, xv–xvi, xvii–xix; and Caius Martius Coriolanus, 3–4; in "La muerte y la brújula," 39; *The Invisible Man*, 55, 67; *El hablador*, 72, 79, 87; *Yo el Supremo*, 160, 167, 177, 207, 236–38, 240–41

Moon: in "La muerte y la brújula," 40; "Sur," 42–43; "Luna," 43–44, in Borges and Tennyson, 47; in *El hablador*, 74, 82–83, 85, 87; "Silvia," 126; *Yo el Supremo*, 173, 175, 190, 221, 250, 252

Mother (motherhood): in "El Sur," 28–31, 41; "La muerte y la brújula," 41–42; "Luna," 43–44; in *El hablador*, 74, 78, 82, 87; as dangerous, 83–84; and incest taboo as bonding, 88; in "Cefalea," 114; "Los venenos," 140; "Bestiario," 147, 150; and kinship reading of, 152–55; in "Las armas secretas," 158; and perversion, 158–59; in *Yo Supremo*, 165; and parthenogenesis and matricide, 169–70; and the Supreme, 173; in alchemy, 176; in *Finnegans Wake*, 187–89; in Chaucer, 205, 210–11; in *Hijo de hombre*, 212; in "Lucha hasta el alba," 214, 248–52; and the *tutorial voice*, 256

Mourning, xvii, xviii; and Benjamin and Borges, 8; in Borges, 18–19; in fetishism and masochism, 20–21; and Dahlmann and the *flâneur*, 36; in "Sur," 42;

"Adrogué," 43; in Ireneo Funes and Griffin, 66; and "Cefalea," 117; in *Yo el Supremo*, 175, 232, 243, 253

Murder, xi, 34, 55, 72; in Cortázar's stories, 122–26, 157–58; in *Yo el Supremo*, 193, 206, 212, 238, 248–49, 253, 256

Myth, xvi, xvii, xviii; and Caius Martius Coriolanus, 4; in "The Work of Art," 10, 16–17; and Borges's early writings, 18; in "La postulación de la realidad," 23–24, 26–28; in "El Sur," as Dahlmann and the *flâneur* compared, 28, 31, 33–34, 36, 38; in "La muerte y la brújula," 40, 41; "Luna," 44–45; and Borges on Tennyson, 45–48; and Borges on Whitman, 49; in *The Invisible Man*, 54, 67–68; and Henry Jekyll's confession, 69; in *El Hablador*, 71, 74–75, 77–82, 87, 92; and *lo fantástico*, 100; in "Cefalea," 102, 114, 134; "Final de juego," 134; "Los venenos," 137–39, 141; "Bestiario," 147–50, 154–55; "Las armas secretas," 158; in *Yo el Supremo*, 165, 169–71; and Patiño and the Supreme, 178–79; and hieroglyphic doubling, 184–85; in *Hijo de hombre*, 210, 212, 214, 222; in contrast with Lévi-Strauss's notions of, 230–31; and genealogical claims, 239–40; and Paraguay's past, 243–44; as *voice* and *gesture*, 245; in "Lucha hasta el alba," 248, 250, 252, 253

Nagy, Gregory, 91–93

Narcissism, xviii, 19, 123, 134, 136, 137, 143, 184, 209

Neitzsche, Friedrich, 49, 51, 77

Nimuendajú, Curt, 247

Nosology (nosography): and "Cefalea," 102–3, 108–9, 113

Nymphs: and "Final de juego," 130; in "Lucha hasta el alba," 250

Nympholepsy: and "Final de juego," 131–32

Oedipal, xv, 19, 78, 80, 87, 126, 160, 169, 190, 253, 255

Orphan (orphanhood), 37, 41, 78; in "Sil-

About the Author
Eduardo González is Professor of Hispanic Studies at Johns
Hopkins University. He is the author of *Alejo Carpentier: El
tiempo del hombre* (Caracas: Monte Avila, 1978) and *La
persona y el relato: proyecto de lectura psicoanalitica* (Madrid:
Porrúa, 1985).

Library of Congress Cataloging-in-Publication Data
González, Eduardo, 1943–
The monstered self : narratives of death and performance in
Latin American fiction / Eduardo Gonzalez.
Includes bibliographical references (p.   ) and index.
ISBN 0-8223-1209-3 (cloth)
1. Spanish American fiction—20th century—History and
criticism. 2. Self in literature. 3. Death in literature.
4. Performance in literature. 5. Metamorphosis in literature.
I. Title.
PQ7082.N7G673   1992
863—dc20   91-27927 CIP